REAL WORLD
BANKING
AND
FINANCE
7TH EDITION

READINGS IN ECONOMICS, BUSINESS, AND SOCIAL POLICY FROM
DOLLARS&SENSE

EDITED BY DOUG ORR, ALEJANDRO REUSS, CHRIS STURR, MARTY WOLFSON,

AND THE *DOLLARS & SENSE* COLLECTIVE

REAL WORLD BANKING AND FINANCE, 7TH EDITION

ISBN: 978-1-939402-10-3

Published by: Economic Affairs Bureau, Inc. d/b/a *Dollars & Sense*
               One Milk Street, Boston, MA 02109
               617-447-2177; dollars@dollarsandsense.org.

Real World Banking and Finance is edited by the *Dollars & Sense* Collective, which also publishes *Dollars & Sense* magazine and the classroom books *Real World Macro, Real World Micro, America Beyond Capitalism, Current Economic Issues, The Economic Crisis Reader, The Economics of the Environment, Grassroots Journalism, Introduction to Political Economy, Labor and the Global Economy, Real World Globalization, Real World Latin America, Real World Labor, Striking a Balance: Work, Family, Life, Unlevel Playing Fields: Understanding Wage Inequality and Discrimination,* and *The Wealth Inequality Reader.*

The 2013 *Dollars & Sense* Collective: Betsy Aron, Arpita Banerjee, Nancy Banks, Ellen Frank, John Miller, Kevin O'Connell, Larry Peterson, Linda Pinkow, Paul Piwko, Smriti Rao, Alejandro Reuss, Dan Schneider, Bryan Snyder, Chris Sturr, and Jeanne Winner.

Co-editors of this volume: Doug Orr, Alejandro Reuss, Chris Sturr, and Marty Wolfson

Cover design: Chris Sturr, based on a design by David Gerratt, dgcommunications.com.

Cover photos: Lettering and columns above the entrance to the Federal Reserve Bank of San Francisco (Wikimedia Commons; photo by Brokensphere, Creative Commons Attribution-Share Alike 3.0 license,); the "Eye of Providence" on reverse side of the Great Seal of the United States, as seen on U.S. dollar bill (Wikimedia Commons; photo is in the public domain); statue of an eagle located on the Marriner S. Eccles Federal Reserve Board Building, Washington, D.C. (Wikimedia Commons; photo by AgnosticPreacherKid, Creative Commons Attribution-Share Alike 3.0 license).

Production: Alejandro Reuss

Printed in U.S.A.

CONTENTS

Chapter 1

MONEY, MONETARY POLICY, AND THE ECONOMY

Article 1.1

WHAT IS MONEY?

BY DOUG ORR
November/December 1993; updated October 2010

We all use money every day. Yet many people do not know what money actually is. There are many myths about money, including the idea that the government "prints" all of it and that it has some intrinsic value. But actually, money is less a matter of value, and more a matter of faith.

Money is sometimes called the universal commodity, because it can be traded for all other commodities. But for this to happen, everyone in society must believe that money will be accepted. If people stop believing that it will be accepted, the existing money ceases to be money. In the early 1990s in Poland, people stopped accepting the zloty, and used vodka as money instead.

In addition to facilitating exchanges, money allows us to "store" value from one point in time to another. If you sell your car today for $4,000, you probably won't buy that amount of other products today. Rather, you store the value as money, probably in a bank, until you want to use it.

The "things" that get used as money have changed over time, and "modern" people often chuckle when they hear about some of them. The Romans used salt (from which we get the word "salary"), South Sea Islanders used shark's teeth, and several societies actually used cows. The "Three Wise Men" brought gold, frankincense and myrrh, each of which was money in different regions at the time.

If money does not exist, or is in short supply, it will be created. In POW camps, where guards specifically outlaw its existence, prisoners use cigarettes instead. In the American colonies, the British attempted to limit the supply of British pounds, because they knew that by limiting the supply of money, they could hamper the development of independent markets in the colonies. Today, the United States uses a similar policy, through the International Monetary Fund, in dealing with Latin America.

To overcome this problem, the colonists began to use tobacco leaves as money. This helped the colonies to develop, but it also allowed the holders of large plots of land to grow their own money! When the colonies gained independence, the new government decreed gold to be money, rather than tobacco, much to the dismay of Southern plantation owners. Now, rather than growing money, farmers had to find or buy it.

To aid the use of gold as money, banks would test its purity, put it in storage, and give the depositor paper certificates of ownership. These certificates, "paper money," could then be used in place of the gold itself. Since any bank could store gold and issue certificates, by the beginning of the Civil War, over 7,000 different types of "paper money" were in circulation in the United States, none of it printed by the government.

Only the bankers knew how much gold was in their vaults. If a customer wanted a loan, rather than give them gold, the bank would just print more paper money. Over time it became obvious that bankers were printing excessive amounts of money. In 1864, the government outlawed the printing of money by private banks, but this attempt to control the amount of money was unsuccessful.

While paper money is easier to use than gold, it is still risky to carry around large amounts of cash. It is safer to store the paper in a bank and simply sign over its ownership to make a purchase. We sign over the ownership of our money by writing a check. When the government outlawed printing money, checking account money became a new form of money and banks make loans by creating new checking accounts.

How Banks Create Money

Banks are central to understanding money, because in addition to storing it, they help to create it. Bankers realize that not everyone will withdraw their money at the same time, so they loan out much of the money that has been deposited. It is from the interest on these loans that banks get their profits, and through these loans the banking system creates new money.

If you deposit $100 cash in your checking account at Chase Manhattan Bank, you still have $100 in money to use, because checks are also accepted as money. Chase must set aside some of this cash as "reserves," in case you or other depositors decide to withdraw money as cash. Current regulations issued by the Federal Reserve Bank (the Fed) require banks to set aside an average of three cents out of each dollar. So Chase can make a loan of $97, based on your deposit. Chase does not make loans by handing out cash but instead by putting $97 in the checking account of the person, say Emily, taking out the loan. So from your initial deposit of $100 in cash, the economy now has $197 in checking account money.

The borrower, Emily, pays $97 for some product or service by check, and the seller, say Ace Computers, deposits the money in its checking account. The total amount of checking account money is still $197, but its location and ownership have changed. If Ace Computer's account is at Citibank, $97 in cash is transferred from Chase to Citibank. This leaves just $3 in cash reserves at Chase to cover your original deposit. However, Citibank now has $97 in "new" cash on hand, so it sets aside three cents on the dollar ($2.91) and loans out the rest, $94.09, as new checking account money. Through this process, every dollar of "reserves" yields many dollars in total money.

If you think this is just a shell game and there is only $100 in "real" money, you still don't understand money. Anything that is accepted as payment for a transaction is "real" money. Cash is no more real than checking account money. In fact, most car rental companies will not accept cash as payment for a car, so for them, cash is not money!

As of June 2010, there was $883 billion of U.S. currency, i.e. "paper money," in existence. However, somewhere between 50% and 70% of it is held outside the United States by foreign banks and individuals. U.S. $100 bills are the preferred currency of choice used to facilitate illegal international transactions, such as the drug trade. The vast majority of all money actually in use in the United States is not cash, but rather checking account money. This type of money, $1,590 billion, was created by private banks, and was not "printed" by anyone. In fact, this money exists only as electronic "bits" in banks' computers. (The less "modern" South Sea Islanders could have quite a chuckle about that!)

The amount of money that banks can create is limited by the total amount of reserves, and by the fraction of each deposit that must be held as reserves. Prior to 1914, bankers themselves decided what fraction of deposits to hold as reserves. Since then, this fraction has been set by the main banking regulator, the Fed.

Until 1934, gold was held as reserves, but the supply of gold was unstable, growing rapidly during the California and Alaska "gold rushes," and very slowly at other times. As a result, at times more money was created than the economy needed, and at other times not enough money could be created. Starting in 1934, the U.S. government decided that gold would no longer be used as reserves. Cash, now printed by the Fed, could no longer be redeemed for gold, and cash itself became the reserve asset.

Banks, fearing robberies, do not hold all of their cash reserves in their own vaults. Rather, they store it in an account at a regional Fed bank. These accounts count as reserves. What banks do hold in their vaults is their other assets, such as Treasury bonds and corporate bonds.

The Fed and Bank Reserves

The only role of the government in creating money is indirectly through the Fed. While the governors and chairman of the Fed are appointed and approved by the government, once approved , they are not directly controlled by either the Congress or the eExecutive branch. If the Fed wants to expand the money supply, it must increase bank reserves. To do this, the Fed buys Treasury bonds from a bank, and pays with a check drawn on the Fed itself. By depositing the check in its reserve account at the Fed, the bank now has more reserves, so the bank can now make more loans and create new checking account money.

By controlling the amount of reserves, the Fed attempts to control the size of the money supply. But as recent history has shown, this control is limited. During the late 1970s, the Fed tried to limit the amount of money banks could create by reducing reserves, but banks simply created new forms of money, just like the POW camp prisoners and colonial farmers. In 1979, there was only one form of checking account money. Today, there are many, with odd names such as NOWs, ATSs, repos, and money market deposit accounts. If there is a profit to be made creating money, banks will find a way.

In 2010, we have the opposite problem. The Fed is trying to expand the money supply, but banks are refusing to create new money. In good times, banks hold as few reserves as possible, so they can profit from making loans. In times of crisis, banks fear that we will lose faith in the commercial banking system and all try to take out our "money" as cash. Since there is far more electronic money than cash, this is impossible. But if the bank cannot give us our money in the form we want it, the bank fails. Most failed banks either close completely or are purchased by other banks. Since the start of 2007, over 300 banks, with assets totaling more than $637 billion, have failed.

Since all banks fear they will be next, they want as many reserves as possible. Excess reserves are any reserves above those required by the Fed. During the 1990s, these averaged about $1 billion for the entire banking system. During the crisis of 2001, they spiked to the then unheard of level of $19 billion. As of June 2010, excess reserves in the banking system were $1,035 billion! This is the classic case of trying to push on a string (see Article 1.7Gerald Freidman "Pushing on Strings," by Gerald Friedman, in this chapter). The Fed can create reserves, but only banks can create money, and they are not yet willing to make any new loans. This is even more truetruer given that the Fed, for the first time, is now paying interest on assets held as reserves, which lowers the incentives to make loans.

These amorphous forms of money function only because we believe they will function, which is why the continued stability of the banking system is so critical. While it is true that the bailout ofcrisis in the banking system was not handled very wellas well as it could have been, and that many people who created the crisis are still profiting from it, preventing the banks from failing abruptly and disrupting the payments system was necessary. In a modern market economy, banks create the money, and no market economy can function without its money. Money only exists if we believe in it, so we have to maintain the faith. To maintain the faith we need more democratic control over money creation. This can only come if regulation of the financial system is greatly expanded. ❏

Sources: Money supply, Federal Reserve Board, http://www.federalreserve.gov/releases/h6/ current/; Excess reserves, St. Louis Federal Reserve Bank, http://research.stlouisfed.org/fred2/ series/EXCRESNS; Bank Failures, Federal Deposit Insurance Corporation (FDIC) http://www. fdic.gov/bank/individual/failed/banklist.html.

Article 1.2

THE "BOND MARKET" VERSUS THE REST OF US

BY DOUG ORR AND ELLEN FRANK
October 1999; revised October 2010

Why should anyone involved in environmental issues, education reform efforts, efforts to house the homeless, or anyone else care about monetary policy? After all, it only affects the financial markets, right? *Wrong.* Monetary policy is holding all other social policy hostage, and is part of the cause of the rapid increase in income inequality in the United States. Whenever any policy change is proposed, be it in health care, housing, or transportation, the first question politicians ask is, "What will the 'bond market' think about this?"

"The bond market" is a euphemism for the financial sector of the U.S. economy and the Federal Reserve Bank (the Fed), which regulates that sector. The Fed is the central bank of the United States. It controls monetary policy, and uses its power to help the banking industry and the holders of financial assets, while thwarting government attempts to deal with pressing social problems.

Since 1979, the Fed has had an unprecedented degree of independence from government control. This independence has put it in a position to veto any progressive fiscal policy that Congress might propose. To understand how this situation developed, we must understand the function of banks, the structure of the Fed, and the role of monetary policy.

Banks and Instability

Government regulates the banking industry because private sector, profit-driven banking is inherently unstable. Banks do more than just store money—they help create it. If you deposit a dollar in the bank, you still have that dollar. Commercial banks will set aside three cents as "reserves" to "cover" your deposit, and the remaining 97 cents is loaned out to someone else who now has "new money." By making loans, banks create new money and generate profit. The drive to maximize profits often leads banks to become overextended: making too many loans and holding too few reserves. This drive for profits can undermine a bank's stability.

If depositors think the bank is holding too few reserves, or is making overly speculative loans, they might try to withdraw their money as cash. Large numbers of depositors withdrawing cash from a bank at the same time is called a "run on the bank." Since banks only hold 3% of their deposit liabilities as cash, even a moderate-sized "run" would be enough to drain the bank of its cash reserves. If a bank has no reserves, it is insolvent and is forced to close. At that point, all remaining deposits in the bank cease to exist, and depositors lose their money.

The failure of a bank affects more than just that bank's depositors. One bank's excesses tend to shake people's faith in other banks. If the run spreads, "bank panics" can occur. During the 1800s, such panics erupted every five to ten years, bankrupting between 10% and 25% of the banks in the United States and creating a major recession each time.

The Creation of the Fed

The panic of 1907 bankrupted some of the largest banks and led to demands by the public for bank reforms that would stabilize the system. Reform proposals ranged from doing almost nothing to nationalizing the entire banking industry. As a compromise, the Federal Reserve was created in 1913. The U.S. government saw the Fed as a way for bankers to regulate themselves, and structured the Federal Reserve System so that it could be responsive to its main constituents: banks and other financial-sector businesses that are now called, euphemistically, "the bond market." While ideally it should serve the interests of the general public when it conducts monetary policy, in reality the Fed balances two, conflicting goals: maintaining the stability of "the bond market" and maximizing financial-sector profits. Over time, Congress and the President have varied the degree of independence that they have given to the Fed to choose between these goals.

Initially, the Fed enjoyed a high degree of independence. During the 1920s, the Fed allowed member banks to engage in highly speculative activities, including using depositor's money to play the stock market. While many banks were very profitable, speculative excesses caused almost 20% of the banks in existence in 1920 to fail during the following decade. With the onset of the Great Depression, between 1929 and 1933, more than 9,000 banks, 38% of the total, failed. Since the Fed had not achieved its first goal, in 1935 Congress responded with laws that put many new regulations on banks, and reduced the Fed's independence.

Fed Independence Lost

Under the new regulations, "investment banks" were not allowed to take deposits, but were allowed to play the markets, while "commercial banks" were restricted to taking deposits and making commercial loans. Deposits were now insured by the FDIC. Thus, the only opportunity for making a profit was to maintain a "spread" between the interest rate paid on deposits and that charged on loans. Loans are made for relatively long terms, and deposits are not. If the short-term interest rate on deposits varies widely, the spread will grow and shrink, which makes bank profits unstable. In order to stabilize bank profits, during the 30 years after 1935, the Treasury mandated that the Fed keep the short-term rate approximately constant.

Under this arrangement, Congress indirectly controlled monetary policy. If Congress wanted to stimulate the economy it could increase government spending or cut taxes. Both led to an increase in spending and an increase in the demand for money. To keep interest rates, which are the price of money, from rising, the Fed had to increase the supply of money. Thus, the Fed "accommodated" fiscal policy decisions made by Congress and the President.

During most of this period, growth was moderate and prices were stable. The Fed went along because this arrangement did not threaten bank profits. Starting in the mid-1960s, however, stimulative fiscal policy started to push up the inflation rate, which did threaten bank profits. A confrontation over Fed independence ensued and grew in intensity throughout the 1970s.

Inflation's Impact

Contrary to the view commonly propagated by the media, inflation does not affect everyone equally. In fact, there are very clear winners and losers. Inflation is an increase in the average level of prices, but some prices rise faster than average and some rise slower. If the price of the thing you are selling is rising faster than average, you win. Otherwise, you lose. Inflation redistributes income, but in an arbitrary manner. This uncertainty makes inflation unpopular, even to the winners. However, one industry always loses from unexpected inflation, and that industry is finance.

Banks make loans today that will be repaid, with interest, in the future. If inflation reduces the value of those future payments, the banks' profits will be reduced. So bankers are interested in the "real interest rate," that is, the actual (nominal) interest rate on the loan minus the rate of inflation. If the interest rate on commercial bank loans is 7% and the rate of inflation is 3%, the real rate of interest is 4%. In the early postwar period, real interest rates were relatively stable at about 2%.

From 1965 on, unexpected increases in inflation reduced the real interest rate. This cheap credit was a boon to home buyers, farmers, and manufacturers, but it greatly reduced bank profits. Banks wanted inflation cut. The Keynesian view of monetary policy offered a simple but unpopular solution: raise interest rates enough to cause a recession. High unemployment and falling incomes would take the steam out of inflation.

But, putting people out of work to help bankers would be a hard sell. The Fed needed a different story to justify shifting its policy from stabilizing interest rates to fighting inflation. That story was "monetarism," a theory that claims that changes in the money supply affect prices, but nothing else in the economy.

The Monetarist Experiment

On October 6, 1979, Fed Chair Paul Volcker, using monetarist theory as a justification, announced that the Fed would no longer try to keep interest rates at targeted levels. He argued that Fed policy should concentrate on controlling inflation, and to do so he would now focus on limiting the money supply growth rate. Since neither Congress nor the President attempted to overrule Volcker, this change ushered in an era of unprecedented independence for Fed monetary policy.

During the next three years, the Fed reduced the rate of growth in the money supply, but this experiment did not yield the results predicted by the monetarists. Instead of a swift reduction in the rate of inflation, the most immediate outcome was a rapid rise in the real interest rate and the start of the worst recession since the Great Depression.

As the Keynesian view predicted, the recession occurred because high interest rates slowed economic growth and increased unemployment. In 1979, the unemployment rate was 5.8%. By 1982 it had reached 10.7%, the first double-digit rate since the Depression. With fewer people working and buying products, the inflation rate, which had been 8.7% in 1979, finally started to slow in 1981 and was approaching 4% by the end of 1982. Tight money policies by the Fed kept nominal interest rates from falling as fast as inflation. This raised real interest rates on commercial loans from 0.5% in 1979 to 10% in 1982.

The Fed's fight against inflation had a severe impact on the entire economy. All businesses, especially farming and manufacturing, run on credit. The rise in interest rates, combined with lower prices, squeezed the profits of farmers and manufacturers.

Both of these industries rely heavily on exports, and so were also hurt by the negative effect of high interest rates on the competitiveness of U.S. exports. Real interest rates in the United States were the highest in the world, thereby attracting financial investment from abroad. In order for foreigners to buy financial assets in the United States, they first had to buy dollars. This demand for dollars drove up their value in international markets. While a "strong" dollar means imports are relatively cheap, it also means that U.S. exports are expensive. Foreign countries could not afford to buy our "costly" agricultural and manufactured exports. As a result, during this period, bankruptcy rates in these two industries were massive, higher than during the 1930s.

Despite its high cost to the rest of the economy, the monetarist experiment did not benefit many banks. Initially, the high real interest rates appeared to help bank profits. Regulations capped the interest rates banks could pay on deposits, but rates charged on loans were not regulated. This increased the profit on loans. Many investors, however, started moving their deposits to less regulated financial intermediaries, such as mutual funds and new forms of "shadow banks" that could pay higher rates on deposits. In addition, the recession forced many borrowers to declare bankruptcy and default on their loans. Both of these factors pushed banks toward insolvency.

Reversing Course

It was bank losses,not the pain in the rest of the economy, that led Volcker to announce in September 1982 that he was abandoning monetarism. His new policy aimed to provide enough reserves to keep most banks solvent and to allow a *slow* recovery from the recession. Unemployment remained high for the next five years, so inflation continued to slow. Real interest rates stayed near 8% through 1986, so interest-sensitive industries, such as farming and manufacturing, did not take part in the recovery.

Volcker made his allegiance to the banking industry very clear during a meeting, in February 1985, with a delegation of state legislators, laborers, and farmers who were demanding easier money and lower interest rates. He told them, "Look, your constituents are unhappy, mine aren't."

Yet by 1985, the crisis in the savings and loan industry was spreading into commercial banking. To provide cash ("liquidity") to the banks, Volcker allowed the money supply to grow by 12% during 1985 and by 17% in 1986. Monetarists raised the specter of a return to double-digit inflation. Instead, the rate of inflation continued to slow, demonstrating that a simple link between the money supply and inflation hypothesized by monetarist theory does not exist.

The Veto

Despite the failure and subsequent abandonment of monetarist policies, the Fed still uses monetarist *theory* to justify its continued focus on "fighting inflation." The myth that monetary policy only affects inflation provides a convenient "cover" that allows the Fed to serve its narrow constituency: "the bond market." From the end of World War II to 1979, real interest rates averaged 2.1%. Since 1980, they have averaged 5.7%. Real interest rates remain high because "the bond market" worries about any possible increase in future inflation, but high rates continue to hollow out the manufacturing sector.

Fighting inflation benefits the bond market. However, despite the near-depression that monetarism caused in the 1980s and the extremely slow rate of economic growth that has occurred since, the Fed continues to claim that fighting inflation serves the interests of the entire country. The public's widespread belief in this myth denies progressives in Congress the support they need to force the Fed back into accommodating fiscal policy. It also provides support for those in Congress that want to block any expansion of social programs.

If Congress decides to spend more for environmental clean-up, housing the homeless, or education, "the bond market" will raise the specter of renewed inflation. The Fed will then raise interest rates, as it did in June 1999 as a "preemptive strike" to prevent inflation, and sent the economy into a recession. The increase in interest rates slowed the economy, increased unemployment, reduced government revenues, and returned the federal budget to a deficit. Since Congress knows it will be incorrectly blamed for this outcome, it won't pass any legislation "the bond market" doesn't like. This is how the bond market holds Congress hostage. As long as Congress and the President allow the Fed to follow an inflation-fighting policy, the Fed can maintain a veto threat over the elected government.

The Fed has not vetoed Obama's fiscal policy stimulus because Fed Chairman Ben Bernanke realizes that the second premise of monetarist theory, that the Fed can always increase the money supply, is also wrong. The Fed has pumped more than $1 trillion in reserves into the banking system, and almost all of them sit as excess reserves. This is a classic example of what Keynes called a "liquidity trap." In this case, monetary policy is powerless to stimulate the economy. Only fiscal policy can bring us out of the "Great Recession." Unfortunately, the veto power of the Fed has been replaced by the veto power of the Republican "Party of No," which has filibustered every attempt to revive the economy. Apparently, making Obama look ineffective is more important to them than the well-being of the American people.

While the Fed has not vetoed Obama's fiscal policy, it has again demonstrated that its banking constituents are more important than the general public and the overall economy. If a commercial bank finds itself short on reserves, it has the option of borrowing reserves from the Fed through what is called the "discount window." It has this name because a member bank would bring assets to an actual Fed bank and trade those assets for reserves "at a discount." The value of assets the Fed received was more than the value of the reserves lent. Historically, the Fed only lent to commercial banks that were members of the Federal Reserve System.

During the current crisis, the Fed has greatly expanded its role. While investment banks and hedge funds cannot borrow at the discount window, the Fed still found a way to help them. The Fed agreed to trade Treasury bonds, which are completely safe from default, for "equal amounts" of mortgage backed securities that have a high probability for default. In this case, the value of assets received by the Fed were far less than the assets they lent to the investment banks and hedge funds because of the higher risk of default.

In both cases, the Fed had the power to impose restrictions on these loans. These restrictions could have included the requirement that banks attempt to renegotiate any mortgage loan, including a reduction in principle owed, before starting the process of foreclosure. This would have helped millions of American families avoid losing their homes. It would have also helped the recovery of the economy from the current Great Recession. But since this requirement would have reduced the profits of member banks, the Fed chose not to do this. Only now that these member banks have been exposed for fraudulently foreclosing on millions of loans has the Fed finally started to "investigate" the problem.

The Fed has also played a large role in the rapid increase in income and wealth inequality that started in the 1980s and has accelerated ever since. The two decades following World War II are often called the "golden age" of the U.S. economy. On average, Gross Domestic Product (GDP) grew 4.3% each year, and unemployment averaged 4.6%. Average real wages, that is, wages adjusted for inflation, grew at an annual rate of 2.1%, rising from $10.86 an hour in 1950 to $18.21 in 1973 (both measured in 2005 dollars). This period saw the creation of a true middle class in the United States.

In the three decades since 1980, GDP growth has averaged 2.7% each year, unemployment has averaged 6.2% (2.3% and 6.7% if we exclude the higher-growth Clinton years). Average real wages *declined* every year from 1980 to 1996. In fact, the real wage in 2009 was $16.40 an hour, exactly the same as in 1966. If wages had continued to grow at 2.1%, the average wage today would be $38.50. Without the slow growth policies of the Fed and the anti-labor policies started under Reagan, the average income of the majority of the people in the United States would be more than twice as large. Instead, we've seen a hollowing out of the middle class, and a rapid transfer of wealth and income to those already wealthy.

Where Do Interest Payments Go?

By focusing on inflation rather than interest rates, the media deflect attention from a critical social issue—how high interest rates transfer income from the indebted middle class to the very rich. If ownership of financial assets was evenly distributed among households, the growth in interest income would not be of much importance. But ownership of financial assets is heavily concentrated. As of 2007, the top 5% of households, those with incomes more than $183,000, controlled 60.5% of all wealth in the U.S. The top 10% controlled 71.6%. Yet these numbers understate the concentration of financial wealth. Almost 80% of families in the United States have almost no assets, outside the equity in their homes and vehicles. Despite the media hype about the "democratization" of the stock market, between 1989 and 1995 the concentration of stock ownership increased. Detailed studies of wealth data collected by the Fed report that in 2007 the wealthiest 5% of households owned 93.6% of all directly owned bonds and 82.4% of all directly owned stocks. The top 10% if households owned 98.4% of all bonds and 90.4% of all stocks.

The "poorest" nine-tenths of the U.S. population—that is, most of us—have virtually no financial assets. Such families gain little from rising interest rates. But the higher mortgage, credit card, and auto payments that result take a real toll on living standards. Each uptick in the real interest rate entails a transfer of income from the lowest 90% of the population to the highest 10%. And most of that income goes to the very, very wealthy, who are yet another part of "the bond market" served by the Fed.

Economist James Galbraith has called today's high interest rates a form of taxation without representation. The term is apt. Tax increases are passed by Congress, which has at least some public oversight. Interest rate hikes are decided by the Fed, an institution over which the President, Congress, and the public have virtually no control.

Like taxes, rising interest rates are a drain on the resources and income of the vast majority of U.S. households. But unlike tax revenues that can be used to provide education, environmental clean-up, homeless shelters, roads, airports, and other infrastructure, interest payments flow into the pockets of the very rich, who become ever so much richer. ❏

Resources: Arthur B. Kennickell, , "Ponds and Streams: Wealth and Income in the U.S,, 1989 to 2007," *Federal Reserve Working Paper 2009-13* (Jan. 2009); Lawrence Mishel, Jared Bernstein, and Heidi Shierholz, *The State of Working America 2008/2009.*

Article 1.3

SHOULD WE BLAME "FRACTIONAL RESERVE" BANKING?

BY ARTHUR MacEWAN
May/June 2013

> Dear Dr. Dollar:
>
> *I have seen various arguments (on the Internet, for example) that a prime cause of our economic problems (inequality, crises, mass unemployment, the immense power of the banks, etc.) is our montary system. In particular, that it is a "fractional reserve system," in which "money is created out of thin air." Could you comment?*
>
> —Mike Smith, New York, NY

The last several years, when banks and the whole financial system have been at the core of economic disruption, could easily lead one to see the monetary system as central to our economic problems.

Keep in mind, however, that we have had essentially the same monetary system for decades, the Federal Reserve has existed for a hundred years, and the "fractional reserve" system existed before the Fed. During these earlier eras, including periods when we relied on the gold standard as the basis of our monetary system, we have had depressions, inflation, severe inequality, and excessive power in the hands of finance and large corporations generally. We have also had some relatively good times—periods of stable economic growth, less economic inequality, lower unemployment, and less power and profits for the banks. So, whatever is wrong with our monetary system (and there are certainly things wrong), the explanation of our economic problems must be more complex.

But what is the fractional reserve system? Basically, it is the system by which banks keep as reserves only a fraction of the amount of deposits that their customers have with the banks. Banks can do this because at any time their customers will demand only a fraction of those total obligations. When, for example, you deposit $100 in the bank, the bank will loan out to someone else perhaps $90 of that $100. This $90 is new money that the bank has created. The person or business taking this loan then deposits the $90 in another account with the bank or another bank, allowing a new loan of $81 to be generated by the banking system; the remaining $9 (10% of the deposit) will be kept as reserves. And so on.

By this process, if people are willing to take out the loans, the banks can create an additional $900 of money based on an original deposit of $100. This is sometimes called "creating money out of thin air." In fact, it is creating money on the basis of 10% reserves.

If banks were left to their own devices, competition would create pressure to push down the reserve ratio—they could, for example, make twice the amount of loans were they to reduce their reserves from 10% to 5% of obligations. However, the Federal Reserve has a great deal of authority over what the banks can do. It sets the reserve ratio. Banks cannot simply lower the amount of reserves to make more loans. (The actual reserve ratio varies depending on type of obligation; 10% is just an example that makes calculations easy.) Most frequently, the Fed affects the supply of money by buying bonds from the banks, thus increasing the banks' reserves (and enabling them to lend more), or selling bonds to the banks, thus reducing the banks' reserves.

That's the formal way it works. Although critics of a fractional reserve system claim it "debases the currency" (i.e., leads to inflation), it does not automatically allow the banks to create more and more money without limits, which could indeed generate severe inflation. The U.S. economy has experienced mild inflation for most of the last century (averaging 3.2% annually), but fractional reserve banking is not generally associated with high "runaway" inflation. Ironically, in light of the claims of the critics, the Fed has often followed policies that work in exactly the opposite direction—restricting the banks' ability to create money, thus restricting the loans they can make, and restraining economic growth and employment. (After all, neither banks nor other large corporations like severe inflation.)

But of course the formal way the system works is not the whole story. The banks themselves and other big firms have a great deal of influence over what the Fed does. So the Fed usually regulates the banks with a very light hand. In the Great Recession, in particular, the Fed (along with the U.S. Treasury) provided the banks with funds to meet their obligations when many of those banks would have otherwise failed. In this respect, the way the Fed works is not so different from the way the government works in general—money has a great deal of influence over policy.

It would be nice if our economic problems were so simple that they could be solved by some reorganization of our monetary system. But the problems are bigger and deeper. ❑

Article 1.4

PUSHING ON STRINGS

*The explosion of U.S. banks' excess reserves since last fall
illustrates the dramatic failure of monetary policy.*

BY GERALD FRIEDMAN
May/June 2009

Monetary policy is not working. Since the economic crisis began in July 2007, the Federal Reserve has dramatically cut interest rates and pumped out over a trillion dollars, increasing the money supply by over 15% in less than two years. These vast sums have failed to revive the economy because the banks have been hoarding liquidity rather than investing it.

The Federal Reserve requires that banks hold money on reserve to back-up deposits and other bank liabilities. Beyond these required reserves, in the past banks would hold very small amounts of excess reserves, holdings that they minimized because they earn very little or no interest. Between the 1950s and September 2008, all the banks in the United States held more than $5 billion in excess reserves only once, after the September 11 attacks. This changed with the collapse of Lehman Brothers. Beginning with less than $2 billion in August 2008, excess reserves soared to $60 billion in September and then to $559 billion in November before rising to $798 b. in January 2009. They hovered around that level for nearly a year until jumping again in the winter of 2009-10.

This explosion of excess reserves represents a signal change in bank policy that threatens the effectiveness of monetary policy in the current economic crisis. Aware of their own financial vulnerability, even insolvency, frightened bank managers responded to the collapse of major investment houses like Lehman Brothers by grabbing and hoarding cash. (The spike in excess reserves also coincides with a

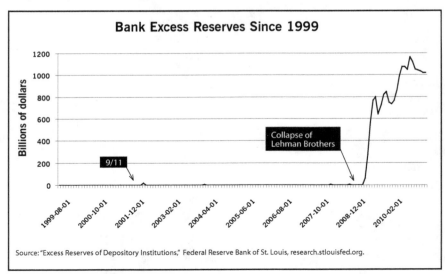

Source: "Excess Reserves of Depository Institutions," Federal Reserve Bank of St. Louis, research.stlouisfed.org.

change in Federal Reserve policy to begin paying interest on required and excess reserves. The rate paid, however—about 0.25%—is so low that it would not deter banks from making real investments and loans. On the other hand, the payment of interest amounts to a subsidy to banks by the Federal Reserve, and, ultimately, the United States Treasury, worth tens of billions of dollars.) At the same time, a general loss of confidence and spreading economic collapse persuaded banks that in any case there are few to whom they could lend with good confidence that they will be repaid. Clearly, our banks have decided that they need, or at least want, the money more than do consumers and productive businesses.

Banks could have been investing this money by lending to businesses needing liquidity to buy inventory or pay workers. Had they done so then monetarist economists would be shouting from the rooftops, at least in the university halls, about how monetary policy prevented another Great Depression. Instead, even the *Wall Street Journal* is proclaiming that "We're All Keynesians Again" because monetary policy has failed. Monetary authorities, the *Journal* explains, can create money but they cannot force banks to lend or to invest it in productive activities. The Federal Reserve confronts a reality shown in the graph above: it can't push on a string.

If the banks won't lend, then we need more than monetary policy to get out of the current crisis. The Obama stimulus was an appropriate response to the failure of string-pushing. But to solve a crisis this large will need much more government stimulus, and we will need programs to move liquidity from bank vaults to businesses and consumers. It may be time to stop waiting on the banks, and to start telling them what to do with our money. ❏

Article 1.5

FED UP

The Federal Reserve's balance sheet is exploding on both ends.

BY ROB LARSON
March/April 2011

After suffering for years from a dizzyingly high unemployment rate, Americans are eager for meaningful increases in hiring. In the past, the government jump-started economic growth with fiscal policy—increasing spending in order to create new demand for goods and services, which companies could fulfill only by hiring. After the nation languished through a decade of depression in the 1930s, the monumental fiscal outlays for World War II created an enormous "stimulus" to total demand and hiring. The massive spending for the war effort, financed in large part by aggressive 80%-plus tax rates on the richest households, created demand that gave employers reason to create millions of jobs.

Most people regard social spending, such as on education or public health, as a more acceptable form of stimulus than military spending. But apart from government programs started in the 1960s due to popular demand, stimulus has proven "politically difficult" unless it takes the form of military adventure or tax cuts that are typically skewed toward the richest households. Unfortunately, tax cuts for the wealthy are the weakest form of stimulus and have relatively little job-creating impact; and non-military stimulus plans, including the inadequate 2009 stimulus bill, are targets for deficit hawks.

Yet in this climate of public-spending cutbacks, policymakers recognize that some new government response to the desperate job-market situation is clearly needed. The traditional alternative to fiscal policy is monetary policy—encouraging growth by lowering short-term interest rates through the Federal Reserve Bank's interventions. But traditional monetary policy has failed—short-term rates remain near zero while the economy continues to show little response. So attention has turned to the Fed's new alternative, "quantitative easing," an enormous program of purchases of financial assets. Fed policymakers hope to make long-term borrowing cheaper and therefore spur hiring, but the result so far has been to load up the Fed's balance sheet while enriching bond investors and rescuing more banks, with little effect on interest rates.

Balancing Act

All companies have balance sheets, listing a company's "liabilities"—what the company owes—and "assets"—what the company owns. Assets and liabilities always balance (as long as the company owner's equity is included with the liabilities), due to how they are counted. For example, on the balance sheet of a typical commercial bank, the main assets are bank loans extended to consumers and businesses, because they provide the bank with interest income. The main liabilities are the depositors' account balances, which the bank is obliged to produce at any time. The Federal

Reserve is different, however, because it can essentially print money by electronically increasing the account balances it owes other banks. With the government's current refusal to run sensible fiscal deficits targeted at creating jobs, the Fed's ability to massively expand its balance sheet (and to even run a profit doing so) has attracted new attention.

Historically, the Fed's main assets have been U.S. Treasury bonds, which are pieces of government debt. This is because the Fed's usual role is to influence interest rates in order to moderate the business cycle. It does this by buying and selling large numbers of Treasury bonds from the largest U.S. banks, which influences interest rates across the economy, as money is pulled in and out of the banking system. This means the Fed generally has large volumes of these interest-bearing government bonds among its assets.

The Fed has historically held a number of liabilities, including the reserve accounts of the many private banks in the Federal Reserve system, held as cushions against losses. The U.S. Treasury Department's own "general account," used for government payments, also falls on this side of the balance sheet. But Fed liabilities also include the U.S. paper currency used across the economy, hence the "Federal Reserve Note" on bills. So the Fed is "liable" for the balances of the rest of the government, the private banks' reserve accounts it maintains, and for U.S. cash, which can be exchanged for other assets.

Throwing Money at the Problem

Over the course of the 2008 financial crisis and the ensuing weak recovery, the Fed's balance sheet has taken on a very different look. It has swollen with "quantitative easing" asset purchases: first, the Fed bought devalued "toxic assets" from the banks in the 2008 bank rescue, and more recently in a large "QE2" program of buying long-term U.S. government bonds. The Fed's current large-scale buying tends to push bond prices up, which lowers long-term interest rates. The Fed is buying great volumes of such assets, with its balance sheet rocketing from $800 billion in 2007 to $2.6 trillion in February 2011, and with QE2 still underway.

The mountain of new Fed assets is composed of three broad asset categories. The first is the extension of short-term credit to financial firms—lending on favorable terms to banks that are in dire need of immediate lending. This is an extension of the Fed's original role of "banker of last resort," lending cheaply to banks in need of money overnight or even facing a "run" of panicking depositors. This role included lending through both the Fed's normal "discount window" and the "Term Auction Facility," set up to allow staggering banks to borrow with more anonymity. "Currency swaps" to foreign central banks, in which the Fed bought foreign currency from banks needing U.S. dollars, were also part of the program. This category of Fed assets reached its high point during and immediately after the 2008 financial crisis, when the short-run lending markets dried up among fears of borrower insolvency, leaving many enormous banks, insurers, and other financial companies on the edge of failure. As the financial industry has recovered its footing, this category has declined as a share of the Fed's balance sheet.

The second category of the Fed's new asset pile is loans to broader borrowers in the economy, primarily short-term corporate bonds, or "commercial paper," from many U.S. corporations. Companies often rely on short-term borrowing to cover regular operating costs, like payroll or supplier bills, while waiting for receivables to come in. During the 2008 crisis, struggling investment groups like money market funds faced huge withdrawals, leaving them without the cash to continue investing in these short-term bonds. Therefore the commercial paper market "locked up": rates spiked and borrowing became almost impossible. The Fed stepped in to supply the market with emergency short-term credit, and its program earned headlines for the "bedrock" corporations—including Caterpillar, GE, McDonald's, Toyota, and Verizon—revealed to have relied heavily on the program. This category of assets also includes the TALF program, which sought to restart "securitization"—the packaging of loans into assets that may be bought and sold. Car loans, credit card debt, and student loans are among the forms of packaged debt the Fed invested in. As these short-term markets have returned to somewhat normal functioning, this component has also diminished as a proportion of the Fed's total assets.

TALF and its related programs have become particularly notorious for being "gamed" by financial firms and what the *New York Times* called "a cross-section of America's wealthy." The super-low interest rates provided by the Fed for desperate and important corporations were also used by canny investors to make enormous sums off

---

A Fed Balance Sheet Glossary

Assets: Tangible or intangible items of value owned by a firm, such as cash or interest-paying loans.

Liabilities: An obligation of a firm to another party, such as a bank depositor; equal to assets minus net equity.

Balance sheet: A financial statement indicating a firm's assets and liabilities at some point in time.

Bond: A tradable piece of an institution's debt. Bond interest rates decrease as prices increase, lowering funding costs.

Liquidity: An institution's access to cash or close equivalents

Reserve account: Deposit accounts kept by private banks with their regional Fed bank, holding the capital the Fed obliges them to maintain.

Open market operations: The Fed's normal practice of influencing interest rates by buying or selling large volumes of government bonds, which tends to decrease/increase short-term rates.

Quantitative easing: The Fed's recent program to lower long-term interest rates by buying massive amounts of Treasury bonds and mortgage-backed securities.

Securities: A general term for a financial asset, such as stocks and bonds.

Term Auction Facility: The Fed's program to extend cheap, short-term credit to financial institutions through a more anonymous process than the discount window, mostly during the 2008 financial crisis.

TALF: Term Asset-Backed Securities Loan Facility, set up by the Fed in 2008 to restart securitization markets, which package existing loans into tradable assets and have become a major source of U.S. credit.

the public aid. One investor, having seen impressive returns of up to 10%, referred to getting "a gift from the Fed." In this connection, it is notable that at every stage the Fed's policy has been to pursue options that preferentially benefit the rich. Bond ownership is skewed toward upper-income households, so supporting bond market conditions is of disproportionate benefit to them. Likewise, the Fed's actions during and after the 2008 financial crisis meant few losses for the well-off creditors of banks and insurers, with their institutions rescued at taxpayer expense. The Fed richly deserves its reputation as a "captured" regulator, being predominantly run by former Wall Street bankers who often return to the finance industry after leaving the Fed.

The third main category of the Fed's asset purchases is what the Fed calls "high-quality" securities, meaning debt instruments with relatively low risk. This

The Federal Reserve System: Left vs. Right Views

The Federal Reserve retains a strong reputation in mainstream circles. Its chairs, like Paul Volcker or Ben Bernanke, are treated with the reverence of high priests, even if their images are later tarnished by their disastrous policy decisions, as with Alan Greenspan.

The left position, however, begins with the recognition that the Fed's policymaking bodies are visibly controlled by Wall Street. From regular staffers to senior policymakers, there is a standard practice of Fed staff working for large commercial or investment banks before joining the Fed, and an expectation that they will likely return to the financial industry later in their careers. Further indicators that the Fed is to a large extent a pawn of Wall Street include its recent surrender of a significant part of its influence, as government deregulation has allowed huge "shadow banking" institutions to grow outside the Fed system, weakening the Fed's monetary policy effectiveness. Despite complaints from Fed leaders, the central bank generally accepted these changes since they were demanded by Wall Street, which is the center of economic power and where many Fed figures hope to return for employment.

So the left picture is of a "captured regulator," a government body run by the industries it's supposed to regulate. From this point of view, moves to reform the Fed would include greater transparency and replacing banking industry influence with democratic governance, along with an increased emphasis on creating jobs instead of treating inflation as the main threat to the economy.

Right-wing criticisms of the Fed, in contrast, are grounded in the traditional conservative insistence on reduced government intervention in the economy, at least for interventions that regulate investment or reduce profit. In this view, the Fed is another government intervention in markets that would operate better if left alone, despite the clear association between financial deregulation and bubbles/crashes over the last thirty years. More recently, the advent of QE1 and 2 have driven the right to decry the "hyperinflation" it will bring about, overcoming the strong deflationary pressures of our slack job market. Conservative efforts to reform the Fed range from demands for more transparency up to Ron Paul's demand to abolish the bank entirely, returning to the era of free-floating interest rates (and presumably the greater volatility that accompanied them).

is the component that has taken on enormous proportions as part of the Fed's QE program. This program of asset purchases, which could reach $3 trillion in total, has made massive purchases of U.S. Treasury bonds, "agency debt" issued by the government mortgage agencies Freddie Mac and Fannie Mae, and mortgage-backed securities.

While these colossal buys were meant to lower long-term interest rates, the bond market has seen rate increases instead, defying Fed policy. Bond investors evidently expect borrowers to have difficulty repaying loans in today's weak recovery, and may also be "spooked" at the huge supply of public and private bonds for purchase today. Higher interest rates, of course, act as a drag on the economic recovery, such as it is. This "overruling" of the Fed by the bond market is parallel to the recent reduction in the Fed's power, as more "shadow" banking among unregulated finance firms has taken the place of the commercial banks the Fed regulates, reducing its ability to influence the economy through interest rate changes for the banks in its system. The Fed's separate QE programs, although not themselves limited to Fed system banks, have also been so far unable to lower the price of in-demand credit.

Notably, the QE program is having a secondary effect as a semi-bailout for America's mid-size banks, which are still failing at a rate on course to swamp the FDIC, which insures their deposits. Since these second-tier banks received relatively little bailout money, the Fed is propping many up by buying their bad mortgage debt. QE is presumably also executed with the expectation that it will contribute to driving down the value of the U.S. dollar relative to other world currencies, as the Fed's buying spree effectively dumps the currency into world markets. This may have a positive effect in encouraging U.S. exports, which are cheaper for foreign buyers when the dollar loses value, but it also risks setting off a global currency war as other nations strive to weaken their own currencies in order to boost exports. Competition among trading blocks to deflate currencies was a prominent feature of the Great Depression and not an encouraging model for world economic recovery.

In the shadow of this still-growing mountain of Federal Reserve asset purchases, the Fed's liabilities have grown in parallel, but with less public attention. This is because most of the Fed's new assets are purchased from banks in the Federal Reserve regulatory system, which maintain their own reserve accounts with the Fed. So when the Fed buys some of a private bank's assets, like U.S. Treasury bills or mortgage-backed debt, rather than mail a check it simply increases the banks' deposit account balance. The Fed may be called on to give the bank the money in its Fed account, so these payments are a liability for the Fed, and have grown as a mirror image of the assets bought in the QE purchase program.

Quantitative Unease

The QE gambit—and its effects on the Fed's balance sheet—is by no means unanimously popular at the Fed. It is widely reported that QE is a contentious move among members of the Federal Reserve Open Market Committee, which decides monetary policy. Prominent Fed members, including the presidents of the Dallas,

Philadelphia, and Minneapolis Federal Reserve Banks, have stated discomfort with QE. Dissenters also include Kansas City Federal Reserve Bank President Thomas Hoenig, who has described QE as "risky," and prefers breaking up the "too-big-to-fail" banks. And in language rather unusual for a Fed bank president, he openly discusses the "Wall Street-Washington axis of influence" and decries the "enormous power" of the "oligarchy" of powerful banks.

But most of QE's critics are inflation "hawks"—investors and FOMC members who advocate an aggressively anti-inflationary posture. They oppose QE for two reasons. The first is a fear of runaway inflation caused by injecting so much money into the economy. However, this concern seems remote in an economy with a double-digit real unemployment rate and usage of manufacturing capacity at an embarrassing 72%. Also, the inflation rate itself has not reached 3% since the financial crisis, although significant inflation could originate in imported products should the dollar fall quickly. The hawks' second concern about QE is that the Fed will become unwilling to raise interest rates in the future. Increasing interest rates would reduce the value of the Fed's own large bond investments, when investors sell them for higher-yielding assets. Furthermore, higher rates would mean the Fed would have to pay more in interest to banks with deposits at the Fed. For these twin reasons the hawks fear a loss of the Fed's willingness to raise rates later, thus damaging its inflation-fighting "credibility."

Conservative critics also fear that QE jeopardizes the large payments the Fed makes to the government. By law, any profit the Federal Reserve Bank makes on its now-large investments must be paid to the U.S. Treasury, after covering the Fed's own costs. In 2009 the Fed made $78 billion from its huge investments, politically valuable income in a time of widening budget deficits. A Fed rate increase could eliminate that payment, and indeed the Fed could ultimately lose money on its investment—as the bond market has declined, the Fed's portfolio was recently down a few percent.

Whatever the long-term impact on the Fed of its asset-purchasing campaign, it is difficult to see significant positive effects on the broader economy. Even if the Fed ultimately succeeds in pushing down long-term interest rates, cheap borrowing won't boost the economy the way a targeted spending program would. Companies may appreciate cheap borrowing, but they still won't create jobs when there is not sufficient demand for goods: who would buy new workers' output? Likewise, while cash-strapped and indebted consumers will benefit from low interest rates, they're unlikely to increase spending again without the feeling of security that comes from a steady job. Aggressive fiscal outlays in energy and infrastructure would create far more jobs than quantitative easing is likely to do. No wonder popular discontent with the Fed has reached the point that it's a featured villain in many Tea Party and progressive protests (see sidebar), and now even faces limited audits. Now that the Fed has been disbursing literally trillions in aid to the rich and their institutions for years, with a pitiful trickle going to the majority, the public is getting fed up with the Federal Reserve.

So as the economy staggers on, instead of asking your neighborhood employer for a stimulus-driven job consider asking your neighborhood bank if you can borrow a cup of money. ❏

Sources: Binyamin Applebaum, "Mortgage Securities It Holds Pose Sticky Problem for Fed," *New York Times*, July 22, 2010; Agnes Crane and Robert Cyran, "Rising Interest Rates and the Fed's Red Ink," *New York Times*, December 15, 2010; Michael Derby, "Treasury Fall Poses Long-Term Dilemma for Fed Balance Sheet," *Wall Street Journal*, December 10, 2011; Peter Goodman, "Policy Options Dwindle as Economic Fears Grow," *New York Times*, August 28, 2010; Sewell Chan, "Fed Pays a Record $78.4 Billion to Treasury," *New York Times*, January 10, 2011; "Fed's Fisher: Bond Buying Likely to Run Its Course," *Wall Street Journal*, January 10, 2011; Luca Di Leo, "Yellen Staunchly Defends Fed's Bond Program," *Wall Street Journal*, January 8, 2011; Jon Hilsenrath, "Fed Chief Gets a Likely Backer," *Wall Street Journal*, January 10, 2011; Sewell Chan, "Fed's Contrarian Has a Wary Eye on the Past," *New York Times*, December 13, 2010; Christine Hauser, "A Bond Rush as Treasury Prices Fall," *New York Times*, December 8, 2010; Mark Gongloff, "Bond Market Defies Fed," *Wall Street Journal*, November 16, 2010; Sewell Chan and Jo Craven McGinty, "Fed Papers Show Breadth of Emergency Measures," *New York Times*, December 1, 2010; Jon Hilsenrath, "Fed Fires $600 Billion Stimulus Shot," *Wall Street Journal*, November 4, 2010; Sewell Chan and Ben Protess, "Cross Section of Rich Invested With the Fed," *New York Times*, December 2, 2010.

Article 1.6

LIBOR LIABILITY

A scandal unfolds that has already affected millions of people.

BY MAX FRAAD WOLFF
July/August 2012

The summer of 2012 is heating up for leading financial firms. HSBC is poised to settle money-laundering charges. JPMorgan is struggling to put billions of bad trade losses behind it. Wells Fargo is settling on mortgage discrimination charges. And now, a growing scandal surrounding leading banks' alleged manipulation of key reference interest rates has claimed large fines, senior executives' careers, and the attention of both regulators and the public.

The London InterBank Offered Rates, known as "Libor," are the interest rates at which banks borrow funds from each other. Each day, the British Bankers' Association (BBA) compiles and reports 150 Libor rates (for ten different currencies and fifteen different "maturities," or borrowing terms) with the business-data provider Thomson Reuters. Libor rates are the most widely cited and influential rates for setting adjustable interest rates on trillions of dollars in loans and derivative contracts.

Since 1986, the BBA has arranged to have between eight and sixteen leading banks report the interest rates at which they can borrow in different currencies. Different committees comprised of multiple leading banks set the rates. The names under investigation read like a roll call of banks that received trillions in assistance from governments during the financial crisis.

Libor rates are set in a self-regulatory process arranged, executed, and policed by private entities (the member banks, the BBA, and Thompson Reuters). Thus, Libor reports are a service by and for financial firms. However, they have impact across the global economy: Libor rates are seen as a measure of bank health and financial-market health, and they affect values and interest rates of hundreds of trillions of dollars worth of financial products and loans—including credit cards, student loans, adjustable-rate mortgage, and small-business loans. When Libor rates rise, individuals, governments, and firms pay more to borrow. When rates fall, they pay less.

Libor rates are created by collecting and averaging individual bank rates from multiple institutions, so each individual bank has only a marginal influence on reported rates. However, investigators have found allegations of traders working to coordinate misreporting and fix interest rates. Emails and calls between traders suggest that some worked to guide reported rates up or down across several years. Although regulators in the United States, the UK, and beyond have long been aware of irregularities in Libor rate reporting, authorities have been slow to take action, and the public is still waiting for details. Reports that regulators encouraged underreporting Libor rates to give an appearance of calm and stability in interbank lending markets during the crisis do not boost public confidence in financial markets.

As of now, authorities in the U.S. and British governments as well as across Asia and Europe are investigating the scandal. Several jurisdictions will bring charges and receive settlements in the many millions of dollars. Barclays has already paid over $450 million and replaced its three most senior executives, and other involved banks are scrambling to reach settlements and avoid serious penalties.

But the Libor scandal is a developing story, with much more still to be told. It appears that separately and together, many of the world's leading banks provided inaccurate and misleading information, possibly in illegal concert, and reported incorrect rates. Sometimes this was done to affect the prices of financial products and make ill-gotten gains. On other occasions, particularly in the depths of the financial crisis 2008-2009, false rates were reported to hide the high rates and low trust among banks.

Since rates were both under- and over-reported, it's difficult to determine the net effect of misreporting. Because Libor literally sets interest rate benchmarks, we can't be sure what the rates would have been without the tampering. But it's clear that regulators, clients, states, cities, and citizens were misled, affecting millions of people and trillions of dollars.

As clients sue and regulators investigate, investor confidence will continue to suffer. The scandal couldn't have come at a worse time for the global economy. Whatever your views on finance and your interest level in the Libor scandal, if you borrow or invest money, this saga has been a part of your life for at least four years. Libor rate-fixing will be added to the swirl of public anger about mortgage securities, ratings agencies, bad trades, and predatory lending. Accumulating incidents suggest our flawed regulatory framework and dependence on large financial institutions remain painful vulnerabilities in the global economic system. ❏

Article 1.7

THE EUROZONE: CAUGHT IN A BIND

From "The ABCs of Free-Trade Agreements and Other Regional Economic Blocs"

BY THE *DOLLARS & SENSE* COLLECTIVE
January/February 2001, updated November 2012

The European Union (EU) forms the world's largest single market—larger than the United States or even the three NAFTA countries together. From its beginnings in 1951 as the six-member European Coal and Steel Community, the association has grown both geographically (now including 27 countries) and especially in its degree of unity. All national border controls on goods, capital, and people were abolished between member countries in 1993. And seventeen of the EU's members now share a common currency (the euro), collectively forming the "eurozone."

The process of European economic integration culminated with the establishment of a common currency (the euro) between 1999 and 2002. The creation of the euro seemed to cap the rise of Europe, over many years, from the devastation of the Second World War. Step by step, Western Europe had rebuilt vibrant economies. The largest "core" economy, Germany, had become a global manufacturing power. Even some countries with historically lower incomes, like Ireland, Italy, and Spain, had converged toward the affluence of the core countries. The euro promised to be a major new world currency, ultimately with hundreds of millions of users in one of the world's richest and seemingly most stable regions. Some commentators viewed the euro as a potential rival to the dollar as a key currency in world trade, and as a "reserve" currency (in which individuals, companies, and national banks would hold financial wealth).

Of the 27 European Union (EU) member countries, only 17 have adopted the euro as their currency (joined the "eurozone"). One of the most important EU economies, the United Kingdom, for example, has retained its own national currency (the pound). The countries that did adopt the euro, on the other hand, retired their national currencies. There is no German deutschmark, French franc, or Italian lira anymore. These currencies, and the former national currencies of other eurozone countries, stopped circulating in 2001 or 2002, depending on the country. Bank balances held in these currencies were converted to euros. People holding old bills and coins were also able to exchange them for euros.

The adoption of the euro meant a major change in the control over monetary policy for the eurozone countries. Countries that have their own national currencies generally have a central bank (or "monetary authority") responsible for policies affecting the country's overall money supply and interest rates. In the United States, for example, the Federal Reserve (or "the Fed") is the monetary authority. To "tighten" the money supply, the Fed sells government bonds to "the public" (really, to private banks). It receives money in return, and so reduces the amount of money held by the public. The Fed may do this at the peak of a business-cycle boom, in order to combat or head off inflation. Monetary tightening tends to raise interest rates, pulling back on demand for goods and services. Reduced overall demand, in turn, tends to reduce upward pressure on prices. To "loosen" the money supply, on the other hand, the Fed buys government bonds back from the banks. This puts more money into the banks' hands, which tends to reduce interest rates and stimulate spending. The Fed may do this during a business-cycle downturn or full-blown recession, in order to raise output and employment. As these examples suggest, monetary policy can be an important lever through which governments influence overall demand, output, and employment. Adopting the euro meant giving up control over monetary policy, a step many EU countries, like the UK, were not willing to make.

For eurozone countries, monetary policy is made not by a national central bank, but by the European Central Bank (ECB). ECB policy is made by 23-member "governing council," including the six members of the bank's executive board and the directors of each of the 17 member countries' central banks. The six executive-board members, meanwhile, come from various eurozone countries. (The members in late 2011 are from France, Portugal, Italy, Spain, Germany, and Belgium.)

While all countries that have adopted the euro are represented on the governing council, Germany has a much greater influence on European monetary policy than other countries. Germany's is the largest economy in the eurozone. Among other eurozone countries, only France's economy is anywhere near its size. (Italy's economy is less than two-thirds the size of Germany's, in terms of total output; Spain's, less than half; the Netherlands', less than one-fourth.) German policymakers, meanwhile, have historically made very low inflation rates their main priority (to the point of being "inflation-phobic"). In part, this harkens back to a scarring period of "hyperinflation" during the 1920s; in part, to the importance of Germany as a financial center. Even during the current crisis, as economist Paul Krugman puts it, "what we're seeing is an ECB catering to German desires for low inflation, very much at the expense of making the problems of peripheral economies much less tractable."

For countries, like Germany, that have not been hit so hard by the current crisis, the "tight money" policy is less damaging than for the harder-hit countries. With Germany's unemployment rate at 6.5% and the inflation rate at only 2.5%, as of late 2011, an insistence on a tight money policy does reflect an excessive concern with maintaining very low inflation and insufficient concern with stimulating demand and reducing unemployment. If this policy torpedoes the economies of other European countries, meanwhile, it may drag the whole of Europe—including the more stable "core" economies—back into recession.

For the harder-hit countries, the results are disastrous. These countries are mired in a deep economic crisis, in heavy debt, and unable to adopt a traditional "expansionary" monetary policy on their own (since the eurozone monetary policy is set by the ECB). For them, a looser monetary policy could stimulate demand, production, and employment, even without causing much of an increase in inflation. When an economy is producing near its full capacity, increased demand is likely to put upward pressure on prices. (More money "chasing" the same amount of goods can lead to higher inflation.) In Europe today, however, there are vast unused resources—including millions of unemployed workers—so more demand could stimulate the production of more goods, and need not result in rising inflation.

Somewhat higher inflation, moreover, could actually help stimulate the harder-hit European economies. Moderate inflation can stimulate demand, since it gives people an incentive to spend now rather than wait and spend later. It also reduces the real burdens of debt. Countries like Greece, Ireland, Italy, Portugal, and Spain are drowning in debt, both public and private. These debts are generally specified in nominal terms—as a particular number of euros. As the price level increases, however, it reduces the real value of a nominal amount of money. Debts can be paid back in euros that are worth less than when the debt was incurred. As real debt burdens decrease, people feel less anxious about their finances, and may begin to spend more freely. Inflation also redistributes income from creditors, who tend to be wealthier and to save more of their incomes, to debtors, who tend to be less wealth and spend most of theirs. This, too, helps boost demand.

The current crisis has led many commentators to speculate that some heavily indebted countries may decide to abandon the euro. This need not mean that they would repudiate (refuse to pay) their public debt altogether. They could, instead, convert their euro debts to their new national currencies. This would give them more freedom to pursue a higher-inflation policy, which would reduce the real debt burden. (Indeed, independent countries that owe their debt in their own currency need not ever default. A country that controls its own money supply can "print" more money to repay creditors—with the main limit being how the money supply can be expanded without resulting in unacceptably high inflation. Adopting the euro, however, deprived countries in the eurozone of this power.) The current crisis, some economists argue, shows how the euro project was misguided from the start. Paul Krugman, for example, argues that the common currency was mainly driven by a political (not economic) aim—the peaceful unification of a region that had been torn apart by two world wars. It did not make much sense economically, given the real possibility for divergent needs of different national economies. Today, it seems a real possibility that the eurozone, at least, will come apart again. ❏

Sources: Paul Krugman, "European Inflation Targets," *New York Times* blog, January 18, 2011 (krugman.blogs.nytimes.com); European Central Bank, Decision-making, Governing Council (www.ecb.int/); European Central Bank, Decision-making, Executive Board (www.ecb.int/); Federal Statistical Office (Statistisches Bundesamt Deutschland), Federal Republic of Germany, Short-term indicators, Unemployment, Consumer Price Index (www.destatis.de); Paul Krugman, "Can Europe Be Saved?" *New York Times*, January 12, 2011 (nytimes.com).

Chapter 2

THE BANKING AND FINANCE INDUSTRY

Article 2.1

FINANCIALIZATION: A PRIMER

BY RAMAA VASUDEVAN
November/December 2008

You don't have to be an investor dabbling in the stock market to feel the power of finance. Finance pervades the lives of ordinary people in many ways, from student loans and credit card debt to mortgages and pension plans.

And its size and impact are only getting bigger. Consider a few measures:

• U.S. credit market debt—all debt of private households, businesses, and government combined—rose from about 1.6 times the nation's GDP in 1973 to over 3.5 times GDP by 2007.

• The profits of the financial sector represented 14% of total corporate profits in 1981; by 2001-02 this figure had risen to nearly 50%.

These are only a few of the indicators of what many commentators have labeled the "financialization" of the economy—a process University of Massachusetts economist Gerald Epstein succinctly defines as "the increasing importance of financial markets, financial motives, financial institutions, and financial elites in the operation of the economy and its governing institutions."

In recent years, this phenomenon has drawn increasing attention. In his latest book, pundit Kevin Phillips writes about the growing divergence between the real (productive) and financial economies, describing how the explosion of trading in myriad new financial instruments played a role in polarizing the U.S. economy. On the left, political economists Harry Magdoff and Paul Sweezy had over many years pointed to the growing role of finance in the operations of capitalism; they viewed the trend as a reflection of the rising economic and political power of "rentiers"—those whose earnings come from financial activities and from forms of income arising from ownership claims (such as interest, rent, dividends, or capital gains) rather than from actual production.

From Finance to Financialization

The financial system is supposed to serve a range of functions in the broader economy. Banks and other financial institutions mop up savings, then allocate that capital, according to mainstream theory, to where it can most productively be used. For households and corporations, the credit markets facilitate greatly increased borrowing, which should foster investment in capital goods like buildings and machinery, in turn leading to expanded production. Finance, in other words, is supposed to facilitate the growth of the "real" economy—the part that produces useful goods (like bicycles) and services (like medical care).

In recent decades, finance has undergone massive changes in both size and shape. The basic mechanism of financialization is the transformation of future streams of income (from profits, dividends, or interest payments) into a tradable asset like a stock or a bond. For example, the future earnings of corporations are transmuted into equity stocks that are bought and sold in the capital market. Likewise, a loan, which involves certain fixed interest payments over its duration, gets a new life when it is converted into marketable bonds. And multiple loans, bundled together then "sliced and diced" into novel kinds of bonds ("collateralized debt obligations"), take on a new existence as investment vehicles that bear an extremely complex and opaque relationship to the original loans.

The process of financialization has not made finance more effective at fulfilling what conventional economic theory views as its core function. Corporations are not turning to the stock market as a source of finance for their investments, and their borrowing in the bond markets is often not for the purpose of productive investment either. Since the 1980s, corporations have actually spent more money buying back their own stock than they have taken in by selling newly issued stock. The granting of stock options to top executives gives them a direct incentive to have the corporation buy back its own shares—often using borrowed money to do so—in order to hike up the share price and allow them to turn a profit on the sale of their personal shares. More broadly, instead of fostering investment, financialization reorients managerial incentives toward chasing short-term returns through financial trading and speculation so as to generate ballooning earnings, lest their companies face falling stock prices and the threat of hostile takeover.

What is more, the workings of these markets tend to act like an upper during booms, when euphoric investors chase the promise of quick bucks. During downturns these same mechanisms work like downers, turning euphoria into panic as investors flee. Financial innovations like collateralized debt obligations were supposed to "lubricate" the economy by spreading risk, but instead they tend to heighten volatility, leading to amplified cycles of boom and bust. In the current crisis, the innovation of mortgage-backed securities fueled the housing bubble and encouraged enormous risk-taking, creating the conditions for the chain reaction of bank (and other financial institution) failures that may be far from over.

Financialization and Power

The arena of finance can at times appear to be merely a casino—albeit a huge one—where everyone gets to place her bets and ride her luck. But the financial system carries a far deeper significance for people's lives. Financial assets and liabilities represent claims on ownership and property; they embody the social relations of an economy at a particular time in history. In this sense, the recent process of financialization implies the increasing political and economic power of a particular segment of the capitalist class: rentiers. Accelerating financial transactions and the profusion of financial techniques have fuelled an extraordinary enrichment of this elite.

This enrichment arises in different ways. Financial transactions facilitate the reallocation of capital to high-return ventures. In the ensuing shake-up, some sectors of capital profit at the expense of other sectors. More important, the capitalist class as a whole is able to force a persistent redistribution in its favor, deploying its newly expanded wealth to bring about changes in the political-economy that channel even more wealth its way.

The structural changes that paved the way for financialization involved the squashing of working-class aspirations during the Reagan-Thatcher years; the defeats of the miners' strike in England and of the air traffic controllers' (PATCO) strike in the United States were perhaps the most symbolic instances of this process. At the same time, these and other governments increasingly embraced the twin policy mantras of fighting inflation and deregulating markets in place of creating full employment and raising wages. Corporations pushed through legislation to dismantle the financial regulations that inhibited their profitmaking strategies.

Financialization has gathered momentum amid greater inequality. In the United States, the top 1% of the population received 14.0% of the national after-tax income in 2004, nearly double its 7.5% share in 1979. In the same period the share of the bottom fifth fell from 6.8% to 4.9%.

And yet U.S. consumption demand has been sustained despite rising inequality and a squeeze on real wages for the majority of households. Here is the other side of the financialization coin: a massive expansion of consumer credit has played an important role in easing the constraints on consumer spending by filling the gap created by stagnant or declining real wages. The credit card debt of the average U.S. family increased by 53% through the 1990s. About 67% of low-income families with incomes less than $10,000 faced credit card debt, and the debt of this group saw the largest increase—a 184% rise, compared to a 28% increase for families with incomes above $100,000. Offered more and more credit as a privatized means of addressing wage stagnation, then, eventually, burdened by debt and on the edge of insolvency, the working poor and the middle class are less likely to organize as a political force to challenge the dominance of finance. In this sense, financialization becomes a means of social coercion that erodes working-class solidarity.

As the structures created by financial engineering unravel, the current economic crisis is revealing the cracks in this edifice. But even as a growing number of U.S. families are losing their homes and jobs in the wake of the subprime meltdown, the financial companies at the heart of the crisis have been handed massive bailouts and their top executives have pocketed huge pay-outs despite their role in abetting the meltdown—a stark sign of the power structures and interests at stake in this era of financialization. ❏

Sources: Robin Blackburn, "Finance and the Fourth Dimension," *New Left Review* 39 May-June 2006; Robert Brenner, "New Boom or Bubble," *New Left Review* 25 Jan-Feb 2004; Tamara Draut and Javier Silva, "Borrowing to make ends meet," *Demos*, Sept 2003; Gerald Epstein, "Introduction" in G. Epstein, ed., *Financialization and the World* Economy, 2006; John Bellamy Foster, "The Financialization of Capitalism," *Monthly Review*, April 2007; Gretta Krippner, "The financialization of the US economy," *Socio-Economic Review* 3, Feb. 2005; Thomas Palley, "Financialization : What it is and why it matters," Political Economy Research Institute Working Paper #153, November 2007; A. Sherman and Arin Dine, "New CBO data shows inequality continues to widen," Center for Budget Priorities, Jan. 23, 2007; Kevin Phillips, *Bad Money: Reckless Finance, Failed Politics, and the Global Crisis of American Capitalism*, 2008.

Article 2.2

NOT TOO BIG ENOUGH
Where the big banks come from.

BY ROB LARSON
July/August 2010

The government bailout of America's biggest banks set off a tornado of public anger and confusion. When the House of Representatives initially rejected the bailout bill, the *Wall Street Journal* attributed it to "populist fury," and since then the public has remained stubbornly resentful over the bailout of those banks considered "too big to fail." Now, the heads of economic policy are trying to gracefully distance themselves from bailouts, claiming that future large-scale bank failures will be avoided by stronger regulation and higher insurance premiums.

Dealing with the collapse of these "systemically important banks" is a difficult policy issue, but the less-discussed issue is how the banking industry came to this point. If the collapse of just one of our $100 billion megabanks, Lehman Brothers, was enough to touch off an intense contraction in the supply of essential credit, we must know how some banks became "too big to fail" in the first place. The answer lies in incentives for bank growth. After the loosening of crucial industry regulations, these incentives have driven the enormous waves of bank mergers in the last thirty years.

Geographical Growth

Prior to the 1980s, American commercial banking was a small-scale affair. State-chartered banks were prohibited by state laws from running branches outside their home state, or sometimes even outside their home county. Nationally chartered banks were likewise limited, and federal law allowed interstate acquisitions only if a state legislature specifically decided to permit out-of-state banks to purchase local branches. No states allowed such acquisition until 1975, when Maine and other states began passing legislation allowing at least some interstate banking. The trend was capped in 1994 by the Riegle-Neal Act, which removed the remaining restrictions on interstate branching and allowed direct cross-state banking mergers.

This geographic deregulation allowed commercial banks to make extensive acquisitions, in state and out. When Wells Fargo acquired another large California bank, Crocker National, in 1986 it was the largest bank merger in U.S. history. Since "the regulatory light was green," a single banking company could now operate across the uniquely large U.S. market, opening up enormous new opportunities for economies of scale in the banking industry.

Economies of scale are savings that companies enjoy when they grow larger and produce more output. The situation is similar to a cook preparing a batch of cookies for a Christmas party, and then preparing a batch for New Year's while all the ingredients and materials are already out. Producing more output (cookies) in one afternoon is more efficient than taking everything out again later to make the New Year's batch separately. In enterprise, this corresponds to spreading the large costs of startup investment over more and more output, and is often thought of as lower per-unit costs as the level of production increases. In other words, there's less effort per cookie if you make them all at once. Economies of scale, when present in an industry, create a strong incentive for firms to grow larger, since profitability will improve. But they also give larger, established firms a valuable cost advantage over new competitors, which can put the brakes on competition.

Once unleashed by the policy changes, these economies of scale played a major role in the industry's seemingly endless merger activity. "In order to compete, you need scale," said a VP for Chemical Bank when buying a smaller bank in 1994. Of course, in 1996 Chemical would itself merge with Chase Manhattan Bank.

Economies of Scale in Banking and Finance

Economies of scale are savings that companies benefit from as they grow larger and produce more output. While common in many industries, in banking and finance, these economies drove bank growth after industry deregulation in the 1980s and 90s. Some of the major scale economies in banking are:

- **Spreading investment over more output.** With the growth in importance of large-scale computing power and sophisticated systems management, the costs of setting up a modern banking system are very large. However, as a firm grows it can "spread out" the cost of that initial investment over more product, so that its cost per unit decreases as more output is produced.

- **Consolidation of functions.** The modern workforce is no stranger to the mass firings of "redundant" staff after mergers and acquisitions. If one firm's payroll staff and computer systems can handle twice the employees with little additional expense, an acquired bank may see its payroll department harvest pink slips while the firm's profitability improves. When Citicorp merged with the insurance giant Travelers Group in 1998, the resulting corporation laid off over 10,000 workers—representing 6% of the combined company's total workforce and over $500 million in reduced costs for Citigroup. This practice can be especially lucrative in a country like the United States, with a fairly unregulated labor market where firms are quite free to fire. Despite the economic peril inflicted on workers and their families, this consolidation is key to increasing company efficiency post-merger. Beyond back-office functions, core profit operations may also benefit from consolidation. When Bank of America combined its managed mutual funds into a single fund, it experienced lower total costs, thanks to trimming overhead from audit and prospectus mailing expenses. Consolidating office departments in this fashion can yield savings of 40% of the cost base of the acquired bank.

- **Funding mix.** The "funding mix" used by banks refers to where banks get the capital they then package into loans. Smaller institutions, having only limited deposits from savers, must "purchase funds" by borrowing from other institutions. This increases the funding cost of loans for banks, but larger banks will naturally have access to larger pools of deposits from which to arrange loans. This funding cost advantage for larger banks relative to smaller ones represents another economy of scale.

- **Advertising.** The nature of advertising requires a certain scale of operation to be viable. Advertising can reach large numbers of potential customers, but if a firm is small or local, many of those customers will be too far afield to act on the marketing. Large firm size, and especially geographic reach, can make the returns on ad time worth the investment.

Spreading big investment costs over more output is the main source of generic economies of scale, and in banking, the large initial investments are in sophisticated computer systems. The cost of investing in new computer hardware and systems development is now recognized as a major investment obstacle for new banks, although once installed by banks large enough to afford them, they are highly profitable. The *Financial Times* describes how "the development of bulk computer processing and of electronic data transmission…has allowed banks to move their back office operations away from individual branches to large remote centers. This had helped to bring real economies of scale to banking, an industry which traditionally has seen diseconomies set in at a very modest scale."

Economies of scale are common in manufacturing, and in the wake of deregulation the banking industry was also able to exploit a number of them. Besides spreading out the cost of computer systems, economies of scale may be present in office consolidation, in the funding mix used by banks, and in advertising. (See sidebar.)

Industry-to-Industry Growth

BusinessWeek's analysis is that the banking industry "has produced large competitors that can take advantage of economies of scale…as regulatory barriers to interstate banking fell," although not until the banks could "digest their purchases." The 1990s saw hundreds of bank purchases annually and hundreds of billions in acquired assets.

But an additional major turn for the industry came with the Gramm-Leach-Bliley Act of 1999 (GLB), which further loosened restrictions on bank growth, this time not geographically but industry-to-industry. After earlier moves in this direction by the Federal Reserve, GLB allowed for the free combination of commercial banking, insurance, and the riskier field of investment banking. These had been separated by law for decades, on the grounds that the availability of commercial credit was too important to the overall economy to be tied to the volatile world of investment banking.

GLB allowed firms to grow further, through banks merging with insurers or investment banks. The world of commercial credit was widened, and financial mergers this time exploited economies of scope—where production of multiple products jointly is cheaper than producing them individually. As commercial banks, investment banks, and insurers have expanded into each others' fields in the wake of GLB, their different lines of business can benefit from single expenses—for example, banks perform research on loan recipients that can also be used to underwrite bond issues. Scope economies such as these allow the larger banks to both run a greater profit on a per-service basis and attract more business. Thanks to the convenience of "one stop shopping," Citigroup now does more business with big corporations, like IT giant Unisys, than its component firms did pre-merger.

Exploiting economies of scope to diversify product lines in this fashion can also help a firm by reducing its dependence on any one line of business. Bank of America weathered the stock market downturn of 2001 in part because its corporate debt underwriting business was booming. Smaller, more specialized banks can become "one-trick ponies" as the *Wall Street Journal* put it—outdone by larger competitors with low-cost diversification thanks to scope economies.

These economies of scope are parallel to the scale economies, since both required deregulatory policy changes to be unleashed. Traditionally, banking wasn't seen as an industry with the strong economies of scale seen in, say, manufacturing. But the deregulation and computerization of the industry have allowed these firms to realize returns to greater scale and wider scope, and this has been a main driver of the endless acquisitions in the industry in recent decades.

Market Power

The enormous proportions that the banking institutions have taken on following deregulation have meant serious consequences for market performance. A number of banks have reached sufficient size to exercise market power—the ability of firms to influence prices and to engage in anticompetitive behavior. The market power of our enormous banks allows them to take positions as price leaders in local markets, where large firms use their dominance to elevate prices (i.e., increase fees and rates on loans, and decrease interest rates on deposits). Large firms can do this because smaller firms may perceive that lowering their prices to take market share could be met by very drastic reductions in prices from the larger firm in retaliation. Large firms, having deeper pockets, may be able to withstand longer periods of operating at a loss than the smaller firms.

Small banks are likely to perceive that the colossal size and resources of the megabanks make them unprofitable to cross—better to follow along and charge roughly what the dominant, price-leading firm does. Empirical research by Federal Reserve Board senior economist Steven Pilloff supported this analysis, finding that the arrival of very large banks in local markets tended to increase bank profitability for reasons of price leadership, due to the larger banks' economies of scale and scope, financial muscle, and diversification.

Examples of the use of banking industry market power are easy to find. Several bills now circulating in Congress deal with the fees retail businesses pay to the banks and the credit card companies. When consumers make purchases with their Visas or MasterCards, an average of two cents of each dollar goes not to the retailer but to the credit card companies that run the payment network and the banks that supply the credit. These "interchange fees" bring in over $35 billion in profit in the United States alone, and they reflect the strong market power of the banks and credit card companies over the various big and small retailers. The 2% charge comes to about $31,000 for a typical convenience store, just below the average per-store yearly profit of $36,000, and this has driven a coalition of retailers to press for congressional action.

Visa has about 50% of the credit card market (including debit cards), and MasterCard has 25%, which grants them profound market power and strong bargaining positions. Federal Reserve Bank of Kansas City economists found the United States "maintains the highest interchange fees in the world, yet its costs should be among the lowest, given economies of scale and declining cost trends." The *Wall Street Journal*'s description was that "these fees...have also been paradoxically tending upward in recent years when the industry's costs due to technology and economies of scale have been falling." Of course, there's only a paradox if market power is omitted from the picture. The dominant size and scale economies of the banks and the credit card oligopoly allow for high prices to be sustained—bank muscle in action against a less powerful sector of the economy. The political action favored by the retailers includes proposals for committees to enact price ceilings or (interestingly) collective bargaining by the retailers. As is often the case, the political process is the reflection of the different levels and positions of power of various corporate institutions, and the maneuvering of their organizations.

Market power brings with it a number of other advantages. A powerful company is likely to have a widespread presence, make frequent use of advertising, and be able to raise its profile by contributing to community organizations like sports leagues. This allows the larger banks to benefit from stronger brand identity—their scale and resources make customers more likely to trust their services. This grants a further advantage in the form of customer tolerance of higher prices due to brand loyalty.

Political Clout

Crucially, large firms with market power are free to participate meaningfully in politics—using their deep pockets to invest in electoral campaigns and congressional lobbying. The financial sector is among the highest-contributing industries in the United States, with total 2008 campaign contributions approaching half a billion dollars, according to the Center For Public Integrity. So it's unsurprising that they receive so many favors from the government, since they fund the careers of the decision-making government personnel. This underlying reality is why influential Senator Dick Durbin said of Congress, "The banks own the place."

Finally, banks may grow so large by exploiting scale economies and market power that they become "systemically important" to the nation's financial system. In other words, the scale and interconnectedness of the largest banks is considered to have reached a point where an abrupt failure of one or more of them may have "systemic" effects—meaning the broader economic system will be seriously impaired. These "too big to fail" banks are the ones that were bailed out by act of Congress in the fall 2008. Once a firm becomes so enormous that the government must prevent its collapse for the good of the economy, it has the ultimate advantage of being free to take far greater risks. Riskier investments come with higher returns and profits, but the greater risk of collapse that accompanies them will be less intimidating to huge banks that have an implied government insurance policy.

Some analysts have expressed doubt that such firms truly are too large to let fail, and that the banks have pulled a fast one. It might be pointed out in this connection that in the past the banks themselves have put their money where their mouths are—they have paid out of pocket to rescue financial institutions they saw as too large and connected to fail. An especially impressive episode took place in 1998, when several of Wall Street's biggest banks and financiers agreed to billions in emergency loans to rescue Long Term Capital Management. LTCM was a high-profile hedge fund that borrowed enormous sums of capital to make billion-dollar gambles on financial markets.

America's biggest banks aren't in the habit of forking over $3.5 billion of good earnings, but they had loaned heavily to LTCM and feared losing their money if the fund went under. The Federal Reserve brought the bankers together, and in the end, they paid up to bail out their colleagues, and the *Wall Street Journal* reported that it was the Fed's "clout, together with the self-interest of several big firms that already had lent billions of dollars to Long-Term Capital, that helped fashion the rescue." Interestingly, the banks insisted on real equity in the firm they were pulling out of the fire, and they gained a 90% stake in the hedge fund. Comparing this to the less-valuable "preferred stock" the government settled for in its 2008 bailout package of the large banks is instructive. The banks also got a share of control in the firm they rescued, again in stark contrast to the public bailout of some of the same banks.

Even Bigger?

In fact, the financial crisis and bailout led only to further concentration of the industry. The crisis gave stronger firms an opportunity to pick up sicker ones in another "wave of consolidation," as *BusinessWeek* put it. And a large part of the government intervention itself involved arranging hasty purchases of failing giants by other giants, orchestrated by the Federal Reserve. For example, the Fed helped organize the purchase of Bear Stearns by Chase in March 2008 and the purchase of Wachovia by Wells Fargo in December 2008. Even the bailout's "capital infusions" were used for further mergers and acquisitions by several recipients. The Treasury Department was "using the bailout bill to turn the banking system into the oligopoly of giant national institutions," as the *New York Times* reported.

The monumental growth of the largest banks owes a lot to the industry's economies of scale and scope, once regulations were relaxed so firms could exploit them. While certainly not unique to finance, these dynamics have brought the banks to such enormous size that their bad bets can put the entire economy in peril. Banking therefore offers an especially powerful case for the importance of these economies and the role of market power, since it's left the megabanks holding all the cards.

In fact, many arguments between defenders of the market economy and its critics center on the issue of competition vs. power—market boosters reliably insist that markets mean efficient competition, where giants have no inherent advantage over small, scrappy firms. However, the record in banking clearly shows that banks have enjoyed a variety of real benefits from growth. The existence of companies of great size and power is a quite natural development in many industries, due to the appeal of returns to scale and power. This is why firms end up with enough power to influence government policy, or such absurd size that they can blackmail us for life support.

And leave us crying all the way to the bank. ❏

Sources: Judith Samuelson and Lynn Stout, "Are Executives Paid Too Much?" *Wall Street Journal*, February 26, 2009; Tom Braithwaite, "Geithner Presses Congress for Action on Reform," *Financial Times*, September 23, 2009; Phillip Zweig, "Intrastate Mergers Between Banking Giants Might Not Be Out of the Question Anymore," *Wall Street Journal*, March 25, 1986; Bruce Knecht, "Chemical Banking plans acquisition of Margaretten," *Wall Street Journal*, May 13, 1994; Eric Weiner, "Banks Will Post Good Quarterly Results," *Wall Street Journal*, January 10, 1997; Gabriella Stern, "Four Big Regionals To Consolidate Bank Operations," *Wall Street Journal*, July 22, 1992; "Pressure for change grows," *Financial Times*, September 27, 1996; Tracy Corrigan and John Authers, "Citigroup To Take $900 million charge: Cost-cutting Program to Result in Loss of 10,400 Jobs," *Financial Times*, December 16, 1998; Eleanor Laise, "Mutual-Fund Mergers Jump Sharply," *Wall Street Journal*, March 9, 2006; Steven Pilloff, "Banking, commerce and competition under the Gramm-Leach-Bliley Act," *The Antitrust Bulletin*, Spring 2002; David Humphrey, "Why Do Estimates of Bank Scale Economies Differ?" *Economic Review* of Federal Reserve Bank of Richmond, September/October 1990, note four; Michael Mandel and Rich Miller, "Productivity: The Real Story," *BusinessWeek*, November 5, 2001; John Yang, "Fed Votes to Give 7 Bank Holding Firms Additional Power in Securities Sector," *Wall Street Journal*, July 16, 1987; "Banking Behemoths—What Happens Next: Many companies Like to Shop Around For Their Providers of Financial Services," *Wall Street Journal*, September 14, 2000; Carrick Mollenkamp and Paul Beckett, "Diverse Business Portfolios Boost Banks' Bottom Lines," *Wall Street Journal*, July 17, 2001; *Journal of Financial Services Research*, "Does the Presence of Big Banks Influence Competition in Local Markets?" May 1999; "Credit-Card Wars," *Wall Street Journal*, March 29, 2008; *Economic Review* of the Federal Reserve Bank of Kansas City, "Interchange Fees in Credit and Debit Card Markets: What Role for Public Authorities," January-March 2006; "Credit Where It's Due," *Wall Street Journal*, January 12, 2006; Keith Bradsher, "In One Pocket, Out the Other," *New York Times*, November 25, 2009; Center For Public Integrity, Finance/Insurance/Real Estate: Long-Term Contribution Trends, opensecrests.org; Dean Baker, "Banks own the U.S. government," *Guardian*, June 30, 2009; Anita Raghavan and Mitchell Pacelle, "To the Rescue? A Hedge Fun Falters, So the Fed Persuades Big Banks to Ante Up," *Wall Street Journal*, September 24, 1998; Theo Francis, "Will Bank Rescues Mean Fewer Banks?" *BusinessWeek*, November 25, 2008; Joe Nocera, "So When Will Banks Give Loans?" *New York Times*, October 25, 2008.

Article 2.3

BIG BANK IMMUNITY
When do we crack down on Wall Street?

BY DEAN BAKER
March 2013; Truthout

The Wall Street gang must really be partying these days. Profits and bonuses are as high as ever as these super-rich takers were able to use trillions of dollars of below-market government loans to get themselves through the crisis they created. The rest of the country is still struggling with high unemployment, stagnant wages, underwater mortgages and hollowed out retirement accounts, but life is good again on Wall Street.

Their world must have gotten even brighter last week when Attorney General Eric Holder told the Senate Judiciary Committee that the Justice Department may have to restrain its prosecutors in dealing with the big banks because it has to consider the possibility that a prosecution could lead to financial instability. Not only can the big banks count on taxpayer bailouts when they need them; it turns out that they can share profits with drug dealers with impunity. (The case immediately at hand involved money laundered for the Mexican drug cartel.) And who says that times are bad?

It's hard to know where to begin with this one. First off, we should not assume that just because the Justice Department says it is concerned about financial instability that this is the real reason that they are not prosecuting a big bank. There is precedent for being less than honest about such issues.

When Enron was about to collapse in 2002 as its illegal dealings became public, former Treasury Secretary Robert Rubin, who was at the time a top Citigroup executive, called a former aide at Treasury. He asked him to intervene with the bond rating agencies to get them to delay downgrading Enron's debt. Citigroup owned several hundred million dollars in Enron debt at the time. If Rubin had gotten this delay Citigroup would have been able to dump much of this debt on suckers before the price collapsed.

The Treasury official refused. When the matter became public, Robert Rubin claimed that he was concerned about instability in financial markets.

It is entirely possible that the reluctance to prosecute big banks represents the same sort of fear of financial instability as motivated Robert Rubin. In other words, it is a pretext that the Justice Department is using to justify its failure to prosecute powerful friends on Wall Street. In Washington this possibility can never be ruled out.

However, there is the possibility that the Justice Department really believes that prosecuting the criminal activities of Bank of America or JP Morgan could sink the economy. If this is true then it make the case for breaking up the big banks even more of a slam dunk since it takes the logic of too big to fail one step further.

Just to remind everyone, the simple argument against too-big-to-fail is that it subsidizes risk-taking by large banks. In principle, when a bank or other company is engaged in a risky line of business those who are investing in the company or lending it money demand a higher rate of return in recognition of the risk.

However, if they know that government will back up the bank if it gets into trouble then investors have little reason to properly evaluate the risk. This means that more money will flow to the TBTF bank since it knows it can undertake risky activities without paying the same interest rate as other companies that take on the same amount of risk. The result is that we have given the banks an incentive to engage in risky activity and a big subsidy to their top executives and creditors.

If it turns out that we also give them a get-out-of-jail-free card when it comes to criminal activity then we are giving these banks an incentive to engage in criminal activity. There is a lot of money to be gained by assisting drug dealers and other nefarious types in laundering their money. In principle the laws are supposed to be structured to discourage banks from engaging in such behavior. But when the attorney general tells us that the laws cannot be fully enforced against the big banks he is saying that we are giving them incentive to break the law in the pursuit of profit.

Our anti-trust laws are supposed to protect the country against companies whose size allows them inordinate market power. In principle, we would use anti-trust law to break up a phone company because its market dominance allowed it to charge us $10 a month too much on our cable. How could we not use anti-trust policy to break up a bank whose size allows it to profit from dealing with drug dealers and murderers with impunity? ❑

Article 2.4

VULTURES IN THE E.R.
Private-equity firms target the U.S. health-care industry.

BY NICOLE ASCHOFF
January/February 2013

Public anger over increasing economic polarization and frustration with the seemingly unassailable power of big finance coalesced for a brief moment last summer in the public shaming of Bain Capital, the private-equity firm formerly run by Mitt Romney. Popular journalists like Rolling Stone's Matt Taibbi turned their attention to the activities of powerful, secretive private equity firms, connecting the dots between private-equity investment and job loss, and people got mad. But, as with the leveraged-buyout kings of the 1980s, after the election furor subsided, Bain and its privateequity brethren dropped back under the radar, returning to business as usual.

However, the nature of "business as usual" for private equity warrants another look. Private-equity (PE) firms like Bain, Cerberus, Blackstone, Warburg Pincus, and Kohlberg, Kravis and Roberts (KKR) operate in nearly every sector of the economy, including manufacturing, business and financial services, food, entertainment, and health care. Cutthroat tactics, job loss, and bankruptcy are common themes in the PE world (see John Miller, "Private Equity Moguls and the Common Good," Dollars & Sense, July/August 2012).

Health care is a particularly popular sector for PE firms. After a decline following the 2008 financial crisis, PE investment in health care has rebounded, both in the United States and globally. In particular, medical technology, pharmaceuticals, and medical services (like hospitals and nursing homes) are seeing sharp increases in PE investment. According to a recent report by Bain, the value of global private-equity deals in health care was over $30 billion in 2011, double the investment of 2010.

Growing PE interest in low-profit, or no-profit, sectors like hospitals may come as a surprise to many who assume that private investors prefer to channel their money toward industries with rapid growth or high profit potential, like medical technology and pharmaceuticals. But private-equity firms are not like most investors. Unlike venture capitalists, who bet their own money on the success of a company, in most cases private-equity firms put very little of their own capital into their investments, and instead arrange for outside investors (like pension funds) and the firm being taken over to fund the investment. The PE firms make their money from fees and dividends, which are often debt-financed by the acquired firm. This unique feature of private-equity firms means that any company with steady cash flow (or even just a substantial potential cash flow) is a possible target for acquisition.

The growing appetite for hospital takeovers by PE firms has its roots in the ongoing struggle for survival experienced by many hospitals. Hospitals— particularly small, community hospitals and those serving poor populations—are under intense pressure due to declining Medicare/Medicaid reimbursement rates, new government demands for technological upgrades, increasing numbers of under- and uninsured patients, and restricted access to credit markets. According to the American Hospital Association (AHA), roughly 30% of non-profit hospitals are operating at a loss. Many more hospitals find themselves breaking even each year, but unable to borrow and make investments to keep up with increasing costs and regulation.

The precarious financial situation of many community hospitals has led to a wave of mergers and acquisitions in recent years by for-profit hospital corporations and larger non-profit systems. Community hospitals believe that being absorbed by a larger hospital or hospital chain will result in improved access to capital to make necessary upgrades and maintain their patient base. Meanwhile, big, for-profit, and non-profit hospitals view the acquisition of smaller, community hospitals as an easy way to increase market share and improve economies of scale.

This consolidation trend is similar to the one that occurred in the hospital sector in the 1990s, but with one significant difference—the increasing role of PE investors. PE investors are betting that the growing needs of the baby-boomer generation, in combination with the Affordable Care Act, which will dramatically expand health-insurance coverage (an estimated 15-20 million new insured by 2014, and an additional 15 million by 2016), will create new profit opportunities. For example, in 2006, KKR, Bain, and Merrill Lynch acquired the mammoth Hospital Corporation of America (HCA), a for-profit hospital chain that owns hundreds of hospitals in the United States and England, for $31.6 billion. PE firms are also snapping up non-profit, community hospitals. In December 2010, Vanguard Health (owned at the time by Blackstone), bought the Detroit Medical Center for $1.3 billion. In the same year, Cerberus Capital Management paid $830 million to acquire the Caritas Christi chain of hospitals from the Archdiocese of Boston, folding the hospitals into a new, for-profit entity called Steward Health Care System. Although the AHA estimates that less than 20% of community hospitals are investor-owned, the number is growing rapidly. Josh Kosman, an expert on PE investment, estimates that half of the biggest for-profit hospital chains are now owned by private-equity firms.

One of the strategies followed by PE-backed, forprofit hospital chains like Vanguard and Steward is to gain control over urban market share by aggressively acquiring hospital groups. This strategy is a departure from earlier, more scattered, and somewhat opportunistic, acquisition patterns by for-profit hospital chains like HCA and Essent. Vanguard's purchase of Detroit Medical Center gave it control over 13.4% of Detroit's total market, while its 2010 purchase of Westlake Hospital and West Suburban Medical Center in Illinois gave it 47% of acute care inpatient beds in the immediate health planning area. Steward's recent acquisitions, including its purchase of the Caritas chain, give it control over a quarter of eastern Massachusetts acute care beds.

What's the Difference?

All hospitals are facing similar market conditions and are concerned with minimizing costs and increasing revenues. So what is the difference between not-forprofit systems like Partners, for-profit hospital chains such as Tenet and LifePoint, and

PE-owned hospital chains like Steward? A recent report issued by the Congressional Budget Office suggests that there is little difference in the behavior of non-profit and forprofit hospitals. The report found that not-for-profit hospitals on average provide slightly higher levels of uncompensated care than for-profit hospitals, while for-profit hospitals, on average, serve poorer populations with higher rates of people living with little or no health insurance.

However, Jill Horwitz, a professor at the University of Michigan, argues that nonprofit hospitals and forprofit hospitals exhibit important differences in the types of care they offer. For-profit firms emphasize surgical and acute care services, and cardiac and diagnostic services, while non-profit hospitals often provide less lucrative care such as mental health services, drug-and-alcohol treatment programs, and traumaand- burn centers. When non-profit hospitals are converted into for-profits, they often discontinue or decrease these crucial, but less-profitable, services.

PE-backed hospital firms are particularly likely to jettison less-profitable services given their shorter investment timelines. Like most PE investments, PE firms' hospital acquisitions tend to last a short period (around five years). Then, the PE firm either takes the acquired firm public (offers stock for sale to the general public) or re-sells to other PE firms. For example, HCA was owned by two PE firms (KKR and Bain) for five years before a March 2011 initial public offering of stock (IPO), while Vanguard was owned by Morgan Stanley and Blackstone before going public in June 2011. The PE owners' goal during this period of time is to quickly increase profits and cash flow, enabling the PE firm to collect its fees and dividends, often by accessing credit and bond markets.

This investment timeline pushes PE firms to look for simple, and relatively fast, ways to increase revenues, such as eliminating less-profitable services. For example, in 2004, Vanguard's Weiss Hospital in Chicago failed a spot inspection for maternity-ward security. Staff failed to stop undercover inspectors from removing a baby (actually, for the purpose of the inspection, just an infant doll) from the ward without authorization. Rather than resolve the issue through increased staffing and a reexamination of hospital policy, Vanguard simply closed the maternity wing in 2007, eliminating a vital service for the surrounding community.

At the Vanguard-acquired Phoenix Memorial Hospital, located in a predominately urban, poor area of Phoenix, the company announced the closure of the emergency room despite earlier promises to the contrary. After a public outcry, Vanguard shelved the plan, but just a few years later closed the entire hospital and leased out the space. In the meantime, Vanguard invested heavily in surgical and ambulatory services at a nearby hospital in Phoenix's wealthier western suburbs.

In addition to reducing less-profitable services, PE-owned hospitals look for other ways to increase profits. These include centralizing and improving billing, records management, and financial services, and reducing staff, particularly registered nurses. In late 2011, nurses organized by the Massachusetts Nurses Association (MNA) gathered at Cerberus headquarters in New York to protest cuts of registered nurses on duty at Steward's Morton Hospital in southeastern Massachusetts. Since Steward's creation in 2010, the MNA and Steward have been at loggerheads. The MNA argues that Steward has cut the level of registered nurses to dangerously low levels at a number of its hospitals, including psychiatric units like the one at Carney Hospital in Boston, and has cut back on basics for patients. Nurses at Holy Family Hospital in northeastern Massachusetts complained that they were not allowed to give patients even a cup of coffee, while nurses at Norwood Hospital (in Norwood, Mass., south of Boston) brought loaves of bread to their floor to protest decreased food for patients. Nurses at Merrimack Valley Hospital, also in northeastern Massachusetts, claimed that administrators were turning down the temperature of electric blankets for chemotherapy patients to save pennies. The MNA and Steward are also fighting an ongoing battle over the MNA's pension plan. The MNA argues that Steward has refused to honor the pension agreement the union made with Caritas Christi, the former owner of the Steward chain, prior to the PE firm's 2010 acquisition.

PE-owned hospitals also engage in less-visible strategies to boost profits such as increasing lucrative surgical procedures. In 2005, the former chief compliance officer at the PE-owned Iasis hospital chain filed a complaint under the False Claims Act, alleging that doctors at St. Luke's Medical Center in Phoenix were installing a specific kind of heart implant—the intra-aortic pump—at ten times the normal rate. The alleged motive? Iasis could bill patients an additional $1000. In a 2012 exposé, the New York Times reported that an internal HCA memo showed that the company performed 1,200 cardiac procedures on patients without significant heart disease. The whistleblower, a registered nurse at a Florida HCA hospital, was fired for reporting the abuse.

The Biggest Difference: The Debt Trap

While service and staffing cuts, deteriorating patient care, and potentially unethical medical practices are easy to find at PE-owned hospitals and deserve urgent attention, they are not uniformly present at all PE-owned hospitals, and are also present at many non-PE-owned hospitals, both for-profit and non-profit. There is, however, another much bigger problem particular to PE hospital ownership.

PE firms are often portrayed as "turnaround" specialists and are viewed by many, including the hospitals themselves, as white knights bringing desperately needed investment and credit access. The problem with this view is that PE firms do not actually earn their money by turning around companies and making them successful. A PE firm's return on investment has little relation to whether the acquired hospital succeeds through improved patient care or increased cash flow. Instead, PE firms recoup their investment through fees (management fees, transaction fees, selling fees, etc.) from both the acquired firm and outside institutional investors. In fact, unlike other kinds of investment firms, PE firms generally put only a small percentage of the total equity down themselves, instead getting outside investors to cover the bulk of the initial equity investment. So even if the PE firm's investment fails to yield the imagined profits, the PE firm still earns a profit, or loses little or no money, because the risk is shouldered by outside investors, and in many cases, the acquired firm itself.

The primary source of risk for hospitals being acquired by PE firms is the debt load that comes with PE ownership. PE firms use the acquired hospital as a vehicle to earn profits by forcing it to sell bonds or shares, or take on bank debt, to pay the PE firm fees and dividends. For example, in January 2010, Vanguard took on $1.76 billion in debt, of which $300 million went to pay dividends to Blackstone. In June 2010, the hospital chain issued an additional $250 million in bonds and, in January 2011, the company recapitalized again. It paid a grand total of $775 million in debt-funded dividends to its PE sponsors between January 2010 and summer 2011.

When PE-backed hospital chains like Vanguard and HCA go public, they (and their PE sponsor) are able to make huge profits from their initial public offerings (IPOs). HCA raked in a record $3.8 billion at its 2011 IPO, but the money from the IPO went directly to chip away at the huge debt HCA incurred under KKR and Bain ownership. In the spring of the previous year, HCA's PE owners borrowed $2.5 billion to pay themselves a dividend, and then followed up in December with a junk-bond sale to pay themselves another nearly $2 billion dividend. As a result, under PE ownership, hospital companies like Vanguard and HCA, and all the community hospitals they have acquired along the way, become buried under a mountain of debt that stays with them long after their PE sponsor has moved on to other investments.

High levels of debt make hospitals vulnerable to changes in the industry as well as broader economic shifts. When credit markets are loose and the economy is growing, hospitals can manage their debt by issuing bonds to cover interest payments or by tapping revolving lines of credit from banks, enabling a steady inflow of funds. But these safety valves quickly disappear during broader economic downturns. A contraction in credit markets can make it difficult or impossible for hospitals to service debt by accessing new sources of liquidity. At the same time, because hospitals are saddled with so much debt, profits are channeled toward servicing the debt rather than building up cash reserves or making long-term investments in patient care or technology. This weakens the hospitals' ability to adjust to industry or economic shifts and makes them more likely to end up in bankruptcy.

The pitfalls associated with PE ownership have, in some cases, led to pushback against PE hospital acquisitions. For example, when Steward attempted to acquire Florida's non-profit Jackson Health System in 2011, it was met with public outcry from Miami residents and local politicians and was forced to back out of the deal. Unions have also been vocal opponents. In 2010, Council 31 of AFSCME in Chicago fought hard against the sale of Westlake Hospital and West Suburban Medical Center to Vanguard Health Systems, but ultimately failed to prevent the sale. Some states have attached conditions to deals involving the transformation of non-profit hospitals to forprofit, PE-owned entities. Michigan's attorney general forced Vanguard to agree to continue existing operations and services at the Detroit Medical Center for ten years after the 2010 purchase date, including commitments to charity care and research. However, the Michigan deal is exceptional, and most PE-hospital acquisitions come with few restrictions on the sale or closure of facilities.

The future of PE investment in hospitals depends on a number of factors, including the cost and availability of credit, health care legislation, and the public response to PE ownership. PE interest in the hospital sector hinges on cheap credit. If credit markets contract, and PE firms find it harder to arrange financing for their investment deals, they may lose interest in health care and instead restrict their investments to more profitable ventures. However, growing demand for health care, in the context of increased hospital obligations and restrictions as a result of the Affordable Care Act, may make community hospitals more vulnerable, and actually increase their attractiveness as takeover targets. Ultimately, the most promising avenue for restricting, or ideally, preventing PE takeovers of hospitals is to publicly scrutinize their behavior and demand alternative forms of financial support for the hospitals, doctors, and nurses struggling to provide affordable, high-quality care. ❑

Sources: Tim van Biesen and Karen Murphy, "Global Healthcare Private Equity Report 2012," Bain & Company, 2012; Advisen, "Private equity and hospitals: providence or problem," OneBeacon Professional Insurance, 2011; Lisa Goldstein, "New forces driving rise in not-for-profit hospital consolidation," Moody's Investor Service, 2012; Josh Kosman, *The Buyout of America: How Private Equity Will Cause the Next Great Credit Crisis* (New York: Portfolio, 2009); Congressional Budget Office, "Nonprofit hospitals and the provision of community benefits," Dec., 2006; Jill Horwitz, "Making Profits And Providing Care: Comparing Nonprofit, For-Profit, And Government Hospitals," *Health Affairs*, 24 (3), May 2005; Reed Abelson and Julie Creswell, "Hospital Chain Inquiry Cited Unnecessary Cardiac Work," *New York Times*, Aug. 6, 2012.

Article 2.5

PRIVATE EQUITY EXPOSED

An insider gives a peek at a notoriously secretive industry.

BY ORLANDO SEGURA, JR.

July/August 2008

Today, private equity seems to be everywhere. Enter a Dunkin' Donuts, and you experience private equity. Scan your radio dial, and you're likely to encounter private equity. Purchase gifts for your children at Toys "R" Us, and you engage with private equity. The private equity industry, like other alternative investment industries that have risen to prominence over the last two decades, exerts tremendous economic and political influence in the United States and globally. It is important, then, to understand how this industry works and thrives. For the past three years, I have had the opportunity to see firsthand the inner workings of the industry—first as a consultant to large buyout firms, and then as a financial analyst for one of the firms themselves. Drawing on these experiences, I will try to shed some light on this notoriously secretive industry and answer three important questions: How do private equity firms make money? How do private equity firms affect the distribution of financial risk in society as a whole? And how does the regulatory landscape in the United States give private equity firms an advantage in the market?

How Do Private Equity Firms Make Money?

Specialized transactions called leveraged buyouts are central to what private equity firms do, and it is important to be familiar with the mechanics of these transactions in order to understand how these firms generate profit. Private equity firms are private partnerships that raise money from large investors—pension funds, other investment funds, and wealthy individuals (often the same people who are running the private equity firms)—and use that money to purchase other companies. This is the "buyout" part.

The "leveraged" part is the more important one, however. Private equity firms do not simply employ the money they raise on their own to buy companies. They borrow money from investment banks to complete the transactions. In most instances, this borrowed money constitutes the majority of the funding needed to pay for the company. At one point in the industry's infancy, firms were able to borrow 90% or more of the purchase price of the "target" companies. Today, as credit markets have tightened, that number is lower, but on average it still exceeds 50% of purchase price. When the buyout transaction is completed, the payback for this debt becomes the responsibility of the acquired company and is placed on its balance sheet as a liability. Most private equity firms retain ownership of the businesses they buy for three to five years and then sell them for a profit, often to other private equity firms.

The ability to use such leverage vastly increases the potential returns on private equity firms' investments. A simple analogy helps show how this works. Imagine you decide to buy a house that costs $100,000 in a neighborhood where property values are appreciating. You put a very small $1,000 down payment on the house and borrow the other $99,000 from the bank. In three years' time, the house has doubled in value and you are now able to sell it for $200,000. After you repay the loan, you have $100,000 in profit—a return of 100 times your original $1,000 investment. Now, imagine if you had only been able to borrow $1,000 from the bank; you would have had to make a $99,000 down payment. The house still appreciates to a value of $200,000, but in this scenario you have turned your original $99,000 investment into a $100,000 profit, generating only a return roughly equal to your original investment. In the first scenario, you put much less of your own equity at risk, yet you generate the same absolute profit as in the second scenario. This simple example illustrates the power of leverage, and why private equity firms would want to maximize the share of borrowed money they invest.

Why have investment banks been willing to lend private equity firms so much money? Part of the reason is that they are able to pass the debt along by selling, or "syndicating," it. Banks package the debt into securities called collateralized debt obligations, or CDOs, which they sell on the open market. CDOs have existed since 1987, but did not achieve prominence in the markets until 2001, when banks began devising sophisticated models that allowed them to rapidly price and sell these securities.

The benefit banks derive from their ability to segment and distribute the risks associated with the debt they underwrite for private equity firms cannot be overstated. They lower their downside risk associated with default on these loans because they only hold onto a small portion of the entire loan package, or "facility." So banks can underwrite more debt than they would be able to if they held onto the loans in full. And they can take in more lucrative fees, too. The banks get most of their revenues from fees for originating the loans, generally 2% to 3% of the amount of the loan.

All told, such large amounts of capital being used to purchase companies creates hefty profits for the investment banks and the private equity firms, not to mention the ancillary professional service industries required to complete the deals, including accountants, lawyers, and consultants.

This is simply the tip of the profit iceberg for private equity firms, however. The real money comes in what is called "carry"—the share of profits that the funds' managers are entitled to when they sell a business. Remember, the more these firms borrow for a transaction—the more they "leverage"—the more any increase in value translates into equity profit. The industry norm is for private equity partnerships to keep 20% of the profit that they make when they sell a company.

And apart from the über-profits they "earn" from selling the highly leveraged businesses they own, private equity firms charge hefty management fees to *both* the investors in the fund and to the companies they buy. The "market" management fee that private equity firms charge their investors ranges between 2% and 2.5% of the total fund size. The companies they purchase must likewise pay a quarterly "management fee," usually around 2% of the purchase price of the company. Effectively, private equity firms earn money in return for being given money *and* for spending money. As the value of many of the companies that private equity firms buy can soar into the hundreds of millions, or even billions, of dollars, this represents a low-risk, assured stream of income. On a fund of $10 billion, these fees alone can translate into hundreds of millions of dollars in revenue a year.

How do private equity firms affect the distribution of financial risk in society?

The profits that financial players like private equity firms and investment banks enjoy come at a price. Today, there are hundreds of billions of dollars in CDOs that are spread throughout the economy, most owned by individual investors. Of course, it is the businesses private equity firms own that are carrying the underlying loans that were bundled to create the CDOs. These businesses risk default if they are not able to make the payments on these debts. And the more the private equity firm was able to borrow to purchase the company, the greater the risk the business faces because it will have to manage larger debt payments on an ongoing basis. An ordinary business downturn that the business might have been able to weather may now thrust it into default if it cannot manage the high debt payments resulting from the leveraged buy-out. And if enough of these businesses get into trouble, the holders of the CDOs will see the value of their investments tumble. We are seeing this happen now with the sub-prime crisis, which was fueled by devaluation in mortgage-backed securities.

The ability of banks and private equity firms to siphon the benefits while distributing the risks of leverage is rooted in the legal frameworks that "incentivize" such behavior (to use the industry jargon). Private equity firms are shielded from the extreme downside financial risks because of their peculiar form of corporate governance. Private equity firms set up each company they buy as a separate corporation with limited liability. This means that if one of the highly leveraged businesses experiences a downturn and is unable to pay its loans, the only equity that is at stake is what was used to purchase that business. Thus, a private equity fund can still post healthy returns even if some businesses in its portfolio go bankrupt.

As we've seen, private equity firms have an incentive to leverage their business buyouts as much as possible. But this increases the risk of default for the individual businesses they own because they are forced to pay such large principal and interest payments to support the debt that has been placed on their shoulders. Thus, not only do private equity firms increase the systemic risk across the economy by issuing publicly traded CDOs that provide their leverage, they also increase the more immediate risk for those who work for the businesses they own by saddling them with heavy debt obligations.

The "loosening" of the credit markets, fueled partly through the ascendance of CDOs, predictably led private equity firms to execute ever-larger transactions. In 2007, the Blackstone Group purchased Equity Office Properties for $39 billion and in one fell swoop became one of the largest holders of real estate in the world. Currently, Bain Capital is in the process of completing the purchase of Clear Channel Communications, the largest owner of radio stations in the United States. These are but two of many multi-billion dollar transactions by private equity firms that have occurred over the past decade, and which until now have largely gone unnoticed by the general public. These colossal companies, like all businesses bought up by private equity firms, are now at an increased risk should their profit margins weaken or interest rates rise in a cyclical downturn of the economy. To ensure that their requisite loan payments are made, the new managers of these companies, appointed by and acting on behalf of the private equity firm owner, may cut costs by simply laying off workers and offshoring certain functions. The market implications of contractions in the economy are thus amplified by the actions of private equity firms.

How does the regulatory landscape give private equity firms a market advantage?

With the profits that can be earned in private equity, it is no surprise that the industry has grown as much as it has recently, and it is no surprise that private equity firms are able to attract some of the brightest business minds in the market. Predictably, self-interested individuals are drawn to these firms, aiming to maximize the amount of money they can earn. But that is not the whole story. The regulatory landscape in the United States has given private equity firms a number of advantages in the market—limited transparency into the business dealings of the firms and the businesses they own, capital-gains tax advantages, a lack of consumer protection in the credit markets, lax antitrust law enforcement, among others. In effect, the legal landscape is ripe for private equity firms to thrive.

Since private equity firms have at their disposal all these levers for generating profit so seamlessly, one would imagine that the government would tax their earnings at an effectively higher tax rate than normal business earnings. This could not be further from the truth. Owners of corporations in the United States are afforded numerous tax breaks and incentives from writing off "losses" or deducting "business expenses" from taxable earnings. On this front, private equity firms have cleverly found ways to go above and beyond the call of duty. Virtually all private equity firms are structured as limited liability partnerships, or LLPs. This confers two explicit benefits to the partners. First, they are protected from any downside in their equity investments, meaning that if one of their investments goes bust, they will only lose the equity that they put into that specific business. Second, they are protected under a tax shelter that allows the majority of their profits to be taxed at a very low rate. Because they are partnerships that technically earn "capital gains" on the profitable sale of a business, they are taxed at a flat 15% rate, as opposed to the 28% to 33% income tax rate that ordinary individuals pay. Thanks to this loophole, private equity managers are taxed at lower rates than their secretaries and administrative assistants who make as much money in a year as their bosses make in a day.

Many European countries have recently instituted laws in recognition of the legal and regulatory advantages that private equity owners have enjoyed since the industry's inception. In the UK this past year, for example, Parliament passed a law that took away private equity firms' tax advantages, which incidentally were very similar to what currently exists in the United States. Here, House Democrats recently introduced a bill to do away with the capital gains tax structure for private equity firms and tax them at ordinary income tax rates. This would have raised private equity firms' tax rates on their carry from a flat 15% to a flat 35%. But Charles Schumer (D-N.Y.), head of the Senate Finance Committee, came out against the bill, killing it for now.

It is no coincidence that, as a senator from New York, Schumer receives tens of thousands of dollars from private equity bosses and relies on their support for an ever-increasing portion of his campaign funding. Of course, he is not alone. The private equity industry created its own PAC in 2007, the Private Equity Council, to lobby against efforts to increase taxes on the industry. To date, they have succeeded; there is every reason to believe they will continue to succeed. Schumer's fellow senator from New York, Hillary Clinton, is a loyal recipient of private equity money and joined him in opposing the bill. On the Republican side, former New York City mayor Rudy Giuliani has taken a predictable pro-private-equity stance, as did his competitor in the Republican presidential primaries, Mitt Romney, who made hundreds of millions of dollars as a partner of Bain Capital, one of the leading private equity firms in the world. The political muscle of the industry is as strong as its economic success.

The legal framework that actively encourages this industry to thrive has spawned a new breed of capitalism, one in which businesses are treated as assets to be bought and sold rather than as social institutions that are sources of people's livelihood. Perhaps we should ask: What value do these firms confer upon the economy, and through it, on society? Private equity firms do not foster innovation in the economy, they do not create jobs, and for the most part they do not actively manage the businesses they own. Rather, they redirect the benefits of equity ownership to a small and insular group of people instead of creating social value for everyone. It is time to learn more about how and why these institutions exert their power and, at the very least, to demand more transparency, thoughtful regulation, and fairer taxation in return for the privilege of being able to operate in our economy. ❑

Sources: Tomas Krüger Andersen, "Legal Structure of Private Equity and Hedge Funds," 2007 (available at isis.ku.dk/kurser/blob.aspx?feltid= 155330); Martin Arnold, "Doubt Cast on Buy-Out Firms' Huge Profits," *Financial Times*, November 23, 2007; Neil Hodge, "Private Equity: A Debt to Society?" *Financial Management*, September 2007.

Article 2.6

HEDGE FUNDS

BY ARTHUR MacEWAN
July/August 2008

> Dear Dr. Dollar:
> *When one hedge fund makes $3 billion, who has lost $3 billion? Where does the money come from that hedge funds capture? Who produced the value?*
> — Peter Marcuse, Waterbury, Conn.

As with any "winnings" in the financial markets, the money obtained by hedge funds comes directly from some losers who are also operating in the financial markets. On the surface, the situation might appear like a poker game: when one player wins the pot, some other players lose. Those of us not sitting at the table neither win nor lose.

However, while financial markets do involve a lot of gambling, the analogy to a poker game is limited. Those of us who are not sitting in on "the game" do suffer some substantial losses from the operations of hedge funds. Hedge fund operators, along with other operators in the financial system, have taken an active role in increasing the size of their "pot"—that is, in shifting the income distribution upward, moving money from lower-income workers to business owners and high-salaried professionals. So value created by the rest of us becomes the hedge funds' billions.

Contrary to their popular image, however, hedge funds are not making billions and billions of dollars for their investors. In fact, the performance of hedge funds is not significantly better than the performance of other types of investment funds. Nonetheless, although the investors in hedge funds are not doing especially well, the *managers* of the hedge funds are making off with billions.

The key to the incomes of hedge fund managers lies more in the nature of what the funds are than in how well they do. After all, aside from some notable exceptions, hedge funds as a group have not done especially well.

So what are hedge funds? Hedge funds are a category of mutual funds. In all mutual funds, the money of multiple investors is pooled and invested according to the decisions of the funds' managers. Regular mutual funds are subject to various government regulations, as are some other financial institutions, for example, commercial banks. The rationale for these regulations is that they protect the individual investors.

Hedge funds, however, avoid most regulations by limiting participation to a small number of "qualified" individuals and institutions (e.g., pension funds or college endowment funds) with large sums of money. To be "qualified," an investor must have a net worth of at least $5 million, excluding his or her home. Because they have large sums of money, these wealthy investors supposedly do not need the protection that regulation is assumed to provide.

Largely unregulated, hedge funds can undertake highly risky types of investments that would be off limits to regular mutual funds. With these more risky investments, they are *sometimes* able to obtain very high returns. They can also operate with a good deal of secrecy, exempt from the reporting requirements of regular mutual funds.

Like other investment funds, hedge funds charge a fee to the individuals and institutions that provide them with money. But hedge funds have been able to charge relatively high fees, including performance fees on top of the basic management fees. The basic fees run 1.5% to 2% of the total investment, and the performance fees typically run 20% of positive returns—sometimes higher. In some cases, management fees run to 5% combined with performance fees of over 40%. Furthermore, while hedge fund managers get their hefty performance fees when their funds achieve positive returns, they do not lose anything when their funds have negative returns. In effect, they are saying to their investors: If I perform well, we both win; if I perform poorly, you lose. So it is not difficult to see why the managers of hedge funds do so well.

It is difficult, however, to see why so many investors put their money into hedge funds. Part of the explanation lies in the fact that rich individuals are often not smart investors, and they are drawn in by the popular image, the billions made by some funds, and the aura of success surrounding the stories of hedge fund managers who take home billions. And the institutional investors in hedge funds—local pension funds or college endowment funds, for example—are not especially "smart" either. Perhaps it is also the case that investors with large sums of money are willing to put at least some of their money into hedge funds, looking for the higher returns that the funds do sometimes obtain.

But whatever returns are obtained "sometimes," overall hedge funds do not do significantly better than other types of investment funds. While the secrecy of hedge funds makes it difficult to determine their overall returns, one 2006 study concludes: "...overall performance of hedge funds ... is about the same as that of U.S. equities [as measured by the Standard and Poor's Index of 500 equities] ...[H]edge funds underperformed the stock market ... during the six year, 'bull market' run-up to 1999, while on average they outperformed the stock market during the six year 'bear market' (or lull period) through 2005."

And recently the story has been quite poor: in the period from January 2007 up to May of 2008, hedge funds returned on average 3.1% and were out-performed by rich-world corporate bonds. (These figures are only for hedge funds that are open to new investors and thus, presumably, report how they have been doing. Hedge funds that are not accepting new investors are more opaque.) One might conclude that hedge funds are an undistinguished group of investments.

There are, however, some things that distinguish hedge funds—most particularly the huge payments that are often obtained by the people who run the funds. The most outstanding recent example is John Paulson, who in 2007 took in $3.7 billion running his Paulson & Co. hedge funds. Several others did pretty well also: George Soros was number two last year, at $2.9 billion, and James Simons was third at $2.8 billion

The top 25 hedge fund managers got themselves $22.3 billion in 2007, up substantially from a meager $14 billion in 2006. It is, we may assume, the stories of these individuals that generates the aura of success surrounding hedge funds.

How did hedge fund managers do so well when the economy was moving into bad times? In Paulson's case, according to Bloomberg.com, "Paulson & Co., which oversees about $28 billion, made money betting on the collapse of subprime mortgages in 2007. The Paulson Credit Opportunities Fund soared almost sixfold, helped by bets on slumping housing and subprime mortgage prices, according to investor letters obtained by Bloomberg." More generally, the hedge fund managers rely on their fee structure, as described above, to assure that, regardless of bad times, they come out well.

If rich individuals and institutional investors were the only ones to take the hit when the John Paulsons take home their astronomical fees, perhaps the rest of us could shrug it off. If they want to pay excessive fees to take part in the glitter—and possible large returns—of high stakes finance, that's their problem.

But the rest of us do pay a price. First of all, there is the ridiculously favorable tax treatment that hedge fund managers have been able to garner. Most important, they are allowed to classify their payments as capital gains rather than as salaries, and thereby they pay a low tax rate on their incomes—typically only 15%, compared to the top tax rate of 35%.

There is simply no good reason for this favorable treatment of hedge fund managers' incomes—other than the apparent power they are able to wield. The result is that the rest of us either pay more in taxes or get by with fewer public services.

Also important, hedge fund managers are not passive investors. They do not accept as a given the current profit levels of the companies they invest in, and simply try to claim a larger share of those profits. Instead, at least at times (but their secrecy makes it difficult to determine how often and to what extent), they take an active role in attempting to push up their profits. Along with private equity funds, with which the hedge funds are closely associated and sometimes overlap, they can push firms to downsize and reorganize, lay off workers, outsource, or alter their overall investment strategies.

For instance, according to a May 15, 2008 report in the "Silicon Alley Insider," John Paulson, who through his funds owns 4% of Yahoo stock, has joined corporate raider Carl Icahn in a proxy fight, an attempt to force Yahoo to accept a Microsoft buy-out offer.

There is no reason to think that any general social interest is served when hedge fund managers attempt to affect the operation of the firms in which they have holdings. In the Yahoo example, the impact on the rest of us may be obscure, but when it comes to layoffs, downsizing, outsourcing, and the like, it is clear that many people outside of the financial markets—people who have no seat at the gambling tables—pay a large price for the gains of hedge funds, and especially of fund managers.

Stagnant wages of workers in recent decades and the increased share of total national income going to corporate profits are the consequence of large, long-run economic forces—the decline of unions, globalization, conservative government policies, and technological shifts to name a few. But the hedge funds are one of the instruments by which these forces have their impact on the rest of us, shifting the value that we create into the financial markets and then taking as large a share as they can. ❑

Sources: Andy Baker, "Better than beta? Managers' superior skills are becoming harder to prove," *The Economist*, February 28, 2008; Arindam Bandopadhyaya and James L. Grant, *A Survey of Demographics and Performance In the Hedge Fund Industry*, Working Paper 1011, Financial Services Forum, College of Management, University of Massachusetts Boston, July, 2006; "Hedge-Fund Performance," *The Economist*, May 15, 2008; Tom Cahill and Poppy Trowbridge, "Paulson's $3.7 Billion Top Hedge Fund Pay, Alpha Says," Bloomberg.com, April 16, 2008; Henry Blodget, "Hedge-Fund Mogul Paulson Joins Icahn in Yahoo Siege; 30% of Proxy Vote in Bag," Silicon Alley Insider, May 15, 2008.

Article 2.7

A DIRTY JOB NO ONE SHOULD DO

A lawyer's self-serving defense of Wall Street pay doesn't add up.

BY JOHN MILLER
May/June 2011

> WALL STREET LAWYER: DON'T BLAME PAY
>
> Steve Eckhaus just wanted to get some deals done. He has negotiated hundreds of high-profile pay packages, some of which were met with scorn and scrutiny in Washington and beyond.
>
> "I hate to say it, but I have friends who blame me for the financial crisis," says Mr. Eckhaus, who estimates he has negotiated well over $5 billion in banker pay over the years, including several $100 million pay deals.
>
> "It was understandable why there was anger," says Mr. Eckhaus, but "the crisis was not caused by Wall Street fat cats." In general, he said his clients are "pure as the driven snow" and doing work that supports the economy and justifies their pay.
>
> "There's nothing helpful or healing in the midst of a financial crisis to talk about Wall Street 'fat cats,'" added Mr. Eckhaus. "To blame Wall Street for the financial meltdown is absurd."
>
>   —Steve Eder, "Wall Street Lawyer: Don't Blame Pay," *Wall Street Journal*, February 5, 2011

Pure as the driven snow? How about as dirty as what remains of the Northeast's snow piles, covered with filth a month after record storms? Eckhaus and his fat-cat clients richly deserve the scorn that even his friends have heaped upon them. The pay packages Eckhaus negotiated are obscene. They cushioned financial fat cats from the often-disastrous consequences of their actions. And Eckhaus's protestations notwithstanding, the finance industry's compensation structures lie at the heart of the financial crisis. Banking execs and other key decision-makers all along the mortgage securitization process were induced to take excessive risks because of the way they were compensated.

Let's start with the first link in the process—the people who made the mortgage loans to homebuyers. It's standard practice to pay mortgage brokers based on the volume of loans they originate, not the performance or quality of those loans. And since the banks and mortgage companies who employ the brokers bundled up the loans and sold them off as mortgage-backed securities, they too had little interest in the quality of the loans.

The fees garnered by the financial-services industry from home mortgage lending and mortgage securitization were enormous, as much as $2 trillion in the six years from 2003 to 2008, according to estimates by economist James Crotty. That figure includes the fees paid to mortgage brokers as well as the fees collected by investment bankers who packaged the loans into securities, the fees paid to the ratings agencies who gave the securities their seal of approval, and the fees paid to yet others who serviced the securities. Those massive sums were paid out for short-term success even when the decisions those sums rewarded resulted in long-term losses or failures, a point Securities and Exchange Commission chair Mary Schapiro confirmed for the Financial Crisis Inquiry Commission, the ten-member panel appointed by Congress to examine the causes of the financial crisis.

That the compensation system has "no rhyme or reason" is the conclusion Andrew Cuomo, then attorney general of New York, reached in his 2009 report on compensation practices in the U.S. banking system. The record of Bank of America, for Cuomo, shows just how little compensation had to do with bank performance. In 2006, as the bank raked in profits during the housing bubble, it paid out $18 billion in compensation. In 2008, after the bubble had burst, Bank of America continued to make compensation payments at the $18 billion level—even as its net income plummeted from $14 billion to $4 billion. That fall Bank of America took over Merrill Lynch, which had just brought a new investment banking chief on board—Mr. Eckhaus's client Tom Montag—by guaranteeing him a $39.4 million bonus.

Those giant bonuses paid out to Wall Street high rollers provoked the ire of many, especially when they came from financial firms that received TARP (Troubled Asset Relief Program) bailout funds from the federal government, as was the case with Mr. Montag's millions. The Cuomo report pays special attention to the bonuses paid out by the original TARP recipients. For two of the nine, Citigroup and Merrill Lynch, the disconnect between the banks' earnings and executive bonuses was especially alarming. Together, these two corporations in 2008 lost $54 billion, paid out nearly $9 billion in bonuses, and then received TARP bailouts totaling $55 billion. At Merrill Lynch, 700 employees received bonuses in excess of $1 million in 2008. The top four recipients alone received a total of $121 million. Merrill's reported losses for 2007 and 2008, as Crotty points out, were enough to wipe out 11 years of earnings previously reported by the company.

The Cuomo report rails against this "heads I win, tails you lose" bonus culture. As Cuomo put it, when banks did well, executives and traders were showered with bonuses. When the banks lost money, taxpayers bailed them out, and bonuses and overall compensation remained sky-high.

The consequences of such a perverse compensation system are disastrous, as Crotty explains:

> It becomes rational for top financial firm operatives to take excessive risk in the bubble even if they understand that their decisions are likely to cause a crash in the intermediate future. Since they do not have to return their bubble-year bonuses when the inevitable crisis occurs and since they continue to receive substantial bonuses even in the crisis, they have a powerful incentive to pursue high-risk, high-leverage strategies.

So go ahead and blame Wall Street for the crisis. Not to would indeed be absurd. The bonuses Eckhaus's clients and others took home were the most deformed element of a compensation system that enabled the risk-taking that pushed the financial industry into crisis. Those bonus babies deserve your scorn. Throwing them out with their dirty bathwater, the whole compensation system, is the first step toward curbing the destructive behavior they helped to perpetuate. ❑

Sources: Steve Eder, "Wall Street Lawyer: Don't Blame Pay," *Wall Street Journal*, Feb. 5, 2011; James Crotty, "The Bonus-Driven 'Rainmaker' Financial Firm," Political Economy Research Institute Working Paper 209, revised August 2010 (peri.umass.edu); Andrew Cuomo, *No Rhyme Or Reason: The Heads I Win, Tails You Lose Bank Bonus Culture*, State of New York, 2009; *The Financial Crisis Inquiry Report: Final Report of the National Commission on the Causes of the Financial and Economic Crisis in the United States*, January 2011 (fcic.gov).

Article 2.8

WHAT WERE THE BANKERS THINKING?

BY ARTHUR MacEWAN
March/April 2010

> Dear Dr. Dollar,
> *As I understand it, the main cause of the current economic mess was that banks made a lot of bad housing loans. When the people who took out those loans couldn't make their payments, the banks got in trouble and then the whole economy got in trouble. So why did the bankers make all those bad loans? What were they thinking!?*
> —Sara Boyle, Manchester, Conn.

They were thinking they could make a lot of money. To a large extent, they were right. Sure, they finally started losing. But you won't see many bankers in soup kitchen lines.

Here's how it worked. The actual makers of the mortgage loans were willing to make high-risk loans because they quickly put these loans into bundles (electronic bundles) and sold the bundles to investors. So the makers of the mortgages—mortgage companies, commercial banks, savings and loans, and credit unions—were not harmed when someone stopped payment on a mortgage. These bundles are called mortgage-backed securities, a form of Collateralized Debt Obli-gations (CDOs). CDOs are a type of derivative—a financial instrument (i.e., a vehicle for financial investment) the value of which is derived from some other financial instrument, in this case the set of mortgages in the bundle.

The underwriters—the financial firms handling the marketing of these CDOs, usually large investment banks—then had to get them rated by one of the rating agencies. Moody's, Standard & Poor's, and Fitch are the three big firms, controlling 85% of the market, that evaluate the risk involved in financial instruments. The rating agencies, however, are paid by the underwriters, so they have a conflict of interest that gave them an incentive to rate the CDOs too high, indicating less risk than was really involved. Also, the underwriters could shop among the rating agencies to get the best rating. In general, the rationale for good ratings was that the mortgage-based CDOs were relatively safe because they included many mortgages, creating at least an aura of diversity. Diversity is always taken as implying low risk. (Except, of course, when there is a general failure.)

Also, buyers of the CDOs could buy insurance on these investments, just in case something did go wrong. The insurance policies on the CDOs are called "credit default swaps"—another set of derivatives, the value of which is derived from the value of the CDOs. The credit default swaps, like the CDOs themselves, were then treated in the financial market as another type of financial instrument.

Many investment banks made a lot of money holding these derivatives as well as in buying and selling them. The banks got high returns on the derivatives they held and they got fees for buying and selling derivatives. Bear Stearns and Lehman

Brothers, the two investment banks that went under in 2008, had made lots of money on these activities between 2002 and 2006.

To understand the actions of the banks, it is important to recognize that the salaries and, especially, the large bonuses that the bankers obtained in these operations were based on the immediate, short-run profits that they generated. If in one year (say in 2005) they made lots of money through the fees on buying and selling the derivatives and through the returns on holding the derivatives, then it didn't matter that things fell apart soon after (in 2007). None of the bankers had to give back their salaries or bonuses. (These operations were facilitated by the general lack of regulation of derivative trading.)

Of course when things did fall apart, no one would buy the CDOs or the credit default swaps. These were the "toxic assets" that were held by many large banks and other investors and which "poisoned" the financial system. Some of the people who had made lots of money in salaries and bonuses also held stock in, for example, Bear Stearns or Lehman Brothers, and they lost money on those stocks.

There was, however, still a problem. Lots of financial institutions had taken out loans for which these CDOs and credit default swaps were collateral. With the value of these derivatives collapsing, it looked as though the creditors might lose their money. This was when people started talking about a collapse of the financial system.

Not to worry. The government stepped in and made sure that the creditors got their money.

So, it turns out that a whole set of arrangements—from the initial making of the mortgage to the salary-bonus system to the government bail- out—protected the bankers and other actors from the risks of their actions. The arrangements encouraged excessively risky behavior that ultimately placed a huge cost on the rest of us.

But the bankers? They pretty much came out OK. No, you won't see many bankers in soup kitchen lines. ❑

Article 2.9

ETHICS FOR ECONOMISTS? IT'S ABOUT TIME!

BY GERALD EPSTEIN AND JESSICA CARRICK-HAGENBARTH
May/June 2011

U.S. banks have been accused of lacking transparency in their use of the bailout money given to them by the federal government. Does anyone actually believe that the banks that received bailouts have been adequately forthcoming in telling us about their use of these huge funds? One person who thinks they have is Laura Tyson, a University of California-Berkeley professor of business and economics who appeared on the Rachel Maddow Show on MSNBC in December, 2008. She said that banks were not at fault for failing to tell us how they have used our money. The Treasury should have made clearer rules, Tyson told Maddow's viewers.

It turns out that Laura Tyson is on the board of Morgan Stanley, a bank that received around $10 billion in bailout money. Tyson makes more than $340,000 a year in total compensation from her position with the bank. When the producers of the Rachel Maddow Show became aware of this potential conflict of interest, they contacted Tyson, who submitted the following comment: "I am a professional economist and business school professor. I appeared on the show and answered the questions in this capacity. My answers reflect my professional opinion and I am solely responsible for them. They do not represent the views of Morgan Stanley or any other private company."

Tyson's attitude is all too common among academic economists with ties to Wall Street. The Oscar-winning documentary film Inside Job brought the issue of undisclosed conflicts of interest to the public's attention by asking embarrassing questions to such prominent economists such as Martin Feldstein of the Harvard economics department and Glenn Hubbard, president of the Columbia Business School.

Our study of conflicts of interest in the profession confirms what Inside Job suggests—that there's a real problem. Thirteen of nineteen prominent academic financial economists we reviewed had private financial affiliations. What's more, eight of the thirteen did not disclose any potential or real conflicts of interest when writing for the media, testifying publicly on financial topics, or in their academic publications. Instead, they identified themselves as prominent professors from important universities, implying both objectivity and expertise in the field.

Our findings motivated us to write a letter to the primary professional association in our field, the American Economics Association (AEA), calling for the AEA to adopt a code of ethics that prescribes proper conduct for dealing with a real or potential conflict of interest. Over 300 economists have now signed our letter, which seems a clear statement that economists might welcome a code of professional ethical behavior and might well follow such a code if it were put in place.

The proposal that the AEA adopt a code of ethics has raised several criticisms. Some say an AEA code of ethics would be unenforceable, since unlike the professional associations for law and medicine, the AEA does not license its members. This means that the AEA would not have license revocation as a tool to punish wayward economists. However, legal enforceability is not essential in order to make a differ-ence. Even without the power of law or licensure, a widely acknowledged standard of ethical professional behavior would empower colleagues, journal- ists, students and the public to demand disclosure. The very existence of clear official rules for ethical conduct, known to both economists and the public, could be a powerful deterrent to unethical practices, whether or not the AEA was able to punish transgressors.

Another criticism is that there is no need for a code of ethics. Economists' work will be proven or disproven on the basis of how well the arguments stand the test of time and scholarly discourse, regardless of any conflict of interest or other bias that could influence an economist's work. In fact, even hard sciences like physics and chemistry have guidelines of conduct or codes of ethics. The guidelines for professional conduct for physics have a section addressing conflicts of interest: "Any professional relation-ship or action that may result in a conflict of interest must be fully disclosed. When objectivity and effectiveness cannot be maintained, the activity should be avoided or discontinued." When so many other professions have recognized the possibility that scholarship may be influenced by power and money, doesn't it seem like hubris for economists to think they are immune to such influences?

Disclosure of private financial affiliations that pose potential conflicts of interest is only one of many ethical conundrums faced by economists. (George DeMartino of the University of Denver has written eloquently about the broader subject of ethics in economics in his new book An Economist's Oath.) We have focused on disclosure because we feel it is a timely and central issue in our profession. The ques-tion of ethics and disclosure was taken up by the AEA Executive Committee at its annual meeting in January of this year. Members of the executive committee voted unanimously to create an ad hoc committee to look at current AEA ethical stan-dards and standards for disclosure. Existing standards are limited to the American Economic Review, a journal published by the AEA, requiring authors to disclose any conflicts of interest upon submitting a paper.

The AEA only recently disclosed the membership of the committee, which includes economist and Nobel laureate Robert Solow and former Harvard University president Derek Bok. One hopes that, in a break with the habits typical of the pro-fession, the AEA will soon fully disclose the process the committee will follow, its timeline for deliberation, and information on how members of the profession and the general public can be part of the conversation. ❏

Sources: The Rachel Maddow Show, December 22 and 23, 2008, MSNBC; Proxy Statement 2010, Morgan Stanley SEC filings (morganstanley.com); Inside Job (insidejob.com); Gerald Epstein and Jessica Carrick-Hagenbarth, 2010, "Financial Economists, Financial Interests and Dark Corners of the Meltdown: It's Time to Set Ethical Standards for the Economics Profession," Political Economy Research Institute, Working Paper #239 (peri.umass.edu); Gerald Epstein and Jessica Carrick-Hagenbarth, "Letter to the AEA", hosted at the Political Economy Research Institute (peri.umass.edu); Ethics and Values, APS Guidelines for Professional Conduct (aps.org); George DeMartino, An Economist's Oath: On the Need for and Content of Professional Economic Ethics (Oxford University Press, 2011); American Economics Association, AEA Committees and Representatives, Ad Hoc Committee on Ethical Standards for Economists (aeaweb.org).

Chapter 3

FINANCIAL MARKETS

Article 3.1

THE GREAT STOCK ILLUSION

BY ELLEN FRANK
November/December 2002

During the 1980s and 1990s, the Dow Jones and Standard & Poor's indices of stock prices soared ten-fold. The NASDAQ index had, by the year 2000, skyrocketed to 25 times its 1980 level. Before the bubble burst, bullish expectations reached a feverish crescendo. Three separate books—Dow 36,000, Dow 40,000 and Dow 100,000—appeared in 1999 forecasting further boundless growth in stock prices. Bullish Wall Street gurus like Goldman's Abby Cohen and Salomon's Jack Grubman were quoted everywhere, insisting that prices could go nowhere but up.

But as early as 1996, skeptics were warning that it couldn't last. Fed chair Alan Greenspan fretted aloud about "irrational exuberance." Yale finance professor Robert Shiller, in his 2001 book titled Irrational Exuberance, insisted that U.S. equities prices were being driven up by wishful thinking and self-fulfilling market sentiment, nourished by a culture that championed wealth and lionized the wealthy. Dean Baker and Marc Weisbrot of the Washington-based Center for Economic and Policy Research contended in 1999 that the U.S. stock market looked like a classic speculative bubble—as evidence they cited the rapidly diverging relationship between stock prices and corporate earnings and reckoned that, to justify the prices at which stocks were selling, profits would have to grow at rates that were frankly impossible.

In 1999 alone, the market value of U.S. equities swelled by an astounding $4 trillion. During that same year, U.S. output, on which stocks represent a claim, rose by a mere $500 billion. What would have happened if stockholders in 1999 had all tried to sell their stock and convert their $4 trillion into actual goods and services? The answer is that most would have failed. In a scramble to turn $4 trillion of paper gains into $500 billion worth of real goods and services, the paper wealth was bound to dissolve, because it never existed, save as a kind of mass delusion.

The Illusion of Wealth Creation

Throughout the 1990s, each new record set by the Dow or NASDAQ elicited grateful cheers for CEOs who were hailed for "creating wealth." American workers, whose retirement savings were largely invested in stocks, were encouraged to buy more stock—even to bet their Social Security funds in the market—and assured that stocks always paid off "in the long run," that a "buy-and-hold" strategy couldn't lose. Neither the financial media nor America's politicians bothered to warn the public about the gaping disparity between the inflated claims on economic output that stocks represented and the actual production of the economy. But by the end of the decade, insiders saw the writing on the wall. They rushed to the exits, trying to realize stock gains before the contradictions inherent in the market overwhelmed them. Prices tumbled, wiping out trillions in illusory money.

The case of Enron Corp. is the most notorious, but it is unfortunately not unique. When Enron filed for bankruptcy protection in November of 2001 its stock, which had traded as high as $90 per share a year before, plummeted to less than $1. *New York Times* reporter Jeffrey Seglin writes that the elevators in Enron's Houston headquarters sported TV sets tuned to CNBC, constantly tracking the firm's stock price and acclaiming the bull market generally. As Enron stock climbed in the late 1990s, these daily market updates made employees— whose retirement accounts were largely invested in company shares—feel quite wealthy, though most Enron workers were not in fact free to sell these shares. Enron's contributions of company stock to employee retirement accounts didn't vest until workers reached age 50. For years, Enron had hawked its stock to employees, to pension fund managers, and to the world as a surefire investment. Many employees used their own 401(k) funds, over and above the firm's matching contributions, to purchase additional shares. But as the firm disintegrated amid accusations of accounting fraud, plan managers froze employee accounts, so that workers were unable to unload even the stock they owned outright. With employee accounts frozen, Enron executives and board members are estimated to have dumped their own stock and options, netting $1.2 billion cash—almost exactly the amount employees lost from retirement accounts.

Soon after Enron's collapse, telecommunications giant Global Crossing imploded amid accusations of accounting irregularities. Global Crossing's stock, which had traded at nearly $100 per share, became virtually worthless, but not before CEO Gary Winnick exercised his own options and walked away with $734 million. Qwest Communications director Phil Anschutz cashed in $1.6 billion in the two years before the firm stumbled under a crushing debt load; the stock subsequently lost 96% of its value. The three top officers of telecom equipment maker JDS Uniphase collectively raked in $1.1 billion between 1999 and 2001. The stock is now trading at $2 per share. An investigation by the *Wall Street Journal* and Thompson Financial analysts estimates that top telecommunications executives captured a staggering $14.2 billion in stock gains between 1997 and 2001. The industry is now reeling, with 60 firms bankrupt and 500,000 jobs lost. The Journal reports that, as of August 2002, insiders at 38 telecom companies had walked away with gains greater than the current market value of their firms. "All told, it is one of the greatest transfers of wealth from investors—big and small—in American history," reporter Dennis Berman writes. "Telecom executives ... made hundreds of millions of dollars, while many investors took huge, unprecedented losses."

Executives in the energy and telecom sectors were not the only ones to rake in impressive gains. Michael Eisner of Disney Corp. set an early record for CEO pay in 1998, netting $575 million, most in option sales. Disney stock has since fallen by two-thirds. Lawrence Ellison, CEO of Oracle Corp., made $706 million when he sold 29 million shares of Oracle stock in January 2001. Ellison's sales flooded the market for Oracle shares and contributed, along with reports of declining profits, to the stock's losing two-thirds of its value over the next few months. Between 1999 and 2001, Dennis Kozlowski of Tyco International sold $258 million of Tyco stock back to the company, on top of a salary and other compensation valued near $30 million. Kozlowski defended this windfall with the claim that his leadership had "created $37 billion in shareholder wealth." By the time Kozlowski quit Tyco under indictment for sales tax fraud in 2002, $80 billion of Tyco's shareholder wealth had evaporated.

Analyzing companies whose stock had fallen by at least 75%, Fortune magazine discovered that "executives and directors of the 1035 companies that met our criteria took out, by our estimate, roughly $66 billion."

The Illusion of Retirement Security

During the bull market, hundreds of U.S. corporations were also stuffing employee savings accounts with corporate equity, creating a class of captive and friendly shareholders who were in many cases enjoined from selling the stock. Studies by the Employee Benefit Research Council found that, while federal law restricts holdings of company stock to 10% of assets in regulated, defined-benefit pension plans, 401(k)-type plans hold an average 19% of assets in company stock. This fraction rises to 32% when companies match employee contributions with stock and to 53% where companies have influence over plan investments. Pfizer Corporation, by all accounts the worst offender, ties up 81% of employee 401(k)s in company stock, but Coca-Cola runs a close second with 76% of plan assets in stock. Before the firm went bankrupt, WorldCom employees had 40% of their 401(k)s in the firm's shares. Such stock contributions cost firms virtually nothing in the short run and, since employees usually aren't permitted to sell the stock for years, companies needn't worry about diluting the value of equity held by important shareholders—or by their executive option-holders. Commenting on recent business lobbying efforts to gut legislation that would restrict stock contributions to retirement plans, Marc Machiz, formerly of the Labor Department's retirement division, told the *Wall Street Journal*, "business loves having people in employer stock and lobbied very hard to kill this stuff."

Until recently, most employees were untroubled by these trends. The market after all was setting new records daily. Quarterly 401(k) statements recorded fantastic returns year after year. Financial advisers assured the public that stocks were and always would be good investments. But corporate insiders proved far less willing to bank on illusory stock wealth when securing their own retirements.

Pearl Meyer and Partners, an executive compensation research firm, estimates that corporate executives eschew 401(k) plans for themselves and instead negotiate sizable cash pensions—the average senior executive is covered by a defined-benefit plan promising 60% of salary after 30 years of service. Under pressure from the board, CEO Richard McGinn quit Lucent at age 52 with $12 million in severance and a cash pension paying $870,000 annually. Lucent's employees, on the other hand, receive a 401(k) plan with 17% of its assets invested in Lucent stock. The stock plunged from $77 to $10 after McGinn's departure. Today it trades at around $1.00. Forty-two thousand Lucent workers lost their jobs as the firm sank.

When Louis Gerstner left IBM in 2002, after receiving $14 million in pay and an estimated $400 million in stock options, he negotiated a retirement package that promises "to cover car, office and club membership expenses for 10 years." IBM's employees, in contrast, have been agitating since 1999 over the firm's decision to replace its defined benefit pension with a 401(k)-type pension plan that, employee representatives estimate, will reduce pensions by one-third to one-half and save the firm $200 million annually. Economist Paul Krugman reports in the *New York Times* that Halliburton Corp. eliminated its employee pensions; first, though, the company "took an $8.5 million charge against earnings to reflect the cost of its parting gift" to CEO Dick Cheney. *Business Week*, surveying the impact of 401(k)s on employee retirement security, concludes that "CEOs deftly phased out rich defined-benefit plans and moved workers into you're-on-your-own 401(k)s, shredding a major safety net even as they locked in lifetime benefits for themselves."

Since 401(k)s were introduced in the early 1980s their use has grown explosively, and they have largely supplanted traditional defined-benefit pensions. In 2002, three of every four dollars contributed to retirement accounts went into 401(k)s. It is thanks to 401(k)s and other retirement savings plans that middle-income Americans became stock-owners in the 1980s and 1990s. It is probably also thanks to 401(k)s, and the huge demand for stocks they generated, that stock prices rose continuously in the 1990s. And it will almost certainly be thanks to 401(k)s that the problems inherent in using the stock market as a vehicle to distribute income will become glaringly apparent once the baby-boom generation begins to retire and liquidate its stock.

If stocks begin again to rise at historical averages—something financial advisors routinely project and prospective retirees are counting on—the discrepancy between what the stock market promises and what the economy delivers will widen dramatically. Something will have to give. Stocks cannot rise faster than the economy grows, not if people are actually to live off the proceeds.

Or rather, stock prices can't rise that fast unless corporate profits—on which stocks represent a legal claim—also surpass GDP gains. But if corporate earnings outpace economic growth, wages will have to stagnate or decline.

Pension economist Douglas Orr believes it is no accident that 401(k)s proliferated in a period of declining earnings and intense economic insecurity for most U.S. wage-earners. From 1980 until the latter half of the 1990s, the position of the typical American employee deteriorated noticeably. Wages fell, unemployment rose, benefits were slashed, stress levels and work hours climbed as U.S. firms "downsized" and "restructured" to cut costs and satiate investor hunger for higher profits.

Firms like General Electric cut tens of thousands of jobs and made remaining jobs far less secure in order to generate earnings growth averaging 15% each year. Welch's ruthless union-busting and cost-cutting earned him the nickname "Neutron Jack" among rank-and-file employees. GE's attitude towards its employees was summed up by union negotiator Steve Tormey: "No matter how many records are broken in productivity or profits, it's always 'what have you done for me lately?' The workers are considered lemons and they are squeezed dry." Welch was championed as a hero on Wall Street, his management techniques widely emulated by firms across the nation. During his tenure, GE's stock price soared as the firm slashed employment by nearly 50%.

The Institute for Policy Studies, in a recent study, found that rising stock prices and soaring CEO pay packages are commonly associated with layoffs. CEOs of firms that "announced layoffs of 1000 or more workers in 2000 earned about 80 percent more, on average, than the executives of the 365 firms surveyed by *Business Week*."

Throughout the 1980s and 1990s, workers whose jobs were disappearing and wages collapsing consoled themselves by watching the paper value of their 401(k)s swell. With labor weak and labor incomes falling, wage and salary earners chose to cast their lot with capital. In betting on the stock market, though, workers are in reality betting that wage incomes will stagnate and trying to offset this by grabbing a slice from the profit pie. This has already proved a losing strategy for most.

Even at the peak of the 1990s bull market, the net wealth—assets minus debts—of the typical household fell from $55,000 to $50,000, as families borrowed heavily to protect their living standards in the face of stagnant wages. Until or unless the nation's capital stock is equitably distributed, there will always be a clash of interests between owners of capital and their employees. If stocks and profits are routinely besting the economy, then either wage-earners are lagging behind or somebody is cooking the books.

Yet surveys show that Americans like 401(k)s. In part, this is because savings accounts are portable, an important consideration in a world where workers can expect to change jobs several times over their working lives. But partly it is because savings plans provide the illusion of self-sufficiency and independence. When retirees spend down their savings, it feels as if they are "paying their own way." They do not feel like dependents, consuming the fruits of other people's labor. Yet they are. It is the nature of retirement that retirees opt out of production and rely on the young to keep the economy rolling. Pensions are always a claim on the real economy—they represent a transfer of goods and services from working adults to non-working retirees, who no longer contribute to economic output. The shift from defined-benefit pensions to 401(k)s and other savings plans in no way changes the fact that pensions transfer resources, but it does change the rules that will govern how those transfers take place—who pays and who benefits.

Private defined-benefit pensions impose a direct claim on corporate profits. In promising a fixed payment over a number of years, corporations commit to transfer a portion of future earnings to retirees. Under these plans, employers promise an annual lifetime benefit at retirement, the amount determined by an employee's prior earnings and years of service in the company. How the benefit will be paid, where the funds will come from, whether there are enough funds to last through a worker's life—this is the company's concern. Longevity risk—the risk that a worker will outlive the money put aside for her retirement—falls on the employer. Retirees benefit, but at a cost to shareholders. Similarly, public pension programs, whether through Social Security or through the civil service, entail a promise to retirees at the expense of the taxpaying public.

Today, the vast majority of workers, if they have pension coverage at all, participate in "defined-contribution" plans, in which they and their employer contribute a fixed monthly sum and invest the proceeds with a money management firm. At retirement, the employee owns whatever funds have accrued in the account and must make the money last until she dies. Defined-contribution plans are a claim on nothing. Workers are given a shot at capturing some of the cash floating around Wall Street, but no promise that they will succeed. 401(k)s will add a huge element of chance to the American retirement experience. Some will sell high, some will not. Some will realize gains. Some will not.

Pearl Meyer and Partners estimate that outstanding, unexercised executive stock options and employee stock incentives today amount to some $2 trillion. Any effort to cash in this amount, in addition to the stock held in retirement accounts, would have a dramatic impact on stock prices. American workers and retirees, in assessing their chances for coming out ahead in the competition to liquidate stock, might ponder this question: If, as employees in private negotiations with their corporate employers, they have been unable to protect their incomes or jobs or health or retirement benefits, how likely is it that they will instead be able to wrest gains from Wall Street where corporate insiders are firmly in control of information and access to deals? ❏

Article 3.2

FROM TULIPS TO MORTGAGE-BACKED SECURITIES

BY GERALD FRIEDMAN
January/February 2008

Thirty years ago, economist Charles Kindleberger published a little book, *Manias, Panics, and Crashes*, describing the normal tendency of capitalist financial markets to fluctuate between speculative excess (or "irrational exuberance" in the words of a recent central banker) and panic. Kindleberger describes about 40 of these panics over the nearly 260 years from 1720–1975, or one every seven years. Following Kindleberger's arithmetic, we were due for a panic because it had been seven years since the high-tech bubble burst and the stock market panic of 2000–1. And the panic came, bringing in its wake a tsunami of economic woe, liquidity shortages, cancelled investments, rising unemployment, and economic distress.

Of course, more than mechanics and arithmetic are involved in the current financial panic. But there is a sense of inevitability about the manias and panics of capitalist financial markets, a sense described by writers from Karl Marx to John Maynard Keynes, Hyman Minsky, John Kenneth Galbraith, and Robert Shiller. The problem is that financial markets trade in unknown and unknowable future returns. Lacking real information, they are inevitably driven by the madness of crowds.

Unlike tangible commodities whose price should reflect its real value and real cost of production, financial assets are not priced according to any real returns, nor even according to some expected return, but rather according to expectations of what others will pay in the future, or, even worse, expectations of future expectations that others will have of assets' future return. Whether it is Dutch tulips in 1637, the South Sea Bubble of 1720, Florida real estate in the 1920s, or mortgage-backed securities today, it is always the same story of financial markets floating like a manic-depressive from euphoria to panic to bust. When unregulated, this process is made still worse by market manipulation, and simple fraud. Speculative markets like these can make some rich, and can even be exciting to watch, like a good game of poker; but this is a dangerous and irresponsible way to manage an economy.

There was a time when governments understood. Learning from past financial disasters, the United States established rules to limit the scope of financial euphoria and panic by strictly segregating different types of banks, by limiting financial speculation, and by requiring clear accounting of financial transactions. While they were regulated, financial markets contributed to the best period of growth in American history, the "glorious thirty" after World War II. To be sure, restrictions on speculative behavior and strict regulations made this a boring time to be a banker, and they limited earnings in the financial services sector. But, limited to a secondary role, finance served a greater good by providing liquidity for a long period of steady and relatively egalitarian economic growth.

Of course, over time we forgot why we had regulated financial markets, memory loss helped along by the combined efforts of free-market economists and self-interested bankers and others on Wall Street. To promote "competition," we lowered the barriers between different types of financial institutions, widening the scope of financial markets. We moved activities such as home mortgage lending onto national markets and allowed a rash of bank mergers to create huge financial institutions too large to be allowed to fail, but never too large to operate irresponsibly. Despite the growing scope and centralization of financial activity, the government accepted arguments that we could trust financial firms to self-regulate because it was in their interest to maintain credible accounting.

So we reap the whirlwind with a market collapse building to Great Depression levels. Once again, we learn history's lesson from direct experience: capitalist financial markets cannot be trusted. It is time to either re-regulate or move beyond. ❑

Article 3.3

STOCK VOLATILITY

BY ELLEN FRANK
May/June 2002

Dear Dr. Dollar:
During the course of a single day, a stock can go up and down frequently. These changes supposedly reflect the changing demand for that stock (and its potential resale value) or changing expectations of a company's profitability. But this seems too vague to me. How can these factors be so volatile? Who actually decides, or what is the mechanism for deciding, when a stock price should go up or down and by how much?
—Joseph Balszak, Muskegon, Mich.

Let's start with your last question first—how are stock prices determined? Shares in most large established corporations are listed on organized exchanges like the New York or American Stock Exchanges. Shares in most smaller or newer firms are listed on the NASDAQ—an electronic system that tracks stock prices.

Every time a stock is sold, the exchange records the price at which it changes hands. If, a few seconds or minutes later, another trade takes place, the price at which that trade is made becomes the new market price, and so on. Organized exchanges like the New York Stock Exchange will occasionally suspend trading in a stock if the price is excessively volatile, if there is a severe mismatch between supply and demand (many people wanting to sell, no one wanting to buy) or if they suspect that insiders are deliberately manipulating a stock's price. But in normal circumstances, there is no official arbiter of stock prices, no person or institution that "decides" a price. The market price of a stock is simply the price at which a willing buyer and seller agree to trade.

Why then do prices fluctuate so much? The vast bulk of stock trades are made by professional traders who buy and sell shares all day long, hoping to profit from small changes in share prices. Since these traders do not hold stocks over the long haul, they are not terribly interested in such long-term considerations as a company's profitability or the value of its assets. Or rather, they are interested in such factors mostly insofar as news that would affect a company's long-term prospects might cause *other traders* to buy the stock, causing its price to rise. If a trader believes that others will buy shares (in the expectation that prices will rise), then she will buy as well, hoping to sell when the price rises. If others believe the same thing, then the wave of buying pressure will, in fact, *cause* the price to rise.

Back in the 1930s, economist John Maynard Keynes compared the stock market to a contest then popular in British tabloids, in which contestants had to look at photos and choose the faces that *other contestants* would pick as the prettiest. Each contestant had to look for photos "likeliest to catch the fancy of the other competitors, all of whom are looking at the problem from the same point of view." Similarly, stock traders try to guess which stocks other traders will buy. The successful trader is the one who anticipates and outfoxes the market, buying before a stock's price rises and selling before it falls.

Financial firms employ thousands of market strategists and technical analysts who spend hours poring over historical stock data, trying to divine the logic behind these price changes. If they could unlock the secret of stock prices, they could arm their traders with the ability to always buy low and sell high. So far, no one has found this particular holy grail. And so traders continue to guess and gamble and, in doing so, send prices gyrating.

For small investors, who do hold stock for the long term and will need to cash in their stocks at some point to finance their retirements, the volatility of the market can be a source of constant anxiety. Every time a share in, say, General Electric is traded, the new price is used to revalue all outstanding shares—just as the value of your home appreciates when the house down the block sells for more than a similar house sold last week. But the value of your home wouldn't be so high if every house on your block were suddenly put up for sale. Similarly, if all ten billion outstanding shares of General Electric—or even a small fraction of them—were put up for sale, they wouldn't fetch anywhere near the current market price. Small investors need to keep in mind that the gains and losses on their 401(k) statements are just hypothetical paper gains and losses. You won't know the true value of your stocks until you actually try to sell them. ❑

Article 3.4

"PRESSURE FROM THE BOND MARKET"

BY ARTHUR MacEWAN
May/June 2010

Dear Dr. Dollar:
With the crisis in Greece and other countries, commentators have said that governments are "under pressure from the bond market" or that bond markets will "punish" governments. What does this mean?
—Nikolaos Papanikolaou, Queens, N.Y.

It means that money is power.

The people and institutions that buy government bonds have the money. They are "the bond market." By telling governments the conditions under which they will make loans (i.e., buy the governments' bonds), they are able to greatly influence governments' policies.

But let's go back to some basics. When a government spends more than it takes in as taxes, it has to borrow the difference. It borrows by selling bonds, which are promises to pay. So the payments for the bonds are loans.

A government might sell a bond that is a promise to pay $103 a year from the date of sale. If bond buyers are confident that this promise will be kept and if the return they can get on other forms of investments is 3%, they will be willing to pay $100 for the bond. That is, they will be willing to loan the government $100 to be paid back in one year with 3% interest. This investment will then be providing the same return as their other investments.

But what if they are not confident that the promise will be kept? What if the investors ("the bond market") think that the government of Greece, for example, may not be able to make the payments as promised and will default on the bonds? Under these circumstances the investors will not pay $100 for the bonds that return $103 next year. They may be willing to pay only $97.

If the government then does meet its promise, the bond will provide a 6.2% rate of return. But if the "bond market's" fear of default turns out to be correct, then these bonds will have a much lower rate of return—or, in the extreme case, they will be a total loss. The "bond market" is demanding a higher rate of return to compensate for the risk. (The 3% - 6.2% difference was roughly the difference between the return on German and Greek bonds in March, when this column was written. By mid-April Greece was paying 9%.)

However, if the Greek government—or whatever government is seeking the loans—can sell these bonds for only $97, it will have to sell more bonds in order to raise the funds it needs. In a year, the payments (that 6.2%) will place a new, severe burden on the government's budget.

So the investors say, in effect, "If you fix your policies in ways that we think make default less likely, we will buy the bonds at a higher price—not $100, but maybe at $98 or $99." It is not the ultimate purchasers of the bonds who convey this message; it is the underwriters, the large investment banks—Goldman Sachs for example. As underwriters they handle the sale of the bonds for the Greek government (and take hefty fees for this service).

Even if the investment banks were giving good, objective advice, this would be bad enough. However, the nature of their advice—"the pressure from the bond market"—is conditioned by who they are and whom they represent.

Foremost, they push for actions that will reduce the government's budget deficit, even when sensible economic policy would call for a stimulus that would be provided by maintaining or expanding the deficit. Also, investment bankers will not tell governments to raise taxes on the rich or on foreign corporations in order to reduce the deficit. Instead, they tend to advocate cutting social programs and reducing the wages of public-sector workers.

It does not require great insight to see the class bias in these sorts of actions.

Yet the whole problem does not lie with the "pressure from the bond market." The Greek government and other governments have followed policies that make them vulnerable to this sort of pressure. Unwilling or unable to tax the rich, governments borrowed to pay for their operations in good times. Having run budget deficits in good times, these authorities are in a poor position to add more debt when it is most needed—in the current recession in particular. So now, when governments really need to borrow to run deficits, they—and, more important, their people—are at the mercy of the "bond markets."

Popular protests can push back, saving some social programs and forcing governments to place a greater burden on the wealthy. A real solution, however, requires long-term action to shift power, which would change government practices and reduce vulnerability to "the pressure from the bond market." ❑

Article 3.5

DOW'S REBOUND AFTER THE GREAT RECESSION INCONSEQUENTIAL FOR MOST AMERICANS

BY SYLVIA A. ALLEGRETTO
October 2010

The Dow has rebounded nicely following the bursting of the housing bubble in 2008 and the Great Recession that followed. As of October 2010, the Dow was just above 11,000—a significant improvement over its recent low of 6,630 in March 2009. The Dow has surpassed the 10,000 mark for the greater part of 2010 even as there has not been much improvement in the overall economy. It is clear that there is a disconnect between the stock market and the broader economy, as measured in terms of job growth or the unemployment rate. Thus, it is important to put stock market gains into perspective for average working families. Fostered by the constant focus and widespread attention given to the performance of the stock market, conventional wisdom has it that everyone in the United States is heavily invested in the stock market. However, the data tell a different story.

The most recent triennial data from the Survey of Consumer Finances show that the historically increasing trend in the shares of all households owning any stock was reversed after 2001, when just over half (51.9%) were in the stock market in some form. In 2004 the share fell to just under half (48.6%), which was the first such decline on record (Figure 1), and there was little improvement in 2007 when the share was about the same (49.1%).

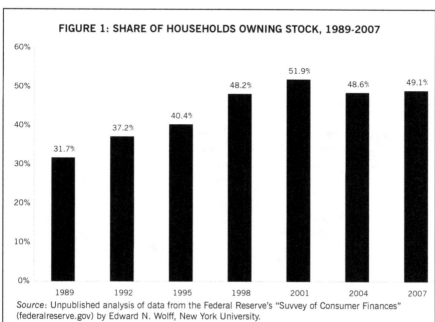

FIGURE 1: SHARE OF HOUSEHOLDS OWNING STOCK, 1989-2007

Source: Unpublished analysis of data from the Federal Reserve's "Suvvey of Consumer Finances" (federalreserve.gov) by Edward N. Wolff, New York University.

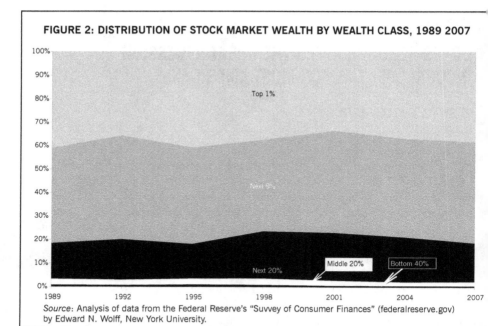

FIGURE 2: DISTRIBUTION OF STOCK MARKET WEALTH BY WEALTH CLASS, 1989 2007

Source: Analysis of data from the Federal Reserve's "Suvvey of Consumer Finances" (federalreserve.gov) by Edward N. Wolff, New York University.

The distribution of stocks by value is highly tilted to the wealthiest Americans, as shown in Figure 2. In 2007, the wealthiest one percent owned 38.2% of all stocks, while the next 9% owned 43.0%. Hence, the wealthiest 10% controlled about 80% of all stocks while the bottom 90% owned just over 20%. Given the starkness and persistence of inequality in stock holdings, there is no reason to think those in the bottom 90% are doing any better in 2010.

For the most part, lower-, middle-, and even upper-middle-income working-age households depend on their paychecks, not stock portfolios, to meet their everyday needs. Typical working families that own stock do so in retirement plans that are costly to turn into cash. Therefore, increasing stock value does little to help them make ends meet at a time when wages for most workers have been stagnant for decades. ❑

Sources: The figures are unpublished updates of Figure 5F and Table 5.7 from *The State of Working America 2006/2007* by Lawrence Mishel, Jared Bernstein, and Sylvia Allegretto, an Economic Policy Institute Book (Ithaca, N.Y.: ILR Press, an imprint of Cornell University Press, 2007).

Article 3.6

HOW HAVE BANKS MANAGED TO REPAY THE BAILOUT?

BY ARTHUR MacEWAN
May/June 2012

Dear Dr. Dollar:

Many of the banks that were bailed out by the Bush and Obama admin-istrations—to the tune of some trillions of dollars (no one seems to know exactly how much)—have, according to news reports, already paid back the huge sums of money they were loaned to avoid bank-ruptcy. How is this possible if, as the news reports also tell us, the banks have been extremely reluctant to loan money in these recessionary times? Since banks only make money by making loans, how were they able to pay off their huge debts to the U.S. Treasury in so short a period of time?
—Clifford Anderson, Sacramento, Calif.

Actually, banks make money in lots of ways, and for the big banks, making loans is not the main way that they make money.

Which raises the question: What is a bank? Consider the infamous Wall Street firm of Goldman Sachs, generally viewed as a bank and a recipient of substantial bailout funds from the federal government. In 2010, Goldman Sachs had revenues of $39.2 billion, but a tiny fraction of this was interest income from loans. The larg-est share of its revenues, $21.8 billion, came from "Institutional Client Services," fees for handling financial transactions for institutional clients (other firms, invest-ment funds, and governments). Activity involving "Investment and Lending" provided Goldman with $7.5 billion, but this does not mean making new loans; it means mainly buying and selling existing loans—for example, those packages of mortgages, called "collateralized debt obligations," which were so important in the financial meltdown of 2008.

Another example is provided by JPMorgan Chase, which differs from Goldman Sachs in that its operations include a large amount of what we usually view as banking—that is, commercial banking operations of holding checking and savings deposits and making loans to individuals and businesses. Still, in 2010 slightly more than half of the firm's $102.7 billion revenue was non-interest revenue. (And much of the interest revenue, we may assume, was not from mak-ing new loans.) The largest component of JPMorgan Chase's 2010 non-interest revenue, $13.5 billion, is listed in its annual report as "Asset management, admin-istration and commissions."

In 2010, Goldman reported $8.3 billion in after-tax profits and JPMorgan Chase reported $17.4 billion. So they had a good deal of money with which to reward their stockholders, pay something back to the U.S. Treasury, and provide bonuses to executives—though bonuses would come as expenses, not deductions from profits. (It appears that these firms and large banks generally did not do so well in 2011, but final figures are not yet available).

There is a good deal of controversy over how much money was actually provided to the banks and other financial firms. So it is difficult to figure out how much has been paid back. In a December 6, 2011, letter to Congress, Ben Bernanke, chairman of the Federal Reserve Bank, wrote:

> ... one article asserted that the Federal Reserve lent or guaranteed more than $7.7 trillion during the financial crisis. Others have estimated the amounts to be $16 trillion or even $24 trillion. All of these numbers are wildly inaccurate. As disclosed on the Federal Reserve's balance sheet, published weekly and audited annually by independent auditors, total credit outstanding under the liquidity programs was never more than about $1.5 trillion; that was the peak reached in December 2008.

There is not necessarily a conflict between Bernanke's $1.5 trillion and the larger estimates. If the Fed provided $1 trillion in ten other months—money which was paid back each month— and $1.5 trillion in December 2008, the total provision of funds would be $11.5 trillion, but the peak, as Bernanke says, would still be $1.5 trillion.

Also, in what is called "quantitative easing," the Fed bought a large amount of long-term securities form the banks, which put money into the banks' hands— another way of keeping them afloat, but not through providing loans to the banks.

How does one count all this? It all depends on how you want to spin it.

However, if Bernanke's claim is correct, this means that, while a lot more than $1.5 billion was provided to the banks, the great majority of it was short term and was paid back—so the peak never rose above that $1.5 trillion.

The bottom line? The Fed provided several trillion dollars to the banks at very low interest rates. These funds allowed many banks, most of the big ones in particular, to stay in operation, make lots of money by pursing their investment strategies (but not much by making new loans), and pay back a large share of what they borrowed from the Fed.

Did this save us from an even worse financial crisis? Probably yes. Were there other ways to do it that would have bailed out the banks but not the bankers who led us into this crisis? Other ways that would have put conditions on the banks, preventing them from enriching their executives and leading us towards another crisis? Probably yes again. ❑

Article 3.7

THE BIG CASINO

BY DOUG ORR
November 2013

Speculators may do no harm as bubbles on a steady stream of enterprise. But the position is serious when enterprise becomes the bubble on a whirlpool of speculation. When the capital development of a country becomes a by-product of the activities of a casino, the job is likely to be ill-done.
— John Maynard Keynes (1936)

Every night on the evening news we hear something like this: "In economic news, the Dow is up by 1.5%, the S&P is up by 1.2% and the NASDAQ is down by 0.3%, based on ...." Reporting these numbers so prominently and giving a supposed link to the events of the day gives the impression that the stock market plays a central role in moving the economy forward and that everyone has a stake in these daily changes. In fact, the movement of these stock indices on a day-to-day basis has almost nothing to do with the actual economy and, except in times of economic crisis, the stock market has almost no impact on the lives of most Americans. Fewer than half of American families own a single share of stock, and only about a third own shares totaling more than $5000. The stock market is the realm of the elite, and for the past several decades has had a negative impact on the real economy.

Who are the "Investors"?

Economic textbooks tell us that financial markets play an important role in the economy, linking saving to investment. Some individuals have more income than they currently want to spend, so they engage in saving. Other individuals need money to engage in investment. "Investment" in this context means the creation of new, physically productive resources. If a firm builds a new factory, installs new machines, or buys new software to do its accounting, that is investment. When you, as a student, learn new skills that make you more productive, that is investment. So when a bank takes people's savings and lends it to the owner of a restaurant to buy a new stove, the bank plays an important economic role. Further, savers can get their money back if they need it in the future, because loans get repaid.

When you put money in the bank you receive interest. This is your reward for saving and giving the bank the use of your money. But you are not engaging in investment. The person who borrows the money and puts it to productive use is the investor. When you put money in the bank, you are a saver, not an investor.

Corporations, however, can bypass banks and gain access to financial capital by issuing stock. When a company issues new shares of stock, the money raised from the sale can be used to engage in productive investment. The issuing of new shares is called an "initial public offering," or IPO. IPOs are not done on stock exchanges. They are handled by investment banks. But no one would buy a share of stock if they could not get their money back when they needed it. The useful role of the stock exchanges, what we call the "stock market," is to provide "liquidity." One individual who has money to save today can buy a share of stock from someone who needs to get their past savings back.

The words we use to describe things matter. Investors are usually seen as contributing to the economy because they hire workers to build new factories, new machines and other productive assets, and these assets can make the real economy more productive. Workers create the assets, and the investors are given the credit. On the other hand, gamblers and speculators are usually seen as frivolous and destructive.

The biggest propaganda coup of the 20th century was convincing the media and the general public to call the speculators on the New York Stock Exchange (NYSE) "investors." They did it by blurring the positive role of the stock market with the speculative role. If you buy a share of Pacific Gas and Electric (PG&E) stock on the stock exchange, you will get a quarterly dividend payment, just like the interest you get from the money you put in a bank. But, PG&E does not get any new money to use for actual investment. The price you pay for the stock goes to the previous owner of the stock, not PG&E.

On November 8, 2013, the Dow-Jones index hit a record high of 15,761.78, on news that the unemployment rate was up, median family incomes were falling and, six years after the start of the last recession, the economy has not yet recovered. That day, NYSE market volume was 823 million shares, and another 1.96 billion shares were traded on the NASDAQ. More than $50 billion changed hands, yet not a penny of all this money went to a corporation for use as productive investment.

The biggest casino in the world is located at the corner of Wall Street and Broad Street in New York City. Calling the players on the NYSE "investors" completely changes our understanding of the role they play. Consider rewording some recent stories: "Gamblers bet big on new Genentech drug," or "Speculators made 73% in one day buying Twitter's IPO in the morning and reselling later in the day to suckers caught up in the excitement." The *Wall Street Journal* does occasionally tell us the truth when they report on the "bets" made by "players" on the NYSE. Speculators betting that the price of a share will rise want to buy it and those betting that the price will fall want to sell it. If there are more buyers than sellers, the price will rise, regardless of anything that is happening in the real economy. Reporting a record high for the NYSE has about as much importance as reporting a record amount of gambling in Las Vegas. Except the gambling on the NYSE can have a much larger negative impact on the real economy.

Big Gambling Does Big Damage

The reason why the volume on the NYSE is so high is because speculators engage in high-frequency trading. An analyst predicts that, based on breaking news, the price of a particular stock may go up. If you can be the first to buy the stock before the price goes up, you can sell it a few minutes later (or even seconds, or fractions of a second, later) and make a profit. This is why brokerage houses now rely on "program trading." Computers can see price differentials and make trades much faster than humans can. Brokerage firms need to have the fastest possible computers and the fastest network connections because milliseconds matter. By 2010, this type of high-frequency, or "quant" trading made up 70% of the bloated stock trading volume.

If you buy a share of stock for $100 and sell it 30 minutes later for $100.50, you make a profit of 50 cents, or 0.5%. If you buy a million shares, you make half a million dollars for a half an hour of "work." But the "work" was done by a computer program and you have done nothing to make the economy more productive, to create jobs, or to increase GDP. All you have done is to bring a large pile of money to the table at the casino. You have redistributed money from one person at the table to another, and for this, the *Wall Street Journal* calls you an "investor." You can use your winnings to hire the best and brightest minds to give you an edge at the table, and you will pay them well.

We are being told how important it is to get students into STEM (science, technology, engineering and math). Yet government funding for these fields is being cut and jobs prospects are uncertain. Stock market speculation diverts the best and brightest minds away from solving the real problems facing the world. Instead they are writing software to "read" news feeds looking for key phrases that might indicate a change in speculators' sentiment toward a particular stock, so that instantaneous trades can be made. They are writing algorithms to find the most minute correlations between economic indicators and changes in share prices. Landing a job at a big Wall Street firm can lead to annual bonuses in the millions of dollars. Jobs in basic scientific research and engineering cannot hope to compete.

Corporate managers are rewarded with bonuses for increases in stock prices, regardless of the long-term impacts on the firm. Cutting jobs and driving down wages can increase stock prices, but this has devastating impacts on the lives of ordinary people. If the price of a company's stock starts to fall, management may use the cash held by the company to buy back shares in order to prop up the price. This diverts resources that could have been used for productive investment into the hands of stock market speculators.

If enough of these speculators believe prices will continue to rise, they will pour more money into stocks, and share prices will rise. Speculation can be self-fulfilling and create price bubbles. But if speculators turn pessimistic, they can also create stock market crashes. If this only affected the gamblers it would not be a problem. But as a company's stock price falls, it may be harder for the firm to borrow from banks or the bond market to pay for day-to-day operations. This can crash the real economy and drive up unemployment. As stock prices fall, the retirement savings of millions of workers (who have seen their defined-benefit pensions stolen and converted into 401(k) savings accounts) will also decline. Ordinary people reap little benefit from the daily speculation on the stock market, but millions experience real losses when the bets go bad. The Big Casino does very real damage to the real economy.

One way to reduce the damage would be to put a tax on the socially destructive behavior. We tax cigarettes and alcohol because of the damage they do. We tax gambling in Atlantic City at 8% and in Las Vegas at 6.25%. The sales taxes on socially useful items like shoes and computers are often more than 7%. There should also be a sales tax on stock market transactions, i.e., speculation.

To be sure, Wall Street lobbyists will try to scare the pubic in thinking that taxing speculation will somehow kill "investment" and jobs. Because unemployment is still high, anything that reduces employment growth will be seen as negative. But this tax will not reduce job creation. Stock market speculation already does that. Between 2008 and 2013, the dollar value of shares repurchased by corporations was higher than the amount raised by IPOs. So the stock market has actually drained resources away from real investment and job creation.

In 2007, the year before the most recent collapse of a speculative bubble, $43.8 trillion in stocks changed hands on just the NYSE and the NASDAQ. That same year, only $65.1 billion was raised in IPOs. That is $673 dollars of speculation for every $1 allocated from savers to real investors. Putting a tax on stock speculation will have almost no impact on productive investment by businesses, but it will raise much needed revenue for public investments in education and infrastructure.

What we need is a "speculation-reduction tax." Gamblers and speculators are seen as frivolous and destructive, and a tax that would restrict their behavior would be positively received. To be fully effective, the tax should be "progressive" with respect to time. If a stock is held for less than a day, the tax on the trade should be 5% of the value of the trade. The tax on a stock held for a week would be 2%; for a month, 1%; and, for a year, 0.5%. But opponents will make the case that this is too complex and too costly, so a flat-rate tax is more feasible.

The European Union is likely to implement a FTT rate of 0.1% in 2014. This rate is too small to have much of an impact on speculation. The UK has had a tax rate of 0.5% since 1986. It has not restricted the basic functioning of their stock market, but a tax of this amount makes the short-term trade described above unprofitable. Since 2009, ten different FTT bills have been introduced in the U.S. House and four in the Senate, most at a rate less than 0.5%. If a 0.5% tax were implemented in the United States, the Congressional Research Service estimates revenue generation of $164 to $264 billion per year, depending on the decline in speculative trading. The liberal Center for Economic and Policy Research (CEPR) estimates revenues will be between $110 to $220 billion for a 0.5% tax.

If we implement this type of speculation-reduction tax, it will reallocate much needed resources to productive public investment and away from job-killing stock speculation. This idea, first proposed by John Maynard Keynes in 1936, is long over-due. As Dean Baker, co-director of CEPR, put it in 1994: "Government is perfectly willingly to tax Las Vegas, Atlantic City and the lotteries, where working people place their bets with virtually no consequence to the country's economic future. Why then should it not also tax the preferred gambling venue of the wealthy, especially given the serious costs their activities impose on the economic prospects of the majority?" ❑

Sources: Dean Baker, et.al., "The Potential Revenue from Financial Transactions Taxes," Center for Economic and Policy Research, Dec. 2009; "A securities Transactions Tax: Brief Analytic Overview with Revenue Estimates," Congressional Research Service, June 2012; Stephany Griffith-Jones, "Germany wants the Robin Hood tax," *The Guardian*, Oct. 2013; Robert Pollin and James Heintz, "Transaction Costs, Trading Elasticities and the Revenue Potential of Financial Transaction Taxes for the United States," Political Economy Research Institute, Dec. 2011; Dean Baker, Robert Pollin and Marc Schaberg, "Taxing the Big Casino," *The Nation*, May 1994; NYSE Technologies Market Data (nyxdata.com); NASDAQ Trader (NASDAQtrader.com); PriceWaterhouse IPO Watch (pwc.com).

Article 3.8

TRANSACTION TAX: SAND IN THE WHEELS, NOT IN THE FACE

Why a transaction tax is a really good *idea.*

BY JOHN MILLER
March/April 2010

WHY TAXING STOCK TRADES IS A REALLY BAD IDEA

[S]urely it is "socially useful" to let free people transact freely, without regulators and legislators micromanaging them. ... It's Economics 101 that the free actions of market participants cause supply and demand to reach equilibrium. And isn't that what investors—indeed even speculators—do? Can they do it as well when facing the dead-weight costs of a transaction tax?

If not, then trading volume in our stock markets will fall. Beyond the tax, everyone—investors and speculator, great and small—who buys or sells stocks will pay more to transact in markets that are less liquid. In such a world, markets would necessarily be more risky, and the cost of capital for business would necessarily rise. The consequence of that is that innovation, growth, and jobs would necessarily fall. That would be the full and true cost of the trading tax.

—Donald L. Luskin and Chris Hynes, "Why Taxing Stock Trades Is a Really Bad Idea," *Wall Street Journal*, Jan. 5, 2010

"**S**ome financial activities which proliferated over the last 10 years were socially useless," Britain's Finance Service Authority Chairman Adiar Turner told a black-tie gathering of financial executives in London in September 2009. That is why he had proposed a transaction tax for the United Kingdom and why British Prime Minister Gordon Brown would propose an international transaction tax at the November G-20 summit.

The gathered bankers "saw red," as one report described their reaction. Investment bankers Donald L. Luskin and Chris Hynes are still irate.

In some ways their reaction is surprising. A financial transaction tax is nothing other than a sales tax on trading stocks and other securities. Transaction taxes are already in place in about 30 countries, and a transaction tax applied to the sale of stock in the United States from 1914 to 1964.

In addition, the transaction tax rates on a single trade are typically quite low. For instance, the "Let Wall Street Pay for the Restoration of Main Street Act of 2009," proposed by U.S. Representative Peter DeFazio (D-Ore.), would assess a one quarter of one percent (.25%) tax on the value of stock transactions, and two one hundredths of one percent (.02%) tax on the sale on a variety of derivative assets—including credit default swaps, which played such a large role in the mortgage crisis. To target speculators, the bill exempts retirement accounts, mutual funds, education and health savings accounts, and the first $100,000 of transactions annually.

In other ways, Luskin's and Hynes's reaction is not surprising at all. At its heart, a transaction tax is a radical measure. Its premise is that faster-acting financial markets driven by speculation don't bring relief to the economy—instead, they loot the economy. Its purpose, as Nobel Prize-winning economist James Tobin put it when he proposed his original transaction tax on international money markets during the 1970s, is to "throw sand in the wheels" of our financial markets.

Also, while its tax rate is low, the burden of a transaction tax adds up as securities are repeatedly traded, as is the practice on Wall Street today. For instance, even after accounting for its exemptions and allowing for a sizable decline in trading, the DeFazio bill would still raise $63.5 billion annually, according to the estimates of Dean Baker, co-director of the Center for Economic Policy Research.

Luskin and Hynes have two main objections to the transaction tax. The first is that a transaction tax would affect every single person who owns and invests in stocks, not just speculators. Customers would not have to pay a tax to buy or sell mutual funds, but, as Luskin and Hynes emphasize, the mutual funds themselves would have to pay a tax every time they trade stocks. So everyone holding mutual funds would still end up paying the tax.

What Luskin and Hynes don't say is this: Mutual funds that actively trade stocks would pay three times the transaction taxes of an average fund, as the Investment Company Institute, the fund industry trade group, reports. And stock index funds, which hold a sample of all stocks but seldom trade them, are taxed the least. Those funds have historically outperformed other mutual funds. So a transaction tax would work to push mutual fund customers to invest their savings more wisely, providing some with higher rates of return with a transaction tax than their previous funds provided without it. And that would mean fewer broker fees and lower profits for the fund industry.

But what really sticks in Luskin's and Hynes's craw is the assertion that financial trading is not socially useful. That claim flies in face of the long-held contention, buttressed by much of finance theory, that the equilibrium outcomes of financial markets are efficient. And if financial markets are efficient, there is no need for a tax that will reduce trading.

But much of what Luskin and Hynes have to say is not right. First, as anyone who *paid attention* in Economics 101 would know, reaching an equilibrium is not in and of itself desirable. To endorse the outcomes of today's speculative financial markets as desirable because they reach an equilibrium is the equivalent of describing a gambler in a poker game raking in a big pot as desirable because it clears the table. And the gamblers in our financial markets did rake in some awfully big pots betting that subprime borrowers would default on their loans. The last few years show us just how undesirable that equilibrium turned out to be.

Second, speculation dwarfs financing investment in U.S. stock markets. During the 1970s, for every dollar of new investment in plants and equipment, $1.30 in stocks were traded on the U.S. exchanges, reports Robert Pollin, co-director of the Political Economy Research Institute. But from 1998 to 2007, $27 in stocks were traded on the U.S. exchanges for every dollar of corporate investment in plant equipment. Such a rapid stock turnover has diverted the attention of managers of enterprises from long-term planning. Whatever damage that churning caused on Main Street, it paid off handsomely on Wall Street. From 1973 to 2007, the size of the financial (and insurance) sector relative to the economy doubled, financial sector profits went from one-quarter to two-fifths of domestic profits, and compensation in the finance industry went from just about average to 180% of the private industry average.

By counteracting these trends, a transactions tax can actually enhance, not diminish, the efficiency of financial markets. If it forces the financial sector to fulfill its function of transferring savings to investment with less short-term churning, then the tax will have freed up resources for more productive uses.

A transaction tax would surely be a step in the right direction toward reducing the bloat of the finance industry, righting the balance of speculation over enterprise, and restoring the focus on long-term planning and job-creation in the economy.

None of that will happen unless every last grain of the decades' worth of sand the bullies on Wall Street have kicked in our faces gets thrown into the wheels of finance. That is a tall order. But as DeFazio's and Turner's example shows, some of today's policymakers are up to the task. ❏

Sources: Dean Baker, "The Benefits of a Financial Transaction Tax," Center For Economic and Policy Research, December 2008; Robert Pollin and Dean Baker, "Public Investment, Industrial Policy, and U.S. Economic Renewal," Political Economy Research Institute, December 2009; Caroline Binham, "Turner Plan on 'Socially Useless' Trades Make Bankers See Red," Bloomberg. com; Yaiman Onaran, "Taxing Wall Street Today Wins Support for Keynes Idea (Update 1)," Bloomberg.com; Dean Baker, Robert Pollin, Travis McArthur, and Matt Sherman, "The Potential Revenue from Financial Transactions Taxes, Political Economy Research Institute, Working paper no. 212, December 2009; Donald L. Luskin and Chris Hynes, "Why Taxing Stock Trades Is a Really Bad Idea," *Wall Street Journal*, Jan. 5, 2010; John McKinnon, "Lawmakers Weigh A Wall Street Tax," *Wall Street Journal*, Dec. 19, 2009; Tobin Tax (freerisk.org); text of HR 4191—"Let Wall Street Pay for the Restoration of Main Street Act of 2009" (govtrack.us).

Chapter 4

MORTGAGES, CONSUMER CREDIT, AND PREDATORY LENDING

Article 4.1

AMERICA'S GROWING FRINGE ECONOMY

BY HOWARD KARGER
November/December 2006

Financial services for the poor and credit-challenged are big business.

Ron Cook is a department manager at a Wal-Mart store in Atlanta. María Guzmán is an undocumented worker from Mexico; she lives in Houston with her three children and cleans office buildings at night. Marty Lawson works for a large Minneapolis corporation. What do these three people have in common? They are all regular fringe economy customers.

The term "fringe economy" refers to a range of businesses that engage in financially predatory relationships with low-income or heavily indebted consumers by charging excessive interest rates, superhigh fees, or exorbitant prices for goods or services. Some examples of fringe economy businesses include payday lenders, pawnshops, check-cashers, tax refund lenders, rent-to-own stores, and "buy-here/pay-here" used car lots. The fringe economy also includes credit card companies that charge excessive late payment or over-the-credit-limit penalties; cell phone providers that force less creditworthy customers into expensive prepaid plans; and subprime mortgage lenders that gouge prospective homeowners.

The fringe economy is hardly new. Pawnshops and informal high-interest lenders have been around forever. What we see today, however, is a fringe-economy sector that is growing fast, taking advantage of the ever-larger part of the U.S. population whose economic lives are becoming less secure. Moreover, in an important sense the sector is no longer "fringe" at all: more and more, large mainstream financial corporations are behind the high-rate loans that anxious customers in run-down storefronts sign for on the dotted line.

The Payday Lending Trap

Ron and Deanna Cook have two children and a combined family income of $48,000—more than twice the federal poverty line but still $10,000 below Georgia's median income. They are the working poor.

To make ends meet, the Cooks borrow from payday lenders. When Ron and Deanna borrow $300 for 14 days they pay $60 in interest—an annual interest rate of 520%! If they can't pay the full $360, they pay just the $60 interest fee and roll over the loan for another two weeks. The original $300 loan now costs $120 in interest for 30 days. If they roll over the loan for another two-week cycle, they pay $180 in interest on a $300 loan for 45 days. If the payday lender permits only four rollovers, the Cooks sometimes take out a payday loan from another lender to repay the original loan. This costly cycle can be devastating. The Center for Responsible Lending tells the tale of one borrower who entered into 35 back-to-back payday loans over 17 months, paying $1,254 in fees on a $300 loan.

The Cooks take out about ten payday loans a year, which is close to the national average for payday loan customers. Although the industry claims payday loans are intended only for emergencies, a 2003 study of Pima County, Ariz., by the Southwest Center for Economic Integrity found that 67% of borrowers used their loans for general non-emergency bills. The Center for Responsible Lending found that 66% of borrowers initiate five or more loans a year, and 31% take out twelve or more loans yearly. Over 90% of payday loans go to borrowers with five or more loans a year. Customers who take out 13 or more loans a year account for over half of payday lenders' total revenues.

The Unbanked

María Guzmán and her family are part of the 10% of U.S. households—more than 12 million—that have no relationship with a bank, savings institution, credit union, or other mainstream financial service provider. Being "unbanked," the Guzmáns turn to the fringe economy for check cashing, bill payment, short-term pawn or payday loans, furniture and appliance rentals, and a host of other financial services. In each case, they face high user fees and exorbitant interest rates.

Without credit, the Guzmáns must buy a car either for cash or through a "buy-here/pay-here" (BHPH) used car lot. At a BHPH lot they are saddled with a 28% annual percentage rate (APR) on a high-mileage and grossly overpriced vehicle. They also pay weekly, and one missed payment means a repossession. Since the Guzmáns have no checking account, they use a check-casher who charges 2.7% for cashing their monthly $1,500 in payroll checks, which costs them $40.50 a month or $486 a year.

Like many immigrants, the Guzmáns send money to relatives in their home country. (Money transfers from the United States to Latin America are expected to reach $25 billion by 2010.) If they sent $500 to Mexico on June 26, 2006, using Western Union's "Money in Minutes," they would have paid a $32 transfer fee. Moreover, Western Union's exchange rate for the transaction was 11.12 pesos for the U.S. dollar, while the official exchange rate that day was 11.44. The difference on $500 was almost $14, which raised the real costs of the transaction to $46, or almost 10% of the transfer amount.

Without a checking account, the Guzmáns turn to money orders or direct bill pay, both of which add to their financial expenses. For example, ACE Cash Express charges 79 cents per money order and $1 or more for each direct bill payment. If the Guzmans use money orders to pay six bills a month, the fees total nearly $57 a year; using direct bill pay, they would pay a minimum of $72 in fees per year.

All told, the Guzmáns spend more than 10% of their income on alternative financial services, which is average for unbanked households. To paraphrase James Baldwin, it is expensive to be poor and unbanked in America.

The Cooks and the Guzmáns, along with people like Marty Lawson caught in a cycle of credit card debt (see sidebar on next page), may not fully appreciate the economic entity they are dealing with. Far from a mom-and-pop industry, America's fringe economy is largely dominated by a handful of large, well-financed multinational corporations with strong ties to mainstream financial institutions. It is a comprehensive and fully formed parallel economy that addresses the financial needs of the poor and credit-challenged in the same way as the mainstream economy meets the needs of the middle class. The main difference is the exorbitant interest rates, high fees, and onerous loan terms that mark fringe economy transactions.

Credit Cards, College Students, and the Fringe Economy

Marty Lawson is one of the growing legions of the credit poor. Although he earns $65,000 a year, his $50,000 credit card debt means that he can buy little more than the essentials. This cycle of debt began when Marty received his first credit card in college.

Credit cards are the norm for today's college students. A 2005 Nellie Mae report found that 55% of college students get their first credit card during their freshman year; by senior year, 91% have a credit card and 56% carry four or more cards.

College students are highly prized credit card customers because of their high future earnings and lifetime credit potential. To ensnare them, credit card companies actively solicit on campus through young recruiters who staff tables outside university bookstores and student centers. Students are baited with free t-shirts, frisbees, candy, music downloads, and other come-ons. Credit card solicitations are stuffed into new textbooks and sent to dormitories, electronic mailboxes, and bulletin boards. According to Junior Achievement, the typical college freshman gets about eight credit card offers in the first week of the fall semester. The aggressiveness of credit card recruiters has led several hundred colleges to ban them from campus.

Excited by his newfound financial independence, Marty overlooked the fine print explaining that cash advances carried a 20% or more APR. He also didn't realize how easily he could reach the credit limit, and the stiff penalties incurred for late payments and over-the-credit-limit transactions. About one-third of credit card company profits come from these and other penalties.

Marty applied for a second credit card after maxing out his first one. The credit line on his second card was exhausted in only eight months. Facing $4,000 in high-interest credit card bills, Marty left college to pay off his debts. He never returned. Dropping out to repay credit card debt is all too common, and according to former Indiana University administrator John Simpson, "We lose more students to credit card debt than academic failure." Not coincidentally, by graduation the average credit card debt for college seniors is almost $3,000. Credit card debt worsens the longer a student stays in school. A 2004 Nellie Mae survey found the average credit card debt for graduate students was a whopping $7,831, a 59% increase over 1998. Fifteen percent of graduate students carry credit card balances of $15,000 or more.

The Scope of the Fringe Economy

The unassuming and often shoddy storefronts of the fringe economy mask the true scope of this economic sector. Check-cashers, payday lenders, pawnshops, and rent-to-own stores alone engaged in at least 280 million transactions in 2001, according to Fannie Mae Foundation estimates, generating about $78 billion in gross revenues. By comparison, in 2003 combined state and federal spending on the core U.S. social welfare programs—Temporary Aid to Needy Families (AFDC's replacement), Supplemental Security Income, Food Stamps, the Women, Infants and Children (WIC) food program, school lunch programs, and the U.S. Department of Housing and Urban Development's (HUD) low-income housing programs—totaled less than $125 billion. Revenues in the combined sectors of the fringe economy—including subprime home mortgages and refinancing, and used car sales—would inflate the $78 billion several times over and eclipse federal and state spending on the poor.

There can be no doubt that the scope of the fringe economy is enormous. The Community Financial Services Association of America claims that 15,000 payday lenders extend more than $25 billion in short-term loans to millions of households each year. According to Financial Service Centers of America, 10,000 check-cashing stores process 180 million checks with a face value of $55 billion.

The sheer number of fringe economy storefronts is mind-boggling. For example, ACE Cash Express—only one of many such corporations—has 68 locations within 10 miles of my Houston zip code. Nationwide there are more than 33,000 check-cashing and payday loan stores, just two parts of the fringe economy. That's more than the all the McDonald's and Burger King restaurants and all the Target, J.C. Penney, and Wal-Mart retail stores in the United States combined.

ACE Cash Express is the nation's largest check-casher and exemplifies the growth and profitability of the fringe economy. In 1991 ACE had 181 stores; by 2005 it had 1,371 stores with 2,700 employees in 37 states and the District of Columbia. ACE's revenues totaled $141 million in 2000 and by 2005 rose to $268.6 million. In 2005 ACE:

- cashed 13.3 million checks worth approximately $5.3 billion (check cashing fees totaled $131.6 million);
- served more than 40 million customers (3.4 million a month or 11,000 an hour) and processed $10.3 billion in transactions;
- processed over 2 million loan transactions (worth $640 million) and generated interest income and fees of $91.8 million;
- added a total of 142 new locations (in 2006 the company anticipates adding 150 more);
- processed over $410 million in money transfers and 7.6 million money orders with a face value of $1.3 billion;
- processed over 7.8 million bill payment and debit card transactions, and sold approximately 172,000 prepaid debit cards.

Advance America is the nation's leading payday lender, with 2,640 stores in 36 states, more than 5,500 employees, and $630 million this year in revenues. Dollar Financial Corporation operates 1,106 stores in 17 states, Canada, and the United Kingdom. Their 2005 revenues were $321 million. Check-into-Cash has more than 700 stores; Check N' Go has 900 locations in 29 states. Almost all of these are publicly traded NASDAQ corporations.

There were 4,500 pawnshops in the United States in 1985; now there are almost 12,000, including outlets owned by five publicly traded chains. In 2005 the three big chains—Cash America International (a.k.a Cash America Pawn and SuperPawn), EZ Pawn, and First Cash—had combined annual revenues of nearly $1 billion. Cash America is the largest pawnshop chain, with 750 locations; the company also makes payday loans through its Cash America Payday Advance, Cashland, and Mr. Payroll stores. In 2005, Cash America's revenues totaled $594.3 million.

The Association of Progressive Rental Organizations claims that the $6.6 billion a year rent-to-own (RTO) industry serves 2.7 million households through 8,300 stores in 50 states. Many RTOs rent everything from furniture, electronics, major appliances, and computers to jewelry. Rent-A-Center is the largest RTO corporation in the world. In 2005 it employed 15,000 people; owned or operated 3,052 stores in the United States and Canada; and had revenues of $2.4 billion. Other leading RTO chains include Aaron Rents (with 1,255 stores across the United States and Canada and gross revenues of $1.1 billion in 2005) and RentWay (with 788 stores in 34 states and revenues of almost $516 million in 2005).

These corporations represent the tip of the iceberg. Low-income consumers spent $1.75 billion for tax refund loans in 2002. Many lost as much as 16% of their tax refunds because of expensive tax preparation fees and/or interest incurred in tax refund anticipation loans. The interest and fees on such loans can translate into triple-digit annualized interest rates, according to the Consumer Federation of America, which has also reported that 11 million tax filers received refund anticipation loans in 2000, almost half through H&R Block. According to a Brookings Institution report, the nation's largest tax preparers earned about $357 million from fringe economy "fast cash" products in 2001, more than double their earnings in 1998. All for essentially lending people their own money!

The fringe economy plays a big role in the housing market, where subprime home mortgages rose from 35,000 in 1994 to 332,000 in 2003, a 25% a year growth rate and a tenfold increase in just nine years. (A subprime loan is a loan extended to less creditworthy customers at a rate that is higher than the prime rate.) According to Edward Gramlich, former member of the Board of Governors of the Federal Reserve System, subprime mortgages accounted for almost $300 billion or 9% of all mortgages in 2003.

While the fringe economy squeezes its customers, it is generous to its CEOs. According to *Forbes*, salaries in many fringe economy corporations rival those in much larger companies. In 2004 Sterling Brinkley, chairman of EZ Corp, earned $1.26 million; ACE's CEO Jay Shipowitz received $2.1 million on top of $2.38 million in stocks; Jeffrey Weiss, Dollar Financial Group's CEO, earned $1.83 million; Mark Speese, Rent-A-Center's CEO, made $820,000 with total stock options of $10 million; and Cash America's CEO Daniel Feehan was paid almost $2.2 million in 2003 plus the $9 million he had in stock options.

Fringe-economy corporations argue that the high interest rates and fees they charge reflect the heightened risks of doing business with an economically unstable population. While fringe businesses have never made their pricing criteria public, some risks are clearly overstated. For example, ACE assesses the risk of each check-cashing transaction and reports losses of less than 1%. Since tax preparers file a borrower's taxes, they are reasonably assured that refund anticipation loans will not exceed refunds. To further guarantee repayment, they often establish an escrow account into which the IRS directly deposits the tax refund check. Pawnshops lend only about 50% of a pawned item's value, which leaves them a large buffer if the pawn goes unclaimed (industry trade groups claim that 70% of customers do

---

A Glossary of the Fringe Economy

- **Payday loans** are small, short-term loans, usually of no more than $1,500, to cover expenses until the borrower's next payday. These loans come with extremely high interests rates, commonly equivalent to 300% APR. The Center for Responsible Lending conservatively estimates that predatory payday lending practices cost American families $3.4 billion annually.
- **Refund anticipation loans (RALs)**, provided by outlets of such firms as H&R Block, Western Union, and Liberty Tax Service, are short-term loans, often with high interest rates or fees, secured by an expected tax refund. Interest rates can reach over 700% APR-equivalent.
- **Check cashing stores** (ACE Cash Express is the biggest chain) provide services for people who don't have checking accounts. These stores are most often located in low-income neighborhoods and cash checks for a fee, which can vary greatly but is typically far higher than commercial banks charge for the same service. Check cashing fees have steadily increased over the past ten years.
- **Money Transfer companies** (outlets of such companies as Western Union, Moneygram, and Xoom) allow people to make direct bill payments and send money either to a person or bank account for a fee, typically 10% of the amount being sent, not including the exchange rate loss for money sent internationally. the total cost can reach up to 25% of the amount sent.
- **Pawnshops** give loans while holding objects of value as collateral. The pawnbroker returns the object when the loan is repaid, usually at a high interest rates. If the borrower doesn't repay the loan within a specified period, the pawnbroker sells the item. For example, the interest charge on a 30-day loan of $10 could be $2.20, equivalent to a 264% APR. Most pawnshops are individually owned but regional chains are now appearing.
- **Rent-to-own (RTO) stores**—two leading chains are Rent-A-Center and Aaron Rents—rent furniture, electronics, and other consumer goods short-term or long-term. The consumer can eventually own the item after paying many times the standard retail price through weekly rental payments with an extremely high interest rate, commonly around 300% APR. If the consumer misses a payment, the item is repossessed.
- **Buy here/pay here (BHPH) car lots** offer car loans on used cars on-site, with interest rates much higher than auto loans issued by commercial banks. Customers are often saddled with high-interest loans for high-mileage, overpriced vehicles. If a customer misses one payment, the car is repossessed. The largest BHPH company is the J.D. Byrider franchise, with 124 dealerships throughout the country.

redeem their goods). The rent-to-own furniture and appliance industry charges well above the "street price" for furniture and appliances, which is more than enough to offset any losses. Payday lenders require a post-dated check or electronic debit to assure repayment. Payday loan losses are about 6% or less, according to the Center for Responsible Lending.

Much of the profit in the fringe economy comes from financing rather than the sale of a product. For example, if a used car lot buys a vehicle for $3,000 and sells it for $5,000 cash, their profit is $2,000. But if they finance that vehicle for two years at a 25% APR, the profit jumps to $3,242. This dynamic is true for virtually every sector of the fringe economy. A customer who pays off a loan or purchases a good or service outright is much less profitable for fringe economy businesses than customers who maintain an ongoing financial relationship with the business. In that sense, profit in the fringe economy lies with keeping customers continually enmeshed in an expensive web of debt.

Funding and Exporting America's Fringe Economy

Fringe economy corporations require large amounts of capital to fund their phenomenal growth, and mainstream financial institutions have stepped up to the plate. ACE Cash Express has a relationship with a group of banks including Wells Fargo, JP Morgan Chase Bank, and JP Morgan Securities to provide capital for acquisitions and other activities. Advance America has relationships with Morgan Stanley, Banc of America Securities LLC, Wachovia Capital Markets, and Wells Fargo Securities, to name a few. Similar banking relationships exist throughout the fringe economy.

The fringe economy is no longer solely a U.S. phenomenon. In 2003 the HSBC Group purchased Household International (and its subsidiary Beneficial Finance) for $13 billion. Headquartered in London, HSBC is the world's second largest bank and serves more than 90 million customers in 80 countries. Household International is a U.S.-based consumer finance company with 53 million customers and more than 1,300 branches in 45 states. It is also a predatory lender. In 2002, a $484 million settlement was reached between Household and all 50 states and the District of Columbia. In effect, Household acknowledged it had duped tens of thousands of low-income home buyers into loans with unnecessary hidden costs. In 2003, another $100 million settlement was reached based on Household's abusive mortgage lending practices.

HSBC plans to export Household's operations to Poland, China, Mexico, Britain, France, India, and Brazil, for starters. One shudders to think how the fringe economy will develop in nations with even fewer regulatory safeguards than the United States. Presumably, HSBC also believes that predatory lending will not tarnish the reputation of the seven British lords and one baroness who sit on its 20-member board of directors.

What Can be Done?

The fringe economy is one of the few venues that credit-challenged or low-income families can turn to for financial help. This is especially true for those facing a penurious welfare system with a lifetime benefit cap and few mechanisms for emergency assistance. In that sense, enforcing strident usury and banking laws to curb the fringe economy while providing no legal and accessible alternatives would hurt the very people such laws are intended to help by driving these transactions into a criminal underground. Instead of ending up in court, non-paying debtors would wind up in the hospital. Simply outlawing a demand-driven industry is rarely successful.

One strategy to limit the growth of the fringe economy is to develop more community-based lending institutions modeled on the Grameen Bank or on local cooperatives. Although community banks might charge a higher interest rate than commercial banks charge prime rate customers, the rates would still be significantly lower than in the existing fringe sector.

Another policy option is to make work pay, or at least make it pay better. In other words, we need to increase the minimum wage and the salaries of the lower middle class and working poor. One reason for the rapid growth of the fringe economy is the growing gap between low and stagnant wages and higher prices, especially for necessities like housing, health care, pharmaceuticals, and energy.

Stricter usury laws, better enforcement of existing banking regulations, and a more active federal regulatory system to protect low-income consumers can all play a role in taming the fringe economy. Concurrently, federal and state governments can promote the growth of non-predatory community banking institutions. In addition, commercial banks can provide low-income communities with accessible and inexpensive banking services. As the "DrillDown" studies conducted in recent years by the Washington, D.C., non-profit Social Compact suggest, low-income communities contain more income and resources than one might think. If fringe businesses can make billions in low-income neighborhoods, less predatory economic institutions should be able to profit there too. Lastly, low and stagnant wages make it difficult, if not impossible, for the working poor to make ends meet without resorting to debt. A significant increase in wages would likely result in a significant decline in the fringe economy. In the end, several concerted strategies will be required to restrain this growing and out-of-control economic beast. ❏

Sources: "2003 Credit Card Usage Analysis" (2004) and "Undergraduate Students and Credit Cards in 2004" (2005) (Nellie Mae); Alan Berube, Anne Kim, Benjamin Forman, and Megan Burns, "The Price of Paying Taxes: How Tax Preparation and Refund Loan Fees Erode the Benefits of the EITC" (Brookings Institution and Progressive Policy Institute, May 2002); James H. Carr and Jenny Shuetz, "Financial Services in Distressed Communities: Framing the Issue, Finding Solutions," Financial Services in Distressed Communities: Issues and Answers (2001, Fannie Mae Foundation); "Making the Case for Financial Literacy: A Collection of Current Statistics Regarding Youth and Money" (Junior Achievement); Amanda Sapir and Karen Uhlich, "Pay Day Lending in Pima County Arizona" (Southwest Center for Economic Integrity, 2003); Keith Urnst, John Farris, and Uriah King, "Quantifying the Economic Cost of Predatory Payday Lending" (Center for Responsible Lending, 2004).

Article 4.2

THREE MILLION AMERICANS ARE DEBT POOR

BY STEVEN PRESSMAN AND ROBERT SCOTT
July/August 2007

Signs of the debt crisis facing a growing number of U.S. households are not hard to find. The subprime lending debacle, with its mushrooming rates of mortgage default and foreclosure, has been front-page news for months—perhaps because it has made victims of Wall Street firms as well as Main Street homeowners. Although less of a focus in the media, consumer debt—that is, household debt excluding mortgages and home-equity loans—is rising as well. Consumer indebtedness has reached record levels in the United States, currently averaging more than $21,000 per household, according to Federal Reserve data.

Rising consumer indebtedness can put families from across the income spectrum into precarious financial straits. However, it is poor and low- to middle-income families for whom the combination of stagnating incomes and rising debt creates the greatest risks. Yet the standard approach to calculating a poverty level of income and estimating the number of Americans who are poor fails to account for rising debt and the interest payments on that debt. If it did, about three million more Americans, including over half a million children, would be recognized as living below the poverty line.

Weighing Debt, Measuring Poverty

Consumer debt comes in many shapes and sizes (see sidebar). To measure the burden of household debt, economists generally look at the consumer debt-to-income ratio. Households with high incomes generally have lower debt-to-income ratios (see "Household Debt-to-Income Ratios"). Poor and near-poor households, on the other hand, are heavily in debt. The average amount of consumer debt per poor household is over $7,300, with debt-to-income ratios exceeding 60%.

Such high levels of consumer debt are new. For the median U.S. household, consumer debt has increased nearly tenfold in real terms (i.e., adjusted for inflation) since the early 1960s and is now growing at over 5% a year. Debt levels and debt-to-income ratios for low-income households have risen even faster than for more prosperous households. And predictably, interest payments (relative to income) have now reached their highest level ever. In 2005, the average household spent over 4% of its income servicing consumer debt, compared to just 0.8% in 1959 (see "Servicing Consumer Debt").

Rising debt and interest payments distort much economic data; most noteworthy is how they affect estimates of poverty. In 2005 (the most recent year for which data are available), 12.6% of Americans were poor according to the official U.S. Census Bureau tabulation. The poverty rate stood at 11.7% in 2001, when the Bush administration took office; it rose each year, hitting 12.6% in 2004 and again in 2005. But even these disheartening figures are too optimistic. Policymakers assume that when income (adjusted for inflation) goes up, households' living standards rise as well. But this assumption ignores the problem of rising debt. When more income must go to pay down debt or even just to cover interest charges, households have less money to meet day-to-day expenses and their living standards stagnate or fall.

The U.S. government's official definition of poverty was developed in the early 1960s by economist Mollie Orshansky of the Social Security Administration. In Orshansky's model, still used by the federal government today, the poverty-level income is equal to a basic food budget for a family of a given size multiplied by three. The model assumes, in other words, that food represents about one-third of a family's budget. Every year, the poverty threshold is adjusted based on the annual rise in consumer prices.

For a single person under age 65, the poverty threshold was $10,488 in 2006; for a single mother with two children, it was $16,242. For a family of four, the 2006 figure was $20,444—equal in real dollars, i.e., in purchasing power, to the 1962 poverty line of $3,100 for a family of four.

The current poverty thresholds are widely seen as unrealistic at best. So how to measure poverty has become a contentious issue, and Orshansky's methodology has for some time been criticized on a number of grounds by academics and policy-makers. Some have pointed out that the food budgets Orshansky used were meant for emergency purposes only and could not sustain people for an extended period of time. Indeed, the food budgets she used were set at 80% of a permanent nutrition-ally adequate diet. Others have complained that her estimates fail to account for taxes paid by the poor and the near-poor, who may pay little or no income tax but are still subject to payroll taxes. Still others criticize the model for overlooking gov-ernment benefits that low-income families receive, such as Food Stamps, Medicaid,

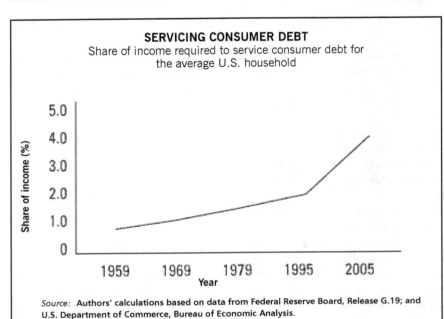

SERVICING CONSUMER DEBT
Share of income required to service consumer debt for the average U.S. household

Source: **Authors' calculations based on data from Federal Reserve Board, Release G.19; and U.S. Department of Commerce, Bureau of Economic Analysis.**

Types of Consumer Debt

Families take on consumer debt for many reasons and in many ways. Here are the most significant forms of consumer debt:

Installment debt— The largest category of consumer debt for the average household, amounting to more than $8,000 per household (2004). These loans are used for large purchases (computers, televisions, furniture, home appliances) and typically have long repayment periods and low interest rates.

Vehicle debt— Averaging more than $5,000 per household, the second largest category of consumer debt. With increasing sprawl, people rely on their cars more and more to get to work and school; U.S. households now have on average 1.9 vehicles—for 1.8 drivers. But vehicles are expensive; few people can afford to buy one (let alone two or three) outright. Those with strong credit histories may qualify for optimal terms on car loans, including very low interest rates, but others can borrow only in the subprime market, at far higher rates.

Education debt— A relatively new phenomenon, but one that has been rising rapidly. College tuitions have risen far faster than inflation over the past two decades, in part because the government has reduced aid to colleges and universities. At the same time, financial aid for students has increasingly come in the form of loans rather than grants. These factors, in combination, account for the fact four-year college students today graduate with a median debt of about $16,000.

Revolving credit card debt— Different from installment debt in that monthly payments and interest rates can both vary over time. Unless a credit card bill is paid in full each month, interest charges are applied to the remaining balance. Interest rates on credit card debt range from 0% to over 30%, with a national average of 14%; the average U.S. household owes about $3,000 in credit card debt.

and housing vouchers, arguing that the value of these benefits should be added to household income.

In all these debates, Americans' rising indebtedness has gone unnoticed. Many Americans have incomes above the poverty line, but because they must use a portion of their income to service their debt, they cannot buy the goods and services needed to escape poverty. These people are debt poor, and they should be recognized as poor by the government.

Using the Federal Reserve's *Survey of Consumer Finances*, we calculated that indebtedness of households with incomes up to 50% above the poverty line increased from $150 (the equivalent of around $1,000 today) in the early 1960s to over $4,000 in 2005. At the going interest rate, a typical low-income household in 2005 spent more than $400 servicing its past debt, compared to interest payments of just $10 to $20 (around $100 today) in the early 1960s. In the late 1950s, when poverty was first measured, both consumer debt and interest were negligible for poor households—mostly because the poor had limited access to formal credit markets.

Taking account of higher interest payments by American households, we calculate that the poverty rate for 2005 should have been around 13.6%, nearly 8% higher than the official rate. Put into concrete terms, this means that three million additional Americans should be counted as poor due to their high consumer debt and interest payments.

HOUSEHOLD DEBT-TO-INCOME RATIOS, BY INCOME (2004)				
Income Range	$35,000 to $40,000	$40,000 to $45,000	$45,000 to $50,000	$50,000 to $55,000	$55,000 and more
D-I Ratio	61%	44%	48%	39%	29%

Source : Federal Reserve Board, Survey of Consumer Finances, 2004.

The effect of consumer debt on child poverty rates is particularly worrisome. Ayana Douglas-Hall and Heather Koball of the National Center for Children in Poverty already refer to children as the United States' "new poor" because 18% of children (13.4 million, in 2005) live in households with incomes below the poverty level. This marks an increase of 12% over the past five years. But again, this figure is too low. When interest on consumer debt is factored in, child poverty rises to 19%. Over half a million children in the United States are debt poor today, none of whom are included in official government poverty estimates.

Lifting the Burden

There are several reasons for the growing phenomenon of debt poverty. The federal minimum wage has been set at $5.15 an hour since 1997 and, until the increase Congress enacted this year takes effect, is at its lowest level in real terms (i.e., in purchasing power) in the past 50 years. At the same time, globalization, the skill requirements of a global economy, and an administration hostile to U.S. workers have all been forces restraining real income gains for low- and middle-income households.

A number of policy changes would help to remedy the problem. In addition to the minimum-wage increase, Congress should raise the child care tax credit and enact limits on credit-card interest rates. We also need to educate low-— and middle-income people about the potential dangers of consumer credit. Finally, the government must provide more money to colleges and universities, especially those that cater to middle- and low-income students, so that they can keep their tuition and fee increases under the rate of inflation. Doing so would both reduce families' debt and increase college attendance and future earnings.

Unless the problem of fast-rising consumer indebtedness is recognized and addressed in short order with steps such as these, George W. Bush is likely to become one of the very few presidents since the Great Depression to preside over rising poverty rates. And if we take rising consumer debt into account, he is likely to preside over the largest increase in poverty since the government began to measure it. ❏

Resources: Jeffrey J. Williams, "Debt Education: Bad for America, Bad for the Young," *Dissent*, Summer 2006; Leslie Miller, "Cars, Trucks Now Outnumber People," *Salon*, Aug. 29, 2003; Federal Reserve Board, *Survey of Consumer Finances*, 2004.

Article 4.3

THE HOMEOWNERSHIP MYTH

BY HOWARD KARGER
Spring 2007, updated October 2013

Subprime mortgages were designed for people who couldn't qualify for main-stream mortgages due to shaky financial histories, poor credit scores, or being newly employed (or employed in temporary or non-traditional employment). These loans were marketed to vulnerable home-buyers using gimmicks such as no income verification (called "liar loans"), low or no down payments, no interest payments for a set number of years, and other tricks designed to get people into homes they couldn't afford. Subprime mortgages gave property developers a built-in market for their over-priced housing, while mortgage brokers earned large upfront loan fees. These risky—and often worthless—mortgages were packaged and sold to investors. By 2007, the value of subprime mortgages was estimated at $1.3 trillion.

Investors were stuck with millions of nonviable mortgages when the global financial crisis struck in 2007-2008. In response, the subprime mortgage industry virtually collapsed, as dozens of subprime lenders quit the business or went bankrupt. The two largest subprime lenders— Countrywide and New Century Financial—went bust, as did Lehman Brothers (the largest Chapter 11 bankruptcy in U.S. history).

The net result was as dire as it was predictable. More than 9% of all U.S. mortgages were either delinquent or in foreclosure in 2008; by 2009, that number had risen to 14%. From 2008 to 2012, there were approximately 4 million completed foreclosures, and by late 2012, about 1.4 million U.S. homes (3% of all mortgages) were in some stage of foreclosure. The foreclosure rate would have been much higher had the Obama administration not implemented a $73 billion program to help millions of home-owners refinance and avoid foreclosure (supplemented by $200 billion for Fannie Mae and Freddie Mac). By 2013, housing prices began to creep upward—the inflation-adjusted average home price rose more than 5% from 2012 to 2013. With that price rise comes the omnipresent danger that subprime mortgages may make a comeback in the same way as derivatives. According to the business-and-economy radio program "Marketplace," one large former subprime lender has already resumed its business.

What's conspicuously absent from the hard data is the effect of the subprime lending debacle on poor and working-class families who bought into the dream of homeownership, regardless of the price. Sold a false bill of goods, many of these families now face foreclosure and the loss of the savings they invested in their homes. It's critical to examine the housing crisis not only from the perspective of the banks and the financial marketplace, but also from the perspective of the families whose homes are on the line. It is also critical to uncover the systemic reasons for the burst of housing-market insanity that saw thousands of families signing up for mortgage loans that were likely to end in failure and foreclosure.

Like most Americans, I grew up believing that being a homeowner represented a rite of passage in U.S. society. Americans widely view homeownership as the best choice for everyone, everywhere and at all times. The common wisdom is that the more people who own their own homes, the more robust the economy, the stronger the community, and the greater the collective and individual benefits. Homeownership is the ticket to the middle class through asset accumulation, stability, and civic participation.

For the most part, this is an accurate picture. Homeowners get a foothold in a housing market with an almost infinite price ceiling. They enjoy important tax benefits. Owning a home is often cheaper than renting. Most important, homeownership builds equity and accrues assets for the next generation, in part by promoting forced savings. These savings are reflected in the data showing that, according to the National Housing Institute's Winton Picoff, the median wealth of low-income homeowners is 12 times higher than that of renters with similar incomes. Plus, owning a home is a status symbol: homeowners are seen as winners compared to renters.

Homeownership may also have positive effects on family life. Ohio University's Robert Dietz found that owning a home contributes to household stability, social involvement, environmental awareness, local political participation and activism, good health, low crime, and beneficial community characteristics. Homeowners are better citizens, are healthier both physically and mentally, and they have children who achieve more and are better behaved than those of renters.

Johns Hopkins University researchers Joe Harkness and Sandra Newman looked at whether homeownership benefits kids even in distressed neighborhoods. Their study concluded that "homeownership in almost any neighborhood is found to benefit children. ... Children of most low-income renters would be better served by programs that help their families become homeowners in their current neighborhoods instead of helping them move to better neighborhoods while remaining renters." Harkness and Newman also found that the positive effects of homeownership on children are weaker in unstable low-income neighborhoods. Moreover, the study cannot distinguish whether homeownership leads to positive behaviors or whether owners were already predisposed to these behaviors.

Faith in the benefits of homeownership—along with low interest rates and a range of governmental incentives—produced a surge in the number of low-income homeowners. In 1994, Bill Clinton set, and ultimately surpassed, a goal to raise the nation's overall homeownership rate to 67.5% by 2000. By 2003, 48% of black households owned their own homes, up from 34.5% in 1950. Much of this gain was among low-income families using subprime loans.

Government efforts to increase homeownership for low-income families include both demand-side (e.g., homeowner tax credits, housing cost assistance programs) and supply-side (e.g., developer incentives) strategies. Federal housing programs insure more than a million loans a year to help low-income homebuyers. Fannie Mae and Freddie Mac—the large, federally chartered corporations that buy mortgages from lenders, guarantee the notes, and then resell them to investors—increasingly turned their attention to low-income home-buyers as the upper-income housing market became more saturated. Banking industry regulations, such as the Community Reinvestment Act and the Home Mortgage Disclosure Act, encourage homeownership by reducing lending discrimination in underserved markets.

The Department of Housing and Urban Development (HUD) adapted some of its programs, originally designed to help renters, to focus on homeownership. For instance, cities and towns were able to use the federal dollars they receive through HOME (the Home Investment Partnerships Act) and Community Development Block Grants to provide housing grants, down payment loans, and closing cost assistance. The American Dream Downpayment Initiative, passed by Congress in 2003, authorized up to $200 million a year for down payment assistance to low-income families. Private foundations followed suit. The Ford Foundation focused its housing-related grants on homeownership rather than rental housing since it viewed homeownership as an important form of asset-building and the best option for low-income people.

While homeownership has undeniable benefits, it is not the best option for everyone or for every family. For many low-income families, buying a home imposes cost burdens that end up outweighing the benefits. As such, it is useful to reassess the emphasis on homeownership, which has been driven by an honest belief in its advantages, but also by numerous business interests who gain when a new cohort of buyers enters the housing market.

The Downsides of Homeownership

Low-income families can run into a range of pitfalls when they buy homes, including the kinds of houses they can afford to purchase (often in poor condition, with high maintenance costs), the neighborhoods they can afford to buy in (often economically distressed), the financing they can get (often with high interest rates, high fees, and risky gimmicks), and their jobs (often unstable). Taken together, these factors can make buying a home a far riskier proposition for low-income families than for middle- and upper-income households.

Most low-income families only have the financial resources to buy rundown houses in distressed neighborhoods marked by scant jobs, high crime rates, few services, and poor schools. Few middle-class homebuyers would commit to 30-year mortgages in these kinds of communities.

Homeownership is no automatic hedge against rising housing costs. On the contrary: lower-end affordable housing stock is typically old, in need of repair, and expensive to maintain. Low-income families often end up paying inflated prices for homes that are beset with major structural or mechanical problems that are cosmetically covered up. A University of North Carolina study sponsored by the national nonprofit organization, NeighborWorks, found that almost half of low-income homebuyers experienced major unexpected costs due to the age and condition of their homes. While renters can hold landlords legally accountable for needed repairs, homeowners can't take themselves to court because the roof leaks, the plumbing is bad, or the furnace or hot water heater stopped working.

Besides maintenance and repairs, homeownership expenses also include property taxes and insurance, both of which have skyrocketed. Between 1997 and 2002 property-tax rates rose nationally by more than 19%. Ten states (including giants Texas and California) saw their property tax rates rise by 30% or more. From 2000 to 2004, property tax rates grew two to three times faster than personal income in New York City suburbs.

Nationally, the average homeowner's annual insurance premiums rose a whopping 62% from 1995 to 2005—twice as fast as inflation. Low-income homeowners in distressed neighborhoods were hit especially hard by high insurance costs. According to a Conning and Co. study, 92% of large insurance companies run credit checks on potential customers. These credit checks translate into insurance scores that are used to determine whether the carrier will insure an applicant, and if so, what they will cover and how much they will charge. Those with poor or no credit are denied coverage, while those with limited credit pay high premiums. Needless to say, many low-income homeowners lack stellar credit scores. Credit scoring may also partly explain why, according to HUD, "Recent studies have shown that, compared to homeowners in predominantly white-occupied neighborhoods, homeowners in minority neighborhoods are less likely to have private home insurance, more likely to have policies that provide less coverage in case of a loss, and are likely to pay more for similar policies."

With few cash reserves, low-income individuals (and their families) are a heartbeat away from financial disaster if they lose their job or their wages drop, property taxes or insurance rates rise, or expensive repairs are needed. With most—or all—of their savings in their homes, low-income families often have no cushion for emergencies. HUD data show that between 1999 and 2001, the only group whose housing conditions worsened—by HUD's definition, the only group in which a larger share of households spent over 30% of gross household income on housing in 2001 than in 1999—were low- and moderate-income homeowners. The National Housing Conference reports that 51% of working families with critical housing needs (i.e., those spending more than 50% of gross household income on housing) are homeowners.

Most people who buy a home imagine they will live there for a long time, thus benefiting from a secure and stable housing situation. This is not the reality for many low-income families. According to a 2005 study by Carolina Katz Reid, nationwide data from 1976 to 1993 reveal that 36% of low-income homeowners gave up or lost their homes within two years and 53% exited within five years. Reid found that very few low-income families ever bought another house after returning to renting. A 2004 HUD research study by Donald Haurin and Stuart Rosenthal reached similar conclusions. Following a national sample of African Americans from youth (ages 14 to 21) in 1979 to middle age in 2000, the researchers found that 63% of the sample owned a home at some point, but only 34% still did in 2000.

Low-income homeowners who are often employed in unstable jobs with stagnant incomes, few health care benefits, limited or no sick days, and little vacation time, may find it almost impossible to keep their homes if they experience a temporary job loss or a change in family circumstances (e.g., the loss of a wage earner). Homeownership can also limit financial opportunities. A 1999 study by economists Richard Green and Patric Hendershott found that states with the highest homeownership rates also had the highest unemployment rates. Their report concluded that homeownership may constrain labor mobility since the high costs of selling a house make unemployed homeowners reluctant to relocate to find work.

Special tax breaks have been a key selling point in homeownership. If mortgage interest and other qualifying expenses come to less than the standard deduction ($12,200 for joint filers in 2013), however, there is zero tax advantage to owning. That is one reason why only 34% of taxpayers itemize their mortgage interest, local property taxes, and other deductions. Even for families who do itemize, the effective tax saving is usually only 10 to 35 cents for every dollar paid in mortgage interest. In other words, the mortgage deduction benefits primarily those in high-income brackets who have a need to shelter their income; it means little to many low-income homeowners.

Finally, homeownership promises growing wealth as home prices rise. But the homes of low-income homeowners generally do not appreciate as much as middle-class housing. Low-income households typically purchase homes in distressed neighborhoods where significant appreciation is unlikely. If financially stressed property owners on the block can't afford to maintain their homes, nearby property values fall. Reid's longitudinal study surveyed low-income minority homeowners from 1976 to 1994 and found that they realized a 30% increase in the value of their homes after owning for 10 years, while middle- and upper-income white homeowners enjoyed a 60% jump. These problems are exacerbated by the loss of subprime mortgages which results in fewer eligible buyers for lower-income housing.

"Funny Money" Mortgages and Other Travesties

Buying a home and taking on a mortgage are scary, and people often leave the closing in a stupor, unsure of what they signed or why. My partner and I bought a house a few years ago, and like many buyers, we didn't retain an attorney. The title company set aside one hour for the closing, and during that time more than 125 single-spaced pages (much of the text in small print) were put in front of us. More than 60 pages required our signature or initials. It would have been difficult for us to digest these documents in 24 hours, much less one hour. When we asked to slow down the process, we were met with impatience. After the closing, my partner asked, "What did we sign?" I was clueless.

Yet buying a home is the largest purchase most families will make in their lifetimes, the largest expenditure in a family budget, and the single largest asset for two-thirds of homeowners. It is also the most fraught with danger, especially for low-income homebuyers.

Homeownership can turn out to be more of a crushing debt than an asset-building opportunity for many low-income families. One reason is the chasm between high home prices and the stagnant incomes of millions of working-class Americans. From the late 1990s until 2007, housing prices rose an unprecedented 35% nationally. While the housing bubble was largely confined to metropolitan areas in the South, the Southwest, and the two coasts (home prices rose 50% in the Pacific states and 60% in New England), there were also bubbles in Midwestern cities like Chicago and Minneapolis. While the housing bubble was most pronounced in high-end properties, the prices of low-end homes also spiked in many markets. Even if the recent rebound in housing prices brings the market back to 2007 levels, it remains well above the financial ability of many prospective homeowners.

Current incomes simply do not support increasing home prices. In 2013, the *New York Times* observed that productivity has risen 23% since 2000 while real hourly pay has stagnated. Only 18% of Californians in 2007 could afford the state's median house price using traditional loan-affordability calculations. The fall in mortgage interest rates in the 1990s and early 2000s was largely neutralized by higher property taxes, higher insurance premiums, and rising utility costs.

Until the big crash of 2007, the chasm between stagnant wages and rising home prices forced the mortgage finance industry to develop creative schemes to squeeze potential homebuyers, albeit often temporarily, into houses they could not afford. It was a sleight of hand that required imaginative and risky financing for both buyers and financial institutions.

Most of the "creative" new mortgage products fell into the category of subprime mortgages that carried interest rates ranging from a few points to ten points or more above the prime or market interest rate, plus onerous loan terms.

Subprime lending was risky. In the 37 years since the Mortgage Bankers Association (MBA) began conducting its annual national mortgage delinquency survey, 2006 saw the highest share of home loans entering foreclosure. In early 2007, 13.5% of subprime

Inside the Subprime Monster

From a review of The Monster: How a Gang of Predatory Lenders and Wall Street Bankers Fleeced America—and Spawned a Global Crisis *by Michael W. Hudson (Times Books, 2010), March/April 2011*

Roland Arnall was there at the beginning, at the helm of a small federal savings bank, and Hudson's main narrative traces how Arnall's lending operations grew into the nation's biggest subprime lending empire. At their peak in 2004, Ameriquest and its affiliates generated $83 billion in subprime loans—and $1.3 billion in profits. The bulk of the profits flowed through to Arnall, elevating him to #73 on the Forbes Four Hundred list of the richest Americans. He took the money and ran, becoming U.S. Ambassador to the Netherlands in early 2006. Ameriquest went out of business the following year.

Arnall's obsession with growth led to an internal culture at Ameriquest that demanded ever-higher loan volumes at all costs. That culture was captured in a memo from one manager to his sales staff: "We are all here to make as much fucking money as possible. Bottom line. Nothing else matters." Those who could meet the ever-increasing sales targets were rewarded with money, luxury vacations, cars, and more. Those who couldn't were fired. And the only way to meet those targets—given the high-cost nature of the loans that they were pushing—was by a combination of deception, psychological manipulation, and fraud. "Bait-and-switch" tactics were routine. Managers monitored sales pitches and berated employees who let potential borrowers escape. Offices had staffers who specialized in forging documents. Those charged with overseeing quality control and preventing fraud soon learned that the only way to hold their jobs was to just say yes. Hudson provides chapter and verse on all this and more in compelling detail.

Still, the explosive growth of subprime lenders like Ameriquest was only possible because of the big Wall Street firms that purchased their loans and packaged them into securities sold to investors. Wall Street's quest for the generous fees gained in this process led them to be no more interested in borrowers' ability to repay their loans than were the lenders. So Hudson's second focus is on Lehman Brothers, the biggest Wall Street backer of subprime lenders, and the picture there was no prettier than it was at Ameriquest. A Lehman executive who visited the now-infamous First American Mortgage Company (FAMCO) in the 1990s reported back that "there is something really unethical about the type of business in which FAMCO is engaged. ... [I]t is a requirement to leave your ethics at the door." Nevertheless, Lehman eagerly sought to finance the company's operations and buy its loans.

The number of staffers quoted and their consistent testimony as to the pervasiveness of the practices that they describe leave no doubt that predation was standard operating procedure, rather than the work of the few "rogue operators" or "bad apples" so dear to the hearts of industry apologists. —Jim Campen mortgages were delinquent (compared to 4.95% of prime-rate mortgages) and 4.5% were in foreclosure. Before the financial collapse, *Forbes* claimed that subprime lenders could realize returns up to six times greater than the best-run banks.

There were traditionally two main kinds of home mortgages: fixed-rate mortgages and adjustable-rate mortgages (ARMs). In a fixed-rate mortgage, the interest rate stays the same throughout the 15- to 30-year loan term. In a typical ARM the interest rate varies over the course of the loan, although there is usually a cap. Both kinds of loans required borrowers to provide thorough documentation of their finances and a down payment of at least 10% (and often 20%) of the purchase price. Adjustable-rate loans are often complicated, and a Federal Reserve study found that fully 25% of homeowners with ARMs were confused about their loan terms. Nonetheless, ARMs are attractive since in the short run they promise a home with an artificially low interest rate and affordable payments.

But even traditional ARMs proved inadequate to the tasks of driving more low-income families into the housing market and keeping home sales up in the face of skyrocketing housing prices. To counter these high prices, the mortgage industry created a wide range of "affordability" products with names like "no-ratio loans," "option ARMS," and "balloon loans" that it doled out like candy to people who were never fully apprised of the intricacies of these complicated loans. These new mortgage options opened the door for almost anyone to secure a mortgage, regardless of their ability to repay it. They also raised the costs and risks of buying a home—sometimes steeply—for the targeted low- and moderate-income families.

Beyond the longer-term high interest rates that characterized the "affordability" mortgages, low-income homebuyers faced other costs as well. For instance, predatory and subprime lenders often required borrowers to carry expensive credit life insurance, which paid off a mortgage if the homeowner died. This insurance was frequently sold either by the lender's subsidiary or by a company that paid the lender a commission.

As many as 80% of subprime loans included prepayment penalties if the borrower paid off or refinanced the loan early, a scam that cost low-income borrowers about $2.3 billion a year and increased the risk of foreclosure by 20%. Pre-payment penalties locked borrowers into a loan by making it difficult to sell or refinance the home with a different lender. While some borrowers faced penalties for paying off their loans ahead of schedule, others discovered that their mortgages had so-called "call provisions" that permitted the lender to accelerate the loan term even if payments were current.

There were also costs outside of the mortgage. Dodgy mortgage products were often not sold by banks directly, but by a crew of mortgage brokers who acted as finders or "bird dogs" for lenders. In 2006, there were approximately 53,000 U.S. mortgage brokerage companies that employed an estimated 418,700 people, according to the National Association of Mortgage Brokers; *BusinessWeek* noted that brokers originated up to 80% of all new mortgages.

Largely unregulated, mortgage brokers lived off loan fees and their transactions were primed for conflicts of interest. For example, borrowers paid brokers a fee to help them secure a loan. Brokers also received kickbacks from lenders for referring a borrower, and many brokers steered their clients to the lenders that paid them the highest referral fees rather than those that offered the lowest interest rates. Closing documents used language like "yield spread premiums" or "service release fees" to hide these kickbacks. Some hungry brokers found even more scurrilous ways to make the sale, including fudging paperwork, arranging for inflated appraisals, or helping buyers find co-signers who had no intention of actually guaranteeing the loan.

Whether or not a broker was involved, lenders often inflated closing costs in a variety of ways, including charging high document-preparation fees, billing for recording fees in excess of the law, or "unbundling" (closing costs were padded by duplicating charges already included in other categories).

All in all, housing is highly susceptible to the predations of the fringe economy. Unscrupulous brokers and lenders had—and continue to have—considerable latitude to ply their trade with vulnerable low-income borrowers.

Time to Change Course

Despite the hype, homeownership is not a cure-all for low-income families who earn less than a living wage and have poor prospects for future income growth. In fact, for some low-income families homeownership only leads to more debt and financial misery. With mortgage delinquencies and foreclosures at high levels, especially among low-income households, millions of people would be better off now if they had remained renters.

Instead of focusing exclusively on homeownership, a more progressive, nuanced and balanced housing policy would address the diverse needs of communities for both homes and rental units, and would facilitate new forms of ownership such as community land trusts and cooperatives. A balanced policy would expand the stock of affordable rental units. Policymakers should also act to protect consumers who opt to buy homes.

The reason the United States lacks a sound housing policy becomes obvious when following the money. Overheated housing markets and rising home prices produce lots of winners. Real estate agents reap bigger commissions while mortgage brokers, appraisers, real estate attorneys, title companies, lenders, builders, home remodelers, and everyone else with a hand in the housing pie does well. Cities raise more in property taxes, and insurance companies enroll more clients at higher premiums. According to Oxford Analytica, housing accounted for only 5% of GDP from 2002 to 2007, but was responsible for up to 75% of U.S. job growth. Housing has historically buffered the economy, and driving more low-income families into homes helps keep the industry ticking, at least in the short run. The only losers are those squeezed by higher rents, those pushed out of rental apartments by the conversion into condo units, young middle-income families trying to buy their first house, and thousands of low-income families for whom buying a home turns into a financial nightmare. ❑

Sources: Carolina Katz Reid, Studies in Demography and Ecology: Achieving the American Dream? A Longitudinal Analysis of the Homeownership Experiences of Low-Income Households, Univ. of Washington, CSDE Working Paper No. 04-04; Dean Baker, "The Housing Bubble: A Time Bomb in Low-Income Communities?" Shelterforce Online, Issue #135, May/June 2004 (nhi.org); Howard Karger, *Shortchanged: Life and Debt in the Fringe Economy* (Berrett-Koehler, 2005); National Multi Housing Council (nmhc.org).

Article 4.4

THE HOUSING BUBBLE WAS NO ACCIDENT
A Primer on the Housing Market

BY DOUG ORR
November 2013

L ibertarians and other conservative economists claim that markets are "natural," and occur spontaneously. In fact, however, all markets are human creations. How they are structured and the incentives they create determine the outcomes of the market. When we change the structure of a market it changes incentives and changes the way the market functions. The market for home mortgages is a perfect example.

The Housing Act and the Expansion of Mortgage Credit

Prior to the Great Depression the majority of home loans were 5-year "balloon" loans requiring a 50% down payment. For these loans, each month the borrower only paid interest on the amount of the loan, but had to pay off the full amount at the end of the fifth year. Monthly payments were low, but the homebuyer had to refinance the loan every five years.

If, as a result of a change in personal circumstances or credit availability, the borrower could not refinance the loan, he would lose the house and the full amount of the down payment. (It was always "he," because in the early 20th century, banks would not make loans to women in their own name) The risk to the borrower was large and the risk to the bank was small. Even so, when the Great Depression hit, not only did millions of families lose their homes, but many banks also failed as a result of mortgage losses. Already-low homeownership rates fell even more.

In 1934, Congress passed the Housing Act, which created the Federal Housing Authority (FHA). The FHA set minimum down payment standards and required mortgage payment insurance for any loan with less than a 20% down payment. The FHA provided loan insurance to the banks. While this stabilized the market, it was not enough to expand bank lending. In 1938, Congress amended the Housing Act to create the Federal Home Loan Administration, Fannie Mae, as a government sponsored entity (GSE). A GSE functions independently of the federal government, but has the financial backing of the government.

Fannie Mae made it possible for banks to create long-term "amortizing" mortgages. The maturity dates of these loans were longer, usually 30 years, and the monthly payment covered both interest and part of the principal amount. Because of the long term of the loan, monthly payments were accessible to a larger number of families. Banks had been unwilling to make this type of loan because they borrow from their depositors at a short term and these loans are long-term. Depositors can take their money out at any time, which puts the bank at risk. As long as a loan conformed to FHA standards (was a "conforming loan"), Fannie Mae would agree to buy the loan from the bank if the bank needed liquidity. Because Fannie Mae is a GSE, it could borrow at very low interest rates and could then purchase loans that paid much higher interest. As a result, Fannie was highly profitable and self-financing, and never needed any funding from the federal government. With the back-stop from Fannie Mae, mortgage lending greatly expanded and homeownership rates grew.

This created a home mortgage system with built-in management of risk. Banks would make loans with the expectation of holding them to maturity, but they could sell them to Fannie Mae if necessary. Both the borrower and the bank expected a long-term relationship. To minimize risk, prior to making the loan, the bank would hire an appraiser to estimate the value of the house, should the need for foreclosure ever arise. Appraisers knew the bank wanted to minimize risk, so they had an incentive to set the appraised value at the low end of the market value. This often irritated potential home sellers and buyers, but it satisfied the banks. Banks charged processing fees to originate the loans, but the value of these fees were dwarfed by the interest payments the bank expected to receive.

Banks issued "safe" loans because those the only loans Fannie Mae would buy. Because the bank held most of the loans it created, if a borrower hit a financial rough patch, he or she could go to the bank to try to work out a temporary forbearance or other solution to avoid foreclosure. As a result, foreclosures were a rare occurrence. Given rising real median family incomes and slowly but steadily rising home values from the 1950s to 1970s, this created a safe system of financing home ownership, which came to be associated with the banks' famous "3-6-3 rule": pay depositors 3%, loan out their money at 6%, and be on the golf course by 3 PM.

The Rise of the Shadow Banks

In 1968, in response to a variety of issues, including the start of the push to deregulate the economy, Congress decided to "privatize" Fannie Mae and turn it into a privately held, for-profit company. Congress also created a much smaller GSE called the Government National Mortgage Association, Ginnie Mae. In 1970, Congress chartered a second private company, the Federal Home Loan Mortgage Corporation, Freddie Mac, to compete with Fannie Mae. Without government backing, both Fannie and Freddie now had somewhat higher borrowing costs, and shareholders demanding higher profits. This changed the operating procedures of both companies and the rest of the mortgage market as well.

To supplement its borrowing, in 1971, Freddie issued its first mortgage-backed security (MBS). An MBS is a bond that "derives" its value from the flow of income generated by a block of mortgages; hence, an MBS is a kind of financial "derivative". A bank makes a loan and "services" the loan by collecting the monthly payments. If the bank sells the loan to Freddie, it passes this money on to Freddie. Freddie then passes on the part of this money it promised to pay to the bond buyers. Fannie and Freddie MBSs were considered safe because the underlying loans generally conformed to FHA standards. At that time, these types of financial derivatives were a tiny part of the activity of financial markets. But they grew in importance as the decade progressed, largely as a result of the creation of a particular type of "shadow bank."

Shadow banks engage in many of the activities of actual banks, but not all. Commercial banks take deposits and make loans. If a business makes loans but does not take deposits, it is not a bank and it avoids government regulation. One of the most famous shadow banks was Countrywide Financial. It borrowed money in the "commercial paper" market, which provides business loans of 90 days or less. It then made mortgage loans to communities that had been systematically excluded from the mortgage market by the FHA and commercial banks, particularly the African-American community. These loans were particularly attractive for Countrywide because they required higher-than-average down payments and charged higher-than-average interest rates. But many African American communities saw Countrywide as a savior because they could now get loans where none had been available previously.

Countrywide could not sell its mortgages to Fannie or Freddie because it was not a bank. As the company grew, it needed access to more funds, so it started to bundle the mortgages it had created and sold them directly in the financial market as MBSs. With access to more funds, it made more mortgage loans, which it sold as MBSs and made more loans. By the 1980s, Countrywide had grown to be one of the largest mortgage lenders in the US. Success breeds imitation and hundreds of new shadow banks entered the market, which put pressure on commercial banks to follow suit..

The World Turned Upside Down

This new process for funding mortgage loans completely changed the incentive structure of the industry and ultimately led to the housing bubble and financial crash of 2007. More and more, commercial banks initiated loans with little or no intention of holding them to maturity. The long-term relationship between lender and borrower was broken. The primary source of income for the lender, especially the shadow banks, was the fees charged to originate the loan. So lenders had the incentive to initiate as many loans as possible. When the bank hired an appraiser, the appraiser had an incentive to over-estimate the value of the house, so the bank could create the loan. If the appraiser was not willing to go along he or she would not get hired again. The bank then tried to sell the loan to either Fannie or Freddie, who as private, for-profit companies, were now competing to see who could buy the most loans. However, to have funds to buy new loans, they had to bundle up older loans as MBSs and sell them.

As the MBSs market grew it became easier for shadow banks to bundle and sell their loans as MBSs, but they still needed a stamp of approval from one of the bond rating agencies: Moodys, Fitch, or Standard and Poors. These ratings agencies have the task of evaluating the likelihood of repayment of bonds issued by corporations, state and local governments, and banks. In other words, they are supposed to determine whether the bonds are safe. But here the incentive structure increased risk rather than reducing it. As MBSs became a larger and larger share of the total bond market, more and more income for these firms came from rating these derivatives. Shadow banks would bundle safe and not-so-safe loans together into a single MBS. This supposedly created diversification, but actually it just hid the not-so-safe loans. If a shadow bank took a MBS to one agency that rated it as risky, it would take it to another agency. The agency that gave the highest rating would get paid, the others would lose business. So the rating agencies started to compete to overestimate the safety of derivatives, just as appraisers were overestimating the value of houses.

The system had now been turned on its head. Rather than reducing risk it increased it. When the lender sold or packaged a loan as a MBS, it hired a "servicing" company to collect the monthly payments to the holder of the loan or MBS. If the borrower hit a financial rough patch, he or she could not go to the bank to work out a forbearance. Foreclosure became the primary outcome.

Heading Off the Cliff

Many liberal economists raised the warning about the risk of the new derivatives markets. But here mainstream economists came to the rescue. The theory of efficient markets claims that diversification can eliminate almost all risk. By bundling safe and not-so-safe mortgages together, risk would be eliminated. Despite the fact that this theory had failed in the collapse of the company Long Term Capital Management in 1998, which led to a global financial crisis, mainstream economists claimed it would work this time. In 1999, a Republican Congress, under a Democratic president passed and implemented the Gramm-Leach-Bliley Act, which specifically forbade any form or regulation of the derivatives industry or of the shadow banking industry.

In the old system, the standard or "prime" loan required 20% down and income high enough that the mortgage payment was no more than 30% of monthly income. As the more and more of loans were repackaged as MBSs, banks and shadow banks were now competing to find customers. At first they lowered the required down payment. Later they loosened the income requirements. These are called "sub-prime" loans. Some of these loans were called "liar loans" because the bank would not try to verify the income or assets of the borrower. Ultimately many banks were issuing NINJA loans: No Income, No Job or Assets. They knew the borrower could never repay the loan, but the lender got its fees and the buyer of the derivative would take the loss. If a lender makes a loan it knows the borrower cannot repay, it is called "predatory lending." Many forms of predatory lending had been made illegal by the regulation of the 1930s, but they came back after the de-regulation of the 1980s and 1990s. In the most egregious cases, lenders sent representatives door to door in low income neighborhoods encouraging families to take out loans that would ultimately destroy their livelihood.

As money flooded into the housing markets, housing prices rose rapidly. The appraisers seemed to be right. If families that could not make their mortgage payments were able to sell their houses at a profit, the MBSs still paid off. An unsustainable housing bubble was growing, but mainstream economists claimed otherwise. Alan Greenspan, arch-libertariarian and Chairman of the Federal Reserve, claimed the rising house prices were evidence of the increased efficiency of the market. He claimed a housing bubble was impossible. At worst it might be a little "froth," like the head on a glass of beer. But at some point, people started to realize that a 2 bedroom, 1 bath house next to the freeway in Fremont, Calif., was not really worth $750,000. Housing prices started to slip and families that could not make their mortgage payments could not sell to get out of the mortgage. The flow of money into the riskiest MBSs slowed or stopped and the bonds dropped in value. Because the rating agencies had given a stamp of approval to all the MBS, bond buyers could not tell which MBS were safe and which were not. The market for MBSs froze up and the whole house of cards came crashing down. Whether it was one big bubble, or hundreds of little bubbles in the froth, it resulted in the financial crisis of 2007.

Mainstream economists want to blame the victims of the crisis by claiming that people entered into mortgages they knew they could not afford. But, in fact, in the majority of cases it was the mortgage brokers who had to convince them to take larger loans. Conservative economists want to blame the Community Reinvestment Act, the 1977 law promoting mortgage lending to low-income communities, for forcing banks to make loans to risky borrowers and, in turn, causing the crisis. But nothing in that act forced banks to reduce the standards on the loans they made. That was the result of greed. It was the blind belief in free markets and the deregulation of the financial sector that caused the housing crisis. Until we learn that lesson, and actually do something to reregulate the industry, it is only a matter of time until the next crisis strikes. ❏

Article 4.5

THE GREAT RECESSION IN BLACK WEALTH

BY JEANNETTE WICKS-LIM
January/February 2012

The Great Recession produced the largest setback in racial wealth equality in the United States over the last 25 years. In 2009 the average white household's wealth was 20 times that of the average black household, nearly double that in previous years, according to a 2011 report by the Pew Research Center.

Driving this surge in inequality is a devastating drop in black wealth. The typical black household in 2009 was left with less wealth than at any time since 1984 after correcting for inflation.

It's important to remember wealth's special role—different from income—in supporting a household's economic well-being. Income pays for everyday expenses—groceries, clothes, and gas. A family's wealth, or net worth, includes all the assets they've built up over time (e.g., savings account, retirement fund, home, car) minus any money they owe (e.g., school loans, credit card debt, mortgage). Access to such wealth determines whether a layoff or medical crisis creates a bump in the road, or pushes a household off a financial cliff. Wealth can also provide families with financial stepping-stones to advance up the economic ladder—such as money for college tuition, or a down payment on a house.

Racial wealth inequality in the United States has always been severe. In 2004, for example, the typical black household had just $1 in net worth for every $11 of a typical white household. This is because families slowly accumulate wealth over their lifetime and across generations. Wealth, consequently, ties the economic fortunes of today's households to the explicitly racist economic institutions in America's past—especially those that existed during key phases of wealth redistribution. For example, the Homesteading Act of 1862 directed the large-scale transfer of government-owned land nearly exclusively to white households. Also starting in the 1930s, the Federal Housing Authority made a major push to subsidize home mortgages—for primarily white neighborhoods. On top of that, Jim Crow Laws—in effect until the mid-1960s—and racial violence severely curtailed efforts by the black community to start their own businesses to generate their own wealth.

The housing market crisis and the Great Recession made racial wealth inequality yet worse for two reasons. First, the wealth of blacks is more concentrated in their

MEDIAN HOUSEHOLD NET WORTH (2009 DOLLARS)

	1984	1988	1991	1993	1995	2004	2009
White	$76,951	$75,403	$68,203	$67,327	$68,520	$111,313	$92,000
Black	$6,679	$7,263	$7,071	$6,503	$9,885	$9,823	$4,900
Ratio of White to Black	12	10	10	10	7	11	19

Source: Taylor et al., *Twenty-to-One: Wealth Gaps to Rise to Record High Between Whites, Blacks and Hispanics*, Pew Research Center.

homes than the wealth of their white counterparts. Homes of black families make up 59% of their net worth compared to 44% among white families. White households typically hold more of other types of assets like stocks and IRA accounts. So when the housing crisis hit, driving down the value of homes and pushing up foreclosure rates, black households lost a much greater share of their wealth than did white households.

Second, mortgage brokers and lenders marketed subprime mortgages specifically to black households. Subprime mortgages are high-interest loans that are supposed to increase access to home financing for risky borrowers—those with a shaky credit history or low income. But these high-cost loans were disproportionately peddled to black households, even to those that could qualify for conventional loans. One study estimated that in 2007 nearly double the share of upper-income black households (54%) had high-cost mortgages compared to low-income white households (28%).

Subprime mortgages drain away wealth through high fees and interest payments. Worse, predatory lending practices disguise the high-cost of these loans with initially low payments. Payments then shoot up, often leading to default and foreclosure, wiping out a family's home equity wealth. In 2006, Mike Calhoun, president of the Center for Responsible Lending, predicted that the surge of subprime lending within the black community would "…likely be the largest loss of African-American wealth that we have ever seen, wiping out a generation of home wealth building." It was a prescient prediction.

To reverse the rise in racial wealth inequality, we need policies that specifically build wealth among black households, such as the "baby bonds" program proposed by economists William Darity of Duke University and Darrick Hamilton of The New School. Baby bonds would be federally managed, interest-bearing trusts given to the newborns of asset-poor families, and could be as large as $50,000 to $60,000 for the most asset-poor. By using a wealth means-test, this program would disproportionately benefit black communities, while avoiding the controversy of a reparations policy. When recipients reach age 18, they could use the funds for a house down payment, tuition, or to start a business. This program would cost about $60 billion per year, which could easily be covered by letting the Bush-era tax cuts expire for the top 1% of income earners. ❏

Sources: Amaad Rivera, Brenda Cotto-Escalera, Anisha Desai, Jeannette Huezo, and Dedrick Muhammad, *Foreclosed: State of the Dream 2008*, United for a Fair Economy, 2008; Citizens for Tax Justice, "The Bush Tax Cuts Cost Two and a Half Times as Much as the House Democrats' Health Care Proposal," CTJ Policy Brief, September 9, 2009; Darrick Hamilton and William Darity, Jr., "Can 'Baby Bonds' Eliminate the Racial Wealth Gap in Putative Post-Racial America?" *Review of Black Political Economy*, 2010; Paul Taylor, Rakesh Kochhar, Richard Fry, Gabriel Velasco, and Seth Motel, *Twenty-to-One: Wealth Gaps to Rise to Record High Between Whites, Blacks and Hispanics*, Washington DC: Pew Research Center, 2011.

Article 4.6

WHOSE HOUSING RECOVERY?

High-finance investors are snapping up tens of thousands of foreclosed homes for rental income and speculation.

BY DARWIN BONDGRAHAM
March/April 2013

The business press has been reporting a "recovery" of the u.s. housing market for over a year now, as the average prices of single-family homes rise across the country. Implied in these stories is the return of a healthy real-estate market, in which the average American family has the resources—in terms of income, savings, and access to credit—to purchase its own slice of the American dream.

The housing recovery we are seeing right now, however, is anything but indicative of broader gains—increased wages, falling unemployment, or renewed access to credit for consumers—being shared across the economy. A growing number of buyers of single-family homes today are not new owner-occupants, but investors. While most of these investors are so-called "mom-and-pop" buyers who own an extra rental house or two in their hometowns, large private investors are also increasingly buying up homes.

These investors are especially focusing on foreclosed properties in the "sun" and "sand" belts—from Florida and Georgia to Arizona, Nevada, and California. Private-equity firms, investment banks, and other high-finance investors are gobbling up housing stocks in these markets by the tens of thousands of units. They have taken to calling single-family rental homes a "new asset class," alongside corporate debt, government bonds, currencies, and financial derivatives.

From Owners to Renters

Under the so-called housing recovery, the foreclosed homeowner is being relegated to the status of renter. Increasingly, the new renters' role will be to pay their new high-finance landlords for shelter, all in order to secure big returns for the millionaire clients and institutional partners who are backing foreclosure purchases with billions of dollars. After decades of hovering around 63-65%, the percentage of Americans who own their homes shot upward starting in 1995. The growth of the subprime-mortgage business created millions of new homeowners, and by 2005 homeownership in the United States peaked at a record 69%. Predatory lending by banks—especially subprime loans whose low "teaser" interest rates ballooned after a couple of years—along with stagnant wages and mounting non-mortgage debt, stretched the finances of many homeowners. When the financial crisis of 2008, centered on securitized mortgage debt, crashed the global economy, a cascade of foreclosures began. Millions lost their homes along with their jobs and retirement savings. This was reflected in a roughly 3-percentage-point drop in the national homeownership rate—from 69% to 66%, according to figures from the Federal Reserve Bank of St. Louis. An influential report by the John Burns Real Estate consulting firm, however, shows that counting homeowners who are now more than 90 days late on their mortgage payments—and are likely to end up foreclosed—the real decline in homeownership is likely to be 7 percentage points. That would take the homeownership rate down to about 62%, substantially lower than before the post-1995 surge.

Homeownership is overly romanticized in American culture, and is not necessarily an intrinsically good thing. (See Howard Karger, "The Homeownership Myth," Dollars & Sense, March/April 2007.) In the United States, however, single-family homes have historically provided a place for families to safely invest and build wealth. In recent decades, rising home prices helped finance college educations and health care for working- and middle-class families, even as wages stagnated.

Being a renter also tends to cost more. Although the mortgage-to-rent ratio (the measure of how much it costs to finance the purchase of a home versus renting one) varies depending on many factors, it is usually true that mortgage payments are well below the rental costs for similar housing. This is especially true now that mortgage rates have dropped to about 3.5% even as rents have risen. In other words, being forced to rent because of a foreclosure means, for millions of Americans, paying a higher percentage of their incomes for housing (and, often, living in smaller quarters).

The millions of foreclosures since 2007 represent a massive upward redistribution of wealth. Millions of families have lost or are on the verge of losing their single largest asset, which has served as a source of security and access to credit. Neither they nor those who would normally be likely first-home buyers are able to buy. Those who are buying are largely investors looking for bargain real estate on which they can turn a profit, both in rents and through eventual sale, after home prices have risen.

Enter the Federal Government

The federal government has lent little assistance to homeowners in danger of foreclosure, or to renters seeking to purchase a first home. Instead it has focused its monetary and policy powers on the well-being of the banks at the center of the financial system. The sum of taxpayer dollars used to bail out the largest banks, which hold millions of mortgage loans, dwarfs the mortgage relief from settlements reached between the federal government and the nation's largest lenders. For example, Citibank received $50 billion in Troubled Asset Relief Program (TARP) payments in 2008, and $426 billion more in other forms of government assistance, according to the Congressional Oversight Panel that tracked Treasury's spending of TARP funds. While Citibank has since repaid the federal government, this public assistance allowed the company to survive, thereby maintaining the incomes and wealth of major shareholders and executives. Under the mortgage-servicer settlement agreed to last year, however, Citigroup is only being made to provide $1.8 billion in relief to borrowers who were defrauded by the bank during the financial crisis.

What's more, it was the combination of the economic collapse in 2008, and more recent interventions by the U.S. Federal Reserve (The Fed) and federal housing agencies, that sowed the seeds of opportunity for powerful investors to purchase homes at historically low prices. The federal government's key housing-market intervention has been a program of purchasing "agency mortgage-backed securities," under a third round of "quantitative easing" (or "QE3"). Mortgage-backed securities (MBSs) are claims on payments from mortgage loans. Only MBSs associated with fixed-rate mortgages backed by agencies like Fannie Mae and Freddie Mac are being purchased under the program. Under QE3, the Federal Reserve is buying upwards of $40 billion in mortgage debt each month. These huge purchases drive up the prices of housing bonds, thereby lowering the yields (interest rates) on the bonds. In theory, this should create conditions for renewed bank lending to homebuyers. As it becomes more expensive to purchase existing mortgage securities, and the returns on these securities decrease, capital should flow into new home loans. But without recovered employment, incomes, and savings, many U.S. households are in no position to make such a big purchase. Worsening this situation is the fact that loan standards have been tightened by all of the major mortgage lenders, making it much more difficult for those with little savings or low incomes to purchase a home.

Big investors are quickly taking advantage of the housing market's peculiar condition. The lack of competition from prospective owner-occupiers makes it easy for them to make bulk purchases of housing. The growing number of renters nationwide means there are people ready to pay to live in the newly purchased homes. And the Fed's recent intervention has led investors to expect home-price increases in the future, potentially creating another source of profit.

The Return of the Financiers

Not all investors waited for the federal government's recent efforts to pump up home prices. One company, Waypoint Homes of Oakland, Calif., began to buy up thousands of foreclosed houses in the Bay Area and Los Angeles as early as 2008. Since 2012, the firm has used a commitment of $400 million to $1 billion from GI Partners, a California private-equity group, to expand nationally. Waypoint now owns upwards of 4,000 homes, mostly in California, Arizona, Illinois, Georgia, and Florida, and is buying dozens more every week. Citibank has extended Waypoint $250 million in credit for its purchases, just one indication of the serious money this industry is now attracting.

In August 2010, the Federal Housing Finance Administration (FHFA) announced that it was seeking input from the real-estate investment industry on how to deal with foreclosed homes sitting on the balance sheets of the government-sponsored loan agencies, Fannie Mae and Freddie Mac. The industry responded with a slew of proposals, all centered on allowing private investors to buy up the government's inventory of over 90,000 foreclosed homes. As a result, the FHFA decided to set up a "pilot program" to sell off its foreclosed housing inventory, and invited investors to submit bids.

In September 2012, the FHFA announced the first of its winning bidders. Pacifica Companies, LLC, took control of 700 homes in Florida. Shortly thereafter, the New York-based Cogsville Group, LLC, took control of 94 homes in Chicago, and the Los Angeles-based Colony Capital took over 970 houses in California, Nevada, and Arizona.

These transactions, however, were small potatoes compared to what has been building in the private housing market, where there are millions of foreclosed homes on the books of banks and mortgage-lending companies. Investor buyouts of entire stocks of regional foreclosed housing inventories began in earnest in 2011 and have shown little sign of slowing.

According to numerous press reports, the Blackstone private-equity fund has been the hungriest purchaser of foreclosed homes, having bought upwards of 16,000 houses across the country. A January 2013 report in Bloomberg News described Blackstone as "rushing" to spend the $2.5 billion the firm has allotted toward foreclosure buyouts. The second largest foreclosure-to-rental mill is Carrington Holding Company, a California-based firm that began as a mortgage servicer during the housing boom of the 2000s, but which has morphed into a private-equity landlord. Carrington reportedly owns 4,500 homes today in Chicago, Miami, Phoenix, and Las Vegas. American Homes 4 Rent, a company set up by Wayne Hughes, the billionaire owner of Public Storage Properties, is chasing Waypoint, Colony, Carrington, and Blackstone, using a $400 million commitment from the state-controlled Alaska Permanent Fund.

Silver Bay Realty, one of the few public corporations to enter the foreclosure-to-rental business, described its business plan in a December 2012 prospectus. "As the housing market recovers and the cost of residential real estate increases, so should the underlying value of our assets," the company's management explained. "We believe that rental rates will also increase in such a recovery due to the strong correlation between home prices and rents. This trend also leads us to believe that the single-family residential asset class will serve as a natural hedge to inflation. As a result, we believe we are well positioned for the current economic environment and for a housing market recovery."

There are perhaps as many as fifteen or twenty other investment firms focused on buying up foreclosed homes and transforming them into assets from which value can be extracted by either rental or sale. No one actually knows how many companies are in this nascent industry, how many homes they have bought, or how much money that have spent. A February 2013 Barclays research report estimates that just over 42,000 foreclosed homes, mostly in California, Arizona, Georgia, Florida, Nevada, and Illinois, have been taken over by private investors. Others have put the figure lower or higher by tens of thousands. What is clear is that the industry is growing quickly.

The $60 Billion Question

More than 40,000 homes is a lot, but given that approximately 4.1 million single-family homes traded hands last year, it would mean that the rise of the private-equity landlord is still a relatively small phenomenon—about 1% of all sales in a market still dominated by owner-occupiers and mom-and-pop investors. The rapid growth of the foreclosure-to-rental mills, however, means that institutional investors could soon overtake other buyers, and dominate particular regional markets. That's what money managers at some of the biggest investment banks are hoping at least.

Analysts at Morgan Stanley call the industry's growth potential the "$60 billion question." Keeping in mind that only about $5 billion has been spent by private equity to buy out foreclosed homes to date, this would mean the U.S. housing market could be poised to see a more than ten-fold increase in foreclosure-to-rental conversions. The analysts at Barclays are even more bullish, saying they think this could grow into a $100 to $200 billion dollar market, encompassing as many as 1.3 million single-family homes.

What this means for many communities, especially residential neighborhoods in Arizona, California, Florida, Georgia, and other hot spots of investor activity, is that home ownership will become an increasingly difficult goal to attain as big-finance investors monopolize the stock of available housing in search of big profits. It also means that as the Fed continues its mortgage-bond buying spree to push up housing values, the parties best poised to reap these gains in equity will be Wall Street investors, rather than owner-occupiers. ❏

Sources: U.S. Census Bureau, Current Population Survey, "Housing Vacancy Survey, Series H-111 Reports," 2012, (census.gov); Peter Coy, "'Real' Homeownership Rate at Nearly 50-Year Low," *Bloomberg Businessweek*, Aug. 29, 2012; Congressional Oversight Panel, "March Oversight Report: The Final Report of the Congressional Oversight Panel," March 16, 2011; U.S. Dept. of Housing and Urban Development, "Fact Sheet: Mortgage Servicing Settlement" (portal.hud.gov); National Association of Realtors, "Single-Family Existing-Home Sales and Prices," (realtor.org); Oliver Chang, Vishwanath Tirupattur, and James Eagan, "Housing Market Insights: A Rentership Society," Morgan Stanley Research, July 20, 2011; Federal Housing Finance Agency, "Request for Information (RFI): Enterprise/FHA REO Asset Disposition Supplemental Data," July 18, 2011, (fhfa.gov); Silver Bay Realty, "Prospectus," Dec. 13, 2012; John Gittelsohn and Heather Perlberg, "Blackstone Rushes $2.5 Billion Purchase as Homes Rise," Bloomberg News, Jan. 9, 2013; Barclays, "Single-Family Rental/REO Rental: The birth of an asset class?"Feb. 1, 2013; Federal Reserve Bank of St. Louis, Home Ownership Rate for the United States (research.stlouisfed.org); John Burns Real Estate Consulting, "Homeownership Plunges to Lowest Rate in 50 Years," Aug. 27, 2012.

Article 4.7

UPDATE ON MORTGAGE LENDING DISCRIMINATION

After a disastrous detour, we're back where we started.

BY JIM CAMPEN

October 2010

In the 1980s and early 1990s, racial discrimination in mortgage lending resulted in less access to home loans for predominantly black and Latino borrowers and neighborhoods. Home mortgages were a fairly standardized product, and the problem was that banks avoided lending in minority neighborhoods (redlining) and denied applications from blacks and Latinos at disproportionately high rates compared to equally creditworthy white applicants (lending discrimination). The preceding article tells this story in some detail, from the vantage point of the mid-1990s.

Soon afterwards, however, a different form of lending discrimination rose to prominence as high-cost subprime loans became increasingly common. Precisely because borrowers and neighborhoods of color had limited access to the traditional prime loans, they were vulnerable for exploitation by predatory lenders pushing the new product.

Redlining was soon over-shadowed by "reverse redlining." Instead of being ignored, borrowers and neighborhoods of color were now aggressively targeted for high-cost subprime loans. Community groups documented and aggressively publicized the problem, and the U.S. Department of Housing and Urban Development (HUD) reported in 2000 that "subprime loans are five times more likely in black neighborhoods than in white neighborhoods." By the final year of the Clinton administration, government regulators were mobilizing to take action against this plague. But once the Bush administration took over in 2001, predatory lenders had nothing to fear from the federal government.

In the early 2000s, predatory lending began to take on a new and more explosive form. Mortgage brokers earned high fees for persuading borrowers to take on high-cost loans from lenders, who then sold the loans to big Wall Street firms, who in turn packaged them into "mortgage-backed securities" that were sold to investors. Everybody earned big fees along the way—in fact, the worse the deal was for borrowers, the bigger the fees for everyone else—and so the system gathered incredible momentum. Wall Street's demand for loan volume led ultimately to a complete lack of lending standards and millions upon millions of loans were made to borrowers who had no realistic prospect of repaying them.

For present purposes, the most important aspect of this appalling story is that these exploitative high-cost loans were strongly targeted to borrowers and neighborhoods of color. My own research on lending in Greater Boston during 2006, the peak year of the subprime lending boom, found that 49% of all home-purchase loans to blacks, and 48% of all home-purchase loans to Latinos, were high-cost loans, compared to just 11% of all loans to whites—and that the share of high-cost loans in predominantly minority neighborhoods was 4.4 times greater than it was in predominantly white neighborhoods. Similar racial and ethnic disparities were documented in numerous studies all across the country. Echoing what researchers at the

Boston Fed did fifteen years earlier (see previous article), the Center for Responsible Lending made use of industry data to demonstrate that these disparities could be only partially accounted for by differences in credit scores and other legitimate measures of borrower risk. In other words, they proved that racial discrimination was at least partly responsible for the observed racial disparities.

Nevertheless, federal regulators again did virtually nothing in response to the abundant evidence of violations of fair housing laws. Their most vigorous action was when the Comptroller of the Currency, the principal regulator of the nation's largest banks, actually went to court to stop New York's attorney general from enforcing that state's anti-discrimination laws against big national banks.

Finally, in 2007, the housing bubble popped and subprime lenders collapsed. Millions of homeowners who had received high-cost subprime loans either lost their homes to foreclosure or are in danger of being foreclosed upon soon. Because they were targeted by the predatory lenders, blacks and Latinos have been hit the hardest by this foreclosure tsunami. For example, researchers at the Center for Responsible Lending estimated that among recent mortgage borrowers, "nearly 8% of both African Americans and Latinos have lost their homes to foreclosures, compared to just 4.5% of whites."

By 2008, borrowers and neighborhoods of color were no longer being targeted by predatory lenders, as that industry had all but disappeared in the aftermath of the subprime meltdown. Instead, the more traditional form of discrimination again rose to the foreground. A recent report by a group of community-based organizations from seven cities across the country found that between 2006 and 2008 prime mortgage lending decreased 60.3% in predominantly minority neighborhoods while falling less than half that much (28.4%) in predominantly white neighborhoods. Home Mortgage Disclosure Act data for 2009, as tabulated by the Federal Reserve, showed that the denial rate for black applicants for conventional mortgage loans was 2.48 times greater than the denial rate for their white counterparts (45.7% vs. 18.4%; the denial rate for Latinos was 35.9%). This denial rate ratio is even higher than those which created such outrage when denial rate data first became public in the early 1990s, as described at the beginning of the preceding article ("Lending Insights").

Geoff Smith, senior vice president of Chicago's Woodstock Institute, summed up the new situation this way: "After inflicting harm on neighborhoods of color through years of problematic subprime loans, banks are now pulling back at a time when these communities are most in need of responsible loans and investment. We are concerned that we have gone from a period of reverse redlining to a period of re-redlining." ❏

Sources: U.S. Dept. of Housing and Urban Development, "Unequal Burden: Income & Racial Disparities in Subprime Lending in America," 2000 (archives.hud.gov/reports/subprime/subprime. cfm); Jim Campen, "Changing Patterns XIV: Mortgage Lending to Traditionally Underserved Borrowers & Neighborhoods in Boston, Greater Boston, and Massachusetts, 2006," Massachusetts Community and Banking Council (www.mcbc.info/files/ChangingPatternsXIV_0.pdf); Center for Responsible Lending, "Unfair Lending: the Effect of Race and Ethnicity on the Price of Subprime Mortgages," 2006, and "Foreclosures by Race and Ethnicity: The Demographics of a Crisis," 2010 (both available at www.responsiblelending.org); California Reinvestment Coalition and six other groups, "Paying More for the American Dream IV: The Decline of Prime Mortgage Lending in Communities of Color," 2010 (available at: www.woodstockinst.org).

Article 4.8

PONZI SCHEMES AND SPECULATIVE BUBBLES

BY ARTHUR MacEWAN
July/August 2009

> Dear Dr. Dollar:
> *What is the difference between a Ponzi scheme and the way the banks and other investors operated during the housing bubble?*
> —Leela Choiniere, Austin, Texas

As badly as our banking system operated in recent years, the housing bubble was not a Ponzi scheme. In some respects, however, it was even worse than a Ponzi scheme!

A Ponzi scheme is based on fraud. The operators of the scheme deceive the participants, telling them that their money is being used to make real or financial investments that have a high return. In fact, no such investments are made, and the operators of the scheme are simply paying high returns to the early participants with the funds put in by the later participants. A Ponzi scheme has to grow—and grow rapidly—in order to stay viable. When its growth slows, the early participants can no longer be paid the returns they expect. At this point, the operators disappear with what's left of the participants' funds—unless the authorities step in and arrest them, which is what happened with Charles Ponzi in 1920 and Bernard Madoff this year.

Fraud certainly was very important in the housing bubble of recent years. But the housing bubble—like bubbles generally—did not depend on fraud, and most of its development was there for everyone to see. With the principal problems out in the open and with the authorities not only ignoring those problems but contributing to their development, one might say that the situation with the housing bubble was worse than a Ponzi scheme. And Madoff bilked his marks out of only $50 billion, while trillions were lost in the housing bubble.

Bubbles involve actual investments in real or financial assets—housing in the years since 2000, high-tech stocks in the 1990s, and Dutch tulips in the 17th century. People invest believing that the price of the assets will continue to rise; as long as people keep investing, the price does rise. While some early speculators can make out very well, this speculation will not last indefinitely. Once prices start to fall, panic sets in and the later investors lose.

A bubble is similar to a Ponzi scheme: early participants can do well while later ones incur losses; it is based on false expectations; and it ultimately falls apart. But there need be no fraudulent operator at the center of a bubble. Also, while a Ponzi scheme depends on people giving their money to someone else to invest (e.g., Madoff), people made their own housing investments—though mortgage companies and banks made large fees for handling these investments.

Often, government plays a role in bubbles. The housing bubble was in part generated by the Federal Reserve maintaining low interest rates. Easy money meant readily obtainable loans and, at least in the short run, low monthly payments. Also,

Fed Chairman Alan Greenspan denied the housing bubble's existence—not fraud exactly, but deception that kept the bubble going. (Greenspan, whose view was ideologically driven, got support in his bubble denial from the academic work of the man who was to be his successor, Ben Bernanke.)

In addition, government regulatory agencies turned a blind eye to the highly risky practices of financial firms, practices that both encouraged the development of the bubble and made the impact all the worse when it burst. Moreover, the private rating agencies (e.g., Moody's and Standard and Poor's) were complicit. Dependent on the financial institutions for their fees, they gave excessively good ratings to these risky investments. Perhaps not fraud in the legal sense, but certainly misleading.

During the 1990s, the government made tax law changes that contributed to the emergence of the housing bubble. With the Taxpayer Relief Act of 1997, a couple could gain up to $500,000 selling their home without any capital gains tax liability (half that for a single person). Previously, capital gains taxes could be avoided only if the proceeds were used to buy another home or if the seller was over 55 (and a couple could then avoid taxes only on the first $250,000). So buying and then selling houses became a more profitable operation.

And, yes, substantial fraud was involved. For example, mortgage companies and banks used deceit to get people to take on mortgages when there was no possibility that the borrowers would be able to meet the payments. Not only was this fraud, but this fraud depended on government authorities ignoring their regulatory responsibilities.

So, no, a bubble and a Ponzi scheme are not the same. But they have elements in common. Usually, however, the losers in a Ponzi scheme are simply the direct investors, the schemer's marks. A bubble like the housing bubble can wreak havoc on all of us. ❑

Article 4.9

SECURITIZATION, THE BUBBLE, AND THE CRISIS

BY ARTHUR MACEWAN
July/August 2009

Dear Dr. Dollar:
What is "securitization" and what role did it play in the emergence and, then, collapse of the housing bubble?
—Anonymous, Boston, Mass.

Fraud in the housing bubble of the early 2000s—which led into the financial crisis that became apparent in 2008—took place partly in the mortgage companies' and banks' use of deceit in getting people to take on mortgages when it was virtually certain that, at some point, the borrowers would not be able to make their payments. While this practice may not always have been fraud in the formal legal sense, it was certainly a deliberate deception. Here's one example, provided in a December 28, 2008, *New York Times* story on the failed Washington Mutual Bank:

> As a supervisor at a Washington Mutual mortgage processing center, John D. Parsons was accustomed to seeing baby sitters claiming salaries worthy of college presidents, and schoolteachers with incomes rivaling stockbrokers'. He rarely questioned them. A real estate frenzy was under way and WaMu, as his bank was known, was all about saying yes.
>
> Yet even by WaMu's relaxed standards, one mortgage four years ago raised eyebrows. The borrower was claiming a six-figure income and an unusual profession: mariachi singer.
>
> Mr. Parsons could not verify the singer's income, so he had him photographed in front of his home dressed in his mariachi outfit. The photo went into a WaMu file. Approved.

But why did WaMu and other financial firms issue loans—the mortgages—to people when the firms knew that many of those loans would never be paid back? The answer to this question lies in "securitization."

Securitization is the practice of putting together several mortgages (or other types of contractual debt) to create a package that is then sold as a single security. The payments on those mortgages go to the buyer(s) of this new security, which is called a collateralized debt obligation or CDO. Because a mortgage-based CDO is made up of many underlying mortgages, perhaps thousands, it is viewed as a diversified investment—and diversification is often a characteristic of safe investments.

So when a financial firm—a mortgage company or a bank—made a mortgage loan, it quickly sold that mortgage to be placed into a CDO. The firm itself, then, would not be hurt if the person who took on the mortgage failed to make payments. At the same time, the firm collected substantial fees for making the mortgage and passing it along in this manner.

The buyers of CDOs viewed them as good investments, partly because the securities contained a diverse set of assets, partly because the buyers failed to recognize the deceptive practices that were widespread in the mortgage market, and partly because the CDOs received good ratings from the major securities rating agencies—Moody's, Standard & Poors, and Fitch. No one seemed to care that the rating agencies were being paid by the large financial firms that were handling the sales of the CDOs—a bit like food critics being paid by the restaurants they are rating.

Nonetheless, buyers of CDOs generally purchased insurance on them, just in case. The insurance policies were called credit default swaps, or simply "swaps" (and are purchased on a wide variety of assets). Unlike other forms of insurance, however, swaps were not regulated. The sellers of swaps did not have to hold funds in reserve in case a large amount of the CDOs failed at the same time. Moreover, as with the mortgages and CDOs, there was an extensive market in the credit default swaps; in fact, people could buy and sell swaps when they had no direct connection to the underlying security that was being insured.

Swaps, CDOs, and even the mortgages are forms of "derivatives." These are securities whose value is derived from the value of some other asset—the value of the swaps derived from the value of the CDOs, the value of the CDOs derived from the value of the mortgages, the value of the mortgages derived from the value of the real properties. So if something happens to the value of the real properties (houses), the whole chain of derivative assets is affected.

When the housing bubble did burst, as all bubbles eventually do, the market for CDOs and swaps fell apart. People and financial institutions stopped buying these assets. The financial markets "froze up" or "melted down" (whichever of these two seemingly contradictory metaphors you like). And there we were, at the financial crisis of 2008, the recession of 2009, and the economic malaise that is still with us. ❑

Article 4.10

STUDENT-LOAN DEBT BY THE NUMBERS

Rising costs and declining job prospects spell trouble.

BY MOLLY CUSANO AND ZACHARY SANTAMARIA
May/June 2012

The total amount of student-loan debt in the United States passed the $1 trillion mark in April 2012, according to the Federal Reserve Bank of New York. Since early 2011, student-loan debt has exceeded total consumer credit-card debt and auto-loan debt combined.

Obtaining a college degree has long been viewed as a secure a path to financial stability, but as cuts in public support for higher education have led to rising tuition costs, students are asking themselves whether a college degree is still worth the financial commitment. Students are paying more for college than ever before, even as job prospects and incomes for recent graduates diminish, leaving the average college graduate laden with debt. Not only are students borrowing more money to finance their educations, but they're also choosing more private loans instead of federal loans because federal loan subsidies have not kept up with tuition increases. Also, new legislation has lowered the maximum income threshold (from $30,000 to $23,000) for students to be eligible for Pell Grants, which do not have to be paid back. This means fewer incoming 2012-2013 students will qualify for these grants.

The first figure below compares the rising cost of attending a four-year private university to the stagnating median income of new graduates with bachelor's degrees. The second figure gives a breakdown of past-due student-loan balance by age group, showing that those under 40 account for most defaults, but that people continue to default on student loans into their 40s, 50s, and even 60s.

FIGURE 1: MEDIAN INCOME, NEW GRADUATES WITH BACHELOR'S DEGREE, AND COST OF PRIVATE FOUR-YEAR COLLEGE, 1990-2008

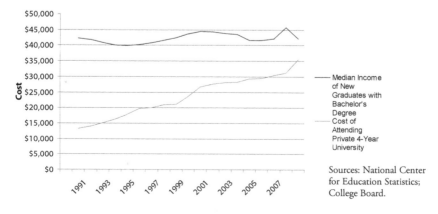

Median Income of New Graduates with Bachelor's Degree

Cost of Attending Private 4-Year University

Sources: National Center for Education Statistics; College Board.

Since the early 1990s, the price of attending college has increased dramatically even as the median starting salary for grads has stagnated. The graph shows a pending convergence of the two numbers, which could earn a year at a private school would cost the same as the first-year salary of a newly hired college graduate. Private college costs have gone from just over $13,000 a year to more than $35,000, while median starting income for college grads has actually gone down slightly from $42,300 to $42,100.

FIGURE 2: PAST-DUE STUDENT DEBT, BY AGE OF DEBTOR, 2011

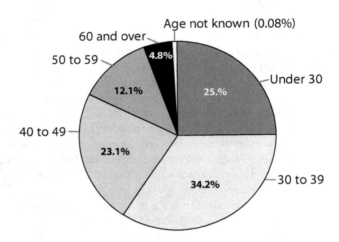

Sources: Federal Reserve Bank of New York Consumer Credit Panel; Equifax.

The total past-due balance of student loans in the United States is now $85 billion, with over 34% of the debt held by people ages 30-39. This shows that excessive student-loan debt, which borrowers are having trouble paying off, is not only owed by recent twenty-something college grads, but also by people further on in their careers. Some 23% of past-due balances are owed by people ages 40-49, and almost 5% of the $85 billion is owed by those age 60 and over. It is becoming clear that some student debt will never be paid off. ❏

Chapter 5

THE FINANCIAL CRISIS

Article 5.1

THE GREED FALLACY

You can't explain a change with a constant.

BY ARTHUR MacEWAN
November/December 2008

Various people explain the current financial crisis as a result of "greed." There is, however, no indication of a change in the degree or extent of greed on Wall Street (or anywhere else) in the last several years. Greed is a constant. If greed were the cause of the financial crisis, we would be in financial crisis pretty much all the time.

But the financial markets have not been in perpetual crisis. Nothing close to the current crisis has taken place since 1929. Yes, there was 1987 and the savings-and-loan debacle of that era. But, the current crisis is already more dramatic—and threatens to get a good deal worse. This crisis emerged over the last decade and appeared full-blown only at the beginning of 2008 (though, if you were looking, it was moving up on the horizon a year or two earlier). The current mess, therefore, is a change, a departure from the normal course of financial markets. So something has to have changed to have brought it about. The constant of greed cannot be the explanation.

So what changed? The answer is relatively simple: the extent of regulation changed.

As a formal matter, the change in regulation is most clearly marked by the Gramm-Leach-Bliley Act of 1999, passed by the Republican-dominated Congress and signed into law by Bill Clinton. This act in large part repealed the Glass-Steagall Act of 1933, which had imposed various regulations on the financial industry after the debacle of 1929. Among other things, Glass-Steagall prohibited a firm from being engaged in different sorts of financial services. One firm could not be both an investment bank (organizing the funding of firms' investment activities) and a commercial bank (handling the checking and savings accounts of individuals and firms and making loans); nor could it be one of these types of banks and an insurance firm.

However, the replacement of Glass-Steagall by Gramm-Leach-Bliley was only the formal part of the change that took place in recent decades. Informally, the relation between the government and the financial sector has increasingly become one of reduced regulation. In particular, as the financial sector evolved new forms of operation—hedge funds and private equity funds, for example—there was no attempt on the part of Washington to develop regulations for these activities. Also, even where regulations existed, the regulators became increasingly lax in enforcement.

The movement away from regulation might be seen as a consequence of "free market" ideology, the belief as propounded by its advocates that government should leave the private sector alone. But to see the problem simply as ideology run amok is to ignore the question of where the ideology comes from. Put simply, the ideology is generated by firms themselves because they want to be as free as possible to pursue profit-making activity. So they push the idea of the "free market" and deregulation any way they can. But let me leave aside for now the ways in which ideas come to dominate Washington and the society in general; enough to recognize that deregulation became increasingly the dominant idea from the early 1980s onward. (But, given the current presidential campaign, one cannot refrain from noting that one way the firms get their ideas to dominate is through the money they lavish on candidates.)

When financial firms are not regulated, they tend to take on more and more risky activities. When markets are rising, risk does not seem to be very much of a problem; all—or virtually all—investments seem to be making money. So why not take some chances? Furthermore, if one firm doesn't take a particular risk—put money into a chancy operation—then one of its competitors will. So competition pushes them into more and more risky operations.

The danger of risk is not simply that one investment—one loan, for example—made by a financial firm will turn out bad-ly, or even that a group of loans will turn out badly. The danger arises in the relation between its loans (obligations to the firm), the money it borrows from others (the firm's obligations to its creditors) and its capital (the funds put in by investors, the stockholders). If some of the loans it has made go bad (i.e., if the debtors default), it can still meet its obligations to its creditors with its capital. But if the firm is unregulated, it will tend to make more and more loans and take on more and more debt. The ratio of debt to capital can become very high, and, then, if trouble with the loans develops, the bank cannot meet its obligations with its capital.

In the current crisis, the deflation of the housing bubble was the catalyst to the general crumbling of financial structures. The housing bubble was in large part a product of the Federal Reserve Bank's policies under the guidance of the much-heralded Alan Greenspan, but let's leave that issue aside for now.

When the housing bubble burst, many financial institutions found themselves in trouble. They had taken on too much risk in relation to their capital. The lack of regulation had allowed them to get in this trouble.

But the trouble is much worse than it might have been because of the repeal of the provisions of Glass-Steagall that prevented the merging of investment banks, commercial banks, and insurance companies. Under the current circumstances, when trouble develops in one part of a firm's operations, it is immediately transmitted throughout the other segments of that firm. And from there, the trouble spreads to all the other entities to which it is connected—through credits, insurance deals, deposits, and a myriad set of complicated (unregulated) financial arrangements.

AIG is the example *par excellence*. Ostensibly an insurance company, AIG has morphed into a multi-faceted financial institution, doing everything from selling life insurance in rural India to speculating in various esoteric types of investments on Wall Street. Its huge size, combined with the extent of its intertwining with other financial firms, meant that its failure would have had very large impacts around the world.

The efforts of the U.S. government may or may not be able to contain the current financial crisis. Success would not breathe life back into the Lehman Brothers, Bear Stearns, and who knows how many other major operators that are on their deathbeds. But it would prevent the financial crisis from precipitating a severe general depression; it would prevent a movement from 1929 to 1932.

The real issue, however, is what is learned from the current financial mess. One thing should be evident, namely that greed did not cause the crisis. The cause was a change in the way markets have been allowed to operate, a change brought on by the rise of deregulation. Markets, especially financial markets, are never very stable when left to themselves. It turns out that the "invisible hand" does some very nasty, messy things when there is no visible hand of regulation affecting the process.

The problem is that maintaining some form of regulation is a very difficult business. As I have said, the firms themselves do not want to be regulated. The current moment may allow some re-imposition of financial regulation. But as soon as we turn our backs, the pressure will be on again to let the firms operate according to the "free market." Let's not forget where that leads. ❑

Article 5.2

CRISIS AND NEOLIBERAL CAPITALISM

BY DAVID KOTZ
November/December 2008; updated October 2013

The Financial Crisis and the Real Economy

In 2008, a severe economic crisis broke out that included a collapse in the financial sector as well as a "Great Recession" in the so-called real sector of the economy (producing ordinary goods and services). This crisis originated in the United States but quickly spread to most of the global economy. While the acute stage of the crisis, during 2008-09, has passed, the fallout persists five years later.

In the fall of 2008, all of the biggest banks in the United States faced bankruptcy and were bailed out by the taxpayers. The real sector of the economy declined from the first quarter of 2008 through the second quarter of 2009, with gross domestic product (GDP) dropping by 4.7% and the unemployment rate rising by 5.6 percentage points to reach 10.0%. By all measures, the Great Recession of 2008-09 was the most severe of any since the Great Depression of the 1930s (apart from a sharp but brief post-World War II "readjustment" as the federal government dramatically cut back spending at war's end).

Both the financial and real-sector dimensions of the current crisis are rooted in a speculative "bubble" that arose in the housing sector of the U.S. economy starting around 2002. By the summer of 2007, housing prices (corrected for inflation) had risen by 70% since 1995. Yet, since 2002, the real value of home rents had been flat. By 2006, the ratio of the Housing Price Index to the Homeowners Equivalent Rent had risen sharply to an all-time high of nearly 170, compared to 110 in 1995. This is clear evidence of a huge asset bubble in the U.S. housing market. This bubble created an estimated $8 trillion in inflated new wealth, which was about 38% of the total housing wealth of $21 trillion at its peak in 2007. When this bubble started to collapse, it set the stage for both a financial crisis and a recession in the real economy.

There are two ways in which a collapsing housing bubble affects the real economy. First, there is a downward "wealth effect" on housing investment and consumer spending. The collapse of housing prices led to a sharp drop in residential investment. In 2007, residential investment declined by 18.7%; in 2008, by 23.9%. Falling home values also caused a reduction in consumer spending, which at some 70% of GDP is a much larger part of the economy than residential investment. Since 2002, American households, pressed by stagnating or declining wages, had been borrowing against their homes to get funds for consumer spending. One study estimated that during 2004-06, Americans took $840 billion per year from their home equity through borrowing and capital gains from the sale of housing. This was almost 10% of disposable personal income in the United States.

As the housing bubble burst, people could no longer supplement their income with funds borrowed against their homes, which led to a large drop in consumer spending, at a rate of 3.8% per year in the third quarter of 2008. This happened before the financial crisis had begun to affect consumer spending. As the $8 trillion of inflated home value disappeared, it produced a big downward impact on the economy. Dean Baker, co-director of the Center for Economic and Policy Research (CEPR) and a respected analyst of the financial crisis, estimated the total effect of the collapsing housing bubble to be a decline of between 3.1% and 7.0% of GDP.

Second, the collapse of the bubble also affects business investment in new plant and equipment. Business fixed investment fell for ten consecutive calendar quarters over two and a half years starting in the second half of 2007, reaching a 28.9% annual rate of decrease in the first quarter of 2009, after which the rate of decline gradually slowed. The bubble-propelled and debt-financed expansions of 1991-2000 and 2001-2007 both produced a growing amount of productive capacity, relative to ordinary income. As the Great Recession developed, industry found it had substantial excess productive capacity, with the industrial capacity-utilization rate falling to just 66.9% in June 2009. As a result, the incentive for business investment has been depressed in the following years. In the previous recession in the United States, in 2001 after the collapse of a stock-market bubble, business fixed investment fell for two consecutive years, and at an accelerating rate, for this reason.

Capitalism and Structural Crises

Every form of capitalism has contradictions that eventually bring about a structural crisis of that form of capitalism. In the 1970s, the system of state-regulated capitalism, having produced rapid growth and high profits for a few decades, stopped working effectively and went into structural crisis. The predominant form of capitalism changed to the "neoliberal" form, which means a type of capitalism in which the role of the market expands greatly while the state, as well as other non-market institutions such as trade unions, play a more limited role in the economy.

It now appears that neoliberal capitalism can no longer work effectively to promote economic expansion and has entered a structural crisis of its own. The high and rising inequality generated by neoliberal capitalism means that the majority of the population has insufficient income to buy the growing output of the economy without relying on an unsustainable buildup of household debt. The deregulated financial system of neoliberal capitalism is inherently unstable, as we saw so clearly in the fall of 2008.

From the late 1940s to 1973, a regulated form of capitalism predominated across the world, including in the United States. Regulated capitalism in the U.S. included extensive government regulation of business and finance, regulation of the macroeconomy (aimed partly at achieving a relatively low unemployment rate), social programs that amounted to a modest welfare state, a significant role for trade unions in setting wages and working conditions through collective bargaining, restrained competition between big corporations, and trade and capital flows regulated by governments and international institutions.

The shift to neoliberal capitalism in the United States involved the deregulation of business and finance, the renunciation of active government macroeconomic policy aimed at keeping unemployment low, sharply reduced social programs, a big business and government attack against labor unions, unrestrained ("cutthroat") competition among large corporations, and relatively free movement of goods, services, and capital across national boundaries. This neoliberal transformation of capitalism was relatively thorough in the United States, the United Kingdom, and in international financial institutions such as the International Monetary Fund and World Bank.

Responses to the Crisis

When the structural crisis of neoliberal capitalism began in the fall of 2008, the reigning free-market ideology, which held that everyone should sink or swim based on their own efforts, was suddenly forgotten—at least for the rich and powerful. Congress was pressured into appropriating $700 billion for the Troubled Assets Relief Program (TARP) to bail out the big banks and other financial institutions. However, while millions of workers lost their jobs and millions of homeowners faced foreclosure, the government did little to help them, passing a job creation bill in February 2009 that was much too small to stop to the job losses and a mortgage relief bill that helped very few homeowners. This began to undermine the legitimacy of the previously dominant free-market ideology. A swell of anger arose, directed at the bankers who were seen as causing the economic crisis.

In the summer of 2009, the powers that be—policy analysts, politicians, the mass media—were able to shift the discourse by pointing to the growing federal budget deficit. From 2007 to 2009, the federal deficit jumped from 1.2% of GDP to 10.1% of GDP. This jump was primarily caused by the economic crisis itself, as rising unemployment and declining incomes meant lower tax revenues, while spending on social programs automatically increased.

Deficit "hawks" warned that the problem facing society was not 25 million unemployed workers but the "spendthrift state" and especially all those "overpaid" government employees and their "powerful unions." Their call for "austerity" diverted attention from the bankers, who had caused the crisis. After being bailed out courtesy of the taxpayers, the banks emerged more powerful than ever and have been able to largely defang the mild Dodd-Frank bank regulatory bill passed in the aftermath of the financial crisis in 2010.

Since 2009. the U.S. economy has expanded, but very sluggishly, at 2.1% per year through the first quarter of 2013. The unemployment rate declined gradually to 7.3% in September 2013, but the ratio of employment to the working age population has not recovered, stuck at 58-59% compared to over 63% in 2007—showing that many workers have given up looking for work. At the rate of job creation over the past year, the economy will not reach a 6.5% unemployment rate until 2021, according to one projection. Although the sluggish recovery calls for increased public spending, the deficit hawks have prevailed so far and blocked any such measures, despite the fact that the deficit has declined as a percentage of GDP every year since 2009, as the economy has gradually expanded.

The rich have been doing well. In the recovery thus far, from 2009-12, the richest 1% have captured 95% of the income gains in the United States, leaving only 5% of total income gains for the remaining 99%. Median household income in June 2013 was still below its level at the lowest point of the Great Recession in June 2009. The rate of profit of the nonfinancial corporate business sector fell sharply in 2008-09, but it bounced back almost to its pre-crisis level by 2011. However, the continuing structural crisis is reflected in the failure of capital accumulation—the rate of increase in the stock of capital goods—to recover to a normal rate despite the recovery in the rate of profit.

If history is any guide, the current crisis will, like past structural crises, result in major economic restructuring during the coming years. However, the outcome of this restructuring process is not pre-determined. So far, austerity advocates have blocked any move toward economic restructuring that might actually address the real problems of the economy.

However, it is still early in the struggle over the response to the economic crisis. We can fight for changes that would benefit the majority rather than the bankers—to assist troubled workers and troubled households rather than just (the owners of) troubled assets. One measure worth fighting for would address the problems of the millions of people who are unable to make the payments on their mortgages. The government should pass an emergency bill to ease mortgage terms to reflect the declining values of homes and the declining economy. This would impose a one-time loss on the financial institutions that invested in the risky new mortgage-based securities, but it would also make it easier to know the value of the mortgage-backed securities, eliminating a source of great uncertainty in the financial system.

A second policy would have the federal government act as employer of last resort, offering a job at a living wage to anyone who cannot find work in the private sector. The federal government would provide the financing, while the jobs could be created by state and local governments, in such areas as infrastructure maintenance and improvement, education, and green technology. Such a policy would have the side benefit of putting pressure on the private sector to pay a living wage.

A third measure would address the problems of the financial system. The financial crisis taught the important lesson that banks and other financial institutions are not ordinary private companies. If General Mills loses money, or even goes bankrupt, it harms its shareholders and workers—but its competitors gain. But if major banks lose money and are in danger of going under, this threatens the entire financial system, and with it the economy as a whole.

The obvious conclusion is that the financial sector should not be operated on a profit-and-loss basis. Instead, it should become part of the public sector, operated to serve the public interest. If banks, which are granted the power to create our money supply, and whose credit is essential to the welfare of the entire public, were made public institutions, then public-policy aims could guide their actions. They could be directed to stay away from speculative activities and instead make loans for socially valuable purposes. This would include steering credit into renewable-energy technologies, fuel-efficient vehicles, low-cost housing, and other good purposes. An advantage of public ownership of the banks over another cycle of government regulation of private banks is that re-regulated private banks can simply press for the elimination of the regulations—as they did successfully starting in the early 1980s.

The ongoing economic crisis has exposed the high-flying financial operators for what they always were—thieves who got rich without doing anything productive. This has also exposed their fallacious free-market ideology. This is a promising time, then, to build popular movements that can fight for progressive changes in our economy. ❏

Article 5.3

INEXCUSABLE: "DR. PHIL'S" FINANCIAL RECESSION

BY JOHN MILLER
March/April 2012

> "The 'Financial Recession ' Excuse"
>
> Never before in postwar America has either real per capita GDP or employment still been lower four years after a recession began.
>
> President Obama first claimed the weakness of the recovery was due to the depth of the recession. But, in fact, the 1981-82 recession was deeper and unemployment was higher. ... [And] President Ronald Reagan's policies ignited a [powerful] recovery.
>
> The most recent excuse for the failed recovery is that financial crises, by their very nature, result in slower, more difficult recoveries.
>
> But today's malaise is similar to that of the Depression ... because of the virtually identical and equally absurd policy prescriptions of the doctors.
>
> Under President Franklin Roosevelt, federal spending jumped by 3.6% of GDP from 1932 to 1936 as the New Deal was implemented. Under President Obama, spending exploded by 4.6% of GDP from 2008 to 2011. ... The regulatory burden mushroomed under Roosevelt, as it has under Mr. Obama.
>
> —Phil Gramm and Mike Solon,
> *Wall Street Journal*, February 2, 2012

Talk about chutzpah. Phil Gramm, one of the chief architects of the financial mess that still haunts our economy, is complaining that the clean-up hasn't gone very well. It sure hasn't.

But listening to the advice of Phil Gramm isn't going to make the tepid and erratic Obama-led recovery from the Great Recession robust. Worse yet, calls for yet another round of the policies that left our economy in shambles, like the one Gramm and Solon issue here, are a large part of what stands in the way of improving the economy.

Dr. Phil's Deregulatory Therapy

He may not have his own TV show like Dr. Phil McGraw, but this Dr. Phil, who does hold a doctorate in economics (although that hardly qualifies someone to dispense advice on the economy these days), is hawking his deregulatory therapy for the economy wherever and whenever he can.

Let's remind ourselves about who we're dealing with here. As an economic advisor to Republican presidential candidate John McCain, Phil Gramm dismissed the 2008 financial crisis as a "mental recession."

As a senator, Phil Gramm was a co-sponsor of the Financial Services Modernization Act of 1999, which marked the high point (well actually, the low point) of the spate of financial deregulation that began back in the 1970s. The

Gramm-Leach-Bliley Act, as it was called for its three Republican co-sponsors, repealed much of the Glass-Steagall Act of 1933. Glass-Steagall had required the separation of different kinds of financial institutions such as commercial banks, investment banks, and insurance companies.

The passage of Gramm-Leach-Bliley and its repeal of Glass-Steagall helped set the stage for the financial crisis of 2008 in two important ways. First, by allowing the conglomeration of different kinds of financial institutions, the law facilitated the spread of financial collapse. As a result, when problems developed with home mortgages, the entire financial industry was brought to its knees. Second, large financial firms were transformed into organizations that were "too big to fail."

It was not just his Republican co-sponsors that bought into the deregulatory, free-market therapy of Dr. Phil. The Gramm-engineered repeal of Glass-Steagall received extensive support from congressional Democrats, was pushed by the Democratic administration, and signed into law by Democratic President Bill Clinton.

Post-Therapy Trauma

So how has deregulatory therapy been working for us? Not so well. Beyond paving the way for the financial crisis a decade later, the performance of the U.S. economy since the repeal of Glass-Steagall has been abysmal.

Today the economy employs fewer people than when Gramm-Leach-Bliley was enacted into law over a decade ago. Non-farm employment stood at 133.4 million in November 1999, but was just 132.9 million in December 2012. The job losses of the Great Recession and wretched job creation during the Obama recovery are surely part of the story. But it couldn't have happened without the six-year Bush economic expansion from 2001 to 2007 that added jobs at about one-third the pace of the typical U.S. economic recovery since World War II.

Nor has the post-Glass-Steagall economic growth record of the U.S. economy been anything to write home about. Take real GDP per capita, gross domestic product corrected for inflation and population growth, the measure favored by Gramm and Solon. It increased just 0.6% a year from 2000 to 2010, the decade following the repeal of Glass-Steagall. That's less than one-third the rate in the previous decade (2.1% annually measured from 1990 to 2000). And once again the Great Recession and the sluggish Obama recovery were only part of the story. Real GDP per capita during the Bush expansion rose just about half as quickly as it had during the Clinton expansion in the decade before repeal of Glass-Steagall.

So not only has the Obama economic recovery fallen flat, but so did the six-year economic expansion under the Bush administration that preceded the Great Recession, something Gramm and Solon fail to mention.

Obama's Excuses

There is no excuse for an economic recovery that does little to put people back to work or to lift their incomes. But what the Obama administration has said about the depth of the Great Recession and the protracted character of recoveries from financial crisis is true.

The Great Recession of 2007 to 2009 is indeed the worst downturn since the Great Depression of the 1930s. That's clearly the case by a vast array of measures, including the unemployment rate once it is corrected for underemployment and those who have given up looking for work. But let's look once again at the two measures Gramm and Solon use in their article. Employment fell by a staggering 6.1% during the Great Recession, the sharpest decline in employment in any recession of the last 60 years, and nearly double that of the 1982 recession (3.1%). Real GDP per capita decreased 2.9% in the 1982 recession but that was well below the 4.1% decline during the Great Recession.

Financial crises have in fact been especially devastating. In their study of recent financial crises across the globe (and the Great Depression in the United States), economists Carmen Reinhart and Kenneth Rogoff found that unemployment rates typically rose seven percentage points and kept rising for four years during financial crises. Also output typically contracted 9.3% and declined for 1.9 years. By those standards, the Great Recession and the financial crisis that began in 2008, at least so far, has not been especially severe or protracted. The unemployment rate rose 5.7 percentage points over two and a half years and output fell 4.1% of output over a year and a half. Nonetheless the Obama administration has faced economic travails far worse than those confronted by any administration since Roosevelt's, including the Reagan administration.

Admittedly that's some heavy lifting. But so far the Obama administration has done little more than get the economy off the ground. Is the problem that Obama administration policies increased government spending and tightened regulation of the financial sector as Gramm and Solon allege? And are they right that the policies the Roosevelt Administration employed to counteract the worst downturn in U.S. economic history, including the Glass-Steagall Act, are a disastrous guide to how best to confront the Great Recession and today's financial crisis?

FDR vs. Reagan

Let's see. Did the U.S. economy collapse into a deeper depression under the increased regulatory burden of Glass-Steagall and the steady ratcheting up of government spending with Roosevelt's New Deal? Quite the opposite. The economic expansion from 1933 to 1937 that followed the passage of Glass-Steagall added jobs at more than six times the rate the Bush expansion of 2001 to 2007 did following the repeal of Glass-Steagall, and increased real GDP per capita by five times as much a year as during the Bush expansion.

How does that record measure up to the Reagan expansion of the 1980s that Gramm and Solon hold up as the robust counterexample to the anemic Obama recovery? In the expansion following the 1982 recession, the economy added jobs and pushed up real GDP per capita at less than half the annual rate of the Roosevelt expansion from 1933 to 1937.

That hardly seems like good reason to give up on the New Deal policies of the Roosevelt administration in favor of the tax-cutting and deregulatory policies begun under the Reagan administration. Furthermore, much of the punch of the Reagan recovery should be attributed to the stimulus provided by what were then record-setting budget deficits. The Reagan administration deficits reached as high as 5.7% of GDP, while the Roosevelt administration deficits during the 1930s never exceeded 4.8% of GDP.

A proper reading of the Roosevelt and Reagan records suggests that financial regulation works and deficit spending is an effective antidote to economic downturns, even severe and protracted ones. Still, the massive loss of output and jobs during the Great Depression was never restored during the 1930s due to the failure to properly calibrate those policies to the depth of the crisis. When spending on World War II enlarged the budget deficit to a whopping 30.3% of GDP, the lost jobs and output were restored.

Enough with the Excuses

Likewise, the failure to restore jobs and real output per capita in the current crisis can be attributed to the timidity of Obama's policies which, like Roosevelt's policies of the 1930s, are not properly calibrated to the severe and protracted downturn that typically follows a financial crisis.

Now is the time to change that, not to turn our economic problems back over to Phil Gramm. Let's not let Dr. Phil do for this decade what he did for the last one. It's time to tune him out. ❏

Article 5.4

UNDERSTANDING THE FINANCIAL CRISIS OF 2008

BY MARTY WOLFSON
November/December 2008

It has become commonplace to describe the current financial crisis as the most serious since the Great Depression. Although we have more tools now to avoid a depression, the current crisis presents in some ways more significant challenges than did the banking crises of the 1930s.

And it's not over.

The form of the current crisis is similar to others we have seen in the past: a speculative increase in asset prices, overly optimistic expectations, and an expansion of debt sustainable only if the speculative bubble continues. Then the bubble pops, debt can't be repaid, and losses mount at financial institutions. The risk of bank failures rises and lenders get scared. They panic, refuse to lend to anyone that seems at all risky, and seek safety in cash or super-safe assets.

In the early 1930s, there was no federal deposit insurance and little federal government intervention. Depositor runs took down the banking system.

In more recent crises, though, the Federal Reserve successfully developed and used its powers as a lender of last resort. Deposit insurance helped to reassure small depositors and, if needed, the Federal Deposit Insurance Corporation stepped in and bailed out threatened banks. It could guarantee all liabilities of a failing bank and arrange mergers with healthier banks. These tools generally worked to reduce panicked reactions and prevent the freezing up of credit.

But this time, after the collapse of the speculative bubble in housing prices, the course of events has been different. The Federal Reserve was forced to expand the concept of a lender of last resort in unprecedented ways. It has lent to investment banks and insurance companies, not just regulated depository institutions. It has taken all kinds of assets as collateral for its loans, not just the high-grade securities it traditionally accepted. It has even lent to nonfinancial corporations (by buying their commercial paper).

What is surprising is that these dramatic actions and expensive bailouts of financial institutions, such as American International Group (AIG) and even Fannie Mae and Freddie Mac, were insufficient to reassure lenders about the ability of financial institutions to honor their repayment commitments. Treasury Secretary Paulson's plan to use $700 billion to buy "toxic assets" from financial institutions, signed into law by President Bush on October 3rd [2008], failed to stop what had become by then a generalized panic and freeze-up of credit. It took a coordinated global initiative to inject capital directly into financial institutions, plus a federal guarantee on bank debt and unlimited FDIC insurance on non-interest-bearing (mostly business) accounts at banks, announced on October 12th [2008], to begin to have an effect on unfreezing credit markets.

The "TED spread," a widely watched measure of credit risk that had spiked sharply during the panic, began to reverse its path following the October 12 [2008] announcement. The TED spread measures the difference between an interest rate that banks charge when lending to each other (the London Interbank Offered Rate, or LIBOR) and the interest rate on U.S. Treasury bills. Because the Treasury is assumed to be "risk-free," the difference between it and LIBOR measures the perceived relative risk of lending to banks.

Why has this panic been so much more difficult to control? The answer has to do with the widespread use of complicated and opaque securities, known as derivatives, in a deregulated, interconnected, and global financial system.

A derivative is a financial contract that derives its value from something else, such as an asset or an index. At the root of the current crisis are derivatives known as mortgage-backed securities (MBSs). MBSs are claims to payments from an underlying pool of mortgages. The ability of MBS issuers to repay their debt, and thus the value of the MBS, is derived from the ability of homeowners to meet their mortgage payments.

In the process leading up to the crisis, a mortgage broker typically extended a mortgage to a borrower, and then turned to a commercial bank to fund the loan. The bank might sell the loan to Fannie Mae, which would pool a group of mortgages together and sell the resulting MBS to an investment bank like Lehman Brothers. Lehman, in turn, repackaged the MBS in various ways, and issued even more complicated derivatives called collateralized debt obligations (CDOs). Buyers of the CDOs might be other banks, hedge funds, or other lenders.

At the base of this complicated pyramid of derivatives might be a subprime borrower whose lender did not explain an adjustable-rate loan, or another borrower whose ability to meet mortgage payments depended on a continued escalation of home prices. As subprime borrowers' rates reset, and especially as housing price speculation collapsed, the whole house of cards came crashing down.

Why were mortgage loans made that could not be repaid? And why did supposedly sophisticated investors buy MBSs and CDOs based on these loans? First of all, the mortgage brokers and commercial banks that made and funded these loans quickly sold them off and no longer had any responsibility for them. Second, rating agencies like Moody's and Standard & Poor's gave these derivatives stellar AAA ratings, signifying a credit risk of almost zero. Recent Congressional hearings have highlighted the conflict of interest that these rating agencies had: they were being paid by the issuers of the derivatives they were rating. Third, financial institutions up and down the line were making money and nobody was limiting what they could do. In the deregulated financial environment, federal regulators stood aside as housing speculation spun out of control and did little to regulate, or even document, the growth of complicated derivatives.

Finally, financial institutions' concerns about the creditworthiness of the derivatives they held were eased because they thought they could protect themselves against possible loss. For example, by using another type of derivative known as a credit default swap, holders of MBSs and CDOs could make periodic premium payments to another financial institution, like American International Group (AIG), to insure themselves against default by the issuers of the MBSs and CDOs. (This insurance contract was technically classified as a derivative rather than insurance in order to escape regulation.) However, if an insurer like AIG is unable to honor all its insurance contracts, then the protection against loss is illusory.

The total value of all the securities insured by credit default swaps at the end of 2007 was estimated by the Bank of International Settlements to be $58 trillion, and by the International Swaps and Derivatives Association to be $62 trillion. (The estimates could vary by as much as $4 trillion because unregulated credit default swaps do not have to be officially reported to regulatory agencies. Moreover, even greater ambiguity surrounds these contracts because insurers can transfer their liability to other parties, and the insured party may be unaware of the creditworthiness or even the identity of the new insurer.)

Surprisingly, though, the value of the actual securities that form the basis of these credit default swaps was only about $6 trillion. How could $6 trillion worth of assets be insured at ten times that amount? The discrepancy is due to the fact that it is possible to speculate on the likelihood of default of a security without actually owning the security: all the speculator has to do is enter into a credit default swap contract with an insurer. The total volume of "insured securities" can thus escalate dramatically.

Because derivatives are so complex, because so much speculation and debt are involved, and because it is so hard to know how much is at risk (and exactly who is at risk), regulators are unsure of the implications of the failure of a particular financial institution. That is why they have been so fearful of the consequences of letting a troubled institution fail.

The exception that did indeed prove the rule was Lehman Brothers. The Federal Reserve and Treasury did not bail it out, and its failure led to an intensification of the problems in credit markets. A money market fund, the Reserve Primary Fund, announced that it would only pay 97 cents on the dollar to its investors, because its investments in Lehman Brothers could not be redeemed. The Treasury moved quickly to announce that it would insure money market funds, in order to prevent a run on the funds. However, the Lehman failure raised further concerns that lenders had about the derivatives portfolios of other banks, and about the possibility that the banks would not have enough capital to cover potential losses.

Secretary Paulson's initial plan to buy "toxic" assets (including MBSs and CDOs) from financial institutions was designed to address these concerns about bank capital. However, his plan was probably also negatively affected by uncertainty. Because these "toxic" assets are complex and nobody wants to buy them, there is no market for them and their value is uncertain. And because the Paulson plan's unstated objective was to boost bank capital by overpaying for these assets, the difficulties in pricing the assets raised the prospects of long delays and questions about whether the plan to increase bank capital would be successful. Lenders continued to hold back. They may also have hesitated because of concern about a political backlash against a taxpayer subsidy for the very banks that many people blamed for the crisis.

By injecting capital directly into the banks, the global initiative announced on October 12th [2008] raised the prospect of returns on the capital investment for taxpayers. It also avoided the uncertainties of buying individual assets and helped to reduce the panic.

But the crisis isn't over. Reducing the panic is only the first step. There is now likely to be a longer-term credit crunch that will continue to threaten the broader economy. Banks and other lenders will be wary for quite some time. Losses on mortgage-related assets will continue as years of housing speculation—financed with heaps of borrowed money—continues to unwind. Bank lending will lag as banks rebuild their capital and overcome their pessimistic expectations.

It will be up to the federal government to pick up the slack that the banks will leave. We will need programs to enable people to stay in their homes and stabilize their communities. We will need to create jobs by investing in infrastructure, renewable energy, and education. We will need a "trickle-up" approach that puts people first and raises living standards and opportunities.

At the same time, we need a regulatory structure for the financial system that puts limits on risk and manipulation. It is clear that deregulation, and the entire neoliberal model that has dominated economic policy for the past 30 years, has run aground. It has sown the seeds of financial crisis, and this crisis has led us to the edge of an abyss. Only by dramatically reorienting our economic and financial structure can we avoid the abyss and create the kind of society that meets our needs. The nature of that new structure should be the subject of intensive democratic discussion and debate in the days to come. ❑

Article 5.5

THE BAILOUT OF FANNIE MAE AND FREDDIE MAC

BY FRED MOSELEY
September/October 2008

It has been a persistent myth, and an article of faith among "free market" conservatives, that Fannie Mae and Freddie Mac—the two government-sponsored mortgage lending giants—were somehow responsible for the housing-market bubble, its subsequent crash, and therefore the worst U.S. recession since the Great Depression. This is a comforting story, for those who want to believe it, since it indicts government involvement in markets as inherently distorting (something they believe anyway) and lets financial deregulation and the private financial industry off the hook.

As economists like Paul Krugman and Mark Zandi point out, however, the facts do not bear out the view that Fannie and Freddie engaged in irresponsible lending or should be blamed for the bubble. Krugman, a Princeton professor and Nobel laureate in economics, notes that the "serious delinquency" rate of Fannie and Freddie's high risk loans was about the same as the national average for all mortgages—and about one third the rate for the "subprime" loans that became stock-in-trade of private mortgage lenders ("Fannie Freddie Phooey," nytimes.com, July 14, 2011). Zandi, co-founder of Moody's Economy.com, points out that Fannie and Freddie rapidly lost market share as the bubble inflated—that is, as private lenders accelerated their indiscriminate subprime lending. "The two giant housing-finance institutions made many mistakes over the decades ...," Zandi concludes, "but causing house prices to soar and then crater during the past decade weren't among them" ("Fannie and Freddie don't deserve blame for bubble," Washington Post, Jan. 24, 2012).

In this article, economist Fred Moseley takes a retrospective look at the ways Fannie and Freddie have operated over the years, what led to their recent troubles, and the eventual bailouts. Moseley draws opposite conclusions from the conservative critics, pointing to the problems caused by Fannie and Freddie's 1968 privatization (which turned them from government-owned to "government-sponsored" entities, with private shareholders but public loan guarantees). And he points to different solutions from either the conservatives who want to see both abolished and those "reformers" who want to see them turned into mortgage-insurance agencies. He calls, instead, for the formation of a fully public mortgage bank. —Eds.

On Sunday, September 7 [2008], Treasury Secretary Henry Paulson announced that the U.S. government was taking control of Fannie Mae and Freddie Mac, the two giant home mortgage companies, which together either own or guarantee almost half of the mortgages in the United States. This takeover stands in striking contrast to the generally laissez-faire philosophy of the U.S. government, especially the Republican Party. Why did Paulson take this highly unusual action? And what will be the future of Fannie and Freddie? To delve into these questions is to underscore the critical fault line between private profits and public aims—in this case, the aim of making homeownership affordable—a fault line that ran right through the hybrid structure of Fannie and Freddie.

A Brief History

Fannie Mae (short for the Federal National Mortgage Association) was created as an agency of the federal government in 1938 in an attempt to provide additional funds to the home mortgage market and to help the housing industry recover from the Great Depression. Fannie Mae purchased approved mortgages from commercial banks, which could then use the funds to originate additional mortgages. It continued to fulfill this function on a modest scale in the early postwar years.

Fannie Mae was privatized in 1968, in part to help reduce the budget deficit caused by the Vietnam War (a short-sighted goal, if ever there was one). In 1970, Freddie Mac (Federal Home Loan Mortgage Corporation) was created as a private company in order to provide competition for Fannie Mae. Chartered by the federal government, both are (or were, until the takeover) so-called government-sponsored enterprises: private enterprises whose main goal is to maximize profit for the shareholders who own them, but also quasi-public enterprises with a mandated goal of increasing the availability of affordable mortgages to families in the United States. In the end, this dual mandate proved to be untenable.

In order to obtain funds to purchase mortgages, Fannie and Freddie sell short-term bonds. In other words, their business plan involves borrowing short-term and lending long-term, because interest rates are higher on long-term loans than on short-term loans. However, such "speculative finance" is risky because it depends on the willingness of short-term creditors to continue to loan to Fannie and Freddie by rolling over or refinancing their short-term loans. If creditors were to lose confidence in Fannie and Freddie and refuse to do so, then they would be in danger of bankruptcy. This is what almost happened in the recent crisis.

Beginning in the 1970s, Fannie and Freddie began to develop and sell "mortgage-backed securities"—hundreds of mortgages bundled together and sold to investors as a security, similar to a bond. They also guaranteed these securities (so that if a mortgage defaulted, they would repurchase it from the investors) and made money by charging a fee for this guarantee (like an insurance premium). This major financial innovation enabled the two companies to buy more mortgages from commercial banks, thereby increasing the supply of credit in the home mortgage market, which in turn was supposed to push mortgage interest rates lower, making houses more affordable. These early mortgage-backed securities consisted entirely of "prime" mortgages—that is, loans at favorable interest rates, typically made to creditworthy borrowers with full documentation and a substantial down payment.

The securities that Fannie and Freddie sold were widely perceived by investors to carry an implicit government guarantee: if Fannie or Freddie were ever in danger of bankruptcy, then the federal government would pay off their debts (even though this government guarantee was explicitly denied in legislation and in the loan agreements them-selves). This perceived guarantee enabled Fannie and Freddie to borrow money at lower interest rates because loans to them were viewed as less risky.

In the 1980s, Wall Street investment banks also began to package and sell mortgage-backed securities. In the 1990s and 2000s, these "private label" mortgage-backed securities expanded rapidly in volume and also in reach, coming to include "subprime" mortgages—loans at higher interest rates with less favorable terms, geared toward less credit-worthy borrowers and typically requiring little or no documentation and little or no down payment.

The subprime innovation was entirely the work of the investment banks; as of 2000, Fannie and Freddie owned or guaranteed almost no subprime mortgages. This innovation greatly increased the supply of credit for home mortgages and led to the extraordinary housing boom of the last decade, and also eventually to the crisis. As a result of these changes, the share of mortgage-backed securities sold by Fannie and Freddie fell to around 40% by 2005.

In the recent housing boom, the companies—especially Freddie—began to take greater risks. While continuing to bundle prime mortgages into securities and sell them to investors, Fannie and Freddie began to buymortgage-backed securities issued by investment banks, including some based on subprime and Alt-A (between prime and subprime) mortgages. Why did they begin buying as well as selling mortgage-backed securities? Buying these private-label securities gave Fannie and Freddie a way to get in on the subprime action—while still avoiding direct purchases of subprime mortgages from the banks and mortgage companies that originated them. It was a way both to increase their profits at the behest of their shareholders, and, in response to pressure from the government, to make more mortgages available to low- and middle-income families. Of course, it also opened them up to the risks of the subprime arena. Moreover, the prime mortgages they continued to buy and guarantee were increasingly at inflated, bubble prices, making them vulnerable to the eventual bust and the decline of housing prices.

Anatomy of a Crisis

When the subprime crisis began in the summer of 2007, Fannie and Freddie at first appeared to be relatively unaffected, and were even counted on to increase their purchases of mortgages in order to support the mortgage market and help overcome the crisis. Congress facilitated this by relaxing some of its regulations on the two companies: the maximum value of mortgages that they could purchase was increased substantially; their reserve capital requirements, already much lower than for commercial banks, were reduced further; and restrictions on their growth were lifted. As a result of these changes and the drying up of private label mortgage-backed securities, the share of all mortgage-backed securities sold by Fannie and Freddie doubled to approximately 80%. Without Fannie and Freddie, the mortgage and housing crises of the last year would have been much worse.

As the overall crisis unfolded, however, the financial situation of Fannie and Freddie deteriorated. Delinquency and foreclosure rates for the mortgages they own or guarantee, while lower than for the industry as a whole, increased rapidly and beyond expectations. The two companies together reported losses of $14 billion in the last year. Their actual losses have been much worse. As of mid-2008, the two had lost about $45 billion due to the decline in the value of their mortgage-backed securities, mostly those backed by subprime and Alt-A mortgages. But by labeling that decline "temporary," they could leave the losses off their balance sheets. If these losses were counted, as they should be, then Freddie's capital would be completely wiped out (a value of -$5.6 billion), and Fannie's would be reduced to a razor-thin margin of $12.2 billion (less than 2% of its assets), likely becoming negative in the coming quarters. In addition, both Fannie and Freddie count as assets "tax deferred losses" that can be used in future years to offset tax bills—if they make a profit. Without this dubious (but legal) accounting trick, the net assets of both Fannie and Freddie would be below zero, -$20 billion and -$32 billion respectively.

The financial crisis of Fannie and Freddie worsened in early July. The price of their stock, which had already fallen by more than half since last summer, declined another 50% in a few weeks, for a total decline of over 80%. Fear spread that Fannie and Freddie's creditors would refuse to roll over their short-term loans to the two. If that were to happen, then the U.S. home mortgage market and the housing construction industry probably would have collapsed completely, and the U.S. economy would have fallen into an even deeper recession. Furthermore, approximately 20% of the mortgage-backed securities and debt of Fannie and Freddie are owned by foreign investors. Mainly these are foreign governments, most significantly China. If these foreign investors became unwilling to continue to lend Fannie and Freddie money, this would have precipitated a steep fall in the value of the dollar which, on top of recent significant declines, would have dealt another blow to the U.S. economy. Clearly, the potential crisis here was serious enough to spur government action.

In late July, Congress passed a law authorizing the Treasury to provide unlimited amounts of money to Fannie and Freddie, either by buying new issues of stock or by making loans, and also to take over the companies in a conservator arrangement if necessary.

Government Takeover

Through August [2008] the financial condition of Fannie and Freddie continued to deteriorate (especially Freddie), and confidence in their ability to survive waned. Foreign investors in particular reduced their purchases of the companies' debt, and mortgage rates increased. The Treasury concluded that it had to implement a takeover in order to reassure creditors and restore stability to the home mortgage market.

The Treasury plan has three main components:

- It commits up to $200 billion over the next 15 months for purchases of preferred shares of Fannie and Freddie as necessary to keep the companies solvent;

- It establishes a special lending facility that will provide emergency loans in case of a liquidity crisis;

- It commits to purchase unspecified amounts of Fannie and Freddie's mortgage-backed securities "as deemed appropriate."

The day after Paulson's announcement, William Poole, ex-president of the Federal Reserve Bank of St. Louis, estimated that the total cost to taxpayers would be in the neighborhood of $300 billion.

The top managers and the boards of directors of both companies will be dismissed and replaced by new, government-appointed managers. Other than that, the Treasury hopes that day-to-day operations at Fannie and Freddie will be "business as usual." They will continue to borrow money from creditors, now reassured by the government's intervention and more willing to lend to them, and they will continue to purchase and guarantee prime mortgages. In fact, Treasury Department plans call for the volume of mortgages purchased by the two companies to increase over the next year in order to push the supply of mortgage loans up and mortgage interest rates down.

The Treasury plan is a complete bailout of the creditors of Fannie and Freddie, who will be repaid in full, with taxpayer money if necessary. In contrast, owners of Fannie or Freddie stock will lose to some degree: dividends will be suspended for the foreseeable future, and their stock is now worth very little. But their stock was not expropriated. Nor was it wiped out entirely; it could regain value in the future as the home mortgage market recovers. Without the intervention, both companies would have gone bankrupt and the stockowners would have lost everything. So the intervention does represent at least a modest bailout for shareholders.

The most controversial issue in the months ahead will be the future of Fannie and Freddie. Should they become public enterprises permanently? Should they be re-privatized? Should they be sold off in pieces and cease to exist? Secretary Paulson made it clear that the government's current conservatorship is a holding action, and that decisions about the companies' ultimate status will only be made once the next administration and the next Congress are in office. Paulson said that Fannie and Freddie's current structure is unworkable because of its dual and conflicting goals of making housing affordable and maximizing profit—a radical statement, if you think about it! And he suggested that the two should either be fully public enterprises, or else they should be fully private enterprises without any government backing.

In the upcoming debate, the left should advocate forcefully for a public home mortgage agency, one whose sole purpose is to provide affordable housing without the conflicting purpose of maximizing profit. This would stabilize the home mortgage market and help it avoid the boom/bust cycle of private mortgage markets that has brought on the current crisis.

More fundamentally, because decent affordable housing is a basic economic right, providing credit for home purchases should be a function of the government rather than of private businesses whose primary goal is maximum profit. The provision of credit for housing should not be an arena where enormous profits are made, as has been the case in recent years. Without these huge profits, mortgages would be cheaper and houses more affordable. Plus, the kinds of fraudulent lending practices that played a significant role in the recent housing boom would be minimized.

With the presidential election just weeks away, the crisis of Fannie, Freddie, and the whole home lending market is poised to become a major campaign issue. McCain has said that he wants Fannie and Freddie to "go away"—i.e., to be broken up and disappear, leaving the mortgage market entirely to private enterprises. Obama has emphasized the conflict between the public aim of making housing widely affordable and the private aim of making a profit, but so far he has not come down on one side or the other. Now he will have to decide. I hope that he will be a strong advocate of a public home mortgage agency, and I think this would help him to get elected.

Update, October 2010

The current recession has clearly demonstrated that private banks and other investors will flee the mortgage market in a serious recession unless there are government guarantees. Without the government guarantee, investors would generally charge a higher rate of interest to finance 30-year fixed rate mortgages for households, and might not be willing to lend at all in economic downturns.

The interest rate "spread" in normal times between a purely private mortgage system (e.g., jumbo loans which exceed the maximum for Fannie-Freddie mortgages) and a mortgage system with government insurance in recent decades has been between .25% and .5%. However, in the current recession, this spread increased sharply to 1.5% and is still today almost 1%. Only about 10% of new mortgages since the recession began have been without government guarantees.

Where would the mortgage market and the economy be today without Fannie and Freddie? The mortgage market would be about one-tenth of its present size, and the economy would be in correspondingly much worse shape.

In spite of the obvious risks, Republicans want to do away with the government role in the mortgage market altogether. They argue that private banks would increase competition, which would lower costs and lower mortgage rates. But this argument is disingenuous, to say the least; everyone but free-market true-believers recognizes that, without explicit government backing, mortgage rates would be higher and in a crisis would be *much* higher. In such a Republican world, houses would be less affordable and home ownership would decline. And in a crisis, new home ownership would become almost impossible. Because of their blind allegiance to the "free market," Republicans are willing to be reckless with our economy and our lives. Obviously, we should not allow them to do this.

Although a government insurance agency (such as had been proposed by the Obama administration) would be much better than a purely private mortgage market, there is an even better way to reduce interest rates on mortgages: transform Fannie and Freddie into a public mortgage bank (rather than an insurance company) that would buy eligible mortgages from originators and hold them in their own portfolio. Actually, this would be a "return to the past" and to the original structure of Fannie Mae from its beginning in the Great Depression (to provide more affordable mortgages) until its privatization in 1968 (to help pay for the Vietnam War).

Such a public bank could charge lower interest rates than private banks (even with government insurance) because the main goal of private banks is to maximize profit and maximize shareholder value, and also to allow for multimillion-dollar salaries of bank executives. A public mortgage bank would have a different objective: not to maximize profit, shareholder value, and executive salaries, but to increase the availability of affordable housing. This goal would not be pursued to the point of losing money, but the profit margin could be less. And the executive salaries would be more in line with high civil servant salaries. Public bank mortgages would also have an upper limit, perhaps $500,000. The public bank provision of low-interest mortgages would not apply to more expensive houses or to second homes.

A relevant comparison is with student loans. The explicit argument of the Obama administration for a "direct lender" model is that they can provide student loans more cheaply than the private companies they have been subsidizing, and can also use the savings to fund more Pell grants for low-income students. What a great idea! The same logic could be applied to housing.

Another related advantage of a public bank over private banks is that its profit would not have to go to private shareholders (there would be none), but would instead become public income that could be used to pursue public policy goals, such as building more affordable housing.

Another advantage of a public bank over an insurance plan is that it would eliminate the risk (which is probably significant) that the insurance premium charged to banks would be too low, and that in the next serious crisis, taxpayers would once again suffer the losses, rather than the private banks that profited from the mortgages during the good times.

A public bank would raise funds to buy mortgages by borrowing money in the capital market (i.e., by selling bonds), the same way that private banks raise funds to finance their mortgages. But this borrowed money would not add to the government deficit, because the money would be invested in mortgages, which would eventually be recovered, together with a modest profit.

The future of Fannie and Freddie will be one of the most important economic policy issues down the road. The Left should attempt to put the public bank option on the table for discussion, and should advocate its adoption, as the best way to achieve the objective of more affordable housing for all Americans and a more stable economy. ❑

Postscript, November 2013

Five years later, the future of Fannie Mae and Freddie Mac is still undecided. President Obama proposed in a speech in August 2013 that the two government agencies be wound down over five years and replaced by a smaller government agency that would only insure mortgages and would not make mortgage loans themselves, thus leaving the housing mortgage market in the hands of private banks. In my view, this would be a significant step backward from the existing Fannie and Freddie. Therefore, my recommended "second best" option at the present time (since a fully public mortgage bank does not seem to be on the agenda) is to leave Fannie and Freddie as they are—both insuring mortgages and issuing mortgages. Dean Baker of the Center for Economic and Policy Research (CEPR) made a similar recommendation soon after Obama's speech, arguing that the goal of "promot[ing] homeownership ... can be best served with Fannie and Freddie continuing as government companies." —*Fred Moseley*

Article 5.6

THE BAILOUTS REVISITED

Who gets bailed out and why? Is there any alternative to "Too Big to Fail"?

BY MARTY WOLFSON

September/October 2009

Bank of America got bailed out, but Lehman Brothers was allowed to fail. The insurance company American International Group (AIG) was rescued, but in July federal authorities refused to bail out a significant lender to small and medium-sized businesses, the CIT Group (not to be confused with Citigroup, which did get bailed out).

What is the logic behind these decisions? Who is being bailed out—and who should be? The AIG story offers an instructive case study, one that sheds light on these and other questions.

Last September, the Federal Reserve Board announced that it was lending AIG up to $85 billion to prevent the firm's collapse. Unless it bailed out AIG, the Fed warned, financial markets could panic, loans could become more difficult to get, and many more businesses, jobs, and homes could be lost. To counter public anger over the bailout, the Fed argued that the ultimate beneficiaries would be the American people.

Citing proprietary information, AIG initially released few details about how it paid out the money it received. But this March, AIG's plan to pay $165 million in bonuses to employees at its Financial Products unit hit the headlines. An angry firestorm erupted: why should public bailout money be used to pay excessive bonuses to the very people who had caused the problem? U.S. officials and AIG CEO Edward Liddy denounced the payments as outrageous, but claimed they could not rescind the bonuses because they were bound by legal contracts. As it turned out, many AIG employees returned the bonuses voluntarily. And in a rare display of bipartisanship, the House of Representatives voted 328 to 93 to enact a 90% tax on bonuses paid to executives at companies that had received at least $5 billion in bailout money.

But the AIG bailout involved billions of dollars. The Financial Products employees only got millions. Who got the rest of the money? Under mounting public pressure, and after consulting with the Federal Reserve, AIG finally revealed who the beneficiaries were.

It's the Banks!

Yes, the money went primarily to large banks, those same banks that took their own large risks in the mortgage and derivatives markets and that are already receiving billions of dollars in federal bailout money. The banks are using AIG's bailout money to avoid taking losses on their contracts with the company.

Why did AIG, an insurance company, have such extensive dealings with the large banks, and why did those transactions cause so much trouble for AIG?

The story begins with AIG's London-based Financial Products unit, which issued a large volume of derivatives contracts known as credit default swaps (CDSs).

These were essentially insurance contracts that provided for payments to their purchasers (known as "counterparties") in the event of losses on collateralized debt obligations (CDOs), another kind of derivative. Many of the CDOs were based in complicated ways on payments on home mortgages. When the speculative housing bubble popped, mortgages could not be repaid, the CDOs lost value, and AIG was liable for payment on its CDSs.

By September 2008, AIG's situation had deteriorated to the point where its credit ratings were downgraded; this meant the company was required to post collateral on its CDS contracts, i.e., to make billions of dollars in cash payments to its counterparties to provide some protection for them against possible future losses. Despite its more than $1 trillion in assets, AIG did not have the cash. Without assistance it would have had to declare bankruptcy. After attempts to get the funding from private parties, including Goldman Sachs and JPMorgan Chase, failed, the Federal Reserve stepped in. The initial $85 billion credit line was followed by an additional $52.5 billion in credit two months later. By March 2009 the Treasury had invested $70 billion directly in the company, after which the Fed cut back its initial credit line to $25 billion.

AIG paid out those billions in several categories. Between September and December of 2008, $22.4 billion went to holders of CDSs as cash collateral. This cash was paid not only to those who sought insurance for CDOs they actually held, but also to speculators who purchased CDSs without owning the underlying securities. (Data to evaluate the extent of speculation involved had not been published by the time this article went to press.)

The largest beneficiaries of these payments were Société Générale, Deutsche Bank, Goldman Sachs, and Merrill Lynch.

Second, in an effort to stop the collateral calls on these CDSs, AIG spent $27.1 billion to purchase insured CDOs from its counterparties in return for their agreement to terminate the CDSs. Again, the largest beneficiaries of this program were Société Générale, Goldman Sachs, Merrill Lynch, and Deutsche Bank.

Third, it turned out that a significant cash drain on AIG was its securities lending program. Counterparties borrowed securities from AIG and in turn posted cash collateral with AIG. When AIG got into trouble, though, the counterparties decided that they wanted their cash back and sought to return the securities they had borrowed. However, AIG had used the cash to buy mortgage-backed securities, the same securities that were falling in value as the housing market crashed. So $43.7 billion of AIG's bailout money went to those counterparties—chiefly Barclays, Deutsche Bank, BNP Paribas, Goldman Sachs, and Bank of America, with Citigroup and Merrill Lynch not too far behind.

Necessary Bailouts?

Without all that bailout money going to the banks via AIG, wouldn't the financial system have crashed, the banks have stopped lending, and the recession have gotten worse? Well, no.

At least, the banks did not need to receive all the money they did. If a regulatory agency such as the Federal Reserve or the Federal Deposit Insurance Corporation had taken over AIG, it could have used the appropriate tools to, as Fed chair Ben

Bernanke told a House committee this March, "put AIG into conservatorship or receivership, unwind it slowly, protect policyholders, and impose haircuts on creditors and counterparties as appropriate. That outcome would have been far preferable to the situation we find ourselves in now." (A haircut in this context is a reduction in the amount a claimant will receive.)

A sudden and disruptive bankruptcy of AIG could indeed have caused a crash of the financial system, especially as it would have come just one day after the sudden fall of Lehman Brothers on September 15. It is the element of surprise and uncertainty that leads to panic in financial markets. On the other hand, an orderly takeover of AIG such as Bernanke described, with clear information on how much counterparties would be paid, likely could have avoided such a panic.

So why didn't the Federal Reserve take over AIG? It said it did not have the legal authority to take over a nonbank financial institution like AIG. Indeed, to his credit, Bernanke frequently asks for such authority when he testifies to Congress. So why didn't the Fed demand it last September? Wasn't such authority important enough to make it a condition of the bailout? And couldn't Congress have passed the necessary legislation as quickly as it passed the bank bailout bill last fall and the tax on AIG bonuses? Even if that took a few weeks, the Fed could have lent money to AIG to keep it from failing until it had the authority to take the company over.

Of course, the Fed already has the authority to take over large troubled banks—but refuses to use it. Now, Fed and Treasury officials claim that since all the major banks passed the recently administered "stress test," such takeovers are unnecessary. However, even some of the banks that passed the test were judged to be in need of more capital. If they can't get it from private markets then, according to Treasury Secretary Timothy Geithner, the government is prepared to supply them with the capital they need.

In other words, the federal government's strategy of transferring extraordinary amounts of public money to large banks that lose money on risky deals will continue. In fact, the same strategy is evident in the Treasury's proposed Public Private Investment Program, which uses public money to subsidize hedge funds and other private investors to buy toxic assets from the banks. The subsidy allows the private investors to pay a higher price to the banks for their toxic assets than the banks could have received otherwise.

Bail Out the People

The consistent principle behind this strategy is that no large bank can fail. This is why the relatively small CIT Group wasn't rescued from potential bankruptcy but Bank of America was. The decision not to bail out Lehman Brothers, which led to panic in financial markets, is now considered a mistake. However, policymakers drew the wrong lesson from the Lehman episode: that all large bank failures must be prevented. They failed to recognize the important distinction between disruptive and controlled failures.

Yes, there are banks that are too big to fail suddenly and disruptively. However, any insolvent bank, no matter what its size, should be taken over in a careful and deliberative way. If this means nationalization, then so be it. Continental Illinois

National Bank, at the time the 11th largest bank in the United States, was essentially nationalized in 1984, ending the turmoil in financial markets that Continental's difficulties had created.

This "too big to fail" strategy equates stabilizing the financial system and promoting the people's welfare with saving the corporate existence of individual large banks. Likewise the auto companies: while GM and Chrysler have been treated much more harshly than the banks, the auto bailout was similarly designed to keep these two corporate entities alive above all else, even at the expense of thousands of autoworker jobs.

The federal government's current bank-bailout strategy may be well-meaning, but there are four problems with it. It uses public money unnecessarily and is unfair to taxpayers. It may not work: it risks keeping alive "zombie banks" that are really insolvent and unwilling to lend, a recipe for repeating Japan's "lost decade" experience. It makes financial reform going forward much more difficult. Protecting the markets for derivative products like CDOs and CDSs allows for a repeat of the risky practices that got us into the current crisis. And finally, by guaranteeing the corporate existence of large banks, we are maintaining their power and priorities and thus are not likely to see gains on predatory lending, foreclosure abuse, and other areas where reform is sorely needed.

If we want to help the people who are suffering in this crisis and recession, then we should make financial policies with them directly in mind. Just throwing money at the banks will not get the job done. ❏

Article 5.7

THE SAD FUTURE OF BANKING

Reforms fail to address the "control fraud" that caused the financial crisis.

BY WILLIAM K. BLACK
October 2010

A truly amazing thing has happened in banking. After the worst financial crisis in 75 years sparked the "Great Recession," we have

- Failed to identify the real causes of the crisis;
- Failed to fix the defects that caused the crisis;
- Failed to hold the CEOs, professionals, and anti-regulators who caused the crisis accountable—even when they committed fraud;
- Bailed out the largest and worst financial firms with massive public funds;
- Covered up banking losses and failures—impairing any economic recovery;
- Degraded our integrity and made the banking system even more encouraging of fraud;
- Refused to follow policies that have proved extremely successful in past crises;
- Made the systemically dangerous institutions (SDIs) even more dangerous;
- Made our financial system even more parasitic, harming the real economy;

And pronounced this travesty a brilliant success.

The Bush and Obama administrations have made an already critically flawed financial system even worse. The result is that the banking industry's future is bad for banking, terrible for the real economy, horrific for the public—and wonderful for the top executives at the largest banks. This is significantly insane. It appears that we will need to suffer another great depression before we are willing to put aside the crippling dogmas that have so degraded the financial system, the real economy, democracy, and the ethical standards of private and public elites.

The Economics Blindfold

Why did most of the experts neither foresee nor understand the forces in the U.S. banking industry that caused this meltdown? The short answer is: their dogmatic belief in neoclassical economic theory that is impervious to the facts, or what I like to call theoclassical economics.

Neoclassical economics is premised on the asserted effectiveness of private market discipline. This (oxymoronic) discipline is the basis for the "efficient markets" and "efficient contracts" hypotheses that are the pillars of faith supporting modern finance theory and much of neoclassical microeconomics. Collectively, these hypotheses lead to absolute faith that markets exclude fraud. "A rule against fraud is not an essential or even necessarily an important ingredient of securities markets," wrote eminent corporate law scholars Frank Easterbrook and Daniel Fischel in their 1991 The Economic Structure of Corporate Law, in a typical statement of that faith.

How are markets supposed to exclude fraud? Easterbrook and Fischel offer two reasons. The first, a circular argument, lies in theoclassical economists' core belief that markets are by nature efficient. Markets that allow frauds cannot be efficient. Therefore, markets must exclude fraud.

The other argument rests on "signaling" theory. The logical premise is that honest firms have a financial incentive to signal to investors and creditors that they are honest. The false premise is that honest firms have the unique ability to signal that they are honest. Easterbrook and Fischel claim that there are three signals of honesty that only honest firms can transmit: hiring a top-tier audit firm, having the CEO own substantial stock in the firm, and operating with extreme leverage, i.e., a high ratio of debt to capital. The reality, which Fischel knew before he co-authored the treatise, was that firms engaging in so-called control fraud can mimic each of these signals. Control fraud occurs when the executives at a seemingly legitimate firm use their control to loot the firm and its shareholders and creditors. In banking, accounting is the weapon of choice for looting. Accounting control frauds have shown the consistent ability to get "clean" accounting opinions from top tier audit firms; their CEOs use their stock ownership to loot the firm; and they love to borrow extensively, as that allows them to loot the firm's creditors.

In fact, the claim that markets inherently exclude fraud runs contrary to all of our experience with securities markets. The role of epidemics of accounting control frauds in driving recent financial crises is well documented. The national commission that investigated the causes of the savings and loan debacle found that at the "typical large failure," "fraud was invariably present." Similarly, the Enron and WorldCom scandals were shown to be accounting control frauds. Savings and loan regulators used their hard-won understanding of accounting control fraud to stop a developing pattern of fraud in California in 1990-1991, involving S&Ls making so-called liar's loans. We recognized that making mortgage loans without adequate underwriting creates intense "adverse selection," i.e., it means more lending to borrowers who are not creditworthy, and that such lending was guaranteed to result in high reported (albeit fictional) income and high real losses. Theoclassical economists, however, refused to acknowledge these frauds because recognizing the existence of control fraud would challenge the assumptions underlying their faith-based economic theories.

This economic dogma was so dominant that it drove regulatory policy in the United States, Europe, and Japan during the last three decades. Regulations ignored control fraud and assumed that paper profits produced by fraud were real. The result, from the mid-1990s on, was regulatory complacency endorsed by economists who actually praised the worst of the emerging control frauds because of their high reported profits. So it is no surprise that the recent U.S. banking crisis was driven by an epidemic of lending fraud, primarily mortgage lenders making millions of "liar's loans" annually. According to Credit Suisse, for instance, 49% of all mortgage originations in 2006 were stated-income loans, meaning loans based on applicants' self-reported incomes with no verification. MARI, the Mortgage Bankers Association experts on fraud, warned in 2006 that these loans caused endemic fraud:

Stated income and reduced documentation loans … are open invitations to fraudsters. It appears that many members of the industry have little historical appreciation for the havoc created by low-doc/no-doc products that were the rage in the early 1990s. Those loans produced hundreds of millions of dollars in losses for their users.

One of MARI's customers recently reviewed a sample of 100 stated income loans upon which they had IRS Forms 4506. When the stated incomes were compared to the IRS figures, the resulting differences were dramatic. Ninety percent of the stated incomes were exaggerated by 5% or more. More disturbingly, almost 60% of the stated amounts were exaggerated by more than 50%. These results suggest that the stated income loan deserves the nickname used by many in the industry, the "liar's loan."

Why would scores of lenders specialize in making liar's loans after being warned by their own exports and even by the FBI that such loans led to endemic fraud? (Not that they needed any warnings. Bankers have known for centuries that underwriting is essential to survival in mortgage lending. Even the label "liar's loan," widely used in the industry, shows that bankers knew such loans were commonly fraudulent.) How could these fraudulent loans be sold to purportedly the most sophisticated underwriters in the history of the world at grossly inflated values blessed by the world's top audit firms? How could hundreds of thousands of fraudulent loans be pooled into securities, the now-infamous collateralized debt obligations (CDOs), and receive "AAA" ratings from the top rating agencies? How could markets that are supposed to exclude all fraud instead accommodate millions of fraudulent loans that hyper-inflated the largest financial bubble in history and triggered the Great Recession?

The answer is that making bad loans allows lenders to grow extremely rapidly and charge premium yields. This maximizes reported accounting income, which in turn boosts executive compensation and optimizes looting. The financial system is riddled with incentives so perverse that it is criminogenic—it creates fraud epidemics instead of preventing fraud. When compensation levels for banking executives and professionals are very large and based substantially on reported short-term income, financial firms become superb vehicles for control fraud. Add in deregulation and desupervision, and the result is an environment ripe for a fraud epidemic.

Accounting is the weapon of choice for financial sector control frauds. The recipe for a lender to maximize (fictional) reported accounting income has four ingredients:

1. Extremely rapid growth
2. Lending regardless of borrower creditworthiness, at premium yields
3. Extreme leverage
4. Minimal loss reserves

The first two ingredients are related. A U.S. housing lender operates in a mature, reasonably competitive industry. A mortgage lender cannot grow extremely rapidly by making high quality mortgages. If it tried to do so, it would have to cut its yield substantially in order to gain market share. Its competitors would respond by cutting their yields and the result would be modest growth and a serious loss of yield, reducing reported profits. Any lender, however, can guarantee extremely rapid growth and charge borrowers a premium yield simply by making loans to borrowers who most likely cannot repay them. Worse, hundreds of lenders can follow this same recipe because there are tens of millions of potential homebuyers in the United States who would not able to repay their loans. Indeed, when hundreds of firms follow the same recipe, they hyper-inflate the resultant financial bubble, which in turn allows borrowers to refinance their loans and thereby delay their defaults for years.

Economists George Akerlof and Paul Romer explained in 1993 that accounting fraud is a "sure thing" and explained why it caused bubbles to hyper-inflate, then burst. Note that the same recipe that produces record fictional income in the short-term eventually produces catastrophic real losses. The lender will fail (unless it is bailed out or able to sell to the "greater fool"), but with their compensation largely based on reported income, the senior officers can walk away wealthy. This paradox—the CEO prospers by causing the firm's collapse—explains Akerlof and Romer's title, Looting: The Economic Underworld of Bankruptcy for Profit.

Senior executives can also use their ability to hire, promote, compensate, and fire to suborn employees, officers, and outside professionals. As Franklin Raines, chairman and CEO of Fannie Mae, explained to *Businessweek* in 2003:

> Investment banking is a business that's so denominated in dollars that the temptations are great, so you have to have very strong rules. My experience is where there is a one-to-one relation between if I do X, money will hit my pocket, you tend to see people doing X a lot. You've got to be very careful about that. Don't just say: "If you hit this revenue number, your bonus is going to be this." It sets up an incentive that's overwhelming. You wave enough money in front of people, and good people will do bad things.

Raines knew what he was talking about: he installed a compensation system at Fannie Mae that produced precisely these perverse incentives among his staff and made him wealthy by taking actions that harmed Fannie Mae.

In an earlier work, Akerlof had explained how firms that gained a competitive advantage through fraud could cause a "Gresham's" dynamic in which bad ethics drove good ethics from the marketplace. The national commission that investigated the savings and loan debacle documented this criminogenic dynamic: "[A]busive operators of S&L[s] sought out compliant and cooperative accountants. The result was a sort of "Gresham's Law" in which the bad professionals forced out the good." The same dynamic was documented by N.Y. Attorney General Andrew Cuomo's 2007 investigation of appraisal fraud, which found that Washington Mutual blacklisted appraisers who refused to inflate appraisals. An honest secured lender would never inflate, or permit the inflation of, appraisals.

Failure to Respond

The U.S. government's response to the meltdown has been not merely inadequate, but actually perverse. The Bush and Obama administrations' banking regulators have left frauds in charge of failed banks and covered up the banks' losses, allowed the behemoths of the industry to become even larger and more dangerous, and passed a "reform" law that fails to mandate the most critical reforms.

In March 2009, Congress, with the explicit encouragement of Federal Reserve Board Chairman Bernanke and the implicit acceptance of the Obama administration, successfully extorted the Financial Accounting Standards Board on behalf of the banking industry to force it to change the banking rules so that banks did not have to recognize losses on their bad assets until they sold them. Normal accounting rules sensibly require banks to recognize losses on bad loans when the problems with the loans are not "temporary." The losses at issue in the recent crisis were caused by system-wide fraud and the collapse of the largest financial bubble in world history. They were not temporary—moreover, they were (and are) massive. If banks had recognized these losses as they were required to do under pre-existing accounting rules, many of them would have had to report that they were unprofitable, badly undercapitalized, or even insolvent.

Gimmicking the accounting rules so bankers could lie about their asset values has caused the usual severe problems. First, it allows CEOs to pretend that unprofitable banks are profitable and so continue to pay themselves massive bonuses. This is not only unfair; it contributes to a broadly criminogenic environment. Second, it leads banks to hold onto bad home loans and other assets at grossly inflated prices, preventing markets from clearing and prolonging the recession. This is the Japanese scenario that led to the country's "lost decade" (now extended). Third, it makes it harder for regulators to supervise vigorously, should they try to do so, because many regulatory powers are triggered only when losses occur with the resulting failure to meet capital requirements. Indeed, the assault on honest accounting was launched with the express purpose of evading the Prompt Corrective Action law, passed in 1991 on the basis of bitter experience: when savings-and-loan CEOs who had looted "their" institutions were allowed to remain in control of them by using fraudulent accounting, the losses and the fallout of the S&L crisis kept growing. Fourth, it embraces dishonesty as an official policy. Indeed, it implies that the solution to the accounting fraud that massively inflated asset valuations is to change the accounting rules to encourage the massive inflation of those same asset values. Effective regulation is impossible without regulatory integrity; lying about asset values destroys integrity.

Even in the case of the roughly 20 massive U.S. financial institutions considered "too big to fail," the public policy response has been perverse. (The Bush and Obama administrations and their economists have claimed that if any of these giant banks were to fail, it would cause a systemic global crisis, hence the "too big to fail" moniker. I am dubious that a systemic crisis would inevitably result, but I agree that these banks are so large that they pose a systemic danger to the global economy.) The terminology itself demonstrates how economists err in their analysis—and how much they identify with the CEOs who helped cause the Great Recession. They refer to the largest banks as "systemically important institutions," as if these banks deserved gold stars. By the prevailing logic, however, the massive banks are the opposite. They are ticking time bombs that can take down the global financial system if they fail. So "systemically dangerous institutions," or SDIs, would be more apt.

It should be a top public policy priority to end the ability of any single bank to pose a global systemic risk. That means that the SDIs should be forbidden to grow, required to shrink over a five-year period to a size at which they no longer pose a systemic risk, and intensively supervised until they shrink to that size. In particular, regulation of the SDIs must end the existing perverse incentives that are so criminogenic—executive compensation systems tied to short-term reported income, the accounting cover-up which has gutted the Prompt Corrective Action law, the use of compensation and hiring and firing powers to create a "Gresham's" dynamic among the SDIs' personnel and outside professionals, and the use of political contributions to impair effective regulation. These reforms are vital for all banks but particularly urgent for the SDIs, with their potential to cause massive damage.

Instead, the opposite has been done. Both administrations have responded to the financial crisis by allowing (indeed, encouraging) SDIs, even insolvent ones, to acquire other failed financial firms and become even larger and more systemically dangerous to the global economy. The SDIs' already perverse incentives were made worse by giving them a bailout plus the accounting cover-up of their losses on terms that made the U.S. Treasury and the Federal Reserve the "fools" in the market.

With small- and medium-size banks likely to continue to fail in high numbers due to residential and commercial real estate losses, the financial crisis has increased the long-term trend toward extreme concentration in the financial industry. The SDIs will pursue diverse business strategies. Some will continue their current strategy of borrowing short-term at extremely low interest rates and reinvesting the proceeds primarily in government bonds. They will earn material, not exceptional, profits but will do little to help the real economy recover. Others will invest in whatever asset category offers the best (often fictional) accounting income. They will drive the next U.S.-based crisis.

What about the long-awaited bank reform law, which Congress finally delivered in July 2010 in the form of the Dodd-Frank Act? The law does not address the fundamental factors that have caused recurrent, intensifying financial crises: fraud, accounting, executive and professional compensation, and regulatory failure. Instead, it deals primarily with the excuses Treasury Secretary Paulson and Federal Reserve Chairman Bernanke offered for their failures. The new law gives regulators (weak) authority to place a failing SDI in receivership. Paulson and Bernanke claimed they had no legal authority to place Lehman in receivership, but they did not place insolvent megabanks over which they had clear legal authority in receivership either. The Bush administration's problem was always a lack of regulatory will, not a lack of authority. The Dodd-Frank Act also creates a regulatory council that is supposed to identify systemic risks. The council, however, will be dominated by economists of the same theoclassical stripe who not only failed to identify the systemic risks that produced the modern financial crises that this essay discusses, but actually praised the criminogenic incentives that caused those crises. The most hopeful part of the Dodd-Frank Act is the creation of a bureau with the mission of protecting financial consumers. No one can predict at this juncture whether it will accomplish its mission.

The chief international reform, the Basel III accord, shares the fundamental deficiency of the Dodd-Frank Act. Dominated as they were by theoclassical economists, the Basel negotiations not surprisingly produced an agreement that ignores the underlying causes of the crisis. Instead, it focuses on one symptom of the crisis—extreme leverage, the third ingredient of the recipe for optimizing accounting control fraud. The remedy was to restore capital requirements to roughly the levels required under Basel I (Basel II eviscerated European banks' capital requirements). Fortunately, the U.S. did not fully implement the Basel II capital reserve reductions, which means that the leverage of non-fraudulent U.S. banks has been significantly lower than their European counterparts. However, capital requirements only have meaning under honest accounting. Once one takes into account the fictional "capital" produced by the accounting fraud that first massively inflated asset values and now hides the losses—along with the revised accounting rules that will be exploited to create fictional income in the future—the irrelevance of the proposed Basel III capital requirements becomes clear.

If the Dodd-Frank Act of 2010 and the Basel III proposals are the limits of our response to the crisis, then the most probable outcome in the near- and medium-term is the Japanese scenario—a weak, delayed, and transitory recovery followed by periodic recessions. Banks will remain weak and a poor provider of capital for economic expansion.

With private market "discipline" having become criminogenic, the only hope for preventing the current crisis was vigorous regulation and supervision. Unfortunately, the dogmatic belief that markets automatically prevent fraud led to complacency and the appointment of anti-regulators chosen for their willingness to praise and serve their banking "customers." (The "reinventing government" initiative championed by former Vice President Al Gore and by George W. Bush when he was Texas' governor indeed instructed banking regulators to refer to bankers as their "customers.") President Obama has generally left in office, reappointed, or promoted the heads (or their "acting" successors) of the Office of the Comptroller of the Currency, the Office of Thrift Supervision, the Federal Reserve, the Federal Reserve Bank of New York, and the Federal Housing Finance Agency. Several of these leaders did not simply fail as federal regulators; they actually made things worse by aggressively preempting state regulatory efforts against fraudulent and predatory mortgage lenders.

None of the reforms to date addresses the fundamental criminogenic incentive structures that have produced recurrent, intensifying financial crises. True, liar's loans have been largely eliminated, and in 2008 the Federal Reserve finally used its regulatory authority under the Home Ownership and Equity Protection Act of 1994 to regulate mortgage bankers (after most of the worst ones had failed), but none of this came soon enough to contain the current crisis and none of it will prevent the next one. The accounting control frauds merely need to switch to a different asset category for a time. ❑

Sources: George A. Akerlof, "The Market for 'Lemons': Quality Uncertainty and the Market Mechanism," Quarterly Journal of Economics 84(3):488–500 (1970); George A. Akerlof and Paul G. Romer, "Looting: The Economic Underworld of Bankruptcy for Profit," in W. Brainard and G. Perry, eds., Brookings Papers on Economic Activity 2:1-73 (1993); William K. Black, "Reexamining the Law-and-Economics Theory of Corporate Governance," Challenge 46(2):22-40 (2003); William K. Black, *The Best Way to Rob a Bank Is to Own One: How Corporate Executives and Politicians Looted the S&L Industry*, Austin: University of Texas Press (2005); Frank Easterbrook and Daniel Fischel, *The Economic Structure of Corporate Law*, Cambridge, Mass.: Harvard University Press (1991); National Commission on Financial Institution Reform, Recovery and Enforcement (NCFIRRE), *Origins and Causes of the S&L Debacle: A Blueprint for Reform*, Washington, D.C.: Government Printing Office (1993).

Article 5.8

WE'RE ALL MINSKYITES NOW

BY ROBERT POLLIN
October 2008; The Nation

As the most severe financial crisis since the 1930s Depression has unfolded over the past eighteen months, the ideas of the late economist Hyman Minsky have suddenly come into fashion. In the summer of 2007, the Wall Street Journal ran a front-page article describing the emerging crisis as the financial market's "Minsky moment." His ideas have since been featured in the Financial Times, BusinessWeek and The New Yorker, among many other outlets. Minsky, who spent most of his academic career at Washington University in St. Louis and remained professionally active until his death, in 1996, deserves the recognition. He was his generation's most insightful analyst of financial markets and the causes of financial crises.

Even so, most mainstream economists have shunned his work because it emerged out of a dissident left Keynesian tradition known in economists' circles as post-Keynesianism. Minsky's writings, and the post-Keynesian tradition more generally, are highly critical of free-market capitalism and its defenders in the economics profession—among them Milton Friedman and other Nobel Prize-winning economists who for a generation have claimed to "prove," usually through elaborate mathematical models, that unregulated markets are inherently rational, stable and fair. For Friedmanites, regulations are harmful most of the time.

Minsky, by contrast, explained throughout his voluminous writings that unregulated markets will always produce instability and crises. He alternately termed his approach "the financial instability hypothesis" and "the Wall Street paradigm."

For Minsky, the key to understanding financial instability is to trace the shifts that occur in investors' psychology as the economy moves out of a period of crisis and recession (or depression) and into a phase of rising profits and growth. Coming out of a crisis, investors will tend to be cautious, since many of them will have been clobbered during the just-ended recession. For example, they will hold large cash reserves as a cushion to protect against future crises.

But as the economy emerges from its slump and profits rise, investors' expectations become increasingly positive. They become eager to pursue risky ideas such as securitized subprime mortgage loans. They also become more willing to let their cash reserves dwindle, since idle cash earns no profits, while purchasing speculative vehicles like subprime mortgage securities that can produce returns of 10% or higher.

But these moves also mean that investors are weakening their defenses against the next downturn. This is why, in Minsky's view, economic upswings, proceeding without regulations, inevitably encourage speculative excesses in which financial bubbles emerge. Minsky explained that in an unregulated environment, the only way to stop bubbles is to let them burst. Financial markets then fall into a crisis, and a recession or depression ensues.

Here we reach one of Minsky's crucial insights—that financial crises and recessions actually serve a purpose in the operations of a free-market economy, even while they wreak havoc with people's lives, including those of tens of millions of innocents who never invest a dime on Wall Street. Minsky's point is that without crises, a free-market economy has no way of discouraging investors' natural proclivities toward ever greater risks in pursuit of ever higher profits.

However, in the wake of the calamitous Great Depression, Keynesian economists tried to design measures that could supplant financial crises as the system's "natural" regulator. This was the context in which the post-World War II system of big-government capitalism was created. The package included two basic elements: regulations designed to limit speculation and channel financial resources into socially useful investments, such as single-family housing; and government bailout operations to prevent 1930s-style depressions when crises broke out anyway.

Minsky argues that the system of regulations and the bailout operations were largely successful. That is why from the end of World War II to the mid-1970s, markets here and abroad were much more stable than in any previous historical period. But even during the New Deal years, financial market titans were fighting vehemently to eliminate, or at least defang, the regulations. By the 1970s, almost all politicians—Democrats and Republicans alike—had become compliant. The regulations were initially weakened, then abolished altogether, under the strong guidance of, among others, Federal Reserve chair Alan Greenspan, Republican Senator Phil Gramm and Clinton Treasury Secretary Robert Rubin.

For Minsky, the consequences were predictable. Consider the scorecard over the twenty years before the current disaster: a stock market crash in 1987; the savings-and-loan crisis and bailout in 1989-90; the "emerging markets" crisis of 1997-98—which brought down, among others, Long-Term Capital Management, the super-hedge fund led by two Nobel laureates specializing in finance—and the bursting of the dot-com market bubble in 2001. Each of these crises could easily have produced a 1930s-style collapse in the absence of full-scale government bailout operations.

Here we come to another of Minsky's major insights—that in the absence of a complementary regulatory system, the effectiveness of bailouts will diminish over time. This is because bailouts, just like financial crises, are double-edged. They prevent depressions, but they also limit the costs to speculators of their financial excesses. As soon as the next economic expansion begins gathering strength, speculators will therefore pursue profit opportunities more or less as they had during the previous cycle. This is the pattern that has brought us to our current situation—a massive global crisis, being countered by an equally massive bailout of thus far limited effectiveness.

Minsky's Wall Street paradigm did not address all the afflictions of free-market capitalism. In particular, his model neglects the problems that arise from the vast disparities of income, wealth and power that are just as endemic to free-market capitalism as are its tendencies toward financial instability, even though he fully recognized that these problems exist.

Yet Minsky's approach still provides the most powerful lens for understanding the roots of financial instability and developing an effective regulatory system.

Minsky understood that his advocacy of comprehensive financial regulations made no sense whatsoever within the prevailing professional orthodoxy of free-market cheerleading. In his 1986 magnum opus, *Stabilizing an Unstable Economy*, he concluded that "the policy failures since the mid-1960s are related to the banality of orthodox economic analysis.... Only an economics that is critical of capitalism can be a guide to successful policy for capitalism." ❏

Article 5.9

GREECE AND THE EUROZONE CRISIS BY THE NUMBERS

BY GERALD FRIEDMAN
July/August 2012

With its surging debt and sinking economy, Greece has been held up as the poster-child for the need for fiscal discipline and austerity. Instead, it should be seen as a case study in the danger of neoliberal financial integration. Greece's economic problems stem from its joining the eurozone, a single-currency region where monetary policy is managed by a largely independent European Central Bank (ECB). The ECB is based in Frankfurt, Germany, and is committed to maintaining stable prices without regard for levels of unemployment or economic growth. Within the eurozone, Greek industry has been unable to compete with its German competitors. If Greece had retained an independent currency, it could have maintained balanced trade and supported domestic industries and employment by devaluing its currency. Membership in the European Union and the eurozone, though, prevents Greece from adjusting its currency value or otherwise imposing trade restraints, even in the face of a rising tide of German imports which have devastated much of Greek industry.

ANNUAL TRADE BALANCE, PERCENTAGE OF GDP, GERMANY AND GREECE, 1996-2010

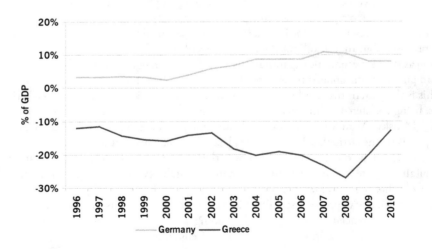

Greece's trade deficits were financed by borrowing, including deposits in Greek banks from Germany and other northern European countries. When the financial crisis began in 2008, however, these countries sought to pull their deposits out of Greek banks and reduce their lending. If Greece had an independent central bank, as it did before joining the euro, that bank would provide liquidity to replace these financial flows and thus guarantee the stability of the Greek banking system. But Greece gave up its own independent monetary authority when it joined the eurozone. Instead, the ECB has used the Greek financial crisis as a tool to drive down Greek wages and living standards.

Binding southern Europe with Germany has allowed Germany to run extraordinary trade surpluses with these other countries. For seven years after 2001, capital flows from Germany balanced German trade surpluses. However, Germany's trade surplus soared with the establishment of the euro in 2002. Most of this surplus was with its eurozone partners, who, without independent currencies, could not adjust to balance their trade.

Greece had a trade deficit even before joining the eurozone, but its deficit soared after it adopted the euro. Germany's surplus and Greece's deficits were balanced with borrowing when Greek banks accepted large deposits from Germans and others.

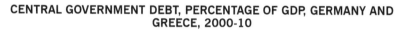

CENTRAL GOVERNMENT DEBT, PERCENTAGE OF GDP, GERMANY AND GREECE, 2000-10

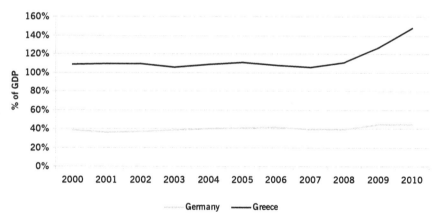

Throughout the 2000s, the Greek government had a relatively high debt burden but remained stable before the economic crisis. Due to falling tax revenues and increased need for government services during the crisis, Greece experienced a sharp rise in its government deficit. Forcing austerity on Greece to stabilize its financial system has led to soaring unemployment. This has led to falling tax revenues and rising expenditures for unemployment relief, which have actually increased the government deficit.

AVERAGE USUAL HOURS WORKED (WEEKLY), EU MEMBERS, 2011

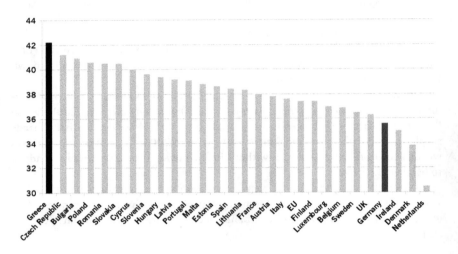

Greece's recent economic troubles come despite the country's work ethic. Relatively poor compared with others in the European Union, Greeks work more hours per week than workers in any other EU member country. By contrast, the relatively affluent Germans work about six hours a week less than the Greeks, and have many more vacation days. ❏

Sources: OECD.stat data base for gross domestic product, government deficits, and unemployment. Eurostat data base for hours worked. International Monetary Fund for trade data.

Chapter 6

RETIREMENT FINANCE

Article 6.1

SOCIAL SECURITY Q&A: SEPARATING FACT FROM FICTION

BY DOUG ORR
May/June 2005; revised October 2010

Is *Social Security going to go bankrupt? I heard that;s going to happen sooner than previously expected.*

Bankruptcy is defined as "the inability to pay ones debts" or, when applied to a business, "shutting down as a result of insolvency." Nothing the Social Security trustees have said or published indicates that Social Security will fold as a result of insolvency.

Until 1984, the system was "pay-as-you-go," meaning current benefits were paid using current tax revenues. In 1984, Congress raised payroll taxes to prepare for the retirement of the baby-boom generation. As a result, the Social Security trust fund, which holds government bonds as assets, grew over time. As the baby boomers retire, these bonds will be sold to help pay their retirement benefits.

Until recently, it appeared that, under reasonably optimistic assumptions about the future of the economy, the trust fund would never run out. The Social Security trustees' report for 2013, however, for the first time shows the trust fund going to zero—in 2068. There are two main reasons:

First, as part of the economic "stimulus" response to the recent recession, the federal government temporarily reduced employee contributions into Social Security from 6.25 to 4.25%. For two years, the tax cut put money in people's pockets, which helped shore up the economy, but it put a big dent in the trust fund. Republicans blocked every proposal for a middle-class tax cut except that one. They went along because they knew a depleted trust fund would help them in their ongoing attack on Social Security as a "broken" system.

Second, the trust fund is only allowed to purchase Treasury bonds. Those bonds have been paying record low interest rates for almost five years, as a result of Federal Reserve policies. These policies were aimed to reduce interest rates to businesses and consumers, and help stimulate spending and economic growth. As an unintended side effect, however, the trust fund has been growing much more slowly than previously projected. Combined, these two effects have lowered the trust fund well below its projected value from even five years ago.

All of this fits nicely into Republican hopes for a "Grand Bargain" that will finally destroy Social Security. Fortunately, so far Democratic leaders have diverted every maneuver aimed at Social Security in the conference committee on the budget.

Even if the trust fund went to zero, however, the consequences would hardly be dire. Social Security would simply revert to pay-as-you-go. It would continue to pay benefits using (then-current) tax revenues, and in doing so, it would be able to cover about 70% of promised benefit levels. According to analysis by the Center for Economic and Policy Research, a 70% benefit level then would actually be higher than 2005 benefit levels in constant dollars (because of wage adjustments). In other words, retirees would be taking home more in real terms than today's retirees do. The system won't be bankrupt in any sense.

I keep hearing about having too few workers to support all the retirees in Social Security. Is that true?

Opponents of Social Security have hated it since its creation in 1935. The first prediction of a Social Security crisis was published in 1936! The Heritage Foundation and Cato Institute are home to many of the program's opponents today, and they fixate on the concept of a "demographic imperative." In 1960, the United States had 5.1 workers per retiree, in 1998 we had 3.4, and by 2030 we will have only 2.1. Opponents claim that with these demographic changes, revenues will eventually be insufficient to pay Social Security retirement benefits.

The logic is appealingly simple, but wrong for two reasons. First, this "old-age dependency" ratio in itself is irrelevant. No amount of financial manipulation can change this fact: all current consumption must come from current physical output. The consumption of all dependents (non-workers) must come from the output produced by current workers. It's the "overall dependency ratio"—the number of workers relative to all non-workers, including the aged, the young, the disabled, and those choosing not to work—that determines whether society can "afford" the baby boomers' retirement years. In the 1960s we had only 0.62 workers for each dependent, and we were building new schools and the interstate highway system and getting ready to put a man on the moon. No one bemoaned a demographic crisis or looked for ways to cut the resources allocated to children; in fact, the living standards of most families rose rapidly. In 2030, we will have 0.98 workers per dependent. We'll have more workers per dependent in the future than we did in the past. While it is true a larger share of total output will be allocated to the aged, just as a larger share was allocated to children in the 1960s, society will easily produce adequate output to support all workers and dependents, and at a higher standard of living.

Second, the "demographic imperative" ignores productivity growth. Average worker productivity has grown by about 2% per year, adjusted for inflation, for the past half-century. That means real output per worker doubles every 36 years. This productivity growth is projected to continue, so by 2040, each worker will produce twice as much as today. Suppose each of three workers today produces $1,000 of real output per week and one retiree is allocated $500 (half of his final salary)—then each worker gets $833. In 2040, two such workers will produce $2,000 real output per week each (real output adjusts for inflation). If each retiree gets $1,000, each worker still gets $1,500. The consumption levels of both workers and retirees go up. Thus, paying for the baby boomers' retirement need not decrease their children's standard of living. A larger share of output going to retirees does not imply that the standard of living of those still working will be lower. Those still working will have a slightly smaller share of a much larger pie.

So that means that there is no funding problem for Social Security?

Not exactly. When the Greenspan Commission (yes, the same Alan Greenspan who helped created the current financial crisis) raised Social Security tax rates in 1984, it claimed that this would solve the funding problem far into the future. Based on past experience that would have been true. Social Security tax revenues are based on the level of wages paid, and historically, real wages (wages adjusted for the effects of inflation) had been growing along with productivity. This is what mainstream economic theory tells us is supposed to happen. But starting in the early 1980s, real wages actually started falling, even as productivity continued to increase. By 2009, the average real wage was just $16.40 (in 2005 dollars), exactly the same as it had been in 1966. So while labor productivity is now more than twice as high, wages have stagnated. If the wage had continued to grow with productivity, the real wage in 2009 would have been $38.50, more than twice as much. If wages paid in 2010 were twice as high as they currently are, the revenues flowing into the Social Security system would also be twice as high. But stagnating wages have put a strain on the system.

How can we address the funding gap that some people claim is going to occur?

One change would be to remove the cap on the Social Security payroll tax. A second option is to follow the lead of other industrialized countries. Social Security funding currently relies on taxing only wage and salary incomes. Over the past three decades, as corporations have driven down the real wages of the vast majority (80%) of employees, the share of total national income going to wages and salaries has declined, and the share going to capital income (from financial assets) has gone up. This erosion of the wage share of total income has reduced the share of total income flowing into the Social Security system. The retirement systems of the rest of the industrialized world are funded out of general tax revenues. The logic is that everyone in society benefits from the efforts of workers, so all should contribute to the support of retired workers. In the two years after the end of the recession in 2001, real wages had gone up by only 2.8%, but corporate profits had gone up by 62.8%. If we expand the Social Security tax to cover all forms of income, the revenue from this vastly increased profit income would allow the tax rate on wages to be significantly lower. This would provide an enormous benefit to small businesses and the self-employed as well as to everyone who works for wages and salaries.

Are there other, more creative, funding ideas?

Yes, but Congress is not even discussing one key idea—a "speculation reduction tax." When we buy a jacket, we pay a sales tax, but when a speculator buys a share of stock, or a collateralized debt obligation (CDO), or a credit default swap, they pay no tax at all. The current economic crisis in the United States was precipitated by massive increases in speculation in the financial sector of the economy in ever more exotic financial instruments. One goal of the ongoing re-regulation of that sector is to reduce this speculation. A speculation reduction tax could solve two problems at once. Many economists, both conservative and liberal, support the idea of a tax on speculation in the financial markets. This is often called a "Tobin tax" after one of its proponents. The tax rate would not have to be very high to have a big impact. The tax rate could go down as the length of time the asset is held goes up. If a speculator buys a stock or CDO and holds it less than a day, the tax could be 5% of the selling price. If they hold it a week, it could be 2%. If they hold it a month it could be one percent, and so on. One recent estimate indicates that a flat rate of just 0.5% on all financial transactions would raise more than $145 billion per year, which is twice the size of the projected Social Security shortfall. If all of this revenue were dedicated to Social Security, the system would be solvent indefinitely. In fact the surplus in the system would be so large we would need to lower the tax rate on wages and raise the level of retirement benefits paid.

I hear the trust fund is just a bunch of government IOUs and therefore worthless. Is this true?

When the trust fund was created in 1935, the law stipulated that any excess revenues coming into the Social Security system must be used to purchase federal government bonds. (At the time, the stock market had just lost over 75% of its value and was understood to be unsafe.) So the trust fund does just contain IOUs, but they're not worthless. If they were, someone should tell that to the very smart and very rich people, and the central banks of Japan, China, and many other countries that hold a large share of their assets in U.S. government bonds.

Federal bonds have historically been considered absolutely safe; the government of the United States has never defaulted on any bond obligation. Recently, however, Republicans in Congress have threatened such default, by holding out on raising the government "debt ceiling," most recently in hopes of rolling back the Affordable Care Act (also known as "Obamacare"). That the U.S. government might not be willing to repay its debt obligations is remarkable and, when it arises as an immediate possibility, threatens to disrupt global financial markets.

Shouldn't we consider benefit cuts today to help prevent a potential shortfall in the future?

Congress, correctly, has not been willing to cut benefits. They don't need to, and they shouldn't. Telling your kids today that they only get to eat one plate of rice each day and have to get their clothes at Goodwill because there is a chance that you might lose your job 50 years from now would be irrational. It would be equally irrational to implement benefit cuts immediately on the chance that the trust fund might go to zero in 2068—especially when future recipients would still be getting more in real terms than recipients do today.

How about lowering benefits to wealthy people, who don't really need Social Security, or indexing benefits to prices rather than to wages as is done now? Are those good ideas?

Lowering benefits just for the wealthy is a bad idea. That's like proposing that, after an accident, someone who drives a Lexus should only get half of the replacement value of their car, while someone who drives a Ford Focus should get the full replacement value. Social Security is a universal insurance system. This change would make the system less universal and pit one group of workers against another.

As for indexation, the formula for Social Security benefits in the first year of retirement is based on an average of the worker's wages over a 35-year period, accounting for productivity increases and for inflation. Productivity is figured in by adjusting the worker's earnings by the change in average annual wages. In effect, the worker's own 35-year average wage is recalculated as if it had been earned in the three years before retirement.

When the opponents of Social Security proposed indexing initial Social Security benefits only to price increases, they were really suggesting stripping out the part of wage increases that result from rising productivity and only allowing for inflation. It's the equivalent of linking your retirement benefits to the very first job you take, rather than the job you hold at retirement. It freezes your retirement standard of living at whatever the standard of living was when you entered the workforce. If this "price indexing" approach were implemented, future retirees would see their retirement income drastically reduced.

Under current law, once you retire, your benefit is adjusted annually for inflation but not for the change in wages since your retirement. This cost of living adjustment (COLA), based on the inflation rate, helps maintain retirees' standard of living at the level they had when they retired, although their standard of living slowly falls behind that of the rest of society as the overall standard of living rises with productivity. Without the COLA, the individual's standard of living would fall even below what it was when he or she retired.

Several countries have converted their public pension systems to private accounts. Would that be a good idea for the United States?
The British experiment with private accounts has failed to provide an adequate and stable retirement income for the majority of citizens. The United Kingdom is now trying to figure out how to switch back to a defined-benefit system of retirement insurance. The problem is that the trillions of pounds that were diverted into the stock market can't be brought back into the defined-benefit system.

In Chile, under the military dictatorship that ruled the country from 1973 to 1989, workers were encouraged to opt out of the system of pension insurance and into private accounts. Over the past 25 years, the return on stocks in Chile has averaged over 10%—a higher return than we can expect in the U.S. stock market over the next 25 years. Yet, even with that extremely high rate of return, the average Chilean retiree relying on private savings will receive a benefit less than half as large as someone who had remained in the old system, and those benefits, unlike those of the old system, last only 20 years. If a retiree is "unlucky" enough to live longer than that, he will simply run out of retirement income. Those in the old system not only receive a higher benefit, but the benefit lasts as long as they live and continues to provide benefits to their surviving spouse.

A recent survey shows that 90% of Chileans who opted for the private accounts wish they had remained in the old system. The only people who have benefited by the new system are the wealthiest top 2% of the population.

The United States' Social Security system is the most efficiently run insurance program in the world, with overhead of only 0.7% of annual benefits. For every $100 paid into the system, $99.30 is paid out in benefits to retirees. In the British and Chilean systems, at retirement, workers convert their private accounts to annuities provided by private insurance companies. In the United States, overhead for annuities provided by private firms average about 20%; for every $100 paid in, $20 gets siphoned off. And almost no annuities are indexed for inflation.

There is a third important experiment with "private accounts" to consider: the United States' own experiment with defined-contribution retirement plans. Since 1975, corporations have been phasing out their old defined-benefit pensions and replacing them with private savings accounts such as 401(k)s. In 1975, 39% of private-sector workers were covered by defined-benefit pensions, and only 6% by defined-contribution savings plans. By 1998 the share covered by real pensions had plummeted to just 18% and the percent relying on private accounts had risen to 38%.

What has this rapid reversal done to retirement income security? A 2002 study by New York University economist Edward Wolff defines retirement income insecurity as having less than half of your final working income in your first year of retirement. In 1989, less than 30% of workers aged 47 to 64 faced retirement income insecurity. Yet by 1999, after the shift to greater reliance on private accounts, even after the most rapid run-up in stock values in U.S. history, almost 43% of workers in this age group faced retirement income insecurity. It has gotten worse since then as a result of the stock market crashes of 2001 and 2007. Private accounts are both risky and unstable. An increasing number of members of the "baby-boom" generation are delaying retirement because they do not have adequate retirement income.

We don't have to look to other countries to see the results of a shift to private accounts. That experiment has already been tried in the United States, and it failed.

How would the U.S. economy be affected if private accounts replaced the current system?

Put simply, moving to a system of private accounts would not only put retirement income at risk—it would likely put the entire economy at risk.

The current Social Security system generates powerful, economy-stimulating multiplier effects. This was part of its original intent. In the early 1930s, the vast majority of the elderly were poor. While they were working, they could not afford to both save for retirement and put food on the table, and most had no employer pension. When Social Security began, elders spent every penny of that income. In turn, each dollar they spent was spent again by the people and businesses from whom they had bought things. In much the same way, every dollar that goes out in pensions today creates about 2.5 times as much total income. If the move to private accounts reduces elders' spending levels, as almost all analysts predict, that reduction in spending will have an even larger impact on slowing economic growth.

The current Social Security system also reduces the income disparity between the rich and the poor. Private accounts would increase inequality—and increased inequality hinders economic growth. For example, a 1994 World Bank study of 25 countries demonstrated that as income inequality rises, productivity growth is reduced. Market economies can fall apart completely if the level of inequality becomes too extreme. The rapid increase in income inequality that occurred in the 1920s was one of the causes of the Great Depression. And the rapid increase in inequality under the Reagan and two Bush administrations was one of the causes of the current "Great Recession."

Young people say they want more control over their Social Security investments. How do you explain the purpose of Social Security to today's young workers?
The best way to explain Social Security is to say what it is. It's an insurance system that protects your income when you retire or face disability, and provides income to your children if you die. Former President Bush wanted you to look at Social Security as an investment, but it is not. It is a form of insurance that guarantees you a constant stream of income in retirement or in case of disability, adjusted to protect against inflation, for as long as you live.

Social Security can be compared to other types of insurance such as home insurance. You insure your home because if it should burn down, you would not be able to afford to rebuild it with your personal income alone. If your house never burns down, you will pay into the insurance fund and never get a penny back. But fire insurance isn't a "bad investment" because it isn't an investment at all. You are purchasing security.

Unlike fire insurance, Social Security inevitably gives most of us our money back. But the fact that we get money back does not change the fact that Social Security is a form of insurance, not an investment. Only the richest of the rich can afford not to have insurance and to rely solely on their own savings and investments to fund their retirement or risk of disability.

Young people must also understand that financial investments are a form of speculation and inherently risky. Many financial investments fail, and when they do, you lose money. Today's 25-year-olds have only seen the stock market go up, except for two (very large) drops. But you don't have to go back to the 1930s to see a different picture: If you put money into the stock market in 1970 and waited until 1980 to take it out, you would have lost money. There is absolutely no guarantee that stock speculators will see the high returns those who support private accounts are falsely promising. ❏

Article 6.2

AFRICAN AMERICANS AND SOCIAL SECURITY
Why the Privatization Advocates Are Wrong

BY WILLIAM E. SPRIGGS
November/December 2004

Proponents of Social Security privatization are trying to claim that the current program is unfair to African Americans and that a privatized program would serve African Americans better. This argument lends support to the privatization agenda while at the same time giving its advocates a compassionate gloss. But the claims about African Americans and Social Security are wrong.

The Old Age Survivors and Disability Insurance Program (OASDI), popularly known as Social Security, was put in place by Franklin Roosevelt to establish a solid bulwark of economic rights for the public—specifically, as he put it, "the right to adequate protection from the economic fears of old age, sickness, accident, and unemployment." Most Americans associate Social Security only with the retirement—or old age—benefit. Yet it was created to do much more, and it does.

As its original name suggests, Social Security is an insurance program that protects workers and their families against the income loss that occurs when a worker retires, becomes disabled, or dies. All workers will eventually either grow too old to compete in the labor market, become disabled, or die. OASDI insures all workers and their families against these universal risks, while spreading the costs and benefits of that insurance protection among the entire workforce. Currently, 70% of Social Security funds go to retirees, 15% to disabled workers, and 15% to survivors.

Social Security is a "pay as you go" system, which means the taxes paid by today's workers are not set aside to pay their own benefits down the road, but rather go to pay the benefits of current Social Security recipients. It's financed using the Federal Insurance Contribution Act (or FICA) payroll tax, paid by all working Americans on earnings of less than about $90,000 a year. While the payroll tax is not progressive, Social Security benefits are—that is, low-wage workers receive a greater percentage of pre-retirement earnings from the program than higher-wage workers.

In the 1980s, recognizing that the baby boom generation would strain this system, Congress passed reforms to raise extra tax revenues above and beyond the current need and set up a trust fund to hold the reserve. Trustees were appointed and charged with keeping Social Security solvent. Today's trustees warn that their projections, which are based on modest assumptions about the long-term growth of the U.S. economy, show the system could face a shortfall around 2042, when either benefits would have to be cut or the FICA tax raised.

Those who oppose the social nature of the program have pounced on its projected shortfall in revenues to argue that the program cannot—or ought not—be fixed, but should instead be fundamentally changed (see box, "Privatization Advocates"). Privatization proponents are seeking to frame the issue as a matter of social

Privatization Advocates

Powerful advocates for privatization include libertarian and conservative think tanks and advocacy groups such as the Cato Institute, the Heritage Foundation, Americans for Tax Reform, and Citizens for a Sound Economy, all driven by an ideological commitment to the abolition of federal social programs.

Wall Street too is thirsty for the $1.4 trillion that privatization would funnel into equities if the taxes collected to support the Social Security system were invested privately rather than reinvested in federal government bonds. That's not to mention the windfall of fees privatization would deliver for banks, brokerage houses, and investment firms.

Just after he took office, President Bush appointed a commission to examine privatizing the Social Security system. The commission could not figure out how to maintain payments to current recipients while diverting tax dollars to the savings of current workers, nor could it resolve how to cover the benefits of the disabled or resolve issues surrounding survivors' benefits. Although the president did not succeed in carrying out Social Security privatization in his first term, he has made the partial privatization of Social Security retirement accounts the top priority of his second-term domestic agenda.

justice, as if Social Security "reform" would primarily benefit low-income workers, blue-collar workers, people of color, and women. Prompted by disparities in life expectancy between whites and African Americans and the racial wealth gap, a growing chorus within the privatization movement is claiming that privatizing Social Security would be beneficial to African Americans.

Opponents attack the program on the basis of an analogy to private retirement accounts. Early generations of Social Security beneficiaries received much more in benefits than they had paid into the system in taxes. Privatization proponents argue those early recipients received a "higher rate of return" on their "investment" while current and future generations are being "robbed" because they will see "lower rates of return." They argue the current system of social insurance—particularly the retirement program—should be privatized, switching from the current "pay-as-you-go" system to one in which individual workers claim their own contribution and decide where and how to invest it.

But this logic inverts the premise of social insurance. Rather than sharing risk across the entire workforce to ensure that all workers and their families are protected from the three inevitabilities of old age, disability, and death, privatizing Social Security retirement benefits would enable high-wage workers to reap gains from private retirement investment without having to help protect lower-wage workers from their (disproportionate) risks of disability and death. High-wage workers, who are more likely to live long enough to retire, could in fact do better on average if they opt out of the general risk pool and devote all their money to retirement without having to cover the risk of those who may become disabled or die, although they would of course be subjecting their retirement dollars to greater risk. But low-wage workers, who are far more likely to need disability or survivors' benefits to help their families and are less likely to live long enough to retire, would then be left with lower disability and survivors' benefits, and possibly no guaranteed benefits. This is what the

Social Security privatization movement envisions. But you wouldn't know it from reading their literature.

And when the myths about Social Security's financial straits meet another American myth—race—even more confusion follows. Here is a look at three misleading claims by privatization proponents about African Americans and Social Security.

Myth #1

Several conservative research groups argue that Social Security is a bad deal for African Americans because of their lower life expectancies. "Lifetime Social Security benefits depend, in large part, on longevity," writes the Cato Institute's Michael Tanner in his briefing paper "Disparate Impact: Social Security and African Americans." "At every age, African-American men and women both have shorter life expectancies than do their white counterparts. ... As a result, a black man or woman earning exactly the same lifetime wages, and paying exactly the same lifetime Social Security taxes, as his or her white counterpart will likely receive a far lower rate of return." Or as the Americans for Tax Reform web site puts it: "A black male born today has a life expectancy of 64.8 years. But the Social Security retirement age for that worker in the future will be 67 years. That means probably the majority of black males will never even receive Social Security retirement benefits."

The longevity myth is the foundation of all the race-based arguments for Social Security privatization. There are several problems with it.

First, the shorter life expectancy of African Americans compared to whites is the result of higher morbidity in mid-life, and is most acute for African-American men. The life expectancies of African-American women and white men are virtually equal. So the life expectancy argument can really only be made about African-American men.

Second, the claim that OASDI is unfair to African Americans because their expected benefits are less than their expected payments is usually raised and then answered from the perspective of the retirement (or "old age") benefit alone. That is an inaccurate way to look at the problem. Because OASDI also serves families of workers who become disabled or die, a correct measure would take into account the probability of all three risk factors—old age, disability, and death. Both survivor benefits and disability benefits, in fact, go disproportionately to African Americans.

While African Americans make up 12% of the U.S. population, 23% of children receiving Social Security survivor benefits are African American, as are about 17% of disability beneficiaries. On average, a worker who receives disability benefits or a family that receives survivor benefits gets far more in return than the worker paid in FICA taxes, notwithstanding privatizers' attempts to argue that Social Security is a bad deal.

Survivors' benefits also provide an important boost to poor families more generally. A recent study by the National Urban League Institute for Opportunity and Equality showed that the benefit lifted 1 million children out of poverty and helped another 1 million avoid extreme poverty (living below half the poverty line).

Federal Policy for Defined-Benefit Plans

For almost a century, the U.S. government has promoted defined-benefit pension plans because they increase productivity and reinforce the employment relationship while stabilizing retirement income. In 1919, the federal government was faced with a meltdown of the defined-benefit plans of legacy railroads that struggled in competition with small, low-cost start-ups that didn't provide pensions to their young workers. This is analogous to regional air carriers like Jet Blue decimating United Airlines and other legacy airlines today. In response, the mandatory, industry-wide Railroad Retirement system was established in 1935, a decade before Social Security, requiring all railroads to pay into a multi-employer pension fund.

During World War II and in the post-war period, court cases and tax laws favored rapid growth in defined-benefit plans. An unusually large pension default at the Studebaker automobile corporation in South Bend, Ind., in 1964, led Congress to pass comprehensive pension regulatory legislation, the Employee Retirement Income Security Act (ERISA), in 1974. ERISA established the PBGC to insure firms' defined-benefit pensions in the event of bankruptcy (which, even before 1974, happened infrequently; one out of 1,000 defined-benefit sponsors had defaulted in 10 years). Since its creation in 1974, the PBGC has operated without ever missing a payment it owes, despite having an overall balance-sheet deficit in most years, using the premium income that every plan sponsor (single employers, multiple employers, or unions) pays to carry the agency through normal cyclical downturns.

In creating an insurance structure, the legislation required companies to fund their defined-benefit promises over time, anticipating "moral hazard" problems (when an insured entity becomes lax, relying on another body to bail it out). ERISA intended companies to have flexibility, contributing more in good times and less in bad. Originally, companies had 40 years to reach 100% funding, using wage, investment returns, and interest-rate projections. In the late 1980s and 1990s, faster funding was required of plans that were less than 70% funded. (A pension's funded status refers to its ratio of assets to liabilities. If a plan is more than 90% funded, that is, if its current assets amount to 90% of the present value of promises, including expected future promises, made to its participants, it is considered fully funded.)

Finally, among workers who do live long enough to get the retirement benefit, life expectancies don't differ much by racial group. For example, at age 65, the life expectancies of African-American and white men are virtually the same.

President Bush's Social Security commission proposed the partial privatization of Social Security retirement accounts, but cautioned that it could not figure out how to maintain equal benefits for the other risk pools. The commission suggested that disability and survivor's benefits would have to be reduced if the privatization plan proceeds.

This vision is of a retirement program designed for the benefit of the worker who retires—only. A program with that focus would work against, not for, African Americans because of the higher morbidity rates in middle age and the smaller share of African Americans who live to retirement.

Myth #2

African Americans have less education, and so are in the work force longer, than whites, and yet Social Security only credits 35 years of work experience in figuring benefits. Tanner says, "benefits are calculated on the basis of the highest 35 years of earnings over a worker's lifetime. Workers must still pay Social Security taxes during years outside those 35, but those taxes do not count toward or earn additional benefits. Generally, those low-earnings years occur early in an individual's life. That is particularly important to African Americans because they are likely to enter the workforce at an earlier age than whites...."

This claim misinterprets the benefit formula for Social Security. Yes, African Americans on average are slightly less educated than whites. The gap is mostly because of a higher college completion rate for white men compared to African-American men. But the education argument fails to acknowledge that white teenagers have a significantly higher labor force participation rate (at 46%) than do African-American teens (29%). The higher labor force participation of white teenagers helps to explain why young white adults do better in the labor market than young African-American adults. (The racial gaps in unemployment are considerably greater for teenagers and young adults than for those over 25.)

These differences in early labor market experiences mean that African-American men have more years of zero earnings than do whites. So while the statement about education is true, the inference from education differences to work histories is false. By taking only 35 years of work history into account in the benefit formula, the Social Security formula is progressive. It in effect ignores years of zero or very low earnings. This levels the playing field among long-time workers, putting African Americans with more years of zero earnings on par with whites. By contrast, a private system based on total years of earnings would exacerbate racial labor market disparities.

Myth #3

A third claim put forward by critics of Social Security is that African-American retirees are more dependent on Social Security than whites. Tanner writes: "Elderly African Americans are much more likely than their white counterparts to be dependent on Social Security benefits for most or all of their retirement income." Therefore, he concludes, "African Americans would be among those with the most to gain from the privatization of Social Security—transforming the program into a system of individually owned, privately invested accounts." Law professor and senior policy advisor to Americans for Tax Reform Peter Ferrara adds, "the personal accounts would produce far higher returns and benefits for lower-income workers, African Americans, Hispanics, women and other minorities."

It's true that African-American retirees are more likely than whites to rely on Social Security as their only income in old age. It's the sole source of retirement income for 40% of elderly African Americans. This is a result of discrimination in the labor market that limits the share of African Americans with jobs that offer pension benefits. Privatizing Social Security would not change labor market discrimination or its effects.

Privatizing Social Security would, however, exacerbate the earnings differences between African Americans and whites, since benefits would be based solely on individual savings. What would help African-American retirees is not privatization, but rather changing the redistributive aspects of Social Security to make it even more progressive.

The current formula for Social Security benefits is progressive in two ways: low earners get a higher share of their earnings than do higher wage earners and the lowest years of earning are ignored. Changes in the formula to raise the benefits floor enough to lift all retired Social Security recipients out of poverty would make it still more progressive. Increasing and updating the Supplemental Security Income payment, which helps low earners, could accomplish the same goal for SSI recipients. (SSI is a program administered by Social Security for very low earners and the poor who are disabled, blind, or at least 65 years old.)

The proponents of privatization argue that the heavy reliance of African-American seniors on Social Security requires higher rates of return—returns that are only possible by putting money into the stock market. Yet given the lack of access to private pensions for African-American seniors and their low savings from lifetimes of low earnings, such a notion is perverse. It would have African Americans gamble with their only leg of retirement's supposed three-legged stool—pension, savings, and Social Security. And, given the much higher risk that African Americans face of both death before retirement and of disability, it would be a risky gamble indeed to lower those benefits while jeopardizing their only retirement leg.

Privatizing the retirement program, and separating the integrated elements of Social Security, would split America. The divisions would be many: between those more likely to be disabled and those who are not; between those more likely to die before retirement and those more likely to retire; between children who get survivors' benefits and the elderly who get retirement benefits; between those who retire with high-yield investments and those who fare poorly in retirement. The "horizontal equity" of the program (treating similar people in a similar way) would be lost, as volatile stock fluctuations and the timing of retirement could greatly affect individuals' rates of return. The "vertical equity" of the program (its progressive nature, insuring a floor for benefits) would be placed in greater jeopardy with the shift from social to private benefits.

Social Security works because it is "social." It is America's only universal federal program. The proposed changes would place Social Security in the same political space as the rest of America's federal programs—and African Americans have seen time and again how those politics work. ❏

Article 6.3

WHY WE NEED UNIVERSAL PENSIONS

BY KATHERINE SCIACCHITANO
September/October 2012

The political economy of the recovery is making the United States even more unequal than it was during the bubble years. Incomes fell across the board during the crisis: median family income is 6.3% below what it was in 2001. But the top 1% garnered 93% of income growth in the first year of recovery. Housing, still the main source of wealth for middle-income families, remains depressed while stocks are close to pre-crash highs. Moreover, the drive for more tax cuts for the wealthy continues. And policy initiatives to cut Social Security, Medicare, and Medicaid would weaken the safety net even as it is most needed.

A spate of attacks on state and local public-sector pensions now threatens to make inequality even more entrenched and painful, and to undermine both short- and long-term economic growth.

The power of labor is dead center in this agenda. Despite a long-term decline in workers covered by union contracts, unions have over 16 million members: they are still the social force most capable of combating the assault on workers' incomes and militating for greater equality. Crippling their political power therefore remains both a tactical and a strategic objective on the right. With only 6.9% of workers in the private sector covered by union contracts, versus 37% in the public sector, public-sector unions are bearing the brunt of the attacks. And public pensions are the battering ram.

Attacking Unions, Eroding Pensions

The trip wire for the assault on pensions was the combined fall in state and local revenues from the bursting of the housing bubble, and the steep losses suffered by pension funds during the resulting stock market slide of 2007-2009: by 2010 there were widely acknowledged public pension funding shortfalls totaling nearly $800 billion.

While pension funds are slowly making back market losses, conservative advocates like Andrew Biggs at the American Enterprise Institute are arguing for new measures of shortfalls that would bring them to over $4 trillion, and using this $4 trillion figure to call for a national movement to slash both public-sector pensions and union rights. The implicit threat is that taxpayers will have to pay these trillions now and into the future, even though they themselves may not have pensions. The stated policy objective is to convince taxpayers and politicians that defined benefit pensions are too expensive in the public sector and should be replaced with defined contribution plans.

Defined benefit pensions are a form of deferred compensation—pay for work performed; they provide guaranteed lifetime payments in retirement. Defined-contribution plans give workers tax breaks for individual savings; workers invest these savings and then pray they don't run out. Over the past three decades, defined benefit pensions have been nearly eradicated in the private sector for non-union workers; their abandonment in the public sector would effectively end defined benefit pensions as a norm for retirement security and shift the burden of retirement savings almost entirely to individuals.

Abandoning public defined benefit pensions would also erode the more than $3 trillion in investment capital controlled and invested by public-sector funds— aggregated capital that gives the funds both a critical role in long-term economic investment and an important shareholder voice in reforming corporate governance and pushing for re-regulation of the financial sector.

While unions remain a powerful voice in defending universal programs like Social Security, declining union density makes defending benefits like defined bene-fit pensions that are mainly enjoyed by union workers more difficult. Union benefits no longer spill over into the non-union sector as they did when non-union employ-ers had to complete with union employers for workers. While 70% of private-sector union workers and almost all public-sector workers still have access to defined ben-efit pensions, only 14% of private-sector non-union workers do, opening the way for a divide-and-conquer strategy for conservative politicians to exploit.

Cutting Edge in Wisconsin

Wisconsin governor Scott Walker is the poster child for the dual attack on public-sector unions and pensions. Elected in late 2010 in a Republican sweep, Walker immediately pushed through over $140 million in tax cuts targeted to corporations and the wealthy, then turned around and blamed an alleged $137 million state budget deficit on public employee pensions and unions. In early February, he introduced legislation to eviscerate state workers' bargaining rights, triggering the now-famous months-long occupation of the state capitol by hundreds of thousands of outraged union and non-union workers.

The facts were with the demonstrators: there were no shortfalls in pension funding for taxpayers to make up, and unions had already offered higher worker contribu-tions to help pay for benefits. When the Republican legislature nevertheless passed legislation eviscerating public-sector bargaining rights and unilaterally raising worker pension contributions, unions launched a yearlong effort to recall the governor.

In the 1930s, Wisconsin had been the birthplace of AFSCME, the nation's largest public-sector union; in the 1950s, it had passed the first state legislation authorizing public-sector bargaining. Yet public pensions remained a wedge issue throughout the campaign.

Wisconsin was once a private-sector union manufacturing stronghold as well, but more recently workers there have been battered with job and benefit losses. As one activ-ist put it, the Walker campaign's uninterrupted message was "cut taxes, create jobs, don't pay for other peoples' pensions." Union workers were almost as vulnerable to the argument as non-union workers: 38% of union households in the state had at least one member who voted to keep Walker in office, handing him a 53% to 47% victory.

Scapegoating in San Jose

The same day as the failed Wisconsin recall, voters in largely Democratic San Jose, California, approved drastic cuts to city workers' pay and pensions with an equally shocking 69% yes vote.

A wealthy community in the heart of Silicon Valley, where the average annual wage is $95,472, San Jose began an ill-timed "Decade of Investment" at the height of the dot-com bubble. Severely limited both in the property tax revenues it could collect, by California's long-standing Proposition 13, and in raising other taxes to compensate, San Jose was buffeted over the next ten years by two recessions, high unemployment, sharp drops in revenue from sales taxes, and repeated budget shortfalls. While city leaders managed to more than double capital expenditures during this decade, spending on services increased less than 1.5% per year (not adjusted for inflation). By 2011, San Jose had endured cumulative workforce reductions of 20% and repeated cuts in services, including closings of 22 community centers.

Having paid for virtually its entire FY 2011-2012 budget shortfall with cuts to payroll, with its FY 2012-2013 budget finally projected to be in balance, the city promptly set about restoring services by slashing pensions.

Like most pension funds, San Jose's were heavily invested in the stock market and suffered large losses from 2007 through 2009, bringing the funds from roughly 90% funded to 75% funded. Although the drop in funding necessitated increased contributions by the city to compensate, the size of the contributions could have been kept reasonable by spreading them out over a longer period of time and bargaining with city unions for appropriate adjustments to benefits and employee contributions.

Instead, San Jose Mayor Chuck Reed magnified pension funding problems to scapegoat workers for revenue shortfalls. Over an 18-month period that coincided with the turmoil in Wisconsin, Reed repeatedly described the city's pension costs as a "cancerous growth" and talked about imminent disaster if benefits weren't cut.

Reed's "Exhibit A" was a figure—eventually exposed by NBC reporters as having been pulled "off the top of the head" of a city retirement official —purporting to show that city pension contributions would more than double over four years, reaching $650 million annually by FY 2015-2016. Forced to do math, the city cut its estimate to $430 million, but still failed to factor in savings from negotiated pay cuts of 10% to 12% and workforce reductions.

The city's final figure—published a year into Reed's campaign, well after the $650 million figure was burned into peoples' brains—was $320 million, less than half the city's original claim. Even this figure included the costs of a voluntary undertaking by the city to pre-fund retiree health care benefits, as well as changed assumptions about future investment returns that increased the size of city pension contributions to be made in the short term – decisions that AFSCME researcher Dan Doonan publicly described as "comically bad timing" for a city recovering from the most severe economic downturn since the Great Depression.

Numbers Games

The pension fight in San Jose highlights the role seemingly arcane actuarial assumptions play in calculating pension shortfalls, and how such assumptions can provide ammunition for public pension battles.

Pension boards invest contributions made by employers and workers and use the returns on these investments to pay for benefits to retirees. They regularly assess the adequacy of returns in relation to benefits that will have to be paid. If pension boards anticipate lower returns over an extended period, they may decide to increase contributions to compensate.

If increased contributions are required, pension boards have several options for minimizing disruptions. They can average gains and losses over a five-year period—a practice called "smoothing." They can lengthen the number of years—or amortization period—over which payments are spread. Lengthening the amortization period is similar to what homeowners do when they choose between a thirty-year mortgage, which spreads payments out over a longer period to keep each payment lower, and a fifteen-year mortgage, which saves money over the long-term, but increases the size of required monthly payments. If boards decide the anticipated rate of return on investments needs to be lowered, they can do that gradually too.

The consequences for taxpayers of these decisions about timing can be enormous. Postponing additional required contributions for too long may mean that small shortfalls become unmanageable. But front-loading payments increases their size, and may force unnecessary tax increases and service cuts, benefit reductions, or all three.

San Jose front-loaded its payments. Pension trustees lowered estimates of future returns without easing in the change. They declined to lengthen the amortization period, spreading increased contributions over a shorter amortization period than they had to. And the city made an enormously expensive decision to pre-fund retiree health care rather than funding it on a pay-as-you-go basis as most other jurisdictions do, voluntarily increasing its immediate payroll costs for retiree health care to 17% of pay, and 15.5% for employees.

Together with the city's earlier inflated estimates of the contributions that would be required to compensate for investment losses, these choices allowed San Jose to magnify pension shortfalls and intensify pressures to reduce benefits.

Pensions and Economic Recovery

San Jose's pension cuts are currently in litigation. If they are upheld, the price for city workers will range from just under 30% to just over 40% of take-home pay: 15.5% for retiree health care; additional contributions for pensions of up to 16%; and a 10% to 12% pay cut—all *in addition* to existing contributions of 13% of pay. Alternatively, city workers, who like many public-sector workers don't participate in Social Security, may be able to opt for a lower tier of benefits being created for new employees, provided the scheme is approved by the IRS. Not surprisingly, San Jose is now having trouble retaining and recruiting personnel.

The price for city residents has also been severe. In addition to what Doonan characterizes as "wrecking the labor market," Reed's divisive campaign increased mistrust of the city by its unions, and of unions by city residents, many of whom might well have worked in coalition with city workers for solutions, including a one-quarter-of-one-cent sales tax increase that could have avoided the bloodletting and improved the city's fiscal position as well. As Bob Brownstein of San Jose-based Working Partnerships USA put it, "When you have a perfect fiscal storm from capital projects you can't staff, a bad economy, falling revenues, and investment losses, then any chance you get to push expenditures off to the future or bring revenues forward, you should probably take. Anytime is going to be better than now."

It's in the context of these votes in Wisconsin and San Jose, and another similar result in San Diego, that AEI's Andrew Biggs is calling for a national movement for to cut public employee pensions by referenda in order to bring them "closer in line with what stressed private sector workers can expect in the 21st century"—a cruel joke, since most private-sector workers have no pensions.

The price of such widespread take-backs would be enormous, not just for future retirees, but for economic recovery and future growth. The real estate bubble was the last stage of a decades-long transformation in which the contribution of manufacturing profits and employment to the U.S. economy fell and the role of the finance industry and debt expanded. The transition was disastrous, both for

Accounting for Liabilities, or Blowing Them Up?

San Jose's choices to magnify its pension problems echo national efforts by conservative advocates to change accounting and reporting of unfunded public-sector pension liabilities in order to increase the appearance of shortfalls and spur a transition from defined benefit to defined contribution pensions.

Unlike corporations, most governments don't go out of business; public-sector pension funds can count on a future stream of contributions from new entrants to maintain funding. As a result, most public-sector pension boards use the long-term average of their funds' actual investment returns—between 7.25% and 8.25% for many funds today—to estimate the rate of future returns. Private pension fund managers use a more conservative rate based on high-grade corporate bonds—recently, approximately 5.5%.

In either case, the projected rate of return is known as the "discount rate"—so called because pension boards count backwards from the amounts they will need to pay benefits, and then discount, or reduce, those amounts by the rate of return they expect on their investments in order to arrive at the amounts they need to invest to fund future benefits. Understanding the concept of a discount rate is important because much of the current war over public-sector pensions is being fought over whether public-sector funds should continue to use a discount rate based on their historical returns, or should use a lower discount rate, similar to the rate used by private-sector pension funds, or even lower. The lower the discount rate, the worse the funded status of public-sector pensions will appear to be, and the more political pressure will be generated to reduce or eliminate defined benefit pensions.

Instead of using past rates of return, advocates such as the AEI's Andrew Biggs argue that public pension funds should use a much lower "riskless rate" based on 30-year treasury bonds—currently at 2.75%—as the discount rate. The argument is that because public-sector pension benefits are usually guaranteed, the rate of return used to assess funding should also be "riskless." Because public-sector pension funds invest in mixed portfolios of stocks and bonds that yield higher returns than treasuries, a "riskless" discount rate makes public-sector funds look much less well funded than they really are. This is especially true today when the economic crisis and monetary policy have driven interest rates into negative territory. Using a riskless rate, state pension liabilities jump from less workers' wages and economic stability. Five years into a severe downturn, the official unemployment rate is still 8.2%. The youth unemployment rate is 16.4%. The critical challenge is economic growth to reduce unemployment and raise wages, not further tax reductions.

Far from just supporting retirees, defined-benefit pensions contribute to economic recovery by providing a long-term, stable source of counter-cyclical spending—spending that continues even during economic downturns. The National Institute on Retirement Security calculates that each dollar of benefits from a defined benefit pension supports $2.37 in economic output. In 2009, defined benefit pension dollars spent in the economy supported 6.5 million jobs nationally, or 4.2% of the labor force.

To the extent that pension funds use dividend income from investments to pay benefits, they also redistribute income that would normally go to high-income

---

than $800 billion to well over $4 trillion nationally. Even fully funded Wisconsin suddenly appears underfunded.

T he Government Accounting Standards Board (GASB) has recently revised its standards to allow public-sector pension funds to use discount rates based on actual rates of investment returns for the "funded" portion of their pension portfolios, but to require the use of discount rates based on high-grade municipal bonds to account for the "unfunded" portions. This achieves a reporting result between current practice and a market-based bond rate.

GASB stresses that its standards are only for reporting on the status of public-sector pension funds. They don't dictate the size or timing of contributions or the actual investment strategies.

Advocates of a riskless rate may be counting on few people understanding the distinction between reporting and funding requirements. The Boston-based Center for Retirement Research calculates that state and local pensions were 76% funded in 2010, but that applying a riskless rate would have yielded a 51% funded status. It cautions that even the new GASB standard would have resulted in a 57% figure for 2010, and could, when it goes into effect in 2014, create unnecessary confusion about differences between reporting and funding requirements, leading politicians to conclude there is a worsening crisis, when in fact pensions are on a more secure footing. More recently, Moody's Investor Service has announced that, among other accounting changes, it is considering using a high-grade corporate bond rate, a discount rate similar to that used by private pension fund managers, to evaluate public-sector pensions when it rates state and local governments. Moody's proposed changes would triple estimates of unfunded liabilities of public-sector pension plans. Since states rely on Moody's for a seal of approval when they borrow in the bond market, if adopted, Moody's proposed discount rate, though only one factor in its evaluation, could put even more concrete pressure on state and local pensions. On top of fueling arguments that public-sector defined benefit pensions are unaffordable, the proposed changes would increase credit costs for states and cities whose rates were lowered. This would add to budget problems just as states and localities are struggling hardest to fund pensions and maintain services. Moody's materials suggest that it views workers' pensions as a rival to bondholders' interests in obtaining more from a shrinking pool of public resources.

investors, making income more equal across the economy. This in turn boosts spending, since lower-income workers spend much more of their income than the wealthy do.

Finally, as David Marchick, managing director of the Carlyle Group, has explained to Congress, defined-benefit funds have a responsibility to actively invest their capital in order to produce long-term returns, not just short-term profits. As a result, they are a critical source of the long-term, patient investment and venture capital needed for sustainable growth and job creation, a role that has been even more vital during the crisis and recovery.

Neither defined-contribution plans nor other kinds of individual savings provide these same benefits. Because workers have to worry about outliving the income from these accounts, they are more reluctant to spend it, limiting its stimulus effect. Small individual accounts don't provide the opportunity for the large-scale, targeted, job-creating investments that pension funds routinely make. And because defined contribution plans are tied to individual savers who have shorter investment horizons and can afford to take fewer risks than professional managers in large funds, they characteristically have 20% to 40% lower returns over their life than defined benefit plans. They also have higher fees.

As a result, defined benefit plans cost half as much to fund as defined contribution plans. Put another way, each dollar contributed to a defined contribution plan delivers half the benefits of a dollar contributed to a defined benefit plan.

Any further large-scale switch from defined benefit to defined contribution plans as currently structured would thus not only undermine retirement security and overall, or aggregate, demand in the economy, it would place heavier burdens on future generations of taxpayers. On the one hand, saving more to achieve the same benefits lowers spending and aggregate demand today, hurting the recovery. On the other hand, *not* saving more and ending up with lower benefits reduces aggregate demand—what will be spent—in the future, hurting long-term growth. To the extent that lower benefits fail to meet basic needs for retirement security, they pave the way for higher poverty rates, raising the need for public assistance down the line, creating longer-term fiscal problem for state and the federal governments—and taxpayers.

The Real Crisis: Retirement Insecurity

Economist Dean Baker of the Center for Economic and Policy Research has calculated that virtually the entire shortfall in public pension funding was caused by the sudden drop in the stock market and cutbacks in contributions during the downturn. The Center for Retirement Research in Boston estimates that if markets continue to recover, pensions are likely to rebound from their crisis low of 75% funded in 2011 to 82% by 2015. The Center for Budget and Policy Priorities calculates that most states can correct remaining shortfalls by easing in increased contributions of up to 1.2% of their budgets over the next five years and modestly scaling back benefits. The exceptions are the handful of states—Illinois, Kentucky, and New Jersey among them—that took "contribution holidays" during the bubble or that promised benefit increases without funding them, where more substantial measures will be needed.

The real pension crisis isn't the acknowledged $800 billion in public pension shortfalls. It's the estimated $6.6 trillion gap in private savings that Retirement USA estimates workers need to achieve retirement security.

Since Social Security's establishment during the Depression, policy makers have viewed retirement security as a "three-legged stool" composed of Social Security, employer pensions, and private savings. Today, less than half of all private-sector workers participate in pensions of any sort. Median-income households with 401(k)s and a head-of-household between 60 and 62 (a group that has lived through two recent stock-market crashes and the bursting of the housing bubble) have saved just one quarter of what they need to maintain their standard of living in retirement. Younger workers face another lost decade of economic growth before they can start saving. In California, 55% of workers aged 25 to 44 can expect to retire on less than $22,000 a year.

The best way to address the real retirement crisis while supporting recovery is to preserve and strengthen Social Security without cutting benefits; defend defined benefit pensions where they exist; and build a universal system to strengthen individual saving among the increasing number of workers who have no pensions.

Saving individually for retirement maximizes three types of risk: longevity risk—the risk of outliving savings; investment risk—the risk of poor diversification or investment choices; and what is referred to as market risk—the risk of retiring in a severe market downturn.

As a result, most proposals for universal coverage start by pooling individual investment accounts into professionally managed funds that can more effectively diversify investments, share longevity risk, and spread gains and losses over much longer periods than individuals can. These techniques for managing risk allow the funds to take appropriate risk to achieve much higher returns, making retirement savings more efficient for individuals and for society.

Senator Tom Harkin of (D-Iowa) has disseminated a proposal for a national system of pooled accounts that would pay annuities based on a combination of the individual contributions workers make and the performance of the investments. To encourage saving, the system would enroll workers automatically, but allow them to opt out or contribute less than the automatic minimum. Because Harkin's program is national, it would be completely portable. Harkin's plan also strengthens Social Security by tailoring its cost-of-living allowance to cover seniors' basic needs, removing the cap on wages subject to the Social Security payroll tax, and modestly boosting benefits by approximately $60 a month for most workers.

Pension economist Teresa Ghilarducci has made proposals for state and national level plans that overlap with Harkin's but would guarantee a minimum return above inflation. Because most tax breaks aimed at encouraging pension saving currently subsidize 401(k) contributions by higher-income savers, Ghilarducci's proposals re-weight assistance towards middle- and low-income savers who would otherwise not be able to save for retirement.

Because of the current political climate that makes expansion of government benefits highly contested, both Ghilarducci's and Harkin's plans are structured to avoid government payment of benefits and to work in tandem with Social Security and existing defined benefit pensions. A number of states, including California, are also developing proposals for universal private-sector pension plans.

Recasting the Debate

A robust defense of pensions is no longer possible without a robust fight for universal coverage linked to the broader fight for economic growth. As Jelger Kalmijn, president of a California local of the Communication Workers of America, put it, "Just fighting to keep the defined benefit plans is like fighting to keep the people who are currently in unions in unions. If you only fight to keep the contracts we have and don't organize anyone new, we've all agreed that's a loser."

The biggest challenge in building a universal pension system is to begin. The challenge in defending existing pensions is to broaden the fight so most workers have a positive stake in winning,

When viewed against the realities of pension economics or the broader macroeconomy, the facts in Wisconsin and San Jose don't support the electoral results achieved. But the electoral results do match the political reality on the ground: the profound anxiety and suffering caused by decades of job losses in manufacturing jobs across the country, the stagnation of hourly wages, and the shredding of benefits. Without concrete solutions many of these workers are holding on to what little they have, which in too many cases comes down to their tax dollars. It's up to unions to lead the fight for those solutions, even though the solutions go beyond traditional union membership or coverage under a contract.

As union density shrinks, fighting for universal benefits will broaden the political playing field. While the educational and political battles will be long, making the fight a concrete one now by making it about pensions for all is what it will take to change the terms of the debate and move from playing defense to playing offense. ❑

Selected sources: California State Auditor, "City of San Jose: Some Retirement Cost Projections Were Unsupported Although Rising Retirement Costs Have Led to Reduced City Services," Bureau of State Audits, August 2012 (bsa.ca.gov); Jenna Susko, et al., "San Jose Pension Estimates Questioned," April 27, 2012 (nbcbayarea.com); Ilana Boivie, "Pensionomics 2012: Measuring the Economic Impact of DB Pension Expenditures," National Institute on Retirement Security, March 2012, (nirsonline.org); Alicia H. Munell, et al., "The Funding of State and Local Pensions: 2011-2015," Center for Retirement Research, Boston College (crr.bc.edu); David Marchick, "The Power of Pensions: Building a Strong Middle Class and Strong Economy," Testimony Before the Senate Committee on Health, Education, Labor and Pensions, July 12, 2011 (help.senate.gov); "The Retirement Income Deficit," Retirement USA (retirement-usa.org); Diane Oakley, Executive Director, National Institute on Retirement Security, "The Power of Pensions: Building a Strong Middle Class and Strong Economy," Testimony before the United States Senate Committee on Health, Education, Labor and Pensions, July 12, 2011 (help.senate.gov); Tom Harkin, Chair, United States Senate Committee on Health, Education, Labor and Pensions, "The Retirement Crisis and a Plan to Solve It" (harkin.senate.gov); Teresa Ghilarducci, "Guaranteed Retirement Accounts: Toward Retirement Income Security," Economic Policy Institute, EPI Briefing Paper #204, November 20, 2007 (gpn.org); Alicia H. Munnell, et al., "The Pension Coverage Problem in the Private Sector," Center for Retirement Research, September 2012 (crr.bc.edu); Alicia H. Munell, et al., "How Would GASB Proposals Affect State and Local Pensions," Center for Retirement Research, Boston College (crr.bc.edu).

Article 6.4

DETROIT'S BANKRUPTCY CRISIS: PENSIONS IN THE BALANCE

BY KATHERINE SCIACCHITANO
October 2013

In July 2013, Detroit Emergency Manager Kevyn Orr filed what could be, at $18 billion, the largest municipal bankruptcy in U.S. history. If the bankruptcy is allowed to proceed, a central issue will be whether the city can jettison up to $3.5 billion in accrued pension benefits owed city workers (which the city claims are unfunded). With accrued state and municipal pension benefits protected by the Michigan constitution, such a ruling would set a chilling precedent for future municipal bankruptcies.

City pension funds—one for police and firefighters and another for non-uniformed city personnel—hotly contest the city's numbers. Fund documents show a combined shortfall of $977 million, $2.5 billion less than Orr claims. They also show the police and fire fund is 96% funded and the general fund is 77% funded, in contrast to Orr's allegations of 78% and 59%, respectively.

The methodology for the Emergency Manager's (EM) calculations takes a page from the playbook of conservatives who argue that public-sector defined-benefit pensions across the country are underfunded and should be eliminated, what one union official calls "the pension busters playbook." (See "Accounting for Liabilities, or Blowing Them Up?" p. 184 of this book.) Like many public and private sector pensions funds, the funds assume rates of return on investments of approximately 8%. The EM lowers those assumptions by at least a full percentage point. Detroit pension funds use a common practice called smoothing to prevent sudden large losses—such as those suffered by funds across the country in 2008-9—from making funds appear more underfunded than they really are. The practice averages losses over a period of years and provides breathing space for markets to recover before recognizing, or locking in, losses. The EM rejects the fund's use of smoothing in its calculations.

Once the size of a shortfall is determined, pension funds also routinely spread out, over a period of years, the contributions needed to eliminate any shortfall, a practice called amortization. Detroit pension funds use 29- and 30-year amortization periods. The EM cuts these periods to 15 and 18 years. While this change doesn't increase the estimates of underfunding, it does push up the size of the annual contributions that would be needed going forward, making the city's overall budget situation appear worse as it moves into bankruptcy, thus boosting the case for cuts to pensions.

With average annual pension benefits for non-uniformed city workers of just $19,000, the problem in Detroit isn't the generosity of city pensions. The problem is the crisis in the city's tax base and the city's repeated failures to make required pension contributions. Heavily dependent on the declining auto industry, Detroit has shrunk from 1.8 million residents in the 1950s to 700,000 today, and has lost fully

25% of its residents since 2000. Detroit has also been devastated by the subprime mortgage crisis. In 2004-6, the last run-up to the crash, 75% of mortgage loans to African Americans in Detroit were subprime loans. Between 2005 and 2009, one in five Detroit homes suffered foreclosure. Ambulance response time in Detroit can be as long as an hour. Unemployment is close to 18%.

Orr frames pension cuts as the only viable alternative to continued severe deterioration in city services. Nationally, the prospect of cuts is portrayed as the choice between paying pensioners or paying investors in Detroit municipal bonds. The explicit threat is that defaulting on payments to bondholders would not only lock Detroit out of the municipal bond market, but also raise borrowing rates for other municipalities across the country.

The Detroit group "Moratorium NOW! Coalition to Stop Foreclosures" has analyzed the role of large financial institutions in Detroit's crisis and argues that Detroit should cease paying debt service to large banks. It takes the position that Detroit's fiscal crisis began with the foreclosure crisis, caused by subprime lending, and that large banks continue to profit from complex financial dealings with the city. Meanwhile, Detroit city workers, residents, and civil life suffer.

In 2005, Detroit issued $1.5 billion in pension obligation certificates to help fund city pensions. The certificates are held by major banks and were accompanied by complex financial arrangements called "interest rate swaps" that favored the banks. Detroit entered other swaps as well, including on water and sewer bonds. The rationale was to hedge against rising future interest rates by swapping a fixed for a variable rate. When interest rates plunged to zero instead, Detroit and the many other cities with similar agreements were left paying the much higher fixed rate. The cost to Detroit of these arrangements has been estimated at close to $1 billion.

Cuts to pensions in the bankruptcy would come on top of $160 million in annual givebacks in wages, pensions, and health-care benefits agreed to by city unions in 2012. Using emergency powers granted by the state, Orr has already announced the elimination of retiree health-care benefits, which are not protected by the state constitution. He also proposes replacing the city's current defined-benefit plans with defined-contribution plans, paying as little as ten cents on the dollar on unfunded liabilities, and eliminating cost-of-living adjustments (COLAs) for retirees. Many retirees from the city, moreover, are not covered by Social Security.

As the bankruptcy proceeds and 80,000 properties lay vacant throughout the city, Detroit's budget problems are touted by conservatives as a microcosm of national public-sector pension problems. In fact, Detroit is a case study of an economy tied to an industry in crisis. It is a microcosm not of the unsustainability of public pensions, but of the devastation wrought by national economic policies that have sacrificed manufacturing to the needs of global capital and the finance industry, and that continue to profit those same players. ❑

Article 6.5

MOODY'S GET FADDISH ON PUBLIC PENSIONS

BY DEAN BAKER
May 2013; Truthout

The bond-rating agency Moody's made itself famous for giving subprime mortgage backed securities triple-A ratings at the peak of the housing bubble. This made it easy for investment banks like Goldman Sachs and Morgan Stanley to sell these securities all around the world. And it allowed the housing bubble to grow ever bigger and more dangerous. And we know where that has left us.

Well, Moody's is back. They announced plans to change the way they treat pension obligations in assessing state and local government debt.

Instead of accepting projections of pension fund returns based on the assets they hold, Moody's wants to use a risk-free discount rate to assess pension fund liabilities. This will make public pensions seem much worse funded than the current method.

While this might seem like a nerdy and technical point, it has very real consequences. If Moody's methodology is accepted as the basis for accounting by state and local governments then they will suddenly need large amounts of revenue to make their pensions properly funded. This will directly pit public-sector workers, who are counting on the pensions they have earned, against school children, low-income families, and others who count on state supported services.

In other words, this is exactly the sort of politics that the Wall Street and the One Percent types love. No matter which side loses, they win. While public sector workers fight the people dependent on state and local services, they get to walk off with all the money.

Wall Street is expert at these sorts of accounting tricks; it is, after all, what they do for a living. And this is not the first time that they have played these sorts of games to advance their agenda.

The current crisis of the Postal Service, which is looking at massive layoffs and cutbacks in delivery, is largely the result of accounting gimmicks. In 2006 ,Congress passed a law requiring an unprecedented level of pre-funding for retiree health care benefits. The Postal Service is not only required to build up a massive level of pre-funding, it also is using more pessimistic assumptions about cost growth than any known plan in the private sector.

This requirement is the basis for the horror stories of multi-billion dollar losses that feature prominently in news stories about the Postal Service. The Postal Service would face difficulties adjusting to rapid declines in traditional mail service in any case (it doesn't help that they are prohibited from using their enormous resources to expand into new lines of business), but this accounting maneuver is imposing an impossible burden. The change in pension fund accounting could have a comparable impact on state and local governments.

Moody's change in accounting is not just bad politics, it is horrible policy. The key question is how we should assess the returns that pension funds can anticipate on the assets they hold in the stock market. Moody's and other bond-rating agencies did flunk the test horribly in the 1990s and 2000s. They assumed that the stock market would provide the historic rate of return even when price-to-earnings ratios were more than twice the historic average at the peak of the stock bubble.

While some of us did try to issue warnings at the time, the bond-rating agencies were not interested. As a result, when the stock market plunged, many pensions that had previously appeared to be solidly funded, suddenly faced substantial shortfalls.

It is possible to construct a methodology that projects future returns based on current market valuations and projected profit growth that maintain proper funding levels, while minimizing the variation in contributions through time. By contrast, if the pension funds adopted the Moody's methodology as the basis for their contribution schedules, they would find themselves making very large contributions in some years followed by years in which they made little or no contribution.

A state or local government that used the Moody's methodology to guide their contributions would effectively be prefunding their pensions in the same way that it would be prefunding education to build up a huge bank account so that K-12 education was paid from the annual interest. While it would be nice to have the cost of these services fully covered for all time, no one thinks this policy makes sense. We would be hugely overtaxing current workers so that future generations could get a huge tax break.

Even worse, Moody's scoring of pensions may discourage pension managers from holding stock as an asset. They would be held accountable for any losses in bad years, but would not get credit for the higher expected returns on stock. For this reason, risk-averse pension managers may decide to hold safe but low-yielding bonds.

This would lead to the perverse situation in which collectively invested funds held in pensions only hold safe bonds, even though market timing carries little risk for them. On the other hand, individual investors, who are hugely vulnerable to market timing, would be holding stock in their 401(k)s.

That outcome makes no sense. But of course it didn't make sense that subprime mortgage backed securities were rated Aaa. This is Moody's we're talking about. ❑

Article 6.6

WHAT HAPPENED TO DEFINED-BENEFIT PENSIONS?

BY ARTHUR MACEWAN
September/October 2013

Dear Dr. Dollar:

What has happened to the defined benefit pensions? Why are they being replaced by defined contribution programs? What are the implications for us (workers!) as we grow older and live longer? —Susan A. Titus, Detroit, Mich.

In large part, the shift from defined benefit pensions to defined contribution pensions is explained by employers shifting risk from themselves to their employees. Increasingly, in recent decades, for the same reasons that employers have been able to hold down wages, employers have shifted pension plans because they have had the power to do so. (See box for definitions of the two types of plans.)

The shift has been dramatic. In 1975, 71% of active workers participating in pension plans had defined benefit plans, and 29% had defined contribution plans. By 2010, the figures had more than reversed: 19% were in defined benefit plans; 81%, in defined contribution plans. Even though the labor force grew by 64% over this 45-year period, the number of workers in defined benefit plans fell by 37%. (See graph.)

In a defined benefit pension system, the employer is obligated to pay the fixed pension regardless of what happens to the economy. The risk for the employer is that bad economic times can make it difficult to make the payments—because the

PERCENTAGE OF NON-RETIRED PENSION-PLAN PARTICIPANTS, DEFINED BENEFIT (DB) VS. DEFINED CONTRIBUTION (DC) PLANS, 1975-2010*

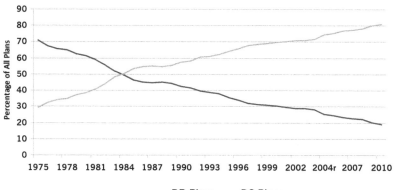

*Many people participate in more than one plan. In 2004 (shown twice) definitions changed.
Sources: U.S. Dept. of Labor, Private Pension Plan Bulletin Historical Tables and Graphs, Nov. 2012.

DEFINED BENEFIT: Employer and employees make contributions to a general pension fund managed by the employer. Based on a formula including years of employment and level of salary, each employee receives a fixed annual amount of money after retirement; that fixed amount does not depend on how well the investment of the fund does. The quality of the plan from the perspective of the employee depends on the amount of employee and employer contributions and on the particulars of the formula for determining benefits.

DEFINED CONTRIBUTION: Employer and employee make contributions to a fund that is identified with the individual and is managed by an investment firm. The money that the employee receives after retirement depends on the amount of money in the individual's fund. The quality of the plan from the perspective of the employee depends on the amount of employee and employer contributions and on how well the investment does, both up to and after the time of retirement.

---

investments made with the pension fund have done poorly, because the firm's revenues are less than anticipated, or both. Even if a private firm goes broke, defined benefit pensions are insured by the federal government, so the private-sector employee bears little or no risk. However, for public sector employees, who now account for most defined benefit plans, there is risk in extreme cases such as—you know it well!—Detroit in 2013. When a public employer goes bankrupt, the pensioners and active workers in the pension system are put in line behind the employer's creditors—mainly banks. (The Detroit situation is being disputed in the courts at this writing, but it does not appear likely that things will come out well for people in the public pension system.)

In defined contribution plans, the risk falls on the employee. The contributions (from both the employee and the employer) go into an investment fund for the individual worker, generally with taxes deferred until the money is taken out of the fund (as in a 401k). But if the economy goes sour— for example, if the stock market crashes— the employee has far less for retirement. This is exactly what happened with the crash of 2008.

There could hardly be a clearer case of conflict of interests between employees and employers. As employers have been able to hold down wages over the last several decades, they have shifted the burden of risk onto employees. There are several aspects of this power shift that have favored employers: the large decline in union membership, the way globalization has been structured to favor large firms, the general shift in political power (of which the decline in the minimum wage is a clear marker), and the way technological changes have been used to displace labor. The result has been a worsening of what workers get—stagnant wages and higher risk.

Social Security alone certainly does not provide a good standard of living. In 2012, the average annual Social Security payment from the Old-Age and Survivors Insurance trust fund was a little more than $14,000 per recipient. A person retiring in 2013 at age 65 who had been earning an annual salary of $70,000 (a bit more than the median family income), would receive about $21,000 annually. Even if all the efforts in Washington to cut Social Security benefits fail, it is easy to see why people need some additional form of retirement income to provide them with a reasonable standard of living during retirement.

Beyond Social Security, in 2010, active workers held 90.6 million pension plans, 17.2 million defined benefit plans and 73.4 million defined contribution plans. These figures involve some double counting, as many people have more than one pension plan, but, with a 2010 labor force of 153.9 million, this means that at least 41% of workers had no pension plan at all (other than Social Security). In fact, according to progressive pension expert Teresa Ghilarducci, a majority of workers do not have pension plans at work and over 75% of Americans nearing retirement age in 2010 had less than $30,000 in their retirement accounts.

While the pressure from business groups in Washington is to reduce Social Security, the current dismal state of retirement prospects for the majority of people in fact provides a strong case for a more extensive public pension system. ❑

Sources: Teresa Ghilarducci, "Don't Cut Pensions, Expand Them," *New York Times*, March 15, 2012; Teresa Ghilarducci, "Our Ridiculous Approach to Retirement, *New York Times*, July 21, 2012; Employee Benefit Research Institute, "The Basics of Social Security, Updated With the 2013 Board of Trustees Report," July 2013.

Article 6.7

THE CASE FOR SOCIAL WEALTH

BY ELLEN FRANK
May/June 2004

Pundits from the political left and right don't agree about war in Iraq, gay marriage, national energy policy, tax breaks, free trade, or much else. But they do agree on one thing: Americans don't save enough. The reasons are hotly disputed. Right-wingers contend that the tax code rewards spenders and punishes savers. Liberals argue that working families earn too little to save. Environmentalists complain of a work-spend rat race fueled by relentless advertising. But the bottom line seems beyond dispute.

Data on wealth-holding reveal that few Americans possess adequate wealth to finance a comfortable retirement. Virtually none have cash sufficient to survive an extended bout of unemployment. Only a handful of very affluent households could pay for health care if their insurance lapsed, cover nursing costs if they became disabled, or see their children through college without piling up student loans. Wealth is so heavily concentrated at the very top of the income distribution that even upper-middle class households are dangerously exposed to the vagaries of life and the economy.

With low savings and inadequate personal wealth identified as the problem, the solutions seem so clear as to rally wide bipartisan support: Provide tax credits for savings. Encourage employers to establish workplace savings plans. Educate people about family budgeting and financial investing. Promote home ownership so people can build home equity. Develop tax-favored plans to pay for college, retirement, and medical needs. More leftish proposals urge the government to redistribute wealth through federally sponsored "children's development accounts" or "American stakeholder accounts," so that Americans at all income levels can, as the Demos-USA website puts it, "enjoy the security and benefits that come with owning assets."

But such policies fail to address the paradoxical role savings play in market economies. Furthermore, looking at economic security solely through the lens of personal finance deflects focus away from a better, more direct, and far more reliable way to ensure Americans' well-being: promoting social wealth.

The Paradox of Thrift

Savings is most usefully envisaged as a physical concept. Each year businesses turn out automobiles, computers, lumber, and steel. Households (or consumers) buy much, but not all, of this output. The goods and services they leave behind represent the economy's savings.

Economics students are encouraged to visualize the economy as a metaphorical plumbing system through which goods and money flow. Firms produce goods, which flow through the marketplace and are sold for money. The money flows into peoples' pockets as income, which flows back into the marketplace as demand for goods. Savings represent a leak in the economic plumbing. If other purchasers don't step up and buy the output that thrifty consumers shun, firms lay off workers and curb production, for there is no profit in making goods that people don't want to buy.

On the other hand, whatever consumers don't buy is available for businesses to purchase in order to expand their capacity. When banks buy computers or developers buy lumber and steel, then the excess goods find a market and production continues apace. Economists refer to business purchases of new plant and equipment as "investment."

In the plumbing metaphor, investment is an injection—an additional flow of spending into the economy to offset the leaks caused by household saving.

During the industrial revolution, intense competition meant that whatever goods households did not buy or could not afford would be snatched up by emerging businesses, at least much of the time. By the turn of the 20th century, however, low-paid consumers had become a drag on economic growth. Small entrepreneurial businesses gave way to immense monopolistic firms like U.S. Steel and Standard Oil whose profits vastly exceeded what they could spend on expansion. Indeed expansion often looked pointless since, given the low level of household spending, the only buyers for their output were other businesses, who themselves faced the same dilemma.

As market economies matured, savings became a source of economic stagnation. Even the conspicuous consumption of Gilded Age business owners couldn't provide enough demand for the goods churned out of large industrial factories. Henry Ford was the first American corporate leader to deliberately pay his workers above-market wages, reasoning correctly that a better-paid work force would provide the only reliable market for his automobiles.

Today, thanks to democratic suffrage, labor unions, social welfare programs, and a generally more egalitarian culture, wages are far higher in industrialized economies than they were a century ago; wage and salary earners now secure nearly four-fifths of national income. And thrift seems a quaint virtue of our benighted grandparents. In the United States, the personal savings rate—the percentage of income flowing to households that they did not spend—fell to 1% in the late 1990s. Today, with a stagnant economy making consumers more cautious, the personal savings rate has risen—but only to around 4%.

Because working households consume virtually every penny they earn, goods and services produced are very likely to find buyers and continue to be produced. This is an important reason why the United States and Europe no longer experience the devastating depressions that beset industrialized countries prior to World War II.

Yet there is a surprisingly broad consensus that these low savings are a bad thing. Americans are often chastised for their lack of thrift, their failure to provide for themselves financially, their rash and excessive borrowing. Politicians and economists constantly exhort Americans to save more and devise endless schemes to induce them to do so.

At the same time, Americans also face relentless pressure to spend. After September 11, President Bush told the public they could best serve their country by continuing to shop. In the media, economic experts bemoan declines in "consumer confidence" and applaud reports of buoyant retail or auto sales. The U.S. economy, we are told, is a consumer economy—our spendthrift ways and shop-til-you-drop culture the motor that propels it. Free-spending consumers armed with multiple credit cards keep the stores hopping, the restaurants full, and the factories humming.

Our schizophrenic outlook on saving and spending has two roots. First, the idea of saving meshes seamlessly with a conservative ideological outlook. In what author George Lakoff calls the "strict-father morality" that informs conservative Republican politics, abstinence, thrift, self-reliance, and competitive individualism are moral virtues. Institutions that discourage saving—like Social Security, unemployment insurance, government health programs, state-funded student aid—are by definition socialistic and result in an immoral reliance on others. Former Treasury Secretary Paul O'Neill bluntly expressed this idea to a reporter for the *Financial Times* in 2001. "Able-bodied adults," O'Neill opined, "should save enough on a regular basis so that they can provide for their own retirement and for that matter for their health and medical needs." Otherwise, he continued, elderly people are just "dumping their problems on the broader society."

This ideological position, which is widely but not deeply shared among U.S. voters, receives financial and political support from the finance industry. Financial firms have funded most of the research, lobbying, and public relations for the campaign to "privatize" Social Security, replacing the current system of guaranteed, publicly-funded pensions with individual investment accounts. The finance industry and its wealthy clients also advocate "consumption taxes"—levying taxes on income spent, but not on income saved—so as to "encourage saving" and "reward thrift." Not coincidentally, the finance industry specializes in committing accumulated pools of money to the purchase of stocks, bonds and other paper assets, for which it receives generous fees and commissions.

Our entire economic system requires that people spend freely. Yet political rhetoric combined with pressure from the financial services industry urges individuals to save, or at least to try to save. This rhetoric finds a receptive audience in ordinary households anxious over their own finances and among many progressive public-interest groups alarmed by the threadbare balance sheets of so many American households.

So here is the paradox. People need protection against adversity, and an ample savings account provides such protection. But if ordinary households try to save and protect themselves against hard times, the unused factories, barren malls, and empty restaurants would bring those hard times upon them.

Social Wealth

The only way to address the paradox is to reconcile individuals' need for economic security with the public need for a stable economy. The solution therefore lies not in personal thrift or individual wealth, but in social insurance and public wealth.

When a country promotes economic security with dependable public investments and insurance programs, individuals have less need to amass private savings. Social Security, for example, provides the elderly with a direct claim on the nation's economic output after they retire. This guarantees that retirees keep spending and reduces the incentive for working adults to save. By restraining personal savings, Social Security improves the chances that income earned will translate into income spent, making the overall economy more stable.

Of course, Americans still need to save up for old-age; Social Security benefits replace, on average, only one-third of prior earnings. This argues not for more saving, however, but for more generous Social Security benefits. In Europe, public pensions replace from 50% to 70% of prior earnings.

Programs like Social Security and unemployment insurance align private motivation with the public interest in a high level of economic activity. Moreover, social insurance programs reduce people's exposure to volatile financial markets. Proponents of private asset building seem to overlook the lesson of the late 1990s stock market boom: that the personal wealth of small-scale savers is perilously vulnerable to stock market downswings, price manipulation, and fraud by corporate insiders.

It is commonplace to disparage social insurance programs as "big government" intrusions that burden the public with onerous taxes. But the case for a robust public sector is at least as much an economic as a moral one. Ordinary individuals and households fare better when they are assured some secure political claim on the economy's output, not only because of the payouts they receive as individuals, but because social claims on the economy render the economy itself more stable.

Well-funded public programs, for one thing, create reliable income streams and employment. Universal public schooling, for example, means that a sizable portion of our nation's income is devoted to building, equipping, staffing, and maintaining schools. This spending is less susceptible than private-sector spending to business cycles, price fluctuations, and job losses.

Programs that build social wealth also substantially ameliorate the sting of joblessness and minimize the broader economic fallout of unemployment when downturns do occur. Public schools, colleges, parks, libraries, hospitals, and transportation systems, as well as social insurance programs like unemployment compensation and disability coverage, all ensure that the unemployed continue to consume at least a minimal level of goods and services. Their children can still attend school and visit the playground. If there were no social supports, the unemployed would be forced to withdraw altogether from the economy, dragging wages down and setting off destabilizing depressions.

In a series of articles on the first Bush tax cut in 2001, the *New York Times* profiled Dr. Robert Cline, an Austin, Texas, surgeon whose $300,000 annual income still left him worried about financing college educations for his six children. Dr. Cline himself attended the University of Texas, at a cost of $250 per semester ($650 for medical school), but figured that "his own children's education will likely cost tens of thousands of dollars each." Dr. Cline supported the 2001 tax cut, the *Times* reported. Ironically, though, that cut contributed to an environment in which institutions like the University of Texas raise tuitions, restrict enrollments, and drive Dr. Cline and others to attempt to amass enough personal wealth to pay for their children's education.

Unlike Dr. Cline, most people will never accumulate sufficient hoards of wealth to afford expensive high-quality services like education or to indemnify themselves against the myriad risks of old age, poor health, and unemployment. Even when middle-income households do manage to stockpile savings, they have little control over the rate at which their assets can be converted to cash.

Virtually all people—certainly the 93% of U.S. households earning less than $150,000—would fare better collectively than they could individually. Programs that provide direct access to important goods and services—publicly financed education, recreation, health care, and pensions—reduce the inequities that follow inevitably from an entirely individualized economy. The vast majority of people are better off with the high probability of a secure income and guaranteed access to key services such as health care than with the low-probability prospect of becoming rich.

The next time a political candidate recommends some tax-exempt individual asset-building scheme, progressively minded people should ask her these questions. If consumers indeed save more and the government thus collects less tax revenue, who will buy the goods these thrifty consumers now forgo? Who will employ the workers who used to manufacture those goods? Who will build the public assets that lower tax revenues render unaffordable? And how exactly does creating millions of little pots of gold substitute for a collective commitment to social welfare? ❑

Chapter 7

THE INTERNATIONAL FINANCIAL SYSTEM

Article 7.1

THE GIANT POOL OF MONEY

BY ARTHUR MacEWAN
September/October 2009

Dear Dr. Dollar:
On May 9, the public radio program This American Life broadcast an explanation of the housing crisis with the title: "The Giant Pool of Money." With too much money looking for investment opportunities, lots of bad investments were made—including the bad loans to home buyers. But where did this "giant pool of money" come from? Was this really a source of the home mortgage crisis?
—Gail Radford, Buffalo, N.Y.

The show was both entertaining and interesting. A good show, but maybe a bit more explanation will be useful.

There was indeed a "giant pool of money" that was an important part of the story of the home mortgage crisis—well, not "money" as we usually think of it, but financial assets, which I'll get to in a moment. And that pool of money is an important link in the larger economic crisis story.

The giant pool of money was the build-up of financial assets—U.S. Treasury bonds, for example, and other assets that pay a fixed income. According to the program, the amount of these assets had grown from roughly $36 trillion in 2000 to $70 trillion in 2008. That's $70 *trillion*, with a T, which is a lot of money, roughly the same as total world output in 2008.

These financial assets built up for a number of reasons. One was the doubling of oil prices (after adjusting for inflation) between 2000 and 2007, largely due to the U.S. invasion of Iraq. This put a lot of money in the hands of governments in oil-producing countries and private individuals connected to the oil industry.

A second factor was the large build-up of reserves (i.e., the excess of receipts from exports over payments for imports) by several low-income countries, most notably China. One reason some countries operated in this manner was simply to keep the cost of their currency low in terms of U.S. dollars, thus maintaining demand for their exports. (Using their own currencies to buy dollars, they were increasing both the supply of their currencies and the demand for dollars; this pushed the price of their currencies down and of dollars up.) But another reason was to protect themselves from the sort of problems they had faced in the early 1980s, when world recession cut their export earnings and left them unable to meet their import costs and pay their debts—thus the debt crisis of that era.

This build-up of dollar reserves by governments (actually, central banks) of other countries was also a result of the budgetary deficits of the Bush administration. Spending more than it was taking in as taxes (after the big tax cuts for the wealthy and with the heavy war spending), the Bush administration needed to borrow. Foreign governments, by buying the U.S. securities, were providing the loans.

Still a third factor explaining the giant pool of financial assets was the high level of inequality within the United States and elsewhere in the global economy. Since 1993, half of all income gains in the United States have gone to the highest-income 1% of households. While the very rich spend a good share of their money on mansions, fancy cars, and other luxuries, there was plenty more money for them to put into investments—the stock market but also fixed-income securities (i.e., bonds).

So there is the giant pool of money or, again, of financial assets.

The financial assets became a problem for two connected reasons. First, in the recovery following the 2001 recession, economic growth was very slow; there were thus very limited real investment opportunities. Between 2001 and 2007, private fixed investment (adjusted for inflation) grew by only 11%, whereas in the same number of years following the recession of the early 1990s, investment grew by 59%.

Second, in an effort to stimulate more growth, the Federal Reserve kept interest rates very low. But the low interest rates meant low returns on financial assets— U.S. government bonds in particular, but financial assets in general. So the holders of financial assets went searching for new investment opportunities, which, as the radio program explained, meant pushing money into high-risk mortgages. The rest, as they say, is history.

So the giant pool of money was the link that tied high inequality, the war, and rising financial imbalances in the world economy (caused in large part by the U.S. government's budgetary policies) to the housing crisis and thus to the more general financial crisis. ❏

Article 7.2

W(H)ITHER THE DOLLAR?

The U.S. trade deficit, the global economic crisis, and the dollar's status as the world's reserve currency.

BY KATHERINE SCIACCHITANO
May/June 2010

For more than half a century, the dollar was both a symbol and an instrument of U.S. economic and military power. At the height of the financial crisis in the fall of 2008, the dollar served as a safe haven for investors, and demand for U.S. Treasury bonds ("Treasuries") spiked. More recently, the United States has faced a vacillating dollar, calls to replace the greenback as the global reserve currency, and an international consensus that it should save more and spend less.

At first glance, circumstances seem to give reason for concern. The U.S. budget deficit is over 10% of GDP. China has begun a long-anticipated move away from Treasuries, threatening to make U.S. government borrowing more expensive. And the adoption of austerity measures in Greece—with a budget deficit barely 3% higher than the United States—hovers as a reminder that the bond market can enforce wage cuts and pension freezes on developed as well as developing countries.

These pressures on the dollar and for fiscal cut-backs and austerity come at an awkward time given the level of public outlays required to deal with the crisis and the need to attract international capital to pay for them. But the pressures also highlight the central role of the dollar in the crisis. Understanding that role is critical to grasping the link between the financial recklessness we've been told is to blame for the crisis and the deeper causes of the crisis in the real economy: that link is the outsize U.S. trade deficit.

Trade deficits are a form of debt. For mainstream economists, the cure for the U.S. deficit is thus increased "savings": spend less and the bottom line will improve. But the U.S. trade deficit didn't balloon because U.S. households or the government went on a spending spree. It ballooned because, from the 1980s on, successive U.S. administrations pursued a high-dollar policy that sacrificed U.S. manufacturing for finance, and that combined low-wage, export-led growth in the global South with low-wage, debt-driven consumption at home. From the late nineties, U.S. dollars that went out to pay for imports increasingly came back not as demand for U.S. goods, but as demand for investments that fueled U.S. housing and stock market bubbles. Understanding the history of how the dollar helped create these imbalances, and how these imbalances in turn led to the housing bubble and subprime crash, sheds important light on how labor and the left should respond to pressures for austerity and "saving" as the solution to the crisis.

Gold, Deficits, and Austerity

A good place to start is with the charge that the Federal Reserve triggered the housing bubble by lowering interest rates after the dot-com bubble burst and plunged the country into recession in 2001.

In 2001, manufacturing was too weak to lead a recovery, and the Bush administration was ideologically opposed to fiscal stimulus other than tax cuts for the wealthy. So the real question isn't why the Fed lowered rates; it's why it was able to. In 2000, the U.S. trade deficit stood at 3.7% of GDP. Any other country with this size deficit would have had to tighten its belt and jump-start exports, not embark on stimulating domestic demand that could deepen the deficit even more.

The Fed's ability to lower interest rates despite the U.S. trade deficit stemmed from the dollar's role as the world's currency, which was established during the Bretton Woods negotiations for a new international monetary system at the end of World War II.

A key purpose of an international monetary system—Bretton Woods or any other—is to keep international trade and debt in balance. Trade has to be mutual. One country can't do all the selling while other does all the buying; both must be able to buy and sell. If one or more countries develop trade deficits that persist, they won't be able to continue to import without borrowing and going into debt. At the same time, some other country or countries will have corresponding trade surpluses. The result is a global trade imbalance. To get back "in balance," the deficit country has to import less, export more, or both. The surplus country has to do the reverse.

In practice, economic pressure is stronger on deficit countries to adjust their trade balances by importing less, since it's deficit countries that could run out of money to pay for imports. Importing less can be accomplished with import quotas (which block imports over a set level) or tariffs (which decrease demand for imports by imposing a tax on them). It can also be accomplished with "austerity"—squeezing demand by lowering wages.

Under the gold standard, this squeezing took place automatically. Gold was shipped out of a country to pay for a trade deficit. Since money had to be backed by gold, having less gold meant less money in domestic circulation. So prices and wages fell. Falling wages in turn lowered demand for imports and boosted exports. The deficit was corrected, but at the cost of recession, austerity, and hardship for workers. In other words, the gold standard was deflationary.

Bretton Woods

The gold standard lasted until the Great Depression, and in fact helped to cause it. Beyond the high levels of unemployment, one of the most vivid lessons from the global catastrophe that ensued was the collapse of world trade, as country after country tried to deal with falling exports by limiting imports. After World War II, the industrialized countries wanted an international monetary system that could correct trade imbalances without imposing austerity and risking another depression. This was particularly important given the post-war levels of global debt and deficits, which could have suppressed demand and blocked trade again. Countries pursued these aims at the Bretton Woods negotiations in 1944, in Bretton Woods, New Hampshire.

John Maynard Keynes headed the British delegation. Keynes was already famous for his advocacy of government spending to bolster demand and maintain employment during recessions and depressions. England also owed large war debts to the United States and had suffered from high unemployment for over two decades. Keynes therefore had a keen interest in creating a system that prevented the build-up of global debt and avoided placing the full pressure of correcting trade imbalances on debtor countries.

His proposed solution was an international clearing union—a system of accounts kept in a fictitious unit called the "bancor." Accounts would be tallied each year to see which countries were in deficit and which were in surplus. Countries with trade deficits would have to work to import less and export more. In the meantime, they would have the unconditional right—for a period—to an "overdraft" of bancors, the size of the overdraft to be based on the size of previous surpluses. These overdrafts would both support continued imports of necessities and guarantee uninterrupted global trade. At the same time, countries running trade surpluses would be expected to get back in balance too by importing more, and would be fined if their surpluses persisted.

Keynes was also adamant that capital controls be part of the new system. Capital controls are restrictions on the movement of capital across borders. Keynes wanted countries to be able to resort to macroeconomic tools such as deficit spending, lowering interest rates, and expanding money supplies to bolster employment and wages when needed. He worried that without capital controls, capital flight—investors taking their money and running—could veto economic policies and force countries to raise interest rates, cut spending, and lower wages instead, putting downward pressure on global demand as the gold standard had.

Keynes's system wouldn't have solved the problems of capitalism—in his terms, the problem of insufficient demand, and in Marx's terms the problems of overproduction and under-consumption. But by creating incentives for surplus countries to import more, it would have supported global demand and job growth and made the kind of trade imbalances that exist today—including the U.S. trade deficit—much less likely. It would also have taken the pressure off deficit countries to adopt austerity measures. And it would have prevented surplus countries from using the power of debt to dictate economic policy to deficit countries.

At the end of World War II, the United States was, however, the largest surplus country in the world, and it intended to remain so for the foreseeable future. The New Deal had lowered unemployment during the Depression. But political opposition to deficit spending had prevented full recovery until arms production for the war restored manufacturing. Many feared that without continued large U.S. trade surpluses and expanded export markets, unemployment would return to Depression-era levels.

The United States therefore blocked Keynes' proposal. Capital controls were permitted for the time being, largely because of the danger that capital would flee war-torn Europe. But penalties for surplus countries were abandoned; pressures remained primarily on deficit countries to correct. Instead of an international clearing union with automatic rights to overdrafts, the International Monetary Fund (IMF) was established to make short-term loans to deficit countries. And instead of the neutral bancor, the dollar—backed by the U.S. pledge to redeem dollars with gold at $35 an ounce—would be the world currency.

Limits of the System

The system worked for just over twenty-five years, not because trade was balanced, but because the United States was able and willing to recycle its huge trade surpluses. U.S. military spending stayed high because of the U.S. cold-war role as "global cop." And massive aid was given to Europe to rebuild. Dollars went out as foreign aid and military spending (both closely coordinated). They came back as demand for U.S. goods.

At the same time, memory of the Depression created a kind of Keynesian consensus in the advanced industrial democracies to use fiscal and monetary policy to maintain full employment. Labor movements, strengthened by both the war and the post-war boom, pushed wage settlements and welfare spending higher. Global demand was high.

Two problems doomed the system. First, the IMF retained the power to impose conditions on debtor countries, and the United States retained the power to control the IMF.

Second, the United States stood outside the rules of the game: The larger the world economy grew, the more dollars would be needed in circulation; U.S. trade deficits would eventually have to provide them. Other countries would have to correct their trade deficits by tightening their belts to import less, exporting more by devaluing their currencies to push down prices, or relying on savings from trade surpluses denominated in dollars (known as "reserves") to pay for their excess of imports over exports. But precisely because countries needed dollar reserves to pay for international transactions and to provide cushions against periods of deficits, other countries would need to hold the U.S. dollars they earned by investing them in U.S. assets. This meant that U.S. dollars that went out for imports would come back and be reinvested in the United States. Once there, these dollars could be used to finance continued spending on imports—and a larger U.S. trade deficit. At that point, sustaining world trade would depend not on recycling U.S. surpluses, but on recycling U.S. deficits. The ultimate result would be large, destabilizing global capital flows.

The Crisis of the Seventies

The turning point came in the early seventies. Europe and Japan had rebuilt from the war and were now export powers in their own right. The U.S. trade surplus was turning into a deficit. And the global rate of profit in manufacturing was falling. The United States had also embarked on its "War on Poverty" just as it increased spending on its real war in Vietnam, and this "guns and butter" strategy—an attempt to quell domestic opposition from the civil right and anti-war movements while maintaining global military dominance—led to high inflation.

The result was global economic crisis: the purchasing power of the dollar fell, just as more and more dollars were flowing out of the United States and being held by foreigners.

What had kept the United States from overspending up to this point was its Bretton Woods commitment to exchange dollars for gold at the rate of $35 an ounce. Now countries and investors that didn't want to stand by and watch as the purchasing power of their dollar holdings fell—as well as countries that objected to the Vietnam War—held the United States to its pledge.

There wasn't enough gold in Ft. Knox. The United States would have to retrench its global military role, reign in domestic spending, or change the rules of the game. It changed the rules of the game. In August 1971, Nixon closed the gold window; the United States would no longer redeem dollars for gold. Countries and individuals would have to hold dollars, or dump them and find another currency that was more certain to hold its value. There was none.

The result was that the dollar remained the global reserve currency. But the world moved from a system where the United States could spend only if could back its spending by gold, to a system where its spending was limited only by the quantity of dollars the rest of the world was willing to hold. The value of the dollar would fluctuate with the level of global demand for U.S. products and investment. The value of other currencies would fluctuate with the dollar.

Trading Manufacturing for Finance

The result of this newfound freedom to spend was a decade of global inflation and crises of the dollar. As inflation grew, each dollar purchased less. As each dollar purchased less, the global demand to hold dollars dropped—and with it the dollar's exchange rate. As the exchange rate fell, imports became even more expensive, and inflation ratcheted up again. The cycle intensified when OPEC—which priced its oil in dollars—raised its prices to compensate for the falling dollar.

Owners of finance capital were unhappy because inflation was eroding the value of dollar assets. Owners of manufacturing capital were unhappy because the global rate of profit in manufacturing was dropping. And both U.S. politicians and elites were unhappy because the falling dollar was eroding U.S. military power by making it more expensive.

The response of the Reagan administration was to unleash neoliberalism on both the national and global levels—the so-called Reagan revolution. On the domestic front, inflation was quelled, and the labor movement was put in its place, with high interest rates and the worst recession since the Depression. Corporate profits were boosted directly through deregulation, privatization, and tax cuts, and indirectly by attacks on unions, unemployment insurance, and social spending.

When it was over, profits were up, inflation and wages were down, and the dollar had changed direction. High interest rates attracted a stream of investment capital into the United States, pushing up demand for the currency, and with it the exchange rate. The inflows paid for the growing trade and budget deficits—Reagan had cut domestic spending, but increased military spending. And they provided abundant capital for finance and overseas investment. But the high dollar also made U.S. exports more expensive for the rest of the world. The United States had effectively traded manufacturing for finance and debt.

Simultaneously, debt was used as a hammer to impose neoliberalism on the Third World. As the price of oil rose in the seventies, OPEC countries deposited their growing trade surpluses—so-called petro-dollars—in U.S. banks, which in turn loaned them to poor countries to pay for the soaring price of oil. Initially set at very low interest rates, loan payments skyrocketed when the United States jacked up its rates to deal with inflation. Third World countries began defaulting, starting with Mexico in 1981. In response, and in exchange for more loans, the U.S.-controlled IMF imposed austerity programs, also known as "structural adjustment programs."

The programs were similar to the policies in the United States, but much more severe, and they operated in reverse. Instead of pushing up exchange rates to attract finance capital as the United States had done, Third World countries were told to devalue their currencies to attract foreign direct investment and export their way out of debt. Capital controls were dismantled to enable transnational corporations to enter and exit at will. Governments were forced to slash spending on social programs and infrastructure to push down wages and demand for imports. Services were privatized to create opportunities for private capital, and finance was deregulated.

Policies dovetailed perfectly. As the high dollar hollowed out U.S. manufacturing, countries in the Global South were turned into low-wage export platforms. As U.S. wages stagnated or fell, imports became cheaper, masking the pain. Meanwhile, the high dollar lowered the cost of overseas production. Interest payments on third world debt—which continued to grow—swelled the already large capital flows into the United States and provided even more funds for overseas investment.

The view from the heights of finance looked promising. But Latin America was entering what became known as "the lost decade." And the United State was shifting from exporting goods to exporting demand, and from recycling its trade surplus to recycling its deficit. The world was becoming dependent on the United States as the "consumer of last resort." The United States was becoming dependent on finance and debt.

Consolidating Neoliberalism

The growth of finance in the eighties magnified its political clout in the nineties. With the bond market threatening to charge higher rates for government debt, Clinton abandoned campaign pledges to invest in U.S. infrastructure, education, and industry. Instead, he balanced the budget; he adopted his own high-dollar policy, based on the theory that global competition would keep imports cheap, inflation low, and the living standard high—regardless of sluggish wage growth; and he continued deregulation of the finance industry—repealing Glass-Steagall and refusing to regulate derivatives. By the end of Clinton's second term, the U.S. trade deficit had hit a record 3.7% of GDP; household debt had soared to nearly 69% of GDP and financial profits had risen to 30% of GDP, almost twice as high as they had been at any time up to the mid 1980s.

Internationally, Clinton consolidated IMF-style structural adjustment policies under the rubric of "the Washington Consensus," initiated a new era of trade agreements modeled on the North American Free Trade Agreement, and led the charge to consolidate the elimination of capital controls.

The elimination of capital controls deepened global economic instability in several ways.

First, eliminating restrictions on capital mobility made it easier for capital to go in search of the lowest wages. This expanded the globalization of production, intensifying downward pressure on wages and global demand.

Second, removing capital controls increased the political power of capital by enabling it to "vote with its feet." This accelerated the deregulation of global finance and—as Keynes predicted—limited countries' abilities to run full-employment policies. Regulation of business was punished, as was deficit spending, regardless of its purpose. Low inflation and deregulation of labor markets—weakening unions and making wages more "flexible"—were rewarded.

Finally, capital mobility fed asset bubbles and increased financial speculation and exchange rate volatility. As speculative capital rushed into countries, exchange rates rose; as it fled, they fell. Speculators began betting more and more on currencies themselves, further magnifying rate swings. Rising exchange rates made exports uncompetitive, hurting employment and wages. Falling exchange rates increased the competitiveness of exports, but made imports and foreign borrowing more expensive, except for the United States, which borrows in its own currency. Countries could try to prevent capital flight by raising interest rates, but only at the cost of dampening growth and lost of jobs. Lacking capital controls, there was little countries could do to prevent excessive inflows and bubbles.

Prelude to a Crash

This increased capital mobility, deregulation, and speculation weakened the real economy, further depressed global demand, and greatly magnified economic instability. From the eighties onward, international financial crises broke out approximately every five years, in countries ranging from Mexico to the former Soviet Union.

By far the largest crisis prior to the sub-prime meltdown took place in East Asia in the mid-nineties. Speculative capital began flowing into East Asia in the mid nineties. In 1997, the bubble burst. By the summer of 1998, stock markets around the world were crashing from the ripple effects. The IMF stepped in with $40 billion in loans, bailing out investors but imposing harsh conditions on workers and governments. Millions were left unemployed as Asia plunged into depression.

When the dust settled, Asian countries said "never again." Their solution was to build up large dollar reserves—savings cushions—so they would never have to turn to the IMF for another loan. To build up reserves, countries had to run large trade surpluses. This meant selling even more to the United States, the only market in the world able and willing to run ever-larger trade deficits to absorb their exports.

In addition to further weakening U.S. manufacturing, the Asia crisis set the stage for the sub-prime crisis in several ways.

First, as capital initially fled Asia, it sought out the United States as a "safe haven," igniting the U.S. stock market and nascent housing bubbles.

Second, the longer-term recycling of burgeoning Asian surpluses ensured an abundant and ongoing source of capital to finance not only the mounting trade deficit, but also the billowing U.S. consumer debt more generally.

Third, preventing their exchange rates from rising with their trade surpluses and making their exports uncompetitive required Asian central banks to print money, swelling global capital flows even more.

Between 1998 and 2007, when the U.S. housing bubble burst, many policy makers and mainstream economists came to believe this inflow of dollars and debt would never stop. It simply seemed too mutually beneficial to end. By financing the U.S. trade deficit, Asian countries guaranteed U.S. consumers would continue to purchase their goods. The United States in turn got cheap imports, cheap money for consumer finance, and inflated stock and real estate markets that appeared to be self-financing and to compensate for stagnating wages. At the same time, foreign holders of dollars bought increasing quantities of U.S. Treasuries, saving the U.S. government from having to raise interest rates to attract purchasers, and giving the United States cheap financing for its budget deficit as well.

It was this ability to keep interest rates low—in particular, the Fed's ability to lower rates after the stock market bubble collapsed in 2000—that set off the last and most destructive stage of the housing bubble. Lower interest rates simultaneously increased the demand for housing (since lower interest rates made mortgages cheaper) and decreased the returns to foreign holders of U.S. Treasuries. These lower returns forced investors to look for other "safe" investments with higher yields. Investors believed they found what they needed in U.S. mortgage securities.

As Wall Street realized what a lucrative international market they had, the big banks purposefully set out to increase the number of mortgages that could be repackaged and sold to investors by lowering lending standards. They also entered into complicated systems of private bets, known as credit default swaps, to insure against the risk of defaults. These credit default swaps created a chain of debt that exponentially magnified risk. When the bubble finally burst, only massive stimulus spending and infusions of capital by the industrialized countries into their banking systems kept the world from falling into another depression.

Deficit Politics

The political establishment—right and center—is now licking its chops, attacking fiscal deficits as if ending them were a solution to the crisis. The underlying theory harks back to the deflationary operation of the gold standard and the conditions imposed by the IMF: Government spending causes trade deficits and inflation by increasing demand. Cutting spending will cut deficits by diminishing demand.

Like Clinton before him, Obama is now caving in to the bond market, fearful that international lenders will raise interest rates on U.S. borrowing. He has created a bipartisan debt commission to focus on long-term fiscal balance—read: cutting Social Security and Medicare—and revived "PAYGO," which requires either cuts or increases in revenue to pay for all new outlays, even as unemployment hovers just under 10%.

By acquiescing, the U.S. public is implicitly blaming itself for the crisis and offering to pay for it twice: first with the millions of jobs lost to the recession, and again by weakening the safety net. But the recent growth of the U.S. budget deficit principally reflects the cost of cleaning up the crisis and of the wars in Iraq and Afghanistan. Assumptions of future deficits are rooted in projected health-care costs in the absence of meaningful reform. And the U.S. trade deficit is driven mainly by the continued high dollar.

The economic crisis won't be resolved by increasing personal savings or enforcing fiscal discipline, because its origins aren't greedy consumers or profligate governments. The real origins of the crisis are the neoliberal response to the crisis of the 1970s—the shift from manufacturing to finance in the United States, and the transformation of the Global South into a low-wage export platform for transnational capital to bolster sagging profit rate. The U.S. trade and budget deficits may symbolize this transformation. But the systemic problem is a global economic model that separates consumption from production and that has balanced world demand—not just the U.S. economy—on debt and speculation.

Forging an alternative will be the work of generations. As for the present, premature tightening of fiscal policy as countries try to "exit" from the crisis will simply drain global demand and endanger recovery. Demonizing government spending will erode the social wage and undermine democratic debate about the public investment needed for a transition to an environmentally sustainable global economy.

In the United States, where labor market and financial deregulation have garnered the most attention in popular critiques of neoliberalism, painting a bulls-eye on government spending also obscures the role of the dollar and U.S. policy in the crisis. For several decades after World War II, U.S. workers benefited materially as the special status of the dollar helped expand export markets for U.S. goods. But as other labor movements throughout the world know from bitter experience, it's the dollar as the world's currency, together with U.S. control of the IMF, that ultimately provided leverage for the United States to create the low-wage export model of growth and financial deregulation that has so unbalanced the global economy and hurt "first" and "third" world workers alike.

Looking Ahead

At the end of World War II, John Maynard Keynes proposed an international monetary system with the bancor at its core; the system would have helped balance trade and avoid the debt and deflation in inherent in the gold standard that preceded the Great Depression. Instead, Bretton Woods was negotiated, with the dollar as the world's currency. What's left of that system has now come full circle and created the very problems it was intended to avoid: large trade imbalances and deflationary economic conditions.

For the past two and a half decades, the dollar enabled the United States to run increasing trade deficits while systematically draining capital from some of the poorest countries in the world. This money could have been used for development in the Global South, to replace aging infrastructure in the United States, or to prepare for and prevent climate change. Instead, it paid for U.S. military interventions, outsourcing, tax cuts for the wealthy, and massive stock market and housing bubbles.

This mismanagement of the dollar hasn't served the long-term interests of workers the United States any more than it has those in of the developing world.

In domestic terms, it has been particularly damaging over the last three decades to U.S. manufacturing, and state budgets and workers are being hit hard by the crisis. Yet even manufacturing workers in the United States cling to the high dollar as if it were a life raft. Many public sector workers advocate cutting back on government spending. And most people in the United States would blame bankers' compensation packages for the sub-prime mess before pointing to the dismantling of capital controls.

After suffering through the worst unemployment since the Depression and paying for the bailout of finance, U.S. unions and the left are right to be angry. On the global scale, there is increased space for activism. Since the summer of 2007, at least 17 countries have imposed or tightened capital controls. Greek workers have been in the streets protesting pension cuts and pay freezes for months now. And a global campaign has been launched for a financial transactions tax that would slow down speculation and provide needed revenue for governments. Together, global labor and the left are actively rethinking and advocating reform of the global financial system, the neoliberal trade agreements, and the role and governance of the International Monetary Fund. And there is increasing discussion of a replacement for the dollar that won't breed deficits, suck capital out of the developing world, impose austerity on deficit countries—or blow bubbles.

All these reforms are critical. All will require more grassroots education. None will come without a struggle. ❏

Sources: C. Fred Bergsten, "The Dollar and the Deficits: How Washington Can Prevent the Next Crisis," Peterson Institute for International Economics, *Foreign Affairs*, Volume 88 No. 6, November 2009; Dean Baker, "The Budget, the Deficit, and the Dollar," Center for Economic Policy and Research, www.cepr.net; Martin Wolf, "Give us fiscal austerity, but not quite yet," *Financial Times* blogs, November 24, 2009; Tom Palley, "Domestic Demand-led Growth: A New Paradigm for Development," paper presented at the Alterantives to Neoliberalism Conference sponsored by the New Rules for Global Finance Coalition, May 21-24, 2002, www.economicswebinstitute.org; Sarah Anderson, "Policy Handcuffs in the Financial Crisis: How U.S. Government And Trade Policy Limit Government Power To Control Capital Flows, " Institute for Policy Studies, February 2009; Susan George, "The World Trade Organisation We Could Have Had," *Le Monde Diplomatique*, January 2007.

Article 7.3

U.S. BANKS AND THE DIRTY MONEY EMPIRE

BY JAMES PETRAS
September/October 2001

Washington and the mass media have portrayed the United States as being in the forefront of the struggle against narcotics trafficking, drug-money laundering, and political corruption. The image is of clean white hands fighting dirty money from the Third World (or the ex-Communist countries). The truth is exactly the opposite. U.S. banks have developed an elaborate set of policies for transferring illicit funds to the U.S. and "laundering" those funds by investing them in legitimate businesses or U.S. government bonds. The U.S. Congress has held numerous hearings, provided detailed exposés of the illicit practices of the banks, passed several anti-laundering laws, and called for stiffer enforcement by public regulators and private bankers. Yet the biggest banks continue their practices and the sums of dirty money grow exponentially. The $500 billion of criminal and dirty money flowing annually into and through the major U.S. banks far exceeds the net revenues of all the information technology companies in the United States. These yearly inflows surpass the net profits repatriated from abroad by the major U.S. oil producers, military industries, and airplane manufacturers combined. Neither the banks nor the government has the will or the interest to put an end to practices that provide such high profits and help maintain U.S. economic supremacy internationally.

Big U.S. Banks and Dirty Money Laundering

"Current estimates are that $500 billion to $1 trillion in illegal funds from organized crime, narcotics trafficking and other criminal misconduct are laundered through banks worldwide each year," writes Senator Carl Levin (D-MI), "with about half going through U.S. banks." The senator's statement, however, only covers proceeds from activities that are crimes under U.S. law. It does not include financial transfers by corrupt political leaders or tax evasion by overseas businesses, since in those cases any criminal activity takes place outside the United States. Raymond Baker, a leading U.S. expert on international finance and guest scholar in economic studies at the Brookings Institution, estimates the total "flow of corrupt money ... into Western coffers" from Third World or ex-Communist economies at $20 to $40 billion a year. He puts the "flow stemming from mis-priced trade" (the difference between the price quoted, for tax purposes, of goods sold abroad, and their real price) at a minimum of $80 billion a year. "My lowest estimate is $100 billion per year by these two means ... a trillion dollars in the decade, at least half to the United States," Baker concludes. "Including other elements of illegal flight capital would produce much higher figures."

The money laundering business, whether "criminal" or "corrupt," is carried out by the United States' most important banks. The bank officials involved in money laundering have backing from the highest levels of the banking institutions. These are not isolated offenses perpetrated by loose cannons. Take the case of Citibank's laundering of Raúl Salinas' $200 million account. The day after Salinas, the brother of Mexico's ex-President Carlos Salinas de Gortari, was arrested and his large-scale theft of government funds was exposed, his private bank manager at Citibank, Amy Elliott, said in a phone conversation with colleagues (the transcript of which was made available to Congressional investigators) that "this goes [on] in the very, very top of the corporation, this was known … on the very top. We are little pawns in this whole thing."

Citibank is the United States' biggest bank, with 180,000 employees world-wide, operating in 100 countries, with $700 billion in known assets. It operates what are known as "private banking" offices in 30 countries, with over $100 billion in client assets. Private banking is the sector of a bank which caters to extremely wealthy clients, with deposits of $1 million or more. The big banks charge customers for managing their assets and for providing the specialized services of the private banks. These services go beyond routine banking services like check clearing and deposits, to include investment guidance, estate planning, tax assistance, off-shore accounts, and complicated schemes designed to secure the confidentiality of financial transactions. Private banks sell secrecy to their clients, making them ideal for money laundering. They routinely use code names for accounts. Their "concentration accounts" disguise the movement of client funds by co-mingling them with bank funds, cutting off paper trails for billions of dollars in wire transfers. And they locate offshore private investment corporations in countries such as the Cayman Islands and the Bahamas, which have strict banking secrecy laws. These laws allow offshore banks and corporations to hide a depositor's name, nationality, the amount of funds deposited, and when they were deposited. They do not require any declarations from bank officials about sources of funds.

Private investment corporations (PICs) are one particulary tricky way that big banks hold and hide a client's assets. The nominal officers, trustees, and shareholders of these shell corporations are themselves shell corporations controlled by the private bank. The PIC then becomes the official holder of the client's accounts, while the client's identity is buried in so-called "records of jurisdiction" in countries with strict secrecy laws. The big banks keep pre-packaged PICs on the shelf awaiting activation when a private bank client wants one. The system works like Russian matryoshka dolls, shells within shells within shells, which in the end can be impenetrable to legal process.

Hearings held in 1999 by the Senate's Permanent Subcommittee on Investigations (under the Governmental Affairs Committee) revealed that in the Salinas case, private banking personnel at Citibank—which has a larger global private banking operation than any other U.S. bank—helped Salinas transfer $90 to $100 million out of Mexico while disguising the funds' sources and destination. The bank set up a dummy offshore corporation, provided Salinas with a secret code-name, provided an alias for a third party intermediary who deposited the money in a Citibank account in Mexico, transferred the money in a concentration account to New York, and finally moved it to Switzerland and London.

Instead of an account with the name "Raúl Salinas" attached, investigators found a Cayman Islands account held by a PIC called "Trocca, Ltd.," according to

Minority Counsel Robert L. Roach of the Permanent Committee on Investigations. Three Panama shell companies formed Trocca, Ltd.'s board of directors and three Cayman shell companies were its officers and shareholders. "Citibank controls all six of these shell companies and routinely uses them to function as directors and officers of PICs that it makes available to private clients," says Roach. Salinas was only referred to in Citibank documents as "Confidential Client No. 2" or "CC-2."

Historically, big-bank money laundering has been investigated, audited, criticized, and subjected to legislation. The banks have written their own compliance procedures. But the big banks ignore the laws and procedures, and the government ignores their non-compliance. The Permanent Subcommittee on Investigations discovered that Citibank provided "services," moving a total of at least $360 million, for four major political swindlers, all of whom lost their protection when the political winds shifted in their home countries: Raúl Salinas, between $80 and $100 million; Asif Ali Zardari (husband of former Prime Minister of Pakistan), over $40 million; El Hadj Omar Bongo (dictator of Gabon since 1967), over $130 million; Mohammed, Ibrahim, and Abba Sani Abacha (sons of former Nigerian dictator General Sani Abacha), over $110 million. In all cases Citibank violated all of its own procedures and government guidelines: there was no review of the client's background (known as the "client profile"), no determination of the source of the funds, and no inquiry into any violations of the laws of the country where the money originated. On the contrary, the bank facilitated the outflow in its prepackaged format: shell corporations were established, code names were provided, funds were moved through concentration accounts, and the funds were invested in legitimate businesses or in U.S. bonds. In none of these cases did the banks practice "due diligence," taking the steps required by law to ensure that it does not facilitate money laundering. Yet top banking officials have never been brought to court and tried. Even after the arrest of its clients, Citibank continued to provide them with its services, including moving funds to secret accounts.

Another route that the big banks use to launder dirty money is "correspondent banking." Correspondent banking is the provision of banking services by one bank to another. It enables overseas banks to conduct business and provide services for their customers in jurisdictions where the bank has no physical presence. A bank that is licensed in a foreign country and has no office in the United States can use correspondent banking to attract and retain wealthy criminal or corrupt clients interested in laundering money in the United States. Instead of exposing itself to U.S. controls and incurring the high costs of locating in the U.S., the bank will open a correspondent account with an existing U.S. bank. By establishing such a relationship, the foreign bank (called the "respondent") and its customers can receive many or all of the services offered by the U.S. bank (called the "correspondent"). Today, all the big U.S. banks have established multiple correspondent relationships throughout the world so they may engage in international financial transactions for themselves and their clients in places where they do not have a physical presence. The largest U.S. and European banks, located in financial centers like New York or London, serve as correspondents for thousands of other banks. Most of the offshore banks laundering billions for criminal clients have accounts in the United States. Through June 1999, the top five correspondent bank holding companies in the United States held correspondent account balances exceeding $17 billion; the total correspondent balances of the 75 largest U.S. correspondent banks was $34.9 billion. For billionaire criminals an important feature of correspondent relationships is that they provide access to international transfer systems. The biggest banks specializing in international fund transfers (called "money center banks") can process up to $1 trillion in wire transfers a day.

The Damage Done

Hundreds of billions of dollars have been transferred, through the private-banking and correspondent-banking systems, from Africa, Asia, Latin America, and Eastern Europe to the biggest banks in the United States and Europe. In all these regions, liberalization and privatization of the economy have opened up lucrative opportunities for corruption and the easy movement of booty overseas. Authoritarian governments and close ties to Washington, meanwhile, have ensured impunity for most of the guilty parties. Russia alone has seen over $200 billion illegally transferred out of the country in the course of the 1990s. The massive flows of capital out of these regions—really the pillaging of these countries' wealth through the international banking system—is a major factor in their economic instability and mass impoverishment. The resulting economic crises, in turn, have made these countries more vulnerable to the prescriptions of the IMF and World Bank, including liberalized banking and financial systems that lead to further capital flight.

Even by an incomplete accounting (including both "criminal" and "corrupt" funds, but not other illicit capital transfers, such as illegal shifts of real estate or securities titles, wire fraud, etc.), the dirty money coming from abroad into U.S. banks amounted to $3.5 to $6.0 trillion during the 1990s. While this is not the whole picture, it gives us a basis for estimating the significance of the "dirty money factor" in the U.S. economy. The United States currently runs an annual trade deficit of over $400 billion. The gap has to be financed with inflows of funds from abroad—at least a third of which is "dirty money." Without the dirty money the U.S. economy's external accounts would be unsustainable. No wonder the biggest banks in the United States and Europe are actively involved, and the governments of these countries turn a blind eye. That is today's capitalism—built around pillage, criminality, corruption, and complicity. ❑

Resources: "Private Banking and Money Laundering: A Case Study of Opportunities and Vulnerabilities," Permanent Subcommittee on Investigations of the Committee on Governmental Affairs, United States Senate, One Hundred Sixth Congress, November 9-10, 1000; "Report on Correspondent Banking: A Gateway to Money Laundering," Minority Staff of the U.S. Senate Permanent Subcommittee on Investigations, February 2001.

Article 7.4

WHY THE UNITED STATES IS *NOT* GREECE

BY JOHN MILLER AND KATHERINE SCIACCHITANO
January/February 2012

For almost two years, we've been hearing a new battle cry in the war against government spending: unless the United States slashes deficits we will become Greece, Europe's poster child for fiscal insolvency and economic crisis. The debt crisis in the eurozone, the 17 European countries that share the euro as their common currency, is held up as proof positive of the perils that await the United States if it continues its supposedly fiscally irresponsible ways.

Take the Heritage Foundation, the Washington-based think tank that specializes in providing red meat for anti-government pro-market arguments. Heritage introduces its 2011 chart on the rising level of government debt (to GDP) with this dire warning: "Countries like Greece and Portugal have suffered or are anticipating financial crises as a result of mounting debt. If the U.S. continues federal deficit spending on its current trajectory, it will face similar economic woes."

Even for those who understand that cutting deficits right now will only weaken a still-fragile recovery, and that weakening the recovery will only increase deficits, getting past the argument that "a eurozone crisis is on its way" is no easy task.

What follows is a self-defense lesson on why the United States is is not Greece—or Europe. The U.S. economy is far larger and more productive than Greece. The United States has many more tools in its macro-economic policy box than countries in the eurozone. And while calls for austerity have kept the United States from undertaking government spending and investment large enough to support a robust economic recovery, at least thus far, the United States hasn't undertaken the same self-defeating austerity measures Europe has. If we learn the right lessons from what is happening in the eurozone now, we never will.

Central Banks and Deficit Spending

When economic activity plummeted during 2008 and 2009 in the United States, Europe, and throughout the world, coordinated stimulus spending of nations across the globe prevented the collapse of world output from becoming another Great Depression. Today, deficit spending remains critical as working people continue to struggle through an economic recovery that has done little to create jobs or to lift wages, but much to restore profits.

Governments finance deficit spending by borrowing. Governments sell bonds—promissory notes—to domestic and foreign investors as well as other government agencies, and then use the proceeds to pay for spending in excess of their tax revenues. In the United States, domestic investors, foreign investors, and government agencies hold near equal shares of government bonds issued by the Treasury and receive the interest paid on those bonds.

The Federal Reserve ("the Fed"), the U.S. central bank, can buy U.S. government bonds as well. The Fed can also create money (sometimes metaphorically called "printing money") simply by entering an appropriate credit on its balance sheet and spending it. When the Fed uses this newly created money to purchase bonds directly from the government, it is financing the government deficit. Economists call the Fed's direct purchase of government bonds "monetizing the deficit." By such direct purchases of bonds that finance the deficit, the Fed can fund government spending in an emergency, should it choose to do so. Monetizing the deficit also significantly expands the money supply, which pushes down interest rates, which can also help stimulate the economy.

In the current crisis, the Fed did precisely that. By purchasing government bonds, the Fed financed public-sector spending, and by pushing down interest rates, it encouraged private-sector borrowing. In doing so, the Fed supported a market recovery, but also helped to keep unemployment from rising even higher than it did.

In seeking to lower unemployment, the Fed was exercising what is known as its "dual mandate" under the law to promote both low inflation and low unemployment.

Nevertheless, the Fed's decision to inject more money into the economy has come under heavy fire from those who worry more about inflation than unemployment, and who think that "printing money" is always inflationary. Neither continued low inflation rates nor persistently high unemployment were enough to change the thinking of these inflation-phobes. Back in August, Rick Perry, the Texas governor and candidate for president in the Republican primary, went so far as to insist that if the Fed "prints more money between now and the election" (in November 2012) it would be "almost treasonous."

The central banks of most other countries have much the same abilities as the Fed has to inject money into their economies and to buy government debt. As with the Fed, they may or may not choose to use this power. But the power is unquestionably there.

Europe's Central Bank Is Different

The 17 countries in the eurozone, however, relinquished their ability to print money, expand their money supplies, and lower interest rates when they adopted the euro as their common currency. Only the European Central Bank—known as the ECB—can authorize the "printing of euros," and the ECB maintains control over the money supply of the eurozone.

Unlike the Fed, the ECB does not have a dual mandate to pursue low employment as well as low inflation. The ECB's authority is limited to maintaining low inflation, known as "price stability," which the ECB defines as an inflation rate below 2%.

And the ECB is prohibited from directly buying government bonds. The ECB is authorized to buy government bonds only on the "secondary" bond market, when original purchasers resell them.

The result of these policies is that eurozone countries must sell their bonds on the open market. That leaves them entirely dependent on private bond buyers (i.e., lenders), whether from their own country or other countries, to finance their government deficits. Governments must offer their bonds for sale with rates of returns (or interest rates) that will attract those bonds buyers. Each uptick in the interest rate adds to the debt burden of these countries, and makes deficit spending to stimulate the economy that much more expensive.

Another way a country can stimulate its economy is by increasing exports. Typically, individual countries' currencies (when not fixed to the value of a dominant currency such as the U.S. dollar) lose value, or "depreciate," when an economy falls into a crisis, such as the crisis Greece is in now. As the value of its currency depreciates, a country's exports become cheaper, and that boosts export sales and domestic production and aids recovery. While currency fluctuations can open the door to speculative excesses, the falling value of a country's currency is yet another way to help turn around a flagging economy not available to the eurozone economies. The problem is that all countries in the eurozone have the same currency. So individual countries can't let their currencies depreciate. Nor can they take steps countries outside the eurozone can take to intentionally lower their exchange rates to become more competitive, known as devaluing.

Similarly, central banks outside the eurozone routinely stimulate economies by pushing down key interest rates at which banks lend to each other. This helps lower other interest rates in the economy, such as rates for business and consumer loans, and can lead to the expansion of borrowing and spending. But the ECB targets one interest rate for lending between banks for the whole eurozone. It is not possible to set one interest rate for Germany to fight inflation, and a second, lower, rate in Greece or Italy to stimulate growth.

Without the ability to use separate exchange rates or interest rates to stimulate lagging economies, the crisis-ridden eurozone had but one public policy left to get their economies going again: expansionary fiscal policy. But even that remaining policy option was constrained. The ECB was not about to ease the burden of increased government spending (or the cost of tax cuts) by directly buying government bonds. Eurozone guidelines prohibit budget deficits that exceed 3% of GDP, or national debt in excess of 60% of their GDP. And there is no central fiscal authority with deep pockets to turn to. Contrast this with the United States, where states also share the same currency and the Fed targets one interest rate, but where states can turn to the federal government for assistance in times of economic stress.

In effect, the eurozone countries were left to confront the global downturn and the sovereign debt crisis with one policy hand tied behind their back, and a couple of digits lopped off the other. Market pressure on interest rates made it yet more difficult for eurozone countries to get out of trouble by undertaking countercyclical, or stimulus, spending when economies slowed.

In the few cases where eurozone authorities have provided loans to indebted countries, they have insisted on austerity measures ranging from slashing government spending to public- and private-sector wage cuts as the pre-condition for providing relief. But since cutting government spending in a downturn leads to both a fall in demand and rise in unemployment, this emergency lending is making it even harder for eurozone countries to recover.

No wonder the global downturn hit the most vulnerable eurozone countries so hard, turning their sovereign (or government) debt as toxic as the mortgage-based securities that sparked the initial global downturn. This is what we're seeing played out with the Greek debt crisis.

Greek Austerity

When the 2008-2009 global collapse pushed down GDP and trade, and pushed up budget deficits around the world, Greece already had a large trade deficit and high government debt. Greece had consistently run government deficits greater than 5% of its GDP, and had carried government debt that just about matched its GDP for nearly a decade, both clear violations of eurozone guidelines. Nonetheless, Greek banks, and then banks elsewhere in Europe (including Germany and France), readily lent money to the Greek government, buying their bonds, which regularly yielded a handsome 5% rate of return (the rate of interest on a ten-year government note), and which presumably carried limited risk as the sovereign debt of a developed country unlikely to default.

But as the Greek economy tumbled downward, Greece had to raise its interest rates to above 12% to sell the additional debt it needed to stay afloat. By the summer of 2010, Greece was pushed to the point of default—not being able to pay its lenders.

The European Union and the IMF gave Greece a $140 billion loan so debt payments to the banks could continue. But both the IMF and the European Union insisted on austerity to reduce deficits and ensure repayment. Greece was forced to agree to sharp cuts in government spending, public employment, and wages and benefits of public employees; to tax increases; and to privatization of government assets. The banks that had happily lent Greece money well beyond the allowable eurozone limits escaped without having to write down the value of their loans to the Greek government.

The Greek economy, on the other hand, dropped like a stone. In the year that followed, Greece lost more output than the United States had during the Great Recession. Unemployment rates reached 18.4%, over one-third of young people were unemployed, and more than one-fifth of the population was poverty stricken. The austerity measures did trim the Greek budget deficit. Nonetheless the ratio of public debt to GDP continued to rise as Greek output plummeted.

One year later, Greece was on the brink of default again. The interest rate on Greek government bonds had skyrocketed to above 20% on ten-year government bonds, only adding to Greece's already unsustainable debt burden.

In October 2011 the IMF and the European Union granted an additional $173 billion loan to Greece in return for a new round of austerity measures. More public-sector workers lost their jobs, public pensions were cut further, and the privatization program expanded. The austerity measures were "equivalent to about 14 percent of average Greek take-home income," according to the Financial Times, the authoritative British newspaper, or an impact about "double that brought about by austerity measures in the other two eurozone countries subject to international bail-out programmes, Portugal and Ireland."

Also as part of the price for its debt reduction, Greece would have to accept monitoring of its fiscal affairs by the European Union. Greek Prime Minister George Papandreou, forced to cancel a referendum on the second round of austerity cuts, resigned in favor of a "government of national unity" headed by Lucas Papademos, a former banker sure to listen to the markets.

This time, banks and other holders of Greek government bonds seemed not to have escaped unharmed. The value of their bonds were to be written down to 50% of their face value, meaning they could still insist on repayment of half the amount lent, although the market value of those bonds was surely far less than that. In addition, the agreement was "voluntary," and it is yet to be seen if the agreement will be enforced.

As 2011 came to a close with this second round of austerity measures and the near collapse of the Greek economy, the Greek government was paying out a crippling 35% interest rate to attract buyers for their ten-year bonds.

Vortex Europe

European banks are the main buyers of European debt. French and German banks hold large quantities of Greek bonds.

So does the ECB, which began buying Greek bonds and other sovereign debt on the secondary (or resale) market in 2010. It resumed the practice in late 2011 to ease pressures on interest rates. Ordinarily, this bond-buying would also stimulate the economy by increasing the money supply, since the ECB creates the money it uses to buy the bonds. But the ECB also "sterilizes" its bond buying by contracting the money supply in the same amount as its purchases. This eliminates any possibility of inflation, but also negates the stimulus effect.

The bottom line is that because of the extensive holdings of Greek and other government debt within the European banking system, a Greek default would cause substantial losses in the European banking system and destabilize it.

In the last weeks of 2011, the ECB did extend a financial lifeline to banks – exactly what it had refused to give to the Greek government. To help buffer them against sudden losses, the ECB offered the banks $638 billion in three-year loans with the bargain basement interest rate of 1%. The majority of eurozone banks, some 523 of them, took out loans. The ECB's backdoor bailout, as a Wall Street Journal editorial called it, was twice the combined size of the two rescue packages for Greece. The banks, unlike governments, would not have to turn to the bond markets for funding if a Greek default occurred. And like banks bailed out in the United States, no requirements were placed on them to continue lending—in Europe's case, to continue lending to governments.

While the ECB move shored up the banks for now, it won't protect them from the large losses that will come with an outright default by Greece or another of the crisis-ridden southern eurozone countries. Such large losses would in turn force countries to bail out banks again, as they did in 2008, to avoid the prospect of cascading banking failures. Because the ECB is prohibited from directly buying European government debt, a new round of bailouts would raise the specter of increasing government deficits, of rising interest rates, and of additional countries defaulting, a sequence that could induce a depression-like downturn.

As a result, private lenders are now insisting on higher interest rates on government bonds not just in Greece, but throughout much of Europe. These interest rate rises began in weaker economies with higher debt levels, including the Italian and Spanish economies, both of which are far larger than the Greek economy. Interest-rate hikes have even spread to France and (very briefly) to Germany, the eurozone's two largest economies.

The spikes in rates not only increase the likelihood of default, they put real roadblocks in the way of the spending and investment needed for recovery and long-term growth.

The danger is not only to Europe. The European Union is the largest economy in the world, accounting for nearly 20% of global economic activity. Every region of the world that trades with Europe will be affected by a slowdown there. The euro-zone is the largest export market for both the United States and China. The default of any European country would cause losses and instability throughout the global economy. The U.S. financial system would also be sharply affected, for European global banks provide much of the credit for the U.S. economy.

To stem the bleeding, many in Europe and beyond have urged and continue to urge the ECB to step up and find a way to act as most normal central banks would in the situation: inject money into these economies by buying government debt in unlimited quantities. That in turn would lower interest rates, and give countries time to rebuild and restart growth. Germany, the largest and the dominant econ-omy in Europe, continues to block this option on the grounds that printing money is not only inflationary but a "moral hazard" and makes borrowing too easy. At the last European summit, Germany successfully insisted instead on a "fiscal stability union" that will require balanced budgets (before taking interest payments into account). In other words, austerity for workers.

Rejecting Austerity

Austerity won't work for Europe: Europe needs growth, and austerity can't pro-duce growth. Austerity also can't work because the proposed cure—budget cuts—assumes the disease is government spending. But excessive social spending by its government did not cause Greece's debt problems. In 2007, the year before the crisis hit, Greece's social expenditures relative to the size of its economy stood at 21.3% of GDP, lower than the social expenditures in France (28.3% of GDP) and Germany (25.2% of GDP), the two countries most responsible for orchestrating the austerity measures that have slashed social spending in Greece.

Europe didn't have a government debt crisis before the subprime collapse of 2008. It had countries like Germany in the north with large permanent trade sur-pluses, and countries in the south like Greece with large permanent trade deficits. Fixing these trade deficits and imbalances can't be done by pushing down wages. In fact, repressive wage and labor policies, especially as practiced in Germany, are what lie at the heart of those imbalances that made the weaker southern eurozone coun-tries so vulnerable to the crisis that followed.

Rather, what's needed is government investment and coordination through-out Europe. A public investment program could modernize the infrastructure of the southern eurozone economies and boost the productivity of their workforce by improving workers' health and education.

A recession—or worse—in Europe will slow down growth and raise budget deficits in the United States as well. It will create political pressure for austerity exactly when we need more investment and more stimulus spending.

If this happens, it will be more important than ever to remember that Europe is in the position it is in, first, because it insisted on austerity for Greece and, second, because Europe has a central bank that is prohibited from financing government deficits and whose sole policy mandate is to limit inflation. Without the insistence on austerity, and without having relinquished these basic tools of economic policy—both of which the United States retains—the mess in Europe could never have happened. The United States is not and will never be Greece.

Yet like the crisis in Europe, the crisis in the United States isn't temporary or fleeting. The outcome will determine what kind of jobs and economic security people will have for a long time to come. It will have a huge effect on public-sector unions. And it will affect democracy itself, especially if we stay silent. Austerity in Europe is being imposed from above. There's no reason to let it be imposed here. ❏

Sources: C. Lapavitsas et al., "Breaking Up? A Route Out of the Eurozone Crisis," Research on Money and Finance, RMF Occasional Report, November 2011; Heiner Flassbeck and Friederike Spiecker, "The Euro—A Story of Misunderstanding," Intereconomics, 2011; "The ECB's Backdoor Bailout," *Wall Street Journal*, December 24, 2011; George Irvin and Alex Izurieta, "Fundamental Flaws in the European Project," *Economic & Political Weekly*, August 6, 2011; C.P. Chandrasekhar, "The Crisis in Europe," *The Frontline*, Jul. 30-Aug. 12, 2011; Robert Skidelsky, "The Euro in a Shrinking Zone," *Project Syndicate*, December 12, 2011; David Enrich, "European Banks Rush to Grasp Lifeline," *Wall Street Journal*, December 22, 2011; Paul Krugman, "Bernanke's Perry Problem," *New York Times*, August 25, 2011; Paul Krugman, "Currency Warnings that Europe Ignored," Krugman & Co., November 22, 2011; Andre Leonard, "The Republican plot to turn the U.S. into Greece," Salon.com, July 18, 2011; Sally Giansbury et al.," Greek austerity plans threaten growth," *Financial Times*, October 17, 2011; James Bullard, "The Fed's Dual Mandate: Lessons of the 1970s," The 2010 Annual Report of the Federal Reserve Bank of St. Louis, April 2011.

Article 7.5

IS CHINA'S CURRENCY MANIPULATION HURTING THE U.S.?

BY ARTHUR MacEWAN
November/December 2010

> Dear Dr. Dollar:
> *Is it true that China has been harming the U.S. economy by keeping its currency "undervalued"? Shouldn't the U.S. government do something about this situation?*
> —Jenny Boyd, Edmond, W.Va.

The Chinese government, operating through the Chinese central bank, does keep its currency unit—the yuan—cheap relative to the dollar. This means that goods imported *from* China cost less (in terms of dollars) than they would otherwise, while U.S. exports *to* China cost more (in terms of yuan). So we in the United States buy a lot of Chinese-made goods and the Chinese don't buy much from us. In the 2007 to 2009 period, the United States purchased $253 billion more in goods annually from China than it sold to China.

This looks bad for U.S workers. For example, when money gets spent in the United States, much of it is spent on Chinese-made goods, and fewer jobs are then created in the United States. So the Chinese government's currency policy is at least partly to blame for our employment woes. Reacting to this situation, many people are calling for the U.S. government to do something to get the Chinese government to change its policy.

But things are not so simple.

First of all, there is an additional reason for the low cost of Chinese goods—low Chinese wages. The Chinese government's policy of repressing labor probably accounts for the low cost of Chinese goods at least as much as does its currency policy. Moreover, there is a lot more going on in the global economy. Both currency problems and job losses involve much more than Chinese government actions—though China provides a convenient target for ire.

And the currency story itself is complex. In order to keep the value of its currency low relative to the dollar, the Chinese government increases the supply of yuan, uses these yuan to buy dollars, then uses the dollars to buy U.S. securities, largely government bonds but also private securities. In early 2009, China held $764 billion in U.S. Treasury securities, making it the largest foreign holder of U.S. government debt. By buying U.S. government bonds, the Chinese have been financing the federal deficit. More generally, by supplying funds to the United States, the Chinese government has been keeping interest rates low in this country.

If the Chinese were to act differently, allowing the value of their currency to rise relative to the dollar, both the cost of capital and the prices of the many goods imported from China would rise. The rising cost of capital would probably not be a serious problem, as the Federal Reserve could take counteraction to keep interest rates low. So, an increase in the value of the yuan would net the United States some jobs, but also raise some prices for U.S. consumers.

It is pretty clear that right now what the United States needs is jobs. Moreover, low-cost Chinese goods have contributed to the declining role of manufacturing in the United States, a phenomenon that both weakens important segments of organized labor and threatens to inhibit technological progress, which has often been centered in manufacturing or based on applications in manufacturing (e.g., robotics).

So why doesn't the U.S. government place more pressure on China to raise the value of the yuan? Part of the reason may lie in concern about losing Chinese financing of the U.S. federal deficit. For several years the two governments have been co-dependent: The U.S. government gets financing for its deficits, and the Chinese government gains by maintaining an undervalued currency. Not an easy relationship to change.

Probably more important, however, many large and politically powerful U.S.-based firms depend directly on the low-cost goods imported from China. Wal-mart and Target, as any shopper knows, are filled with Chinese-made goods. Then there are the less visible products from China, including a power device that goes into the Microsoft Xbox, computer keyboards for Dell, and many other goods for many other U.S. corporations. If the yuan's value rose and these firms had to pay more dollars to buy these items, they could probably not pass all the increase on to consumers and their profits would suffer.

Still, in spite of the interests of these firms, the U.S. government may take some action, either by pressing harder for China to let the value of the yuan rise relative to the dollar or by placing some restrictions on imports from China. But don't expect too big a change. ❑

Article 7.6

CHINA'S DEVELOPMENT BANKS GO GLOBAL: THE GOOD AND THE BAD

BY KEVIN GALLAGHER
November/December 2013

China is redefining the global development agenda. While the West preaches trade liberalization and financial deregulation, China orchestrates massive infrastructure and industrial policies under regulated trade and financial markets. China transformed its economy and brought more than 600 million people out of poverty. Western policies led to financial crises, slow growth and relatively less poverty alleviation across the globe.

China is now exporting its model across the world. The China Development Bank (CDB) and the Export-Import Bank of China (EIBC) now provide more financing to developing countries than the World Bank does. What is more, China's finance doesn't come with the harsh conditions—such as trade liberalization and fiscal austerity—that western-backed finance has historically. China's development banks are not only helping to spur infrastructure development across the world, they are also helping China's bottom line as they make a strong profit and often provide opportunities for Chinese firms.

It is well known that China is taking the lead in developing and deploying clean energy technologies, as it has become the world's leading producer of solar panels. China is pumping finance into cleaner energy abroad as well. According to a new study by the World Resources Institute, since 2002 Chinese firms have put an additional $40 billion into solar and wind projects across the globe.

However, China's global stride may be jeopardized unless it begins to incorporate environmental and social safeguards into its overseas operations. In a policy memorandum for the Paulson Institute, I note how there is a growing backlash against China's development banks on these grounds. By remedying these concerns, China can become the global leader in development finance.

There is a growing number of cases where Chinese financial institutions may be losing ground over social and environmental concerns.

One example is CDB's multibillion-dollar China-Burma oil and gas pipeline projects. The Shwe gas project is coordinated by China National Petroleum Corporation, which has contracted out some operations to Sinohydro (the state-owned hydroelectric company). Local civil society organizations have mounted campaigns against land confiscation with limited compensation, loss of livelihoods, the role of Burmese security forces in protecting the project, and environmental degradation (deforestation, river dredging and chemical pollution).

Another example is the Patuca hydroelectric project in Honduras, supported by EIBC and operated by Sinohydro. Approved by the Honduran government in 2011, one of the projects is said to entail flooding 42 km of rainforest slated to be part of Patuca national park and the Tawahka Asangni biosphere reserve. The project was denounced by local civil society organizations, which cited the shaky foundations of the project's environmental impact assessment. NGOs including International Rivers and The Nature Conservancy have also sought to reevaluate the project. Such campaigns, uniting locally affected communities with globally recognized NGOs that have access to media worldwide, have slowed projects and tainted investors' images.

Extraction from the Belinga iron ore deposit in Gabon was contracted in 2007 between the government in Libreville and the China Machinery Energy Corporation, with financing from EIBC. The project sparked significant local protest over its environmental impact, and, as a result, has been perpetually renegotiated and delayed, and may ultimately be denied.

Environment-related political risk can severely affect the bottom line of the major Chinese development banks to the extent that local skepticism and protests result in delays or even loss of projects. Doing the right thing on the environment and human rights would help maintain China's market access and help mitigate risks to China's development banks.

Adopting established international norms may help China's banks to secure markets in more developed countries. Chinese banks clearly seek to further penetrate markets such as the United States and Europe, where even higher environmental and social standards exist. Establishing a track record of good practice in emerging markets and developing countries could help Chinese banks assimilate, adapt, and ultimately incorporate such practices into their daily operations, an experience that could prove essential as they also seek to navigate markets in Organisation for Economic Co-operation and Development (OECD) countries.

For decades, developing countries have pined for a development bank that provides finance for inclusive growth and sustainable development—without the draconian conditions that the IMF and World Bank have often imposed as a condition of their lending. That conditionality, and the egregious environmental record of early World Bank and other international-financial-institution projects, spurred a global backlash against these institutions. If China's development banks can add substantial social and environmental safeguards, they can become a beacon of 21st century development finance. ❏

Article 7.7

MICROCREDIT AND WOMEN'S POVERTY

BY SUSAN F. FEINER AND DRUCILLA K. BARKER
November/December 2006

The key to understanding why Grameen Bank founder and CEO Muhammad Yunus won the Nobel Peace Prize lies in the current fascination with individualistic myths of wealth and poverty. Many policy-makers believe that poverty is "simply" a problem of individual behavior. By rejecting the notion that poverty has structural causes, they deny the need for collective responses. In fact, according to this tough-love view, broad-based civic commitments to increase employment or provide income supports only make matters worse: helping the poor is pernicious because such aid undermines the incentive for hard work. This ideology is part and parcel of neoliberalism.

For neoliberals the solution to poverty is getting the poor to work harder, get educated, have fewer children, and act more responsibly. Markets reward those who help themselves, and women, who comprise the vast majority of microcredit borrowers, are no exception. Neoliberals champion the Grameen Bank and similar efforts precisely because microcredit programs do not change the structural conditions of globalization—such as loss of land rights, privatization of essential public services, or cutbacks in health and education spending—that reproduce poverty among women in developing nations.

What exactly is microcredit? Yunus, a Bangladeshi banker and economist, pioneered the idea of setting up a bank to make loans to the "poorest of the poor." The term "microcredit" reflects the very small size of the loans, often less than $100. Recognizing that the lack of collateral was often a barrier to borrowing by the poor, Yunus founded the Grameen Bank in the 1970s to make loans in areas of severe rural poverty where there were often no alternatives to what we would call loan sharks.

His solution to these problems was twofold. First, Grameen Bank would hire agents to travel the countryside on a regular schedule, making loans and collecting loan repayments. Second, only women belonging to Grameen's "loan circles" would be eligible for loans. If one woman in a loan circle did not meet her obligations, the others in the circle would either be ineligible for future loans or be held responsible for repayment of her loan. In this way the collective liability of the group served as collateral.

The Grameen Bank toasts its successes: not only do loan repayment rates approach 95%, the poor, empowered by their investments, are not dependent on "handouts." Microcredit advocates see these programs as a solution to poverty because poor women can generate income by using the borrowed funds to start small-scale enterprises, often home-based handicraft production. But these enterprises are almost all in the informal sector, which is fiercely competitive and typically unregulated, in other words, outside the range of any laws that protect workers or ensure their rights. Not surprisingly, women comprise the majority of workers in the informal economy and are heavily represented at the bottom of its already-low income scale.

Women and men have different experiences with work and entrepreneurship because a gender division of labor in most cultures assigns men to paid work outside the home and women to unpaid labor in the home. Consequently, women's paid work is constrained by domestic responsibilities. They either work part time, or they combine paid and unpaid work by working at home. Microcredit encourages women to work at home doing piecework: sewing garments, weaving rugs, assembling toys and electronic components. Home workers—mostly women and children—often work long hours for very poor pay in hazardous conditions, with no legal protections. As progressive journalist Gina Neff has noted, encouraging the growth of the informal sector sounds like advice from one of Dickens' more objectionable characters.

Why then do national governments and international organizations promote microcredit, thereby encouraging women's work in the informal sector? As an anti-poverty program, microcredit fits nicely with the prevailing ideology that defines poverty as an individual problem and that shifts responsibility for addressing it away from government policy-makers and multilateral bank managers onto the backs of poor women.

Microcredit programs do nothing to change the structural conditions that create poverty. But microcredit *has* been a success for the many banks that have adopted it. Of course, lending to the poor has long been a lucrative enterprise. Pawnshops, finance companies, payday loan operations, and loan sharks charge high interest rates precisely because poor people are often desperate for cash and lack access to formal credit networks. According to Sheryl Nance-Nash, a correspondent for Women's eNews, "the interest rates on microfinance vary between 25% to 50%." She notes that these rates "are much lower than informal money lenders, where rates may exceed 10% per month." It is important for the poor to have access to credit on relatively reasonable terms. Still, microcredit lenders are reaping the rewards of extraordinarily high repayment rates on loans that are still at somewhat above-market interest rates.

Anecdotal accounts can easily overstate the concrete gains to borrowers from microcredit. For example, widely cited research by the Canadian International Development Agency (CIDA) reports that "Women in particular face significant barriers to achieving sustained increases in income and improving their status, and require complementary support in other areas, such as training, marketing, literacy, social mobilization, and other financial services (e.g., consumption loans, savings)." The report goes on to conclude that most borrowers realize only very small gains, and that the poorest borrowers benefit the least. CIDA also found little relationship between loan repayment and business success.

However large or small their income gains, poor women are widely believed to find empowerment in access to microcredit loans. According to the World Bank, for instance, microcredit empowers women by giving them more control over household assets and resources, more autonomy and decision-making power, and greater access to participation in public life. This defense of microcredit stands or falls with individual success stories featuring women using their loans to start some sort of small-scale enterprise, perhaps renting a stall in the local market or buying a sewing machine to assemble piece goods. There is no doubt that when they succeed, women and their families are better off than they were before they became micro-debtors.

But the evidence on microcredit and women's empowerment is ambiguous. Access to credit is not the sole determinant of women's power and autonomy. Credit may, for example, increase women's dual burden of market and household labor. It may also increase conflict within the household if men, rather than women, control how loan moneys are used. Moreover, the group pressure over repayment in Grameen's loan circles can just as easily create conflict among women as build solidarity.

Grameen Bank founder Muhammad Yunus won the Nobel Peace Prize because his approach to banking reinforces the neoliberal view that individual behavior is the source of poverty and the neoliberal agenda of restricting state aid to the most vulnerable when and where the need for government assistance is most acute. Progressives working in poor communities around the world disagree. They argue that poverty is structural, so the solutions to poverty must focus not on adjusting the conditions of individuals but on building structures of inclusion. Expanding the state sector to provide the rudiments of a working social infrastructure is, therefore, a far more effective way to help women escape or avoid poverty.

Do the activities of the Grameen Bank and other micro-lenders romanticize individual struggles to escape poverty? Yes. Do these programs help some women "pull themselves up by the bootstraps"? Yes. Will micro-enterprises in the informal sector contribute to ending world poverty? Not a chance. ❏

Resources: Grameen Bank, grameen-info.org; "Informal Economy: Formalizing the Hidden Potential and Raising Standards," ILO Global Employment Forum (Nov. 2001), www-ilo-mirror. cornell.edu/public/english/employment/geforum/informal.htm; Jean L. Pyle, "Sex, Maids, and Export Processing," World Bank, *Engendering Development; Engendering Development Through Gender Equality in Rights, Resources, and Voice* (Oxford University Press, 2001); Naila Kabeer, "Conflicts Over Credit: Re-Evaluating the Empowerment Potential of Loans to Women in Rural Bangladesh," *World Development* 29 (2001); Norman MacIsaac, "The Role of Microcredit in Poverty Reduction and Promoting Gender Equity," South Asia Partnership Canada, Strategic Policy and Planning Division, Asia Branch Canada International Development Agency (June, 1997), www.acdi-cida.gc.ca/index-e.htm.

RESISTANCE AND ALTERNATIVES

Article 8.1

TRANSFORMING THE FED

BY ROBERT POLLIN
November 1992

The U.S. financial system faces deep structural problems. Households, businesses, and the federal government are burdened by excessive debts. The economy favors short-term speculation over long-term investment. An unrepresentative and unresponsive elite has extensive control over the financial system. Moreover, the federal government is incapable of reversing these patterns through its existing tools, including fiscal, monetary, and financial regulatory policies.

I propose a dramatically different approach: transforming the Federal Reserve System (the "Fed") into a public investment bank. Such a bank would have substantial power to channel credit in ways that counter financial instability and support productive investment by private businesses. The Fed would use its powers to influence how and for what purposes banks, insurance companies, brokers, and other lenders loan money.

The U.S. government has used credit allocation policies, such as low-cost loans, loan guarantees, and home mortgage interest deductions, extensively and with success. Its primary accomplishment has been to create a home mortgage market that, for much of the period since World War II, provided non-wealthy households with unprecedented access to home ownership.

I propose increasing democratic control over the Federal Reserve's activities by decentralizing power to the 12 district Fed banks and instituting popular election of their boards of directors. This would create a mechanism for extending democracy throughout the financial system.

My proposal also offers a vehicle for progressives to address two separate but equally serious questions facing the U.S. economy:

- How to convert our industrial base out of military production and toward the development and adoption of environmentally benign production techniques; and

- How to increase opportunities for high wage, high productivity jobs in the United States. The U.S. needs such jobs to counteract the squeeze on wages from increasingly globalized labor and financial markets.

Transforming the Federal Reserve system into a public investment bank will help define an economic path toward democratic socialism in the United States.

My proposal has several strengths as a transitional program. It offers a mechanism for establishing democratic control over finance and investment—the area where capital's near-dictatorial power is most decisive. The program will also work within the United States' existing legal and institutional framework. We could implement parts of it immediately using existing federal agencies and with minimal demands on the federal budget.

At the same time, if an ascendant progressive movement put most of the program in place, this would represent a dramatic step toward creating a new economic system. Such a system would still give space to market interactions and the pursuit of greed, but would nevertheless strongly promote general well-being over business profits.

How the Fed Fails

At present the Federal Reserve focuses its efforts on managing short-term fluctuations of the economy, primarily by influencing interest rates. When it reduces rates, it seeks to increase borrowing and spending, and thereby stimulate economic growth and job opportunities. When the Fed perceives that wages and prices are rising too fast (a view not necessarily shared by working people), it tries to slow down borrowing and spending by raising interest rates.

This approach has clearly failed to address the structural problems plaguing the financial system. The Fed did nothing, for example, to prevent the collapse of the savings and loan industry. It stood by while highly speculative mergers, buyouts, and takeovers overwhelmed financial markets in the 1980s. It has failed to address the unprecedented levels of indebtedness and credit defaults of private corporations and households.

New Roles for the Fed

Under my proposal, the Federal Reserve would shift its focus from the short to the long term. It would provide more and cheaper credit to banks and other financiers who loan money to create productive assets and infrastructure—which promote high-wage, high-productivity jobs. The Fed would make credit more expensive for lenders that finance speculative activities such as the mergers, buyouts, and takeovers that dominated the 1980s.

The Fed would also give favorable credit terms to banks that finance decent affordable housing rather than luxury housing and speculative office buildings. It would make low-cost credit available for environmental research and development so the economy can begin the overdue transition to environmentally benign production. Cuts in military spending have idled many workers and productive resources, both of which could be put to work in such transformed industries.

Finally, the Fed would give preferential treatment to loans that finance investment in the United States rather than in foreign countries. This would help counter the trend of U.S. corporations to abandon the domestic economy in search of lower wages and taxes.

The first step in developing the Fed's new role would be for the public to determine which sectors of the economy should get preferential access to credit. One example, suggested above, is industrial conversion from military production to investment in renewable energy and conservation.

Once the public establishes its investment goals, the Fed will have to develop new policy tools and use its existing tools in new ways to accomplish them. I propose that a transformed Federal Reserve use two major methods:

- set variable cash ("asset reserve") requirements for all lenders, based on the social value of the activities the lenders are financing; and

- increase discretionary lending activity by the 12 district Federal Reserve banks.

Varying Banks' Cash Requirements

The Fed currently requires that banks and other financial institutions keep a certain amount of their assets available in cash reserves. Banks, for example, must carry three cents in cash for every dollar they hold in checking accounts. A bank cannot make interest-bearing loans on such "reserves." I propose that the Fed make this percent significantly lower for loans that finance preferred activities than for less desirable investment areas. Let's say the public decides that banks should allocate 10% of all credit to research and development of new environmental technologies, such as non-polluting autos and organic farming. Then financial institutions that have made 10% of their loans in environmental technologies would not have to hold any cash reserves against these loans. But if a bank made no loans in the environmental area, then it would have to hold 10% of its total assets in reserve. The profit motive would force banks to support environmental technologies without any direct expenditure from the federal budget.

All profit-driven firms will naturally want to avoid this reserve requirement. The Fed must therefore apply it uniformly to all businesses that profit through accepting deposits and making loans. These include banks, savings and loans, insurance companies, and investment brokerage houses. If the rules applied only to banks, for example, then banks could circumvent the rules by redefining themselves as another type of lending institution.

Loans to Banks That Do the Right Thing

The Federal Reserve has the authority now to favor some banks over others by making loans to them when they are short on cash. For the most part, however, the Fed has chosen not to exercise such discretionary power. Instead it aids all banks equally, through a complex mechanism known as open market operations, which increases total cash reserves in the banking system. The Fed could increase its discretionary lending to favored banks by changing its operating procedures without the federal government creating any new laws or institutions. Such discretionary lending would have several benefits.

First, to a much greater extent than at present, financial institutions would obtain reserves when they are lending for specific purposes. If a bank's priorities should move away from the established social priorities, the Fed could then either refuse to make more cash available to it, or charge a penalty interest rate, thereby discouraging the bank from making additional loans. The Fed, for example, could impose such obstacles on lenders that are financing mergers, takeovers, and buyouts.

In addition, the Fed could use this procedure to more effectively monitor and regulate financial institutions. Banks, in applying for loans, would have to submit to the Fed's scrutiny on a regular basis. The Fed could more closely link its regulation to banks' choices of which investments to finance.

Implementing this procedure will also increase the authority of the 12 district banks within the Federal Reserve system, since these banks approve the Fed's loans. Each district bank will have more authority to set lending rates and monitor bank compliance with regulations.

The district banks could then more effectively enforce measures such as the Community Reinvestment Act, which currently mandates that banks lend in their home communities. Banks that are committed to their communities and regions, such as the South Shore Bank in Chicago, could gain substantial support under this proposed procedure.

Other Credit Allocation Tools

The Fed can use other tools to shift credit to preferred industries, such as loan guarantees, interest rate subsidies, and government loans. In the past the U.S. government has used these techniques with substantial success. They now primarily support credit for housing, agriculture, and education. Indeed, as of 1991, these programs subsidized roughly one-third of all loans in the United States.

Jesse Jackson's 1988 Presidential platform suggested an innovative way of extending such policies. He proposed that public pension funds channel a portion of their money into a loan guarantee program, with the funds used to finance investments in low cost housing, education, and infrastructure.

There are disadvantages, however, to the government using loan guarantee programs and similar approaches rather than the Fed's employing asset reserve requirements and discretionary lending. Most important is that the former are more expensive and more difficult to administer. Both loan guarantees and direct government loans require the government to pay off the loans when borrowers default. Direct loans also mean substantial administrative costs. Interest subsidies on loans are direct costs to government even when the loans are paid back.

In contrast, with variable asset reserve requirements and discretionary lending policies, the Fed lowers the cost of favored activities, and raises the cost of unfavored ones, without imposing any burden on the government's budget.

Increasing Public Control

The Federal Reserve acts in relative isolation from the political process at present. The U.S. president appoints seven members of the Fed's Board of Governors for 14-year terms, and they are almost always closely tied to banking and big business. The boards of directors of the 12 district banks appoint their presidents, and these boards are also composed of influential bankers and business people within each of the districts.

The changes I propose will mean a major increase in the central bank's role as an economic planning agency for the nation. Unless we dramatically improve democratic control by the public over the Fed, voters will correctly interpret such efforts as an illegitimate grasp for more power by business interests.

Democratization should proceed through redistributing power downward to the 12 district banks. When the Federal Reserve System was formed in 1913, the principle behind creating district banks along with the headquarters in Washington was to disperse the central bank's authority. This remains a valuable idea, but the U.S. government has never seriously attempted it. Right now the district banks are highly undemocratic and have virtually no power.

One way to increase the district banks' power is to create additional seats for them on the Open Market Committee, which influences short-term interest rates by expanding or contracting the money supply.

A second method is to shift authority from the Washington headquarters to the districts. The Board of Governors would then be responsible for setting general guidelines, while the district banks would implement discretionary lending and enforcement of laws such as the Community Reinvestment Act.

The most direct way of democratizing the district banks would be to choose their boards in regular elections along with other local, regional, and state-wide officials. The boards would then choose the top levels of the banks' professional staffs and oversee the banks' activities.

Historical Precedents

Since World War II other capitalist countries have extensively employed the types of credit allocation policies proposed here. Japan, France, and South Korea are the outstanding success stories, though since the early 1980s globalization and deregulation of financial markets have weakened each of their credit policies. When operating at full strength, the Japanese and South Korean programs primarily supported large-scale export industries, such as steel, automobiles, and consumer electronics. France targeted its policies more broadly to coordinate Marshall Plan aid for the development of modern industrial corporations.

We can learn useful lessons from these experiences, not least that credit allocation policies do work when they are implemented well. But substantial differences exist between experiences elsewhere and the need for a public investment bank in the United States.

In these countries a range of other institutions besides the central bank were involved in credit allocation policies. These included their treasury departments and explicit planning agencies, such as the powerful Ministry of International Trade and Industry (MITI) in Japan. In contrast, I propose to centralize the planning effort at the Federal Reserve.

We could create a new planning institution to complement the work of the central bank. But transforming the existing central banking system rather than creating a new institution minimizes both start-up problems and the growth of bureaucracies.

A second and more fundamental difference between my proposal and the experiences in Japan, France, and South Korea is that their public investment institutions were accountable only to a business-oriented elite. This essentially dictatorial approach is antithetical to the goal of increasing democratic control of the financial system.

The challenge, then, is for the United States to implement effective credit allocation policies while broadening, not narrowing, democracy. Our success ultimately will depend on a vigorous political movement that can fuse two equally urgent, but potentially conflicting goals: economic democracy, and equitable and sustainable growth. If we can meet this challenge, it will represent a historic victory toward the construction of a democratic socialist future. ❏

Resources: Robert Pollin, "Transforming the Federal Reserve into a Public Investment Bank: Why it is Necessary; How it Should Be Done," in G. Epstein, G. Dymski and R. Pollin, eds., *Transforming the U.S. Financial System,* M.E. Sharpe, 1993.

Article 8.2

PROMOTING RECOVERY THROUGH CHEAP CREDIT FOR SMALL BUSINESSES

BY ROBERT POLLIN
September 2010; Political Economy Research Institute

The single most important reason for the failure of the recovery to take hold thus far is that private credit markets are locked up, especially for small businesses. Private business borrowing and lending is at a standstill, while private banks are holding an unprecedented $1.1 trillion in cash reserves in their Federal Reserve accounts. In 2007, before the recession began, the banks held only $20 billion in reserves. The 2007 figure was itself dangerously low. But a nearly $1 trillion turnaround in bank reserve holdings is a new form of Wall Street excess.

The solution is for the federal government to create strong incentives on both the borrowing and lending sides of the market to push affordable credit back into the market—again, especially for small businesses—where these funds will start financing business investments and job creation. The federal government already has the power to accomplish this with minimal impact on the federal budget. It will entail working with existing policy tools and agencies, in particular the loan guarantee program now operating at the Small Business Administration (SBA).

The economic policy debate is now dominated by issues around the federal budget deficit. The deficit hawks are wrong to claim that we are heading toward a fiscal train wreck unless we undertake austerity measures now. At the same time, federal deficits over the past two years, at about 10% of GDP, have been unprecedented in the post World War II era. We need to maintain large deficits now to prevent the economy's floor from collapsing, in particular through avoiding severe cuts in state and local government spending on education, health care, and public safety. But, even more important, we need to push the private credit markets to begin supporting a viable recovery.

In recognition of this situation, Federal Reserve Chairman Ben Bernanke proposed in late August that the Fed should start purchasing securities as a means of lowering long-term interest rates and to also stop paying interest on the private banks' $1.1 trillion in reserves held with the Fed. These are both steps in the right direction, but they are half-measures at a time when bold initiatives are needed.

My proposal includes just two main features, one carrot and one stick. The carrot is an expansion of existing federal loan guarantees by $300 billion, which would roughly double the amount total annual guarantees. Small businesses would be the primarily recipients of the guarantees. The stick is a 1-2% tax on the excess reserves held by banks.

This program could generate about 3 million new jobs, if it succeeds in channeling about $300 billion into new productive investments. The job creation levels would be significantly higher still if a high proportion of the new business spending were for green activities, where the levels of job creation per dollar of expenditure are about 50% greater than the economy-wide average. The impact of the program on the federal budget would be modest, most likely accounting for no more than additional 0.3-0.5% percent increase in federal spending.

How the Program Would Work

Significantly Expand Existing Federal Loan Guarantees for Small Business.
In 2009, the total level of loans guaranteed by the Federal government was about $340 billion. The two largest categories were subsidized mortgage and student loans. About $50 billion went to business loans, through the Small Business Administration and Export-Import Bank. Under this proposal, the federal government would roughly double its overall loan guarantee program—that is, inject another $300 billion in guaranteed loans into the credit market, and shift the focus of the new guarantee programs to the smaller half of businesses operating in the United States. Roughly, this would include businesses with either less than 5,000 employees or less than $70 million in annual receipts.

Terms of Guarantees Should Be Generous.
Existing guarantee programs offer a range of terms, with respect to: a) the level of guarantee; b) the fees for lending institutions; and c) interest rates for borrowers. For this initiative to be effective at reducing risk and encouraging new investment, the terms will have to be generous around all three dimensions—large guarantees, low or no fees, and low interest rate requirements for borrowers. At present, SBA loans offer a guarantee of 85% for the first $150,000 of loans and 75% above that. Given current conditions, guarantees should be kept at 85% for the full amount of the loans. The interest rate on the majority of guaranteed small business loans is currently about 3 percentage points above the prime bank lending rate. To encourage the needed accelerated rate of borrowing, the interest rate on guaranteed loans should be set lower, at 2 percentage points above the prime rate.

Tax Excess Bank Reserves.
An excess reserve tax should create a strong disincentive for banks to continue holding excess reserves. It is difficult to know in advance what the appropriate tax rate should be for this purpose. My judgment is that Congress should set the tax rate initially at between 1-2%. But the law should also allow Congress, operating in conjunction with the Federal Reserve, to adjust the rate as needed for channeling excess reserves into job-generating investments. In undertaking this measure, the Fed would also stop paying positive interest rates on bank reserves, as Chairman Bernanke has already proposed.

Impact on Federal Budget Would Be Modest.
Expanding the existing level of guarantees would entail a modest increase in administrative costs. Beyond this, the government would incur costs only as a result of defaults on the guaranteed loans. If we assume the default rate remained at roughly the 2007 level for the expanded program, this would add about $10 billion, or about

0.3% of the federal budget. Even if, implausibly, the default rate on the new loans doubled relative to the 2007 levels, this would still increase the federal budget by only 0.6%. The revenues generated by the excess reserve tax should be directed toward covering the costs of the loan guarantee program. These revenues should cover a significant share of the total budgetary expense of the loan guarantee program.

Overall, this should be a program that everyone can support. By dramatically lowering the risks for banks of lending money, it benefits the banks themselves, but then also their borrowers, the small businesses, who will receive greatly reduced lending terms. The new wave of small business investments will, in turn, be a major engine of job creation. Finally, all of this can be accomplished with relatively modest costs for the federal government. ❏

Article 8.3

RIGHTING UNDERWATER MORTGAGES

BY DEAN BAKER
July 2012: Truthout

Ever since the housing bubble collapsed, the Federal government has refused to take major initiatives to help underwater homeowners. As a result, we are likely to see close to 1 million foreclosures both this year and next, with the numbers only gradually slipping back to normal levels by the end of the decade.

The inaction cannot be attributed to a lack of opportunity. At the time the TARP bailout was being debated in the fall of 2008 many progressive members of Congress wanted to have a provision that would at least temporarily alter bankruptcy law to allow judges to rewrite the terms of a mortgage.

Under current law, home mortgages are treated differently than any other type of debt. Bankruptcy judges are prohibited from altering the terms of a mortgage in any way. If a homeowner cannot meet the terms of the mortgage, they lose the house. Congress could have allowed bankruptcy judges to rewrite mortgages that were written during the housing bubble frenzy, but it backed away from this opportunity.

Similarly, Congress could have temporarily changed the rules on foreclosure to allow foreclosed homeowners to stay in their homes for a substantial period of time (e.g., five years) as renters paying the market rent. This would have assured underwater homeowners substantial housing security.

Either of these measures would have radically altered the relationship between investors and homeowners. They would have given homeowners a serious weapon that they could use to threaten lenders and hopefully persuade them to agree to modify underwater mortgages. However since Congress did not take any action to shore up the position of homeowners, we are still sitting here with more than 11 million homeowners underwater five years after house prices began their plunge.

This failure at the national level provides the backdrop for a plan by a group of investors, Mortgage Resolution Partners (MRP), to try to get through some of the morass in the housing market. MRP has been working with public officials in San Bernardino, Calif., to arrange to use the government's power of eminent domain to condemn underwater mortgages.

As background, San Bernardino is ground zero in the housing bubble. Prices doubled or even tripled in the bubble years. They then plunged when the bubble burst, with prices now often less than half of their 2006 peaks. Half of the mortgages in the county are underwater.

This collapse has not only destroyed the life savings of hundreds of thousands of homeowners, it also has wrecked the economy of the region. In this context, the prospect of using the power to condemn property to bring many underwater homeowners back above water must sound very appealing.

MRP's plan is to have the county condemn underwater mortgages in private mortgage pools. The logic is that these underwater mortgages are causing serious harm to the community. When people are seriously underwater in their homes they are likely to lack both the means and the incentive to properly maintain their home. Of course, the monthly payment on a mortgage that might exceed the current value of a home by 50% or more (and carry a high interest rate) is a huge drain on the purchasing power of homeowners.

The case for focusing on mortgages in private mortgage pools is that it is generally quite difficult to sell these mortgages out of the pool. This means that even if, in principle, it might be advantageous for both the investors and the homeowners to have pools sell underwater mortgages to third parties like MRP who would rewrite the terms, the rules of the mortgage pools makes it unlikely that the mortgage will be sold.

This is exactly the sort of situation where public action like condemnation is appropriate. The public action allows for a solution that can benefit all the parties but is obstructed by bureaucratic rules that were written to cover a different set of circumstances. (It is important to remember that investors can contest in court the compensation they are provided for condemned mortgages to ensure that they get fair market value.)

It is difficult to see a good argument against this approach. Some have claimed that this sort of tactic will cause lenders to be more reluctant to lend in the future. If the point is that lenders may have second thoughts the next time house prices go into a bubble, then we should certainly hope that condemnation will have this effect.

Others have been critical because MRP is a private company that is doing this to make a profit. I've met with several of the top people at MRP; they certainly don't hide the fact that they expect to make money on this deal. But that hardly seems a reason for nixing the plan. There are very few instances where there has been a public condemnation in which private firms didn't stand to profit in some way.

MRP's plan is not going to rescue the country's underwater homeowners. At best it will directly help the limited segment of this group whose mortgages are in private label securities. However it may serve as an example of the benefits of principal write-downs and perhaps prod Fannie and Freddie, as well as the banks, to be more willing to go this route. ❏

Article 8.4

THE COMMUNITY REINVESTMENT ACT: A LAW THAT WORKS

BY JIM CAMPEN
November/December 1997; updated October 2010 and October 2013

The first potion of this article was originally written in 1997. What appears here is an edited and condensed version. The second portion, under the title "Modernizing the CRA," was orginially written in 2010, and updated in 2013. — Eds.

At an American Bankers Association convention in the early 1980s, bank consultant Ken Thomas was surprised to hear howls of laughter emerge from one of the meeting rooms. He stepped in to find the speaker ending his presentation with a flourish, pointing to the initial letters of the words projected behind him. "In conclusion," he shouted above the laughter and applause, "you can have your Community Reinvestment Act Programs, you can have your Community Reinvestment Act Policies, you can have your Community Reinvestment Act Personnel. But—as you can see—it's all just ... CRAP!"

The bankers' laughter may have been justified at the time, as the Reagan administration and its bank regulators ignored the law that a nationwide grassroots movement of community activists had successfully pushed Congress to enact in 1977. But as the Community Reinvestment Act (CRA) marks its twentieth anniversary this year, no one is laughing at it anymore.

In fact, the CRA is one of the most remarkable success stories of the 1990s. Under strong pressure from a second wave of grassroots activism that began ten years ago, many banks have recognized the potential for profitable business in neighborhoods that they had written off without a second thought not so long ago. Mortgage loans to minority and low-income homebuyers have soared. Hundreds of local partnerships among banks, community-based organizations and government agencies have resulted in tens of thousands of new units of affordable housing.

The CRA has acquired broad and deep support, due to the difference that it has made in hundreds of communities throughout the United States. This support paid off in 1996 when the CRA emerged intact from a determined attempt by congressional Republicans, following their 1994 electoral victory, to gut the law.

A Collection of Laws

In fact, the CRA is the centerpiece of several laws that have worked together to increase flows of credit to borrowers and neighborhoods that banks have traditionally neglected. The CRA itself simply says that banks are obliged to serve the credit needs of all the communities where they are located. It requires regulators to examine each bank's record of doing so and to take this record into account when deciding whether or not to approve applications for new branches or mergers with other banks.

The movement that won passage of the CRA in 1977 was primarily concerned about "redlining" of inner-city neighborhoods by lenders. The term refers to some bankers' practice of actually drawing red lines on maps to indicate areas off-limits for lending. Banks were using deposits collected in these neighborhoods to make loans in the suburbs. Gale Cincotta, of the Chicago-based National People's Action, was probably the most prominent of the many community leaders throughout the country who demanded that this disinvestment be replaced by reinvestment of the community's own money back into the community.

Two years earlier, in 1975, the community reinvestment movement had won passage of the Home Mortgage Disclosure Act (HMDA), which requires each bank to report annually on the number and dollar amount of mortgage loans made in every neighborhood in every metropolitan area. This disclosure made it possible to monitor where banks were and were not making mortgage loans.

Because the driving concern of the community reinvestment movement was saving neighborhoods, both the CRA and HMDA were focused on geographic communities. A separate set of "fair lending laws" prohibits discrimination against individual borrowers on the basis of race, national origin, sex, age, and other characteristics. The two most important of these laws, both legacies of the civil rights movement, are the Fair Housing Act of 1968, which prohibits discrimination in the home purchase and home rental process (including lending), and the Equal Credit Opportunity Act of 1974, which outlaws discrimination in all types of lending.

The Awakening

Until about ten years ago, the government agencies charged with enforcing these laws all but ignored them. As Mildred Brown, president of the national grassroots organization ACORN, testified at a 1988 Senate Banking Committee hearing, "Banks are breaking the law and the regulators are their accomplices."

Two initiatives by community activists during the second half of the 1980s turned the CRA into an effective anti-discrimination tool. First, activists recognized that the emergence of interstate banking provided a new leverage point, as bank holding companies sought regulatory approval for their expansion plans. Community groups challenged these proposals on the grounds of weak performance in meeting community credit needs. Confronted with the resulting uncertainty and delay, most banks responded by negotiating "CRA agreements" that committed them to expand their lending programs in return for withdrawal of the challenges.

The second initiative was the use of HMDA data to document dramatic disparities between the amount of mortgage lending in minority and white neighborhoods. Most significantly, "The Color of Money," a May 1988 *Atlanta Journal-Constitution* series, showed that in 1986 banks made 5.4 times as many mortgage loans per 1,000 homes in Atlanta's white neighborhoods as in comparable black neighborhoods. The Pulitzer Prize-winning series sparked investigations that generated similar findings, and publicity, in several other cities, and led to the Senate hearings later that year that highlighted the bank regulators' indefensible neglect of their responsibilities.

In 1989, the CRA and HMDA were strengthened by important amendments that increased public disclosure and accountability for both banks and regulators.

Starting the next year, each bank's CRA performance rating became publicly available, along with a written report by its regulator. Furthermore, starting with 1990 applications, HMDA data were expanded to contain information on each application received, including the applicant's race and income and whether the application was approved or denied.

When they were released in the fall of 1991, the expanded HMDA data showed that the mortgage denial rate for blacks was more than twice that for whites. Bankers argued that the higher denial rate for blacks might simply reflect their weaker credit histories, smaller down payments, and other factors not included in HMDA data. But just one year later the Federal Reserve Bank of Boston announced the results of a study that proved the bankers wrong. Using statistical methods that separated out the effects of all other known factors, the study found that racial discrimination was a major reason why blacks and Latinos were denied mortgage loans more frequently than whites.

The Fruits of CRA

As publicity and pressure mounted, the laws enacted in the mid-1970s finally began to produce dramatic benefits. Once the spotlight began to shine on mortgage lending patterns, and the Justice Department reached some high-profile settlements in lending discrimination cases, loans to blacks and Latinos soared. Between 1991 and 1995, while conventional home-purchase loans to whites increased by two-thirds, loans to blacks tripled (from 45,000 to 138,000 a year) and those to Latinos more than doubled. During the same period, loans in predominantly minority neighborhoods rose by 137%, while loans in areas where the population was almost all white grew by just 37%.

Meanwhile, all of the mega-mergers that were transforming the banking industry were vulnerable to CRA challenges. In order to ensure regulatory approval, in each case banks negotiated agreements with the community to provide more low-income loans. By mid-1997, according to Comptroller of the Currency Eugene Ludwig (the principal regulator of the nation's largest banks), these CRA agreements had produced total commitments (some extending ten years into the future) for over $215 billion of increased loans and investments in underserved areas.

Fighting to Survive

While some banks recognized that the increased pressures had pushed them to make what turned out to be profitable loans, most resented the growing scrutiny of their performance and called for rollback of the CRA. When the Republicans gained control of Congress after the 1994 elections, bank lobbyists convinced them to make the Community Reinvestment Act a prime target.

The banks' Republican allies offered two main arguments to support their position, neither of which could withstand serious scrutiny. First, CRA opponents claimed that it requires risky loans that could undermine a bank's profitability and threaten its survival. Actually, the reverse is closer to the truth. The 1980s were marked by massive speculative lending to wealthy real estate developers and get-rich-quick schemers that resulted in the failure of more than two thousand banks

CHAPTER 8: RESISTANCE AND ALTERNATIVES | 245

and S&Ls. Yet not a single bank failure had been caused by making too many bad loans to disadvantaged borrowers.

Federal Reserve Board researchers found "no evidence of lower profitability" at banks that specialized in mortgage lending to lower-income borrowers and neighborhoods and, in a nationwide survey by the Kansas City Fed, 98% of banks reported that their CRA lending was profitable. Overall, the look-the-other-way attitude toward CRA enforcement of the 1980s was accompanied by a steady fall in bank profit rates, while the increasingly serious enforcement of the CRA in the 1990s coincided with five straight years of record bank profits.

The other major argument against the CRA—that it was ineffective and that all of the efforts to enforce it in the 1990s had accomplished little—was contradicted not just by statistics but by massive support from cities and towns around the country attesting to how much had, in fact, been accomplished. One open letter to Congress was signed by over 2,000 community-based organizations and more than 200 mayors. The swell of grassroots support overwhelmed pressure from industry lobbyists and produced unanimous opposition by congressional Democrats to every proposal that would have weakened the CRA. In addition, the Clinton administration never wavered from an early pledge to veto any bill containing such provisions. When the dust of battle finally cleared at the end of 1996, the CRA emerged intact.

Modernizing the CRA (October 2013)

In spite of the CRA's many accomplishments, and the success of its defenders in fending off the attack by Congressional Republicans in the mid-1990s, the dramatic ongoing transformation of the banking industry was reducing the law's effectiveness.

The CRA was enacted in 1977 because banks were collecting deposits in inner-city neighborhoods but failing to reinvest the funds back into those same areas. For this reason, CRA performance evaluations were focused on "assessment areas" defined in terms of where bank branches were located. At that time, this covered the great majority of all mortgage lending.

Over time, however, the impact of the CRA eroded as an ever-greater share of total mortgage lending fell outside its reach. This was the result of three developments. First, banks make loans in areas where they didn't have branches—and were therefore not subject to the CRA. Second, banking companies set up mortgage lending affiliates whose lending was not subject to review and evaluation under the CRA. Third, a growing share of total lending was done by independent mortgage companies not related to any bank.

Although this trend was well-established when Congress passed the "Financial Services Modernization Act" of 1999—capping a decades-long process of deregulating banks and other financial companies—lawmakers rejected the compelling arguments by community groups that the CRA needed to be "modernized" as well. The industry-friendly Republicans who controlled the Senate Banking Committee adamantly opposed any strengthening of the CRA.

The Congressional failure to extend the CRA's coverage was an important factor in making possible the explosion of predatory subprime lending that was central to the housing bubble of the mid-2000s and the financial crisis that followed. By 2005, according to the Federal Reserve, only one in four (26%) of all home-purchase loans were made by banks in their CRA assessment areas. The rest of the loans were made by banks in areas where they didn't have branches (Wells Fargo Bank makes loans in all 50 states, although it only has branches in 24), by affiliated companies that didn't have to be included in CRA evaluations (such as Citibank's sister company, CitiFinancial, that specialized in high-cost loans), and by independent mortgage companies not related to banks (including Ameriquest, Countrywide, and other giant predatory lenders).

Don't Blame the CRA

Within its shrinking area of coverage, the CRA continued to have an important impact, encouraging banks to make responsible home loans that borrowers could afford to repay and discouraging predatory subprime loans. The Federal Reserve found that only 7% of the loans that banks made in 2005 in their assessment areas were high-cost loans, compared to 24% of the loans that they made elsewhere, and 38% of the loans made by mortgage companies. My own research in Massachusetts found that in 2006, at the height of the subprime boom, banks whose local lending was covered by the CRA accounted for only 655 out of 40,173 subprime loans in the state (just 1.6% of the total). Conservative claims that the CRA was responsible for the subprime lending crisis have things exactly backwards. If CRA had been expanded to cover the entire mortgage lending industry as part of the 1999 "financial modernization" law, the subprime lending crisis might never have happened.

In the aftermath of the crisis, it remains vital to finally update the CRA—both to prevent predatory lending from re-emerging once the memory of the current crisis fades, and to ensure that those responsible for the crisis provide the credit and capital that local communities need to recover. Accordingly, community-based organizations have continued to campaign for expanding and modernizing the CRA. In 2009, National People's Action and the PICO National Network (together representing more than 70 community-based organizations nationwide) got the Federal Reserve to agree to hold a series of day-long meetings with local leaders and hundreds of activists in nine hard-hit cities across the country, from Richmond, Calif., to Brockton, Mass. In Washington, D.C., meanwhile, the National Community Reinvestment Coalition has led a broad collection of local, regional, and national groups in bringing pressure to bear on regulators and elected officials.

The most important proposals for updating and strengthening the CRA include: extending CRA coverage of bank lending to all of the communities where they do business and to all lending by all affiliated companies; extending CRA coverage to independent mortgage companies; extending CRA-like responsibilities to Wall Street firms such as investment banks and hedge funds; increasing emphasis on basic banking services, including convenient branch offices, affordable small-dollar loans, and inexpensive checking and savings accounts for lower-income families; and expanding the attention given to evaluating performance in meeting the credit and banking needs of people and communities of color.

Some of these long-overdue measures to expand the CRA's coverage and operation would require legislation, which is highly unlikely as long as the Republicans control the House of Representatives. But other important changes could be implemented under the current law, by the bank regulators charged with implementing the CRA. The most important of these is the expansion of assessment areas to include all communities where banks do a significant amount of lending. ❏

Resources: Douglas Evanoff & Lewis Segal, "CRA and Fair Lending Regulations," Economic Perspectives (Federal Reserve Bank of Chicago), November/December 1996; Revisiting the CRA: Perspectives on the Future of the Community Reinvestment Act, Federal Reserve Banks of Boston and San Francisco, 2009 (bos.frb.org); Carolina Reid, et al., "Debunking the CRA Myth – Again," UNC Center for Community Capital, January 2013 (ccc.unc.edu); the National Community Reinvestment Coalition (ncrc.org).

Article 8.5

HOW TO TAKE ON THE CARD SHARKS—AND WIN!

New consumer-protection legislation has reined in predatory credit card lending.

BY JIM CAMPEN
November/December 2013

In the early 2000s, credit card companies, like other lenders, decided that there was lots of money to be made by exploiting vulnerable consumers. Up to that point, the credit card industry was a somewhat boring business that made its money by charging high—but not exorbitant—interest rates to borrowers who it judged likely to be able to make their monthly payments on time. Then, however, the giant banks that provide the bulk of the nation's credit cards switched to a business model based on what Elizabeth Warren, then a professor at Harvard Law School, memorably termed "tricks and traps." These were spelled out in the almost impossible-to-understand small print of the multi-page "agreements" that the banks provided to their customers. Anyone who did manage to read to the end found that the "agreement" allowed the credit card company to change any of its terms "at any time, for any reason."

The unfair and exploitative practices of the credit card companies, affecting millions of households, soon became widely known. Five years ago, it was almost impossible to avoid the avalanche of news articles, radio and TV reports, and Internet postings about them. Today, such stories are few and far between. This isn't because the media became bored with the story. It's because a powerful consumer movement publicized the abuses, built a strong campaign, and won two important legislative victories.

Tricks and Traps

Millions of consumers were enticed with offers of cards with "promotional" interest rates as low as 0% for the first few months and regular interest rates of between 12% and 14% after that, but ended up paying far more. They were slapped with late fees averaging over $33 each time their monthly payment arrived even one day late, even if the due date fell on a Sunday and their payment arrived on Monday. They faced stiff over-limit fees—sometimes multiple charges for a number of small purchases on the same day—if their charges exceeded their credit limit by even a single dollar, even though borrowers were generally not aware that they had exceeded their limit or that the credit card companies would authorize over-limit charges.

Most devastatingly, both of these minor mistakes were among those that could result in their interest rate being switched to a much higher "penalty rate." Some card companies adopted the policy of "universal default" whereby even a problem on an unrelated account (for example, being late on an electric bill) could result in a cardholder being subject to the penalty rate. By 2007, the average penalty rate was 16.9 percentage points higher than the regular interest rate, meaning that a 13% rate would jump to 29.9%.

Worst of all, the penalty rate applied not only to future purchases, but also to money already borrowed. For a household with the average 2008 credit card balance, about $10,700, this would result in additional interest charges of more than $1,800 per year. Once a household fell into this trap, it was almost impossible to get out—which is just the way the banks liked it.

Many of those trapped were low- and middle-income families who used their credit cards to pay for basic living expenses and unexpected medical bills. One recent survey, by the liberal policy organization Dēmos, found that two-fifths of such lower-income families used their credit cards in this way. Many other victims were college students, on their own for the first time, who fell prey to aggressive marketing on college campuses and ended up with debt that they couldn't repay as well as a damaged credit rating.

A Consumer Victory: The Credit CARD Act of 2009

As the credit card industry's abuses grew and spread, millions of outraged consumers demanded change. Led by a coalition of national consumer advocacy groups —including the Center for Responsible Lending, the Consumer Federation of America, Consumers Union, the National Consumer Law Center, and U.S. PIRG —a powerful grassroots movement pushed Congress to take action. The industry argued that the proposed legislation that eventually became the Credit Card Accountability, Responsibility, and Disclosure Act (known as the CARD Act) would end up hurting consumers by raising the cost and reducing the availability of credit card borrowing.

But credit card abuses were so widespread and so offensive that politicians were unwilling to defend them in the light of day. Although many Republicans worked behind the scenes to derail or weaken the bill, when the CARD Act came up for its final votes in May 2009, it passed overwhelmingly in both the Senate (90-5) and the House of Representatives (361-54).

The CARD Act effectively outlaws the worst of the credit card industry's tricks and traps. Most importantly, it prohibits retroactive interest rate increases on existing balances unless a borrower has missed two consecutive monthly payments on the account. And not only that: when a borrower is hit with a penalty rate, the company is required to restore the original interest rate if and when the borrower succeeds in making six consecutive on-time payments.

Late fees have been reduced by requiring that consumers have at least 21 days to make their payments, that payments due on a Sunday or holiday be regarded as on time if they arrive the next business day, that payments be due the same date each month, and that the fees be "reasonable and proportional." Over-limit fees are banned unless a cardholder opts-in to allow approval of charges over their credit limit, and are limited to one fee per month. The initial rate offered on a new account cannot be raised during the first year, and after that the borrower must be provided with 45-day advance notice and given the opportunity to cancel the card and pay off the existing balance over five years.

Credit card companies are prohibited from opening a new account or increasing a borrower's credit limit without assessing the consumer's ability to make timely loan payments. Those under 21 are given special protection from predatory credit card lenders by a prohibition on sending pre-approved offers of credit without advance permission, a ban on marketing on college campuses, and a new rule that no one under 21 years of age can get a card without either proving an independent ability to make the required monthly payments or obtaining a co-signer over 21.

Consumers Win Again: The CFPB

The enactment of the CARD Act was a major accomplishment. But simply passing laws doesn't make a difference unless those laws are enforced. And prohibiting existing abusive practices can't protect consumers against the credit card companies' endless ability to come up with imaginative new abuses that get around the law. The title of a December 2009 report from the Center for Responsible Lending spelled out the problem: "Dodging Reform: As Some Credit Card Abuses are Outlawed, New Ones Proliferate."

That's why a second consumer legislative victory—ensuring that the financial reform law passed in July 2010 (the Dodd-Frank Act) mandated the establishment of a Consumer Financial Protection Bureau (CFPB)—was perhaps even more important than the CARD Act itself.

The CFPB, which came into existence in July 2011, is charged not only with writing and enforcing the regulations that implement the CARD Act and other consumer-protection laws, but also with monitoring the operation of consumer-credit markets and taking action against unfair, deceptive, or abusive acts and practices. It seeks to improve consumers' ability to understand prices and risks upfront when shopping for credit, and to offer them a one-stop location for submitting complaints and seeking remedies for problems with credit card providers.

The Fruits of These Victories

That the CARD Act has produced major benefits for consumers, with none of the dire consequences predicted by the industry, has been documented in numerous reports and studies. For example, the group Consumer Action noted that while complaints about credit cards were regularly the number one reason for calls to its consumer hotline before 2009, they are no longer even among the top ten.

The most comprehensive assessment to date of the Act's impact on consumers and on the industry is provided by a major report released by the CFPB in October 2013. This report found that the average late fee had gone down from $33 to $27 and that over-limit fees had essentially disappeared. Together, these two changes were saving consumers an estimated $4 billion per year.

The CFPB also found that, while credit remains readily available to those with the ability to repay, the number of 18- to 20-year-olds with at least one credit card had fallen by half. (Meanwhile, of course, student loans have soared. These loans have their own problems, but at least their interest rates are much lower than those on credit cards and no repayment is required while students remain in school.)

The CFPB's publicly available consumer complaint database recorded over 36,000 complaints about credit cards in its first two years of operation, resulting in monetary payments to about 6,500 consumers, and increased public scrutiny of card-company performance. J. D. Power's 2013 *Credit Card Satisfaction Study* showed that customer satisfaction had risen every year since 2010, to the highest level since the study began in 2007.

The CFPB's report also highlighted areas where consumers continue to suffer from abusive practices of the credit card industry and promised to address these issues in a timely manner. In one of these areas—the selling of "add-on" products that purport to offer debt protection and identity protection—the CFPB has already required three big lenders (Chase, Capital One, and Discover) to refund over $700 million to consumers and to pay over $100 million in fines for deceptive marketing and charging for services that were never actually provided.

Crying Wolf

Data on what's happened during the three and one-half years since passage of the CARD Act demonstrate beyond any doubt what consumer advocates said at the time: that banks were "crying wolf," rather than warning of real dangers, when they predicted that the pending legislation would cause the cost of credit card borrowing to soar and their own profitability to plummet.

It is theoretically possible that all of the CARD Act's consumer benefits from the lower fees and rates noted earlier could have been offset by increases in other charges. This is what Jamie Dimon, CEO of JPMorgan Chase, was predicting when he said that "If you're a restaurant and you can't charge for the soda, you're going to charge more for the burger." But the CFPB investigated this possibility by measuring what it calls the "total cost of credit"—that is, it added up all fees and interest charges paid by credit card borrowers and calculated what percentage this represented of the total amount of credit card debt outstanding. The CFPB found that the total cost of credit declined from 16.4% in the last quarter of 2008 to 14.4% in the last quarter of 2012. It is impossible to know how much of this reduction is a result of the CARD Act, but it is crystal clear that predictions of an increase in borrowing costs were wrong.

Another October 2013 study on the impact of the CARD Act, this one by four academic economists, concluded that the resulting fee reductions have saved consumers $21 billion per year "with no evidence of an offsetting increase in interest charges or a reduction in access to credit." The savings were particularly great for the riskiest borrowers. While the fee reductions amounted to 2.8% of total credit card balances annually, they came to over ten percent of their credit card balances for the 17% of borrowers who were in the highest risk category as measured by their credit scores at the time they opened their accounts.

Did the consumer benefits from the CARD Act come at the expense of lender profitability? It's possible to get a remarkably clear answer to this question because the FDIC reports quarterly on the performance of different kinds of banks, categorized by specialization or size, and one of its categories consists of "credit card lenders." It turns out that all but one of the six largest credit card lenders (who together account for over two-thirds of total credit card balances) do their lending though separate banks that specialize in credit cards. This is true for Bank of

America, Chase, Capital One, Discover, and American Express; the only exception is Citibank.

Since 2010, "credit card banks" has been the most profitable single category, using the two measures of profitability reported by the FDIC—return on assets (ROA) and return on equity (ROE). In 2012, ROA was 3.14% for credit card banks, more than triple the 1.00% for all banks; ROE was 20.97% for credit card banks, more than double the 8.92% for all banks. The results for 2012 are very similar to those for 2011 and for the first half of 2013, and also to those for 2007, before the onset of the financial crisis and economic downturn.

Perhaps the credit card companies had been outsmarting themselves. A business model based on "tricks and traps" that aggressively pushed money into the hands of borrowers who lacked the ability to repay their debts may have worked in the short run, but ultimately was disastrous to the lenders themselves. Lending money only to those with the ability to repay it would seem like simple common sense. It's too bad that financial hardship for millions of borrowers, an act of Congress, and a new federal agency was necessary to make these lenders behave sensibly. ❑

Sources: The CARD ACT Report, October 1, 2013 (consumerfinance.gov); Sumit Agarwal, et al., "Regulating Consumer Financial Products: Evidence from Credit Cards"; Center for Responsible Lending (responsiblelending.org); Federal Deposit Insurance Corporation (FDIC), *Quarterly Banking Profile* (fdic.gov); Peter Dreier and Donald Cohen, "Credit Sharks Crying Wolf," The Cry Wolf Project, May 2009 (crywolfproject.org).

Article 8.6

TIME FOR *PERMANENT* NATIONALIZATION!
If the big banks are "too big to fail," they should be public.

BY FRED MOSELEY
March/April 2009

The Treasury Department's recent bailouts of major U.S. banks will result in a massive transfer of income from taxpayers to those banks' bondholders.

Under the government's current bailout plan, the total sum of money transferred from taxpayers to bondholders will probably be at least several hundred billion dollars and could be as much as $1 trillion, which is about $3,300 for each man, woman, and child in the United States. These bondholders took risks and made lots of money during the recent boom, but now taxpayers are being forced to bail them out and pay for their losses.

This trillion-dollar transfer of income from taxpayers to bondholders is an economic injustice that should be stopped immediately, and it can be stopped—if the government fully and permanently nationalizes the banks that are "too big to fail."

The TARP program ("Troubled Asset Relief Program") has gone through several incarnations. It was originally intended to purchase high-risk mortgage-backed securities from banks. But this plan floundered because it is very difficult in the current circumstances to determine the value of these risky assets and thus the price the government should pay for them. The main policy for the first $350 billion spent so far has been to invest government capital into banks by buying preferred stock (which is the equivalent of a loan), which receives a 5% rate of return (Warren Buffet gets a 10% rate of return when he buys preferred stocks these days) and has no voting rights. Managers of the banks are not being replaced, and there are usually cosmetic limits on executive pay, unlikely to be enforced. So these bank managers, who are largely responsible for the banking crisis, will continue to be rewarded with salaries of millions of dollars per year, paid for in part with taxpayer money. Existing bank stock loses value as the bank issues stock secured by TARP funds.

But the main beneficiaries of the government bailout money are the bondholders of the banks (see box, "Bank Bonds"). In the event of future losses, which are likely to be enormous, the government bailout money will be used directly or indirectly to pay off the bondholders. This could eventually take all of the available TARP money, and perhaps even more. So the government bailout of the banks is ultimately a bailout of the banks' bondholders, paid for by taxpayers.

The Bush administration's rationale for this approach to the bailout was that if the government did not bail out the banks and their bondholders, then the whole financial system in the United States would collapse. Nobody would lend money to anybody, and the economy would seize up (in the memorable words of George W. Bush: "this sucker would go down"). Bush Treasury Secretary Paulson presented us with an unavoidable dilemma—either bail out the bondholders with taxpayers' money or suffer a severe recession or depression.

If Paulson's assertion were correct, it would be a stinging indictment of our current financial system. It would imply that the capitalist financial system, left on its own, is inherently unstable, and can only avoid sparking major economic crises by being bailed out by the government, at the taxpayers' expense. There is a double indictment here: the capitalist financial system is inherently unstable and the necessary bailouts are economically unjust.

But there is a better alternative, a more equitable, "taxpayer friendly" option: Permanently nationalize banks that are "too big to fail" and run these banks according to public policy objectives (affordable housing, green energy, etc.), rather than with the objective of private profit maximization. The nationalization of banks, if it's done right, would clearly be superior to current bailout policies because it would not involve a massive transfer of wealth from taxpayers to bondholders.

Besides providing a more equitable response to the current banking crisis, nationalizing the biggest banks will help ensure that a crisis like this never happens again, and we never again have to bail out the banks and their bondholders to "save the economy." Once some banks have become "too big to fail" and everyone understands that the government will always bail out these large banks to avoid a systematic collapse, it follows that these banks should be nationalized. Otherwise, the implicit promise of a bailout gives megabanks a license to take lots of risks and make lots of money in good times, and then let the taxpayers pay for their losses in the bad times. Economists call this dilemma the "moral hazard" problem. In this case, we might instead call it the "economic injustice" problem.

The best way to avoid this legal robbery of taxpayers is to nationalize the banks. If taxpayers are going to pay for banks' losses, then they should also receive their profits. The main justification for private profit is to encourage capitalists to invest and to invest wisely because they would suffer the losses if their investment fails. But if the losses fall not on capitalists, but instead on the taxpayers, then this justification for private profit disappears.

Freed from the need to maximize short-term profit, nationalized banks would also make the economy more stable in the future. They would take fewer risks during an expansion to avoid debt-induced bubbles, which inevitably burst and cause so much hardship. For example, there would be fewer housing bubbles; instead, the deposits of these megabanks would be invested in decent affordable housing

---

Bank Bonds

Bank bonds are loans to banks by the bondholders, in contrast to common stocks, which are capital invested in banks by their owners. Bank bonds are a relatively new phenomenon in the U.S. economy (and the rest of the world). Until the 1980s, almost all loans by banks were financed from money deposited in the banks by depositors. Then in the 1980s, banks began to borrow more and more money by selling bonds to bondholders; this became a primary way that banks financed their loans. This debt strategy of banks enabled them to invest ever larger sums and make more profits. However, this debt strategy left the banking system more unstable and vulnerable to collapse because banks would have to repay their bondholders. And when major banks were unable to do so, the banking system fell into crisis.

available to all. With housing more affordable, mortgages would be more affordable and less risky.

The newly nationalized banks could also increase their lending to credit-worthy businesses and households, and thereby help stabilize the economy and lessen the severity of the current recession. As things stand, banks do not want to increase their lending, since the creditworthiness of any borrower is difficult to determine, especially that of other banks that may also hold toxic assets. They have suffered enormous losses over the last year, and they fear that more enormous losses are still to come. Banks prefer instead to hoard capital as a cushion against these expected future losses.

What the government is doing now is giving money to banks in one way or another, and then begging them to please lend this money to businesses and households. Nationalization is clearly the better solution. Instead of giving money to the banks and begging them to lend, the government should nationalize the banks in trouble and lend directly to credit-worthy businesses and households.

How would the nationalization of banks work? I suggest the following general principles and guidelines:

(1) The federal government would become the owner of any "systemically significant" bank that asks for a government rescue or goes into bankruptcy proceedings. The value of existing stock would be wiped out, as it would be in a normal bankruptcy.

(2) The government would itself operate the banks. Top management would be replaced by government banking officials, and the managers would not receive "golden parachutes" of any kind.

(3) Most importantly, the banks' long-term bonds would be converted into common stock in the banks. This would restore the banks to solvency, so they could start lending again. The private common stock would be subordinate to the government preferred stock in the capital structure, which would mean that any future losses would be taken out of the private stock before the government stock. Bondholders could also be given the option of converting their stocks back to bonds at a later date, with a significant write-down or discount, determined by bankruptcy judges.

These "bonds-to-stocks" swaps (often called "debt-to-equity" swaps), or partial write-downs if the bondholders so choose, are a crucial aspect of an equitable nationalization of banks. The bondholders lent their money and signed contracts that stipulated that if the banks went bankrupt, they might suffer losses. Now the banks are bankrupt and the bondholders should take the losses.

This process of accelerated bankruptcy and nationalization should be applied in the future to any banks that are in danger of bankruptcy and are deemed to be "systemically significant." This would include the next crises at Citigroup and Bank of America. Other banks in danger of bankruptcy that are not systemically significant should be allowed to fail. There should be no more bailouts of the bondholders at the expense of taxpayers. In addition, the banks who received some of the first $350 billion should be subject to stricter conditions along the lines that Congress attached to the second $350 billion—that banks should be required to increase their lending to businesses and consumers, to fully account for how they have spent the government capital, and to follow strict limitations on executive compensation. The government should withdraw its capital from any banks that fail to meet these standards.

There is one other acceptable option: the government could create entirely new banks that would purchase good assets from banks and increase lending to credit-worthy borrowers. These government banks are sometimes called "good banks," in contrast to the "bad bank" proposals that have been floated recently, according to which the government would set up a bank to purchase bad ("toxic") assets from banks. The term "good bank" is no doubt more politically acceptable than "government bank," but the meaning is the same. The only difference between the "good bank" proposal and the nationalization proposal I've outlined here is that my proposal would start with existing banks and turn them into government banks.

In recent weeks, there has been more and more talk about and even acceptance of the "nationalization" of banks. the *Washington Post* recently ran an op-ed by NYU economists Nouriel Roubini and Matthew Richardson entitled "Nationalize the Banks! We Are All Swedes Now," and *New York Times* business columnist Joe Nocera has written about how more and more economists and analysts are beginning to call for nationalization: "Nationalization. I just said it. The roof didn't cave in."

Even former Fed chair Alan Greenspan, whom many regard as one of the main architects of the current crisis, recently told the *Financial Times* that (temporary) nationalization may be the "least bad option." He added, "I understand that once in a hundred years this is what you do."

But there are three crucial differences between such pseudo-nationalizations and full-fledged, genuine nationalization:

(1) The pseudo-nationalizations are intended to be temporary. In this, they follow the model of the Swedish government, which temporarily nationalized some major banks in the early 1990s, and has subsequently almost entirely re-privatized them. Real nationalization would be permanent; if banks are "too big to fail," then they have to be public, to avoid more crises and unjust bailouts in the future.

(2) In pseudo-nationalizations, the government has little or no decision-making power in running the banks. In real nationalization, the government would have complete control over the banks, and would run the banks according to public policy objectives democratically decided.

(3) In pseudo-nationalizations, bondholders don't lose anything, and the loans owed by the banks to the bondholders are paid in full, in large part by taxpayers' money. In real nationalization, the bondholders would suffer their own losses, just as they reaped the profits by themselves in the good times, and the taxpayers would not pay for the losses.

In mid-February, Treasury Secretary Timothy Geithner announced the Obama administration's plans for the bank bailout—renamed the "Financial Stability Plan." This plan is very similar to Paulson's two versions of TARP: it includes both purchases of high-risk mortgage-backed securities from banks and also investing capital in banks. The main new feature is that government capital is supposed to be invested together with private capital. But in order to attract private capital, the government will have to provide sufficient guarantees, so most of the risks will still fall on taxpayers. So Geithner's Financial Stability Plan has the same fundamental flaw as Paulson's TARP: it bails out the banks and their bondholders at the expense of taxpayers.

The public should demand that the Obama administration cancel these plans for further bank bailouts and consider other options, including genuine, permanent nationalization. Permanent nationalization with bonds-to-stocks swaps for bondholders is the most equitable solution to the current banking crisis, and would provide a better basis for a more stable and public-oriented banking system in the future. ❏

Sources: Dean Baker, "Time for Bank Rationalization" (cepr.net); Willem Buiter, "Good Bank/New Bank vs. Bad Bank: a Rare Example of a No-Brainer" (blogs.ft.com/maverecon); Krishna Guha and Edward Luce, "Greenspan Backs Bank Nationalization," *Financial Times*, Feb. 18, 2008; Joe Nocera, "A Stress Test for the Latest Bailout Plan," *New York Times*, Feb. 13, 2009; James Petras, "No Bailout for Wall Street Billionaires" (countercurrents.org); Matthew Richardson and Nouriel Roubini, "Nationalize the Banks! We're All Swedes Now," *Washington Post*, Feb. 15, 2009; Joseph Stiglitz, "Is the Entire Bailout Strategy Flawed? Let's Rethink This Before It's Too Late" (alternet.org).

Article 8.7

LABOR'S CAPITAL
Putting Pension Wealth to Work for Workers

BY ADRIA SCHARF
September/October 2005

Pension fund assets are the largest single source of investment capital in the country. Of the roughly $17 trillion in private equity in the U.S. economy, $6 to 7 trillion is held in employee pensions. About $1.3 trillion is in union pension plans (jointly trusteed labor-management plans or collectively bargained company-sponsored plans) and $2.1 trillion is in public employee pension plans. Several trillion more are in defined contribution plans and company-sponsored defined benefit plans with no union representation. These vast sums were generated by—and belong to—workers; they're really workers' deferred wages.

Workers' retirement dollars course through Wall Street, but most of the capital owned *by* working people is invested with no regard *for* working people or their communities. Pension dollars finance sweatshops overseas, hold shares of public companies that conduct mass layoffs, and underwrite myriad anti-union low-road corporate practices. In one emblematic example, the Florida public pension system bought out the Edison Corporation, the for-profit school operator, in November 2003, with the deferred wages of Florida government employees—including public school teachers. (With just three appointed trustees, one of whom is Governor Jeb Bush, Florida is one of the few states with no worker representation on the board of its state-employee retirement fund.)

The custodians of workers' pensions—plan trustees and investment managers—argue that they are bound by their "fiduciary responsibility" to consider only narrow financial factors when making investment decisions. They maintain they have a singular obligation to maximize financial returns and minimize financial risk for beneficiaries—with no regard for broader concerns. But from the perspective of the teachers whose dollars funded an enterprise that aims to privatize their jobs, investing in Edison, however promising the expected return (and given Edison's track record, it wasn't very promising!), makes no sense.

A legal concept enshrined in the 1974 Employee Retirement Income Security Act (ERISA) and other statutes, "fiduciary responsibility" does constrain the decision-making of those charged with taking care of other people's money. It obligates fiduciaries (e.g., trustees and fund managers) to invest retirement assets for the exclusive benefit of the pension beneficiaries. According to ERISA, fiduciaries must act with the care, skill, prudence, and diligence that a "prudent man" would use. Exactly what that means, though, is contested.

The law does *not* say that plan trustees must maximize short-term return. It does, in fact, give fiduciaries some leeway to direct pension assets to worker- and community-friendly projects. In 1994, the U.S. Department of Labor issued rule clarifications that expressly permit fiduciaries to make "economically targeted investments" (ETIs), or investments that take into account collateral benefits like good jobs, housing, improved social service facilities, alternative energy, strengthened infrastructure, and economic development. Trustees and fund managers are free to consider a double bottom line, prioritizing investments that have a social pay-off so long as their expected risk-adjusted financial returns are equal to other, similar, investments. Despite a backlash against ETIs from Newt Gingrich conservatives in the 1990s, Clinton's Labor Department rules still hold.

Nevertheless, the dominant mentality among the asset management professionals who make a living off what United Steelworkers president Leo Gerard calls "the deferred-wage food table" staunchly resists considering any factors apart from financial risk and return.

This is beginning to change in some corners of the pension fund world, principally (no surprise) where workers and beneficiaries have some control over their pension capital. In jointly managed union defined-benefit (known as "Taft-Hartley") plans and public-employee pension plans, the ETI movement is gaining ground. "Taft-Hartley pension trustees have grown more comfortable with economically targeted investments as a result of a variety of influences, one being the Labor Department itself," says Robert Pleasure of the Center for Working Capital, an independent capital stewardship-educational institute started by the AFL-CIO. Concurrently, more public pension fund trustees have begun adopting ETIs that promote housing and economic development within state borders. Most union and public pension trustees now understand that, as long as they follow a careful process and protect returns, ETIs do not breach their fiduciary duty, and may in certain cases actually be sounder investments than over-inflated Wall Street stocks.

Saving Jobs: Heartland Labor Capital Network

During the run-up of Wall Street share prices in the 1990s, investment funds virtually redlined basic industries, preferring to direct dollars into hot public technology stocks and emerging foreign markets, which despite the rhetoric of fiduciary responsibility were often speculative, unsound, investments. Even most collectively bargained funds put their assets exclusively in Wall Street stocks, in part because some pension trustees feared that if they didn't, they could be held liable. (During an earlier period, the Labor Department aggressively pursued union pension trustees for breaches of fiduciary duty. In rare cases where trustees were found liable, their personal finances and possessions were at risk.) But in the past five years, more union pension funds and labor-friendly fund managers have begun directing assets into investments that bolster the "heartland" economy: worker-friendly private equity, and, wherever possible, unionized industries and companies that offer "card-check" and "neutrality." ("Card-check" requires automatic union recognition if a majority of employees present signed authorization cards; "neutrality" means employers agree to remain neutral during organizing campaigns.)

The Heartland Labor Capital Network is at the center of this movement. The network's Tom Croft says he and his allies want to "make sure there's an economy still around in the future to which working people will be able to contribute." Croft estimates that about $3 to $4 billion in new dollars have been directed to worker-friendly private equity since 1999—including venture capital, buyout funds, and "special situations" funds that invest in financially distressed companies, saving jobs and preventing closures. Several work closely with unions to direct capital into labor-friendly investments.

One such fund, New York-based KPS Special Situations, has saved over 10,000 unionized manufacturing jobs through its two funds, KPS Special Situations I and II, according to a company representative. In 2003, St. Louis-based Wire Rope Corporation, the nation's leading producer of high carbon wire and wire rope products, was in bankruptcy with nearly 1,000 unionized steelworker jobs in jeopardy. KPS bought the company and restructured it in collaboration with the United Steelworkers International. Approximately 20% of KPS's committed capital is from Taft-Hartley pension dollars; as a result, the Wire Rope transaction included some union pension assets.

The Heartland Labor Capital Network and its union partners want to expand this sort of strategic deployment of capital by building a national capital pool of "Heartland Funds" financed by union pension assets and other sources. These funds have already begun to make direct investments in smaller worker-friendly manufacturing and related enterprises; labor representatives participate alongside investment experts on their advisory boards.

"It's simple. Workers' assets should be invested in enterprises and construction projects that will help to build their cities, rebuild their schools, and rebuild America's infrastructure," says Croft.

"Capital Stewardship": The AFL-CIO

For the AFL-CIO, ETIs are nothing new. Its Housing Investment Trust (HIT), formed in 1964, is the largest labor-sponsored investment vehicle in the country that produces collateral benefits for workers and their neighborhoods. Hundreds of union pension funds invest in the $2 billion trust, which leverages public financing to build housing, including low-income and affordable units, using union labor. HIT, together with its sister fund the Building Investment Trust (BIT), recently announced a new investment program that is expected to generate up to $1 billion in investment in apartment development and rehabilitation by 2005 in targeted cities including New York, Chicago, and Philadelphia. The initiative will finance thousands of units of housing and millions of hours of union construction work. HIT and BIT require owners of many of the projects they help finance to agree to card-check recognition and neutrality for their employees.

HIT and BIT are two examples of union-owned investment vehicles. There are many others—including the LongView ULTRA Construction Loan Fund, which finances projects that use 100% union labor; the Boilermakers' Co-Generation and Infrastructure Fund; and the United Food and Commercial Workers' Shopping Center Mortgage Loan Program—and their ranks are growing.

Since 1997, the AFL-CIO and its member unions have redoubled their efforts to increase labor's control over its capital through a variety of means. The AFL-CIO's Capital Stewardship Program promotes corporate governance reform, investment manager accountability, pro-worker investment strategies, international pension fund cooperation, and trustee education. It also evaluates worker-friendly pension funds on how well they actually advance workers' rights, among other criteria. The Center for Working Capital provides education and training to hundreds of union and public pension fund trustees each year, organizes conferences, and sponsors research on capital stewardship issues including ETIs.

Public Pension Plans Join In

At least 29 states have ETI policies directing a portion of their funds, usually less than 5%, to economic development within state borders. The combined public pension assets in ETI programs amount to about $55 billion, according to a recent report commissioned by the Vermont state treasurer. The vast majority of these ETIs are in residential housing and other real estate.

The California Public Employees' Retirement System (CalPERS) is an ETI pioneer among state pension funds. The single largest pension fund in the country, it has $153.8 billion in assets and provides retirement benefits to over 1.4 million members. In the mid-1990s, when financing for housing construction dried up in California, CalPERS invested hundreds of millions of dollars to finance about 4% of the state's single-family housing market. Its ETI policy is expansive. While it requires economically targeted investments earn maximum returns for their level of risk and fall within geographic and asset-diversification guidelines, CalPERS also considers the investments' benefits to its members and to state residents, their job creation potential, and the economic and social needs of different groups in the state's population. CalPERS directs about 2% of its assets—about $20 billion as of May 2001—to investments that provide collateral social benefits. It also requires construction and maintenance contractors to provide decent wages and benefits.

Other state pension funds have followed CalPERs' lead. In 2003, the Massachusetts treasury expanded its ETI program, which is funded by the state's $32 billion pension. Treasurer Timothy Cahill expects to do "two dozen or more" ETI investments in 2004, up from the single investment made in 2003, according to the *Boston Business Journal*. "It doesn't hurt our bottom line, and it helps locally," Cahill explained. The immediate priority will be job creation. Washington, Wisconsin, and New York also have strong ETI programs.

In their current form and at their current scale, economically targeted investments in the United States are not a panacea. Pension law does impose constraints. Many consultants and lawyers admonish trustees to limit ETIs to a small portion of an overall pension investment portfolio. And union trustees must pursue ETIs carefully, following a checklist of "prudence" procedures, to protect themselves from liability. The most significant constraint is simply that these investments must generate risk-adjusted returns equal to alternative investments—this means that many deserving not-for-profit efforts and experiments in economic democracy are automatically ruled out. Still, there's more wiggle room in the law than has been broadly recognized. And when deployed strategically to bolster the labor movement, support employee buyouts, generate good jobs, or build affordable housing, economically targeted investments are a form of worker direction over capital whose potential has only begun to be realized. And (until the day that capital is abolished altogether) that represents an important foothold.

As early as the mid-1970s, business expert Peter Drucker warned in *Unseen Revolution* of a coming era of "pension-fund socialism" in which the ownership of massive amounts of capital by pension funds would bring about profound changes to the social and economic power structure. Today, workers' pensions prop up the U.S. economy. They're a point of leverage like no other. Union and public pension funds are the most promising means for working people to shape the deployment of capital on a large scale, while directing assets to investments with collateral benefits. If workers and the trustees of their pension wealth recognize the power they hold, they could alter the contours of capitalism. ❏

Article 8.8

FINANCING THE NEW ECONOMY
The New Hope in Credit Unions and Cooperation

BY ABBY SCHER
November/December 2013

For the last three years, labor organizer Ellen Vera has been piecing together Our Harvest Cooperative, an inspiring project launched primarily by the United Food and Commercial Workers (UFCW) and Mondragon USA, the U.S. arm of the famed Basque co-op network, with the goal of generating 150 to 200 family-wage jobs in farming, food processing and delivery in the rust-belt city of Cincinnati. Regional restaurants and institutions like Cincinnati State University are eager for fresh, locally cultivated food without the huge carbon footprint generated when produce is transported from afar. And through sheer grit, this Cincinnati "food hub" produced a business plan with the help of the Ohio State University Cooperative Development Center and put ten acres into cultivation right in the city. The Cincinnati Central Credit Union and other community members offered small loans to support the project's launch. Farming apprentices paid through the federal Pell Grant program and working with a seasoned organic farmer are growing 40 different types of crops, from corn to melons to tomatoes and "everything you can grow in the area," said Vera.

Despite servicing a CSA and Cincinnati State, the project remains small. The enterprising organizers and extension consultants had gone as far as they could without a big infusion of capital. "We tried with other banks," Vera said, "and didn't get very far." Another pool of funds was also beyond reach: union pensions, which are governed by tight fiduciary rules that discourage risky investment in a startup. A UFCW senior staffer admitted it was hard "to convince union pension funds to look beyond the bait and switch of Wall Street, but you have to convince them this is safe."

Then in August, the venture announced that it had received a large loan from Farm Credit of Mid America and CoBank, a cooperative bank created by the merger of regional rural co-op development banks founded during the New Deal and capitalized by long-term federal loans. With $92 billion in assets, CoBank is huge but focused on rural investment. Now Our Harvest can buy machinery, tractors, and a refrigerator truck, and develop washout and pack-up areas. If the project is successful, its founders hope it can open new horizons in the alternative economy and serve as a prototype for other unionized, worker-owned food hubs throughout the country.

There's a lot to learn about the state of banking and finance from this story. The most obvious lesson is that commercial banks aren't at the center of funding the New Economy—one in which we live sustainably on this earth, wealth is shared equitably, democratic workplaces flourish, and we earn the livings that we all deserve. A second lesson is that the federal government can still be a vital source of funding, even when it is under attack in the Tea Party age. A final lesson is more hopeful. It is that we already have working examples of the kinds of cooperative banking and financial institutions we need in order to scale up our vision of a New Economy beyond corporate control: from cooperative banks to credit unions, to federal loans and the community's own investment. By enriching this sector, we can nurture the power of workers over capital, an age-old struggle that the most recent financial crisis makes only more urgent. But as we will see, this sector, while rich with possibility, faces real constraints.

The Failure of Too-Big-To-Fail Banks

The 2008 financial crisis only made more visible the disconnect between the speculative too-big-to-fail banking sector and the kinds of investment that nurtures good jobs, a resilient and democratic economy, and a sustainable world (see Abby Scher, "Greetings From the New Economy," *D&S*, July/August 2012). The world of speculative finance has nothing to do with productive lending, as economist Michael Hudson, ex-Wall Streeter John Fullerton, and many others have noted. Yet finance makes up 30% of U.S. profits. Important values of solidarity and a healthy earth are pushed out of the calculus, as rapid-fire computerized trading buys and sells stocks and bonds in a great churning where the bottom line is the only thing that matters. Even worse, as Fullerton has argued, "a major lesson of the recent financial crisis is that [financial] firms do not manage risk, they move it" until it "explodes into view."

Banks' traditional lending gives as little consideration to ecological or social goals, including job growth. Bank lending to small businesses—the arena that famously produces the most new jobs, especially during downturns—dropped 18% from June 2008 to June 2011, according to a November 2012 study for the Small Business Administration. During that same period, bank lending overall dropped by about 9%. And big banks were the worst. The smaller banks that didn't get bailouts devoted more funds to small business lending even as the too-big-to-fail banks cut back. For the cooperative businesses that are the heart of the New Economy movement, the credit drought they face in the best of times only worsened.

Meanwhile, big banks take whatever deposits they do receive and leverage them for investments far from the communities where the deposits were made. The Community Reinvestment Act, a 1970s-era law encouraging banks to invest in the poor neighborhoods where they accept deposits, while vital, is clearly not enough.

"The only thing workers own right now is astronomical debt," says Brendan Martin, founder of the co-op lender The Working World, which provided $650,000 in financing to the New Era Windows cooperative (formerly Republic Windows and Doors) in Chicago earlier this year. (See Kari Lydersen and James Tracy, "The Real Audacity of Hope," *D&S*, Jan/Feb 2009.) Instead, the movement needs to "have serious productive capital in the hands of workers." "Banks don't want that," he continued. "They want the peonage state we're in now where most of our interest goes to them."

Building Cooperative Finance for a New Economy

Instead of just battling the big banks, activists are working to strengthen a diverse alternative financial system that pursues social goals and offers affordable lending, but that currently remains undercapitalized and, in the case of credit unions serving low-income communities, is even shrinking. This diverse sector includes community lenders like cooperative and community loan funds, credit unions—nonprofit, democratically run cooperatives whose depositor-owners have one vote no matter how much is in their account—and cooperative banks like CoBank and the National Cooperative Bank in Washington, D.C. Visionaries in 22 states are organizing to replicate the Bank of North Dakota, a state bank founded in the wake of a farmer uprising early in the 20th century. The bank holds government deposits and works through community banks to loan to business enterprises (including the fossil fuel industry), homebuyers, and students (see Abby Scher, "Banking on the Public," dollarsandsense.org).

The alternative financial sector needs strengthening. While the large CoBank and National Cooperative Bank are prominent exceptions, many of the institutions that support cooperatives and other democratic New Economy enterprises remain undercapitalized, are curbed by regulations promoted by commercial banks or are only beginning to create ties of solidarity with other parts of the cooperative sector. But they are taking the best ideas from abroad and getting serious about scaling up.

Credit unions are the most common type of cooperative in the country, with about 94 million members and more than $1 trillion in assets. They operate on tight margins even with tax-exempt earnings and a pay scale far below that of the commercial banking sector. "In good years, credit unions may achieve Return on Average Assets (ROA) or net income of 1%," according to a 2012 Federal Reserve report. They also are less likely than commercial banks to buy securities to generate income.

A 2013 International Labor Organization report argues that financial cooperatives (credit unions and co-op banks, which can serve nonmembers) offer relative resilience during busts because they "aren't involved in risky ventures." Except that sometimes, as in the case of the U.S. and German credit unions that bought mortgage-backed securities, they are.

Five big wholesale credit unions that served like correspondent banks (which processed payments and offered loans and investments to their credit-union members) went under after the crash, largely because of their investments in toxic mortgage-backed securities. This both cut any income the credit unions generated from their membership in these institutions, and led to hikes in their required payments to the depleted federal deposit insurance system for credit unions.

Deposits in the more mainstream, bank-like credit unions grew as people fled the corporate banks during the Move Your Money campaign almost two years ago, as did mergers with failing enterprises. By 2012, the earnings of federally insured credit unions were growing and it was a record year for the industry as a whole, according to the annual report of the National Credit Union Administration (NCUA), a federal agency. Meanwhile, small credit unions—those with assets under $10 million—lost members and labored to find the loan opportunities that provide these low-margin cooperatives with income.

Low-income credit unions, those with majority low-income members, were hit hard by the recession as their members struggled (and continue to struggle); the extra deposit fees to cover the losses in the insurance fund also hit them hard, according to a February 2012 study written by Cliff Rosenthal, then president of the National Federation of Community Development Credit Unions, for the San Francisco Federal Reserve.

Still, because of their social benefit to low-income communities and the challenging economic environment in which they operate, these credit unions have looser restrictions than regular credit unions. American Banking Association lobbying has ensured that business loans over $50,000 issued by credit unions are capped at 12.5% of a credit union's capital. Low-income credit unions are exempt from this cap and the credit union industry as a whole is trying to end it. Low-income credit unions also can accept deposits from nonmembers, which other credit unions cannot, and are eligible for supplemental capital from the NCUA's new Community Development Revolving Loan Fund. They also got a helping hand under the Dodd-Frank banking law, which mandated that credit-union regulators support economic and racial diversity and help preserve the credit unions that are often the lifelines of their communities. Today, 1,915 federal credit unions are designated as serving low-income communities, and 103 received $1.4 million in grants from the fund in 2012, according to the NCUA's annual report.

As the loan fund example shows, the federal government potentially can provide important capitalization, or it does when it feels some heat. Commercial banks succeeded in having credit unions temporarily barred from benefiting from TARP bailout money but after an uproar the Obama administration directed unprecedented amounts into community-development finance institutions that lend in poor communities. The Treasury Department's Community Development Financial Institutions (CDFI) Fund was created in 1994 following a campaign by low-income credit unions and other CDFIs to "economically empower America's underserved and distressed communities" by investing in them. It has awarded more than $1.7 billion in grants, loans and tax credits since then, and got a big boost in funds from the American Recovery and Reinvestment Act of 2009, giving it a total appropriation of nearly $250 million for 2010. Yet only 41 community-development credit unions (largely but not entirely "low income" credit unions) benefited from CDFI Fund awards from 2008 to 2010, amounting to 11.5% of the total distributed, according to the Federal Reserve report. Forty-eight credit unions tapped into $69.9 million in low-cost loans from the CDFI Fund's special Community Development Capital Initiative (a TARP program). This strengthened their balance sheets. But Rosenthal points out many more were in need given the stress on the credit unions from the financial crisis.

Building the New Economy from the Inside

"The industry as a whole is shrinking. It's a strange thing being in that world: every year credit unions disappear and the chartering of credit unions are at a snail's pace of one or two a year," said Deyanira del Rio, co-director of the New Economy Project in New York, who also serves as board chair of the Lower East Side People's Federal Credit Union and board vice-chair of the National Federation of Community Development Credit Unions. "These are the institutions that should be the model for building a new economy but they are facing all these challenges."

Building synergies across cooperatives is a key strategy of the new "horizontalism" seeking to challenge corporate control of the economy through self-management, as seen in Argentina and elsewhere. In the United States, such synergy could help low-income and other credit unions—and those that potentially borrow from them. Member-owned organizations of all sorts, from housing and worker co-ops to food and producer cooperatives, have more than 1 million members and $500 billion in revenue nationwide. That's a lot of potential power, power that the national cooperative banks already support.

"How do we bridge the divide of financial cooperatives, worker cooperatives and consumer cooperatives? There aren't a lot of great examples out there," del Rio said. One easy way? "When a nonprofit or a worker coop becomes a member, it expands their access to services."

The Lower East Side People's Federal Credit Union where del Rio serves as board chair is alreading bridging the divide. "Our credit union is successful primarily because we give loans to low income housing co-ops," says Linda Levy, its CEO. "There are very few lenders who would even lend to them so that's our niche. The New Economy is about co-ops supporting co-ops and it's interesting that that's kept us going." The credit union has worker coop members planning to apply for loans, although it has not yet loaned to this form of enterprise.

With small-business loans often guaranteed by the individual entrepreneur, the structure of collective ownership requires some workarounds when it comes to credit union lending to worker co-ops. For instance, a local bank in Massachusetts provided a co-op with a loan once it tied loan payments to individual workers' pay.

Powerful Models: Cooperative Loan Funds and Co-op Loans

The cooperative sector got another potential boost in federal financing in recent years. Following a concerted campaign by the U.S. Federation of Worker Co-ops and the cooperative movement, in 2012 the Small Business Administration (SBA) clarified that worker co-ops with fewer than 500 staff are small businesses that are eligible for SBA-backed loans. That opens up a wider array of lending institutions to worker co-ops, including community banks. The SBA also gave the Cooperative Fund of New England an unprecedented low-cost loan of $1 million to re-lend to worker co-ops and producer co-ops out of its $30 billion Small Business Lending Fund (created by the Small Business Jobs Act of 2010). The U.S. Department of Agriculture, long a supporter of rural cooperatives, is working on a loan guarantee program for small business conversion into co-ops, reports staffer Bruce Reynolds.

Among worker co-ops, there is a movement to have the co-ops fund their own growth, and build economies of solidarity with food co-ops and credit unions. Common in Quebec, Italy, Spain, and Latin America, such mutual financial support among co-ops would create a new pool of capital, enriching what comes from loan funds, credit unions, banks, or the government. To promote this idea, the Eastern Conference on Workplace Democracy, in collaboration with the Grassroots Economic Organizing newsletter, held a one-day conference on co-op financing in July in Philadelphia. It was one big brainstorm. Worker cooperatives themselves "need to be the primary financers," says Eric Tusz-King, vice president of the Canadian Worker Cooperative Federation, and a member of a cooperative that is building energy-efficient housing in New Brunswick. His federation launched the $20 million National Cooperative Investment Fund. Quebec's Desjardins Solidarity Credit Union is an even stronger model. Created with the support of the CSN labor organization, it holds 40% of the provincial government's deposits and has 2,940 cooperative enterprises among its clients. With $175 billion in assets, it is the sixth biggest financial institution in Canada.

Quebec law also requires worker cooperatives to commit their surpluses to the cooperative movement if they go out of business. The surplus is called "indivisible reserves," and the Canadian Federation is in the midst of a two-year exploration of whether to pursue such laws in other provinces, or at least encourage its members to structure themselves in that way voluntarily. These reserves can be used by the co-op as a whole while it is in operation but not divided among the worker-owners. In the United States, during a recent discussion sponsored by the Canadian Federation, one cooperator suggested it might be possible to pursue tax credits at the state level to promote indivisible reserves; each individual member could get a tax credit if his or her cooperative adopted the policy.

Italy goes further and requires cooperatives by law to contribute 3% of their annual surplus toward the loan fund of their choice to develop the cooperative sector. This depth of support helps explain one of the solidarity economy's biggest success stories: Emilia Romagna, a region the size of New England, has 7,500 cooperatives accounting for one third of its GDP.

In Western Massachusetts, a regional ten-member network of worker co-ops was inspired by Italy's co-op law and is contributing to co-op growth by contributing 5% of their enterprises' surpluses to the Cooperative Fund of New England. In December 2012, the partnership, called the Valley Alliance of Worker Co-operatives (VAWC), launched the VAWC International Cooperative Development Fund to loan to their network and beyond. They join other co-ops, like Cabot Creamery and

Preferred Shares

An interesting arena of alternative finance that more social ventures are exploring is the sale of "preferred shares." An early adopter of the strategy is Equal Exchange, the worker-owned, fair-trade coffee and chocolate company based in West Bridgewater, Mass.

"The economy and capital are far too important to leave to capitalists," said Rodney North, Equal Exchange's "Answer Man" for the media. Equal Exchange has more than 130 worker-owners and more than $10 million in assets. The co-op raised $11.5 million by selling Class B, nonvoting "preferred shares," offering a modest dividend, that buyers must hold for five years. "Clark Arrington of ICA [the consulting group] introduced Class B shares to the founders 25 years ago," said North.

Arrington, now working in Tanzania, told D&S by email that he came up with the strategy "to address the problem of attracting outside capital to a pure worker-owned company without diluting worker control and worker governance of the company. The Class B shares also had the advantage of allowing former worker owners to remain shareholders after leaving the company and for existing worker owners to have a larger equity stake in the company without diluting the control of other worker owners. Additionally, our producer co-ops could own shares and could even elect to be paid with Class B shares."

Equal Exchange, in investing in the Cooperative Fund of New England. Founded in 1975, the Cooperative Fund of New England has $18 million to invest and is growing as much as 20% a year. It is a nonprofit but not a cooperative, which made it eligible for the low cost loan from the SBA while its sister lender in Minneapolis, North Country Cooperative Development Fund, was not.

Sometimes cooperatives have pulled out money—this was the case with the Minneapolis-based North Country—when co-ops felt they were not getting high enough returns, said its director, Christina Jennings. Indeed the economic downturn produced losses for the Fund. Founded in 1978 as a nonprofit, it became a cooperative in 1988 and now gets one-third of its capital from its 170 cooperative members from around the country. It remains quite small, with only $8 million to lend; $190,000 is dedicated to a Worker Ownership Fund launched with USFWC. The average loan is $100,000, a sum too small to be of interest to business lenders at big banks. With only ten to 15 new loans a year, the Fund is not at a scale where it can support itself on fees and interest without grants or low cost loans.

The Working World, the nonprofit lender that came to the aid of Republic Windows workers who were struggling to convert their factory into a cooperative, itself struggles to raise financing. "Getting investors to give to our loan fund is really difficult," said staffer Steve Wong. "We get a small, maybe 5% return, so the workers are the ones who reap the awards," he continued. "We don't get paid unless the cooperative is profitable. With Republic Windows, we're not taking any payments for two years," cutting into fees that help keep the fund going.

A key way CDFIs like community loan funds and low-income credit unions get capital is through low-interest loans or deposits from socially responsible investors for whom a 1-2% return is perfectly OK. Glance at a list of contributors to the Lakotas Fund, working on reservations in South Dakota, or the Cooperative Fund of New England, and you will see the Sisters of St. Francis of Philadelphia, the Christian Brothers, and others. These religious communities are pathbreakers who the CDFIs immediately praise when asked where they get their funds.

The Sisters of St. Francis of Philadelphia lends to both North Country and CFNE. Sister Nora Nash directs the social investment for the Sisters' pension fund, which dedicates several million dollars to "alternative" investments of about $60,000 each. A committee of sisters makes the final decision on the loans, many of which roll over from year to year. "A major part of our investment policy is investing in CDFIs. We believe it is an important mission of the Sisters to invest in community development, sustainability and systemic change."

The Future

Alliances throughout the cooperative sector are only growing, offering promise to New Economy advocates even during this New Gilded Age of disenfranchised workers and despoiled earth. "There's so much momentum now, so much more going on than a year ago," observed Christina Jennings of North Country.

In September, Laboral Kutxa, the Mondragón cooperative's bank with $24 billion in deposits, and the National Cooperative Bank in Washington, D.C., announced they would support each other's customers and exchange best practices in solidarity lending with the goal of revitalizing local economies and community prosperity.

"We can become a new power, creating the structures that allow us to do for ourselves," said Ed Whitfield of the Southern Grassroots Economies Project, which supports the development of co-ops and a solidarity economy. "If the wealth we produce is systematically extracted from these communities, you have what we have today. These questions of ownership structures are key ... for the structural transformation that needs to take place to move from these extractive systems." The goal: democratic ownership of productive spaces and productive opportunities such as that being nurtured in the soil of Cincinnati. ❑

Resources: Clifford Rosenthal, "Credit Unions, Community Development Finance, and the Great Recession," Federal Reserve Bank of San Francisco, February 2012 (frbsf.org); Alan J. Robb, James H. Smith and J. Tom Webb, "Cooperative Capital: What it is and Why Our World Needs It," Financial Cooperative Approaches to Local Development Through Sustainable Innovation, June 10-11, Trento, Italy (smu.ca); Johnston Birchall, *Resilience in a Downturn: The Power of Financial Cooperatives*, International Labour Office, 2013; John Fullerton, et. al., *Economics, Finance, Governance and Ethics for the Anthropocene*, Capital Institute, June 2012; Special Issue on Financing Cooperatives, Grassroots Economic Organizing (geo.coop); Michael Shuman, *Local Dollars, Local Sense: How to Shift Your Money from Wall Street to Main Street and Achieve Real Prosperity* (Chelsea Green Publishing, 2012); David Korten, *Agenda for a New Economy: From Phantom Wealth to Real Wealth* (Berrett Koehler, 2010); National Credit Union Administration 2012 Annual Report, May 2013 (ncua.gov); Michael Hudson, "The Road to Debt Deflation, Debt Peonage, and Neofeudalism," Levy Economics Institute, February 2012; Elissa Yancey, "Cincinnati union co-op Our Harvest grows a national profile from roots in College Hill," WCPO Cincinnati, Aug. 11, 2013 (wcpo.com); "Cincinnati State and Our Harvest Cooperative: Partners in Local Food," Cincinnati State, May 15, 2013 (cincinnatistate.edu); Brian Headd, "An Analysis of Small Business and Jobs: Research Study," Small Business Administration, March 2010 (sba.gov); Rebel A. Cole, "How Did the Financial Crisis Affect Small Business Lending in the United States?" Small Business Administration, November 2012 (sba.gov); "Paying More for the American Dream III," April 2009 (nedap.org).

Article 8.9

THE RETURN OF CAPITAL CONTROLS

BY ARMAGAN GEZICI
January/February 2013

In the wake of the global financial crisis, low interest rates and slow growth in advanced economies have led to a massive influx of capital into so-called emerging markets, where interest rates and growth have been higher. International investors, seeking higher returns, have moved their funds away from advanced economies into emerging-market securities like stocks, bonds, and mutual funds. The governments of many developing countries, as a result, have become increasingly concerned about the effects of these capital inflows—including stronger currencies, asset-price bubbles, and even inflation. In March 2012, Brazil's president Dilma Rousseff accused developed nations of unleashing a "monetary tsunami," which is undermining the competitiveness of emerging economies like her own. These concerns have motivated many countries to introduce measures to cope with cross-border capital flows.

Starting in late 2009, for example, Brazil began to implement "capital controls"—including a tax on capital inflows and other measures—to keep its currency (the real) from growing stronger against the dollar. Several Asian countries, including South Korea, Taiwan, and Thailand, have also implemented controls of various kinds on capital inflows. Suddenly, it appears, capital controls are back.

What Ever Happened to Capital Controls?

The debate about controls on international capital flows goes back to the World War II era. During the Bretton Woods negotiations (1944) establishing the international monetary order for the postwar period, Britain's chief negotiator, John Maynard Keynes, and his U.S. counterpart, Harry Dexter White, agreed that a distinction should be made between "speculative" capital and "productive" capital. Both believed that speculative (or "hot money") capital flows should be subject to controls. Keynes went further, arguing that "control of capital movements, both inward and outward, should be a permanent feature of the post-war system." For much of the postwar period, controls such as restrictions on the types of assets banks could hold and limits on capital outflows (used even by the United States between 1963 and 1973) were, indeed, implemented by many capitalist countries. Beginning in the 1980s, however, international financial institutions like the International Monetary Fund (IMF), many Western governments, and private high finance began to oppose capital controls. The U. S. government and the IMF became staunch advocates of "capital-account liberalization" (that is, the deregulation of international capital flows) during this period.

The recent crisis resulted in widespread recognition, around the world, that deregulated financial activity can result in major economic disruptions. In most of the world's largest economies, possible measures to re-regulate finance on the national level came back on the political agenda. Cross-border finance, however, was largely left out of the discussion, as if it did not require any regulation. Conventional discussions of this issue have also involved a peculiar twist in terminology: financial regulations are typically called "regulations" when purely domestic, yet when they involve cross-border flows, they carry the more ominous-sounding label of "controls"—as if to emphasize the undesirable nature of these regulations from a free-market perspective.

Why Capital Controls?

The essential problem with international capital flows is that they are "pro-cyclical"— that is, they amplify the patterns of the business cycle. Capital tends to flow in when economies are expanding, promoting "overheating" and inflation, and tends to flow out during downturns, exacerbating the decline in output and rise in unemployment. They also narrow the ability of governments to respond to cyclical economic problems. The economic literature on capital flows cites five fears that drive countries to adopt capital controls:

Fear of appreciation: Massive and rapid capital inflows may cause the country's currency to become stronger (increase in value relative to other currencies), making its exports more expensive and damaging its international competitiveness.

Fear of "hot money": Short-term speculative capital inflows may cause financial instability and increase the fragility of the domestic financial system. The short-term nature of these flows leads to a "maturity mismatch" between domestic financial institutions' assets and liabilities. In effect, they have borrowed short-term while lending long-term. As the sudden reversal of hot money occurs at the whim of international investor sentiments, a domestic banking crisis is likely to follow.

Fear of large inflows that can disrupt the financial system, even if they are not all "hot money": Large inflows of foreign capital may feed asset bubbles, such as unsustainable increases in stock or real-estate prices or unsustainable booms in consumer credit.

Fear of loss of monetary autonomy: It is not possible for a country to achieve (simultaneously) full international capital mobility, monetary-policy autonomy, and exchange-rate stability. (This is known as the "trilemma" of international macroeconomics.) If a country does not control international capital flows, inflows can cause exchange-rate appreciation. The government can counteract this by increasing the money supply, but then its monetary policy is not independent. To avoid exchange-rate appreciation and sustain an independent monetary policy, a country should give up full capital mobility.

Fear of capital flight: In the event of a crisis, "herding" behavior by international investors may expose a country to the risk of sharp reversals in capital flows (with capital leaving just as quickly as it came).

What Happened During the Crisis?

Between 2002 and 2007, there were massive flows of capital into emerging markets with high growth rates and relatively developed financial systems. This surge in capital inflows was interrupted after the collapse of the U.S. investment house Lehman Brothers in September 2008, which led global capital to flee to the "safety" of the U.S. market, wreaking havoc in emerging markets. (See figure.) While there was no comparable financial crisis in these economies, more than half of them experienced negative growth in 2009. Countries with already-large trade deficits were among the hardest hit, as they were highly dependent on capital inflows.

Between 2008 and 2011, however, the governments of the industrialized countries lowered interest rates in an attempt to stimulate production and employment. Capital again began to flow into emerging markets, attracted by higher interest rates and growth. The "carry trade" was a key mechanism that triggered these flows. In the carry trade, investors borrow money in one country at a low interest rate and invest it in another country at a higher rate. This strategy allows investors not only to exploit the differences in interest rates, but also take advantage of exchange-rate movements. If the currency of the country with higher interest rates becomes stronger, over time, relative to the currency of the country with lower interest rates, investors stand to make even larger profits.

By late 2008, government policymakers in emerging economies had become alarmed about the problems these inflows could cause—currency appreciation, asset bubbles, inflation, and the sudden turn toward large outflows. From March 2009 to March 2010, Brazil saw the value of the real go up by 30% against the dollar, due at least in part to the carry trade. Under normal circumstances, the conventional macroeconomic tool to stem asset bubbles or inflation would have been an increase in interest rates. By increasing interest rates, monetary authorities would have curbed the appetite to borrow and reduced the amount of money available for spending in the economy. With less spending, the economy would slow down and inflation would decline. However, because of the carry trade, such a policy could actually fuel further inflows and therefore exacerbate these problems. For example, in 2009, interest rates were around 12% in Brazil and less than 1% in the United States; if Brazil had raised interest rates in an attempt to curb asset bubbles and inflation, it could actually have attracted even higher capital inflows.

The Brazilian government was the most vocal critic of these capital flows at the G-20's 2010 summit in Seoul. The Brazilian finance minister declared the surge in capital flows, the subsequent exchange-rate appreciations, and the various policy responses by emerging countries to be the beginning of a "currency war." In late 2009, the Brazilian government imposed a 2% tax on various forms of capital inflows. In October 2010, it twice increased the tax rate, first to 4% and then to 6%. In January 2011, Brazil introduced new reserve requirements on capital inflows (see sidebar) to curb the appreciation of the real against the dollar.

In 2009, nations across Asia also began to deploy controls, having seen large appreciations of their currencies. Between the end of 2008 and early 2010, South Korea's currency (the won) appreciated by over 30% against the dollar. Starting in July 2010, South Korean banks faced new restrictions on their

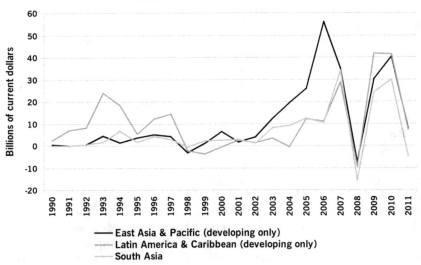

NET PORTFOLIO INVESTMENT—EQUITY, THREE DEVELOPING REGIONS

—— East Asia & Pacific (developing only)
—— Latin America & Caribbean (developing only)
—— South Asia

Source: World Bank, Data, Portfolio equity, net inflows (BoP, current US$), (data.worldbank.org)

international currency holdings. The South Korean government also tried to steer investment away from speculation by permitting bank loans in foreign currencies only for the purchase of raw materials, for foreign direct investment, and for repayment of debts. Meanwhile, in November 2009, the government of Taiwan banned foreign investment funds from investing in certificates of deposit with domestic banks, a move aimed at preventing foreign investors from betting on currency appreciation. At the end of 2010, it also placed restrictions on banks' holdings of foreign currencies. In 2010, Thailand introduced a 15% tax on interest income and capital gains earned by foreign investors. Meanwhile, Indonesia placed limits on short-term external borrowing and introduced a one-month minimum holding period for foreign investors purchasing some types of government-issued securities.

It is still too early to draw final conclusions about the effectiveness of these controls. A study by Kevin Gallagher of the Global Development and Environment Institute (GDAE) provides a preliminary assessment for the cases of Brazil, Taiwan, and South Korea. All three were trying to create a space for independent monetary policy and stem the appreciation of their currencies by placing restrictions on capital mobility. Interest rates between the United States and each of these nations have become less correlated. (A strong correlation between interest rates may indicate that, when the U.S. Fed lowers interest rates, causing capital flows to these other countries, the latter are forced to respond with lower interest rates of their own to stem the appreciation of the currency. That is, they lack monetary independence.) So these findings suggest that the controls have, to some extent, allowed a more autonomous monetary policy.

In the cases of Brazil and Taiwan, there is some evidence that controls have been associated with a slower rate of currency appreciation. But in the case of South Korea, currency appreciation has continued and the rate of appreciation has actually increased since controls were initiated. This difference can be explained by the structural differences across these countries, as well as the different types of controls used. South Korea's strong export performance is an important factor putting upward pressure on the value of its currency. (Demand for a country's exports is one factor determining the demand for its currency, since that country's companies usually require payment in the national currency.) Moreover, unlike

---

How to Impose Capital Controls?

The particular form of capital controls that a government imposes depends on its policy goals. If its main goal is to slow down capital inflows, the types of regulations that it can choose from include:

- Unremunerated reserve requirements: A certain percentage of new capital inflows must be kept on reserve in the country's central bank. "Unremunerated" in this context refers to the fact that no interest would be earned on these funds.
- Taxes on new inflows.
- Limits or taxes on how much domestic banks and other financial institutions can owe in foreign currencies.
- Restrictions on currency mismatches: Borrowing and lending activities of domestic banks or firms should be denominated in the same currency. For example, only firms with foreign-exchange revenues from exports can borrow in foreign currencies.
- Limitations on borrowing abroad: For example, such borrowing may be allowed only for foreign investment and trade activities, or only for firms with positive net revenues in a foreign currency (as from exports).
- Mandatory government approvals for some or all international capital transactions.
- Minimum stay requirements: Foreign investors might be required to stay in the domestic economy for at least a certain length of time.

On the other hand, different measures are available to a country that wants to focus on preventing or slowing down outflows of capital, including:

- Mandatory government approval for domestic residents to invest abroad or hold bank accounts in a foreign currency.
- Requirements for domestic residents to report on foreign investments and transactions done with foreign bank accounts.
- Limits on sectors in which foreign individuals and companies can invest.
- Restrictions on amounts of principal or capital income that foreign investors can send abroad.
- Limits on how much non-residents can borrow in the domestic market.
- Taxes on capital outflows.

In addition to the distinction between controls imposed on outflows or inflows, measures are usually categorized as "price-based" or "quantity-based," depending on the mechanism through which they impact capital flows. Minimum stay requirements, for example, are one kind of quantity-based control. Taxes on inflows or on outflows are one kind of price-based control.

Brazil and Taiwan, South Korean authorities did not use any of the "price-based controls" (see sidebar) that would have automatically placed additional costs on international investors seeking to enter Korean markets. These differences in effectiveness can shed some light on what kinds of capital controls might work in different countries, given their unique conditions.

The IMF and Capital Controls

Not long after developing-country governments began implementing capital controls, official views about controls began to shift. Since 2010, the IMF has produced a series of official papers on capital-account liberalization, on capital inflows and outflows, and on the multilateral aspects of regulating international capital flows. In November 2012, it released a comprehensive "institutional view" on when and how nations should deploy capital-account regulations. The same institution that pushed for the global deregulation of cross-border finance in the 1990s now says that capital-account liberalization is more of a long-run goal, and is not for every country at all times. The IMF now accepts that capital controls—which it has renamed "capital-flow management measures"—are permissible for inflows, on a temporary basis, en route to liberalization; regulations on capital outflows, meanwhile, are permissible only during or just after financial crises.

While more flexible than its previous stances, the new IMF position still insists on the eventual deregulation of global financial flows and emphasizes that controls should only be temporary. Behind this insistence lies the institution's ideological commitment to free markets, as well as the influence of finance capital and Wall Street interests on the institution's decision making. As the experience of developing economies in the recent crisis bears out, rather than being treated as temporary measures, capital controls should be adopted as permanent tools that can be used counter-cyclically—to smooth out economic booms and busts. As described earlier, international capital flows are strongly pro-cyclical. By regulating inflows during a boom, a government can manage booms better, while avoiding exchange-rate problems or additional inflationary pressures. By restricting outflows during a downturn, it can mitigate capital flight, which has the potential of triggering financial crisis, and create some room for expansionary monetary policy.

The IMF guidelines, in addition, give scant attention to policy-design issues related to capital controls. A great deal of international experience shows that controls can lose their effectiveness over time, as foreign investors learn to evade regulation through the use of financial derivatives and other securities. Nations such as Brazil and South Korea have increasingly "fine-tuned" their regulations in an attempt to keep ahead of investors' ability to circumvent them.

The IMF also fails to acknowledge that capital flows should be regulated at "both ends." The industrialized nations are usually the source of international capital flows, but generally ignore the negative spillover effects on other countries. So far, the entire burden of regulation has fallen on the recipients of inflows, mostly developing countries.

Where to Now?

As industrialized nations aim to recover from the crisis, they hope that credit and capital will stay "at home." Meanwhile, the developing world has little interest in having to receive capital inflows. This creates an obvious alignment of interests. Industrialized nations could adjust their tax codes and deploy other types of regulation to keep capital in their countries, as emerging markets deploy capital controls to reduce the level and change the composition of capital flows that may destabilize their economies.

One important obstacle to such coordination is the prohibition, in many trade and investment treaties, on regulation of cross-border finance. For example, in Asia, where capital controls are most prevalent, the Association of South East Asian Nations (ASEAN) requires member countries to eliminate most controls by 2015, with relatively narrow exceptions. Trade and investment agreements with the United States, such as the North American Free Trade Agreement (NAFTA) and the Dominican Republic-Central America Free Trade Agreement (CAFTA-DR), provide the least flexibility. Since the 2003 U.S.-Chile Free Trade Agreement, every U.S. trade or investment agreement has required the free flow of capital (in both directions) between the United States and its trading partners, without exception.

In January 2011, some 250 economists from across the globe called on the United States to recognize that the consensus on capital controls has shifted and to permit nations the flexibility to deploy controls to prevent and mitigate crises. The appeal was rebuffed by prominent U.S. business associations and the U.S. government. Treasury Secretary Timothy Geithner declared that U.S. policy would remain unchanged: "In general, we believe that those risks are best managed through a mix of fiscal and monetary policy measures, exchange rate adjustment, and carefully designed non-discriminatory prudential measures, such as bank reserve or capital requirements and limitations on exposure to exchange rate risk." In other words, he suggested the use of mainly conventional domestic macroeconomic policies and some domestic financial regulation, but excluded controls on international flows.

With the exception of speculators who profit from volatility in the markets, all nations and actors within them would benefit from the financial stability that an international system of financial regulation could help provide. After the opening of capital markets in developing economies, in varying degrees, we have seen extreme volatility of international capital flows. This volatility has been exacerbated by the monetary policies of advanced economies: over the past 30 years expansionary monetary policy in advanced economies has led to capital flows to emerging-market economies, while contractionary policies have produced the reversal of capital flows and, in turn, helped set off the crises of the 1980s and 1990s. The stability provided by an international system of capital controls would not only allow emerging economies to preserve their own growth and stability but also improve the effectiveness of policies in advanced economies.

Some financial interests, however, would have to bear the costs. Capital controls would either make financial transactions more costly, reducing profit margins, or not allow financial companies to take advantage of certain investment opportunities, again reducing potential profits to investors. These "losers" from a capital-controls regime are highly concentrated and very powerful politically. The "winners," in terms of the general public, are comparatively scattered and weaker politically. Despite the optimism that briefly emerged, especially in policy circles, about a future with more effective regulation of international capital flows, these political realities may be the biggest obstacles for 21st-century capital controls. ❏

Sources: Kevin Gallagher, "Regaining Control? Capital Controls and the Global Financial Crisis," Political Economy Research Institute, Working Paper 250, 2011; Stephany Griffith-Jones and Kevin P. Gallagher, "Curbing Hot Money Flows to Protect the Real Economy," Economic and Political Weekly, January 15, 2011, Vol. XLVI, No 3; Ilene Grabel, "Not Your Grandfather's IMF: Global Crisis, Productive Incoherence, and Developmental Policy Space," Political Economy Research Institute, Working Paper 214, 2010; International Monetary Fund, The Liberalization And Management Of Capital Flows: An Institutional View, Washington, D.C., 2011.

Article 8.10

GREECE AND THE CRISIS OF EUROPE: WHICH WAY OUT?

BY MARJOLEIN VAN DER VEEN

The Greek economy has crashed, and now lies broken on the ground. The causes of the crisis are pretty well understood, but there hasn't been enough attention to the different possible ways out. Our flight crew has shown us only one emergency exit—one that is broken and just making things worse. But there is more than one way out of the crisis, not just the austerity being pushed by the so-called "Troika" (International Monetary Fund (IMF), European Commission, and European Central Bank (ECB)). We need to look around a bit more, since—as they say on every flight—the nearest exit may not be right in front of us. Can an alternative catch hold? And, if so, will it be Keynesian or socialist?

The origins of the crisis are manifold: trade imbalances between Germany and Greece, the previous Greek government's secret debts (hidden with the connivance of Wall Street banks), the 2007 global economic crisis, and the flawed construction of the eurozone (see sidebar). As Greece's economic crisis has continued to deepen, it has created a social disaster: Drastic declines in public health, a rise in suicides, surging child hunger, a massive exodus of young adults, an intensification of exploitation (longer work hours and more work days per week), and the rise of the far right and its attacks on immigrants and the LGBT community. Each new austerity package brokered between the Greek government and the Troika stipulates still more government spending cuts, tax increases, or "economic reforms"—privatization, increases in the retirement age, layoffs of public-sector workers, and wage cuts for those who remain.

While there are numerous possible paths out of the crisis, the neoliberal orthodoxy has maintained that Greece had no choice but to accept austerity. The country was broke, argued the Troika officials, economists, and commentators, and this tough medicine would ultimately help the Greek economy to grow again. As Mark Weisbrot of the Center for Economic and Policy Research (CEPR) put it, "[T]he EU authorities have opted to punish Greece—for various reasons, including the creditors' own interests in punishment, their ideology, imaginary fears of inflation, and to prevent other countries from also demanding a 'growth option.'" By focusing on neoliberal solutions, the mainstream press controls the contours of the debate. Keynesian remedies that break with the punishment paradigm are rarely discussed, let alone socialist proposals. These may well gain more attention, however, as the crisis drags on without end.

Neoliberal Solutions

Despite the fact that 30 years of neoliberalism resulted in the worst economic crisis since the Great Depression, neoliberals are undaunted and have remained intent on dishing out more of the same medicine. What they offered Greece were bailouts and haircuts (write-downs of the debt). While the country—really, the country's banks—got bailouts, the money flowed right back to repay lenders in Germany,

Causes of Greece's Deepening Crisis

Trade imbalances. Germany's wage restraint policies and high productivity made German exports more competitive (cheaper), resulting in trade surpluses for Germany and deficits for Greece. Germany then used its surplus funds to invest in Greece and other southern European countries. As German banks shoveled out loans, Greek real estate boomed, inflation rose, their exports became less competitive, and the wealthy siphoned money abroad.

Hidden debt. To enter the eurozone in 2001, Greece's budget deficit was supposed to be below the threshold (3% of GDP) set by the Maastricht Treaty. In 2009 the newly elected Panhellenic Socialist Movement (PASOK) government discovered that the outgoing government had been hiding its deficits from the European authorities, with the help of credit default swaps sold to it by Goldman Sachs during 2002-06. The country was actually facing a deficit of 12% of GDP, thanks to extravagant military spending and tax cuts for (and tax evasion by) the rich.

Global crisis. When the 2007 global economic crisis struck, Greece was perhaps the hardest-hit country. Investments soured, banks collapsed, and loans could not be repaid. Debt-financed household consumption could no longer be sustained. Firms cut back on investment spending, closed factories, and laid off workers. Output has fallen 20% since 2007, the unemployment rate is now above 25%, (for youth, 58%), household incomes have fallen by more than a third in the last three years, and government debt has surpassed 175% of GDP.

The eurozone trap. Greece's government could do little on its own to rescue its economy. With eurozone countries all using the same currency, individual countries could no longer use monetary policy to stimulate their economies (e.g., by devaluing the currency to boost exports or stimulating moderate inflation to reduce the real debt burden). Fiscal policy was also weakened by the Maastricht limits on deficits and debt, resulting in tight constraints on fiscal stimulus.

France, and other countries. Very little actually went to Greek workers who fell into severe poverty. The bailouts invariably came with conditions in the form of austerity, privatization (e.g., water systems, ports, etc.), mass public-sector layoffs, labor-market "flexibilization" (making it easier to fire workers), cutbacks in unemployment insurance, and tax reforms (lowering corporate taxes and raising personal income and sales taxes). In sum, the neoliberal structural adjustment program for Greece shifted the pain onto ordinary people, rather than those most responsible for causing the crisis in the first place.

Austerity and internal devaluation

With steep cuts in government spending, neoliberal policy has been contracting the economy just when it needed to be expanded. Pro-austerity policy makers, however, professed their faith in "expansionary austerity." Harvard economists Alberto Alesina and Silvia Ardagna claimed that austerity (especially spending cuts) could lead to the expectation of increased profits and so stimulate investment. The neoliberals also hoped to boost exports through "internal devaluation" (wage cuts, resulting in lower costs and therefore cheaper exports). An economist with Capital Economics in London claimed that Greece needed a 30–40% decline in real wages to restore competitiveness. A fall in real wages, along with the out-migration of

---

The Role of Goldman Sachs

Greece was able to "hide" its deficits thanks to Goldman Sachs, which had sold financial derivatives called credit-default swaps to Greece between 2002 and 2006. The credit-default swaps operated a bit like subprime loans, enabling Greece to lower its debts on its balance sheets, but at very high borrowing rates. Goldman Sachs had sales teams selling these complicated financial instruments not just to Greece, but to many gullible municipalities and institutions throughout Europe (and the United States), who were told that these deals could lower their borrowing costs. For Greece, the loans blew up in 2008-2009, when interest rates rose and stock markets collapsed. Among those involved in these deals included Mario Draghi (now President of the ECB), who was working at the Greece desk at Goldman Sachs at the time. While these sales generated huge profits for Goldman Sachs, the costs are now being borne by ordinary Greek people in the form of punishing austerity programs. (For more on Goldman Sachs's role, see part four of the PBS documentary "Money, Power, Wall Street.")

---

workers, the neoliberals suggested, would allow labor markets to "clear" at a new equilibrium. Of course, they neglected to say how long this would take and how many workers would fall into poverty, get sick, or die in the process.

Meanwhile, international financial capitalists (hedge funds and private equity firms) have been using the crisis as an opportunity to buy up state assets. The European Commission initially expected to raise €50 billion by 2015 from the privatization of state assets (now being revised downward to just over €25 billion through 2020). The magnitude of the fire sale in Greece is still five to ten times larger than that expected for Spain, Portugal, and Ireland. Domestic private companies on the brink of bankruptcy are also vulnerable. As the crisis drags on, private-equity and hedge-fund "vulture capitalists" are swooping in for cheap deals. The other neoliberal reforms—labor and pension reforms, dismantling of the welfare state, and tax reforms—will also boost private profits at the expense of workers.

Default and exit from the euro

Another possible solution was for Greece to default on its debt, and some individuals and companies actively prepared for such a scenario. A default would lift the onerous burden of debt repayment, and would relieve Greece of complying with all the conditions placed on it by the Troika. However, it would likely make future borrowing by both the public and private sectors more difficult and expensive, and so force the government to engage in some sort of austerity of its own.

Some economists on the left have been supportive of a default, and the exit from the euro and return to the drachma that would likely follow. One such advocate is Mark Weisbrot, who has argued that "a threat by Greece to jettison the euro is long overdue, and it should be prepared to carry it out." He acknowledges there would be costs in the short term, but argues they would be less onerous "than many years of recession, stagnation, and high unemployment that the European authorities are offering." A return to the drachma could restore one of the tools to boost export competitiveness: allowing Greece to use currency depreciation to lower the prices of its exports. In this sense, this scenario remains a neoliberal one. (Many IMF "shock therapy" have included currency devaluations as part of the strategy for countries to export their way out of debt.)

The process of exit, however, could be quite painful, with capital flight, bank runs, black markets, significant inflation as the cost of imports rises, and the destruction of savings. There had already been some capital flight—an estimated €72 billion left Greek banks between 2009 and 2012. Furthermore, the threat of a Greek exit created fear of contagion, with the possibility of more countries leaving the euro and even the collapse of the eurozone altogether.

Keynesian Solutions

By late 2012, Keynesian proposals were finally being heard and having some impact on policymakers. Contrary to the neoliberal austerity doctrine, Keynesian solutions typically emphasize running countercyclical policies—especially expansionary fiscal policy (or fiscal "stimulus"), with deficit-spending to counter the collapse in private demand. However, the Greek government is already strapped with high deficits and the interest rates demanded by international creditors have spiked to extremely high levels. Additional deficit spending would require that the ECB (or the newly established European Stability Mechanism (ESM)) intervene by directly buying Greek government bonds to bring down rates. (The ECB has been lending to private banks at low rates, to enable the banks to buy public bonds.) In any case, a Keynesian approach ideally would waive the EU's deficit and debt limits to allow the Greek government more scope for rescuing the economy.

Alternatively, the EU could come forward with more grants and loans, in order to create employment, fund social-welfare spending, and boost demand. This kind of bailout would not go to the banks, but to the people who are suffering from unemployment, cuts in wages and pensions, and poverty. Nor would it come with all the other conditions the neoliberals have demanded (privatization, layoffs, labor-market reforms, etc). The European Investment Bank could also help stimulate new industries, such as alternative energy, and help revive old ones, such as tourism, shipping, and agriculture. In a European Union based on solidarity, the richer regions of Europe would help out poorer ones in a crisis (much as richer states in the United States make transfers to poorer ones, mostly without controversy).

Even some IMF officials finally recognized that austerity was not working. An October 2012 IMF report admitted that the organization had underestimated the fiscal policy multiplier—a measure of how much changes in government spending and taxes will affect economic growth—and therefore the negative impact of austerity policies. By April 2013, economists at UMass-Amherst found serious mistakes in research by Harvard economists Carmen Reinhart and Kenneth Rogoff, alleging that debt-to-GDP ratios of 90% or more seriously undermine future economic growth. Reinhart and Rogoff's claims had been widely cited by supporters of austerity for highly indebted countries. So yet another crack emerged in the pillar supporting austerity policies.

Keynesians have argued, contrary to the "internal devaluation" advocates, that the reduction in real wages just depressed aggregate demand, and made the recession deeper. Economists such as Nobel laureate Paul Krugman proposed that, instead, wages and prices be allowed to rise in the trade-surplus countries of northern Europe (Germany and the Netherlands). This would presumably make these countries' exports less competitive, at some expense to producers of internationally traded goods, though possibly boosting domestic demand thanks to increased wages. Meanwhile, it would help level the playing field for exporters in the southern countries in crisis, and would be done without the punishing reductions in real wages demanded by the Troika. The Keynesian solution thus emphasized stimulating domestic demand through fiscal expansion in both the northern and southern European countries, as well as allowing wages and prices to rise in the northern countries.

Signs pointing in this direction began to emerge in spring 2013, when some Dutch and German trade unions won significant wage increases. In addition, the Dutch government agreed to scrap its demands for wage restraint in some sectors (such as the public sector and education) and to hold off (at least until August) on its demands for more austerity. (Another €4.5 billion cuts had been scheduled for 2014, after the government spent €3.7 billion in January to rescue (through nationalization) one of the country's largest banks.)

Socialist Solutions

For most of the socialist parties in Greece and elsewhere in Europe, the neoliberal solution was clearly wrong-headed, as it worsened the recession to the detriment of workers while industrial and finance capitalists made out like bandits. Greece's Panhellenic Socialist Movement (PASOK) was an exception, going along with austerity, structural reforms, and privatization. (Its acceptance of austerity lost it significant support in the 2012 elections.) Other socialists supported anything that alleviated the recession, including Keynesian prescriptions for more deficit spending, higher wages, and other policies to boost aggregate demand and improve the position of workers. Greece's SYRIZA (a coalition of 16 left-wing parties and whose support surged in the 2012 elections) called for stopping austerity, renegotiating loan agreements, halting wage and pension cuts, restoring the minimum wage, and implementing a type of Marshall Plan-like investment drive. In many ways, these proposale resemble standard Keynesian policies—which have historically served to rescue the capitalist system, without challenging its inherent exploitative structure or vulnerability to recurrent crisis.

While Keynesian deficit-spending could alleviate the crisis in the short-term, who would ultimately bear the costs—ordinary taxpayers? Workers could end up paying for the corruption of the Greek capitalist class, who pushed through tax cuts, spent government funds in ways that mainly benefited themselves, and hid money abroad. Many socialists argued that the Greek capitalists should pay for the crisis, through increased taxes on wealth, corporate profits, and financial transactions, and the abolition of tax loopholes and havens. As SYRIZA leader Alexis Tsipras put it, "It is common knowledge among progressive politicians and activists, but also among the Troika and the Greek government, that the burden of the crisis has been carried exclusively by public and private sector workers and pensioners. This has to stop. It is time for the rich to contribute their share... ."

Slowly, the right-wing government began making gestures in this direction. In 2010, French finance minister Christine Lagarde had given a list of more than

2,000 Greeks with money in Swiss bank accounts to her Greek counterpart George Papaconstantinou, of the PASOK government, but Papaconstantiou sat on it and did nothing. But in the fall of 2012 the so-called "Lagarde list" was published by the magazine Hot Doc, leading to fury among ordinary Greeks against establishment political leaders (including the PASOK "socialists") who had failed to go after the tax dodgers. Another list of about 400 Greeks who had bought and sold property in London since 2009 was compiled by British financial authorities at the request of the current Greek government. In total, the economist Friedrich Schneider has estimated that about €120 billion of Greek assets (about 65% of GDP) were outside the country, mostly in Switzerland and Britain, but also in the United States, Singapore, and the Cayman Islands. The government also started a clamp down on corruption in past government expenditures. In the Spring of 2013, two politicians (a former defense minister and a former mayor of Thessaloniki, the country's second-largest city) were convicted on corruption charges.

Socialists have also opposed dismantling the public sector, selling off state assets, and selling Greek firms to international private equity firms. Instead of bailouts, many socialists have called for nationalization of the banking sector. "The banking system we envision," SYRIZA leader Alexis Tsipras announced, "will support environmentally viable public investment and cooperative initiatives.... What we need is a banking system devoted to the public interest—not one bowing to capitalist profit. A banking system at the service of society, a banking system that serves as a pillar for growth." While SYRIZA called for renegotiating the Greece's public debt, it favored staying in the euro.

Other socialist parties have put forth their own programs that go beyond Keynesian fiscal expansion, a more equitable tax system, and even beyond nationalizing the banks. For instance, the Alliance of the Anti-Capitalist Left (ANTARSYA) called for nationalizing banks and corporations, worker takeovers of closed factories, and canceling the debt and exiting the euro. The Communist Party of Greece (KKE) proposed a fairly traditional Marxist-Leninist program, with socialization of all the means of production and central planning for the satisfaction of social needs, but also called for disengagement from the EU and abandoning the euro. The Trotskyist Xekinima party called for nationalizing not just the largest banks, but also the largest corporations, and putting them under democratic worker control.

Those within the Marxist and libertarian left, meanwhile, have focused on turning firms, especially those facing bankruptcy, into cooperatives or worker self-directed enterprises. Firms whose boards of directors are composed of worker-representatives and whose workers participate in democratic decision-making would be less likely to distribute surpluses to overpaid CEOs or corrupt politicians and lobbyists, or to pick up and relocate to other places with lower labor costs. While worker self-directed enterprises could decide to forego wage increases or to boost productivity, in order to promote exports, such decisions would be made democratically by the workers themselves, not by capitalist employers or their representatives in government. And it would be the workers themselves who would democratically decide what to do with any increased profits that might arise from those decisions.

Cooperatives Around the World

Efforts at transforming capitalist firms into cooperatives or worker-directed enterprises can draw upon successes in the Basque Country (Spain), Argentina, Venezuela, and elsewhere. The Mondragón Cooperative Corporation, centered in the Basque country, has grown since its founding, in the 1950s, to 85,000 members working in over 300 enterprises. In Venezuela, the Chávez government promoted the development of cooperatives. The total number surged more than 100-fold, to over 100,000, between 1998 and 2006, the last year for which data are available. In Argentina after 2001, failing enterprises were taken over (or "recovered") by workers and turned into cooperatives. The recovered enterprises boasted a survival rate of about 93%. By 2010, 205 of these cooperatives employed a total of almost 10,000 workers.

One Greek company that is trying to survive as a transformed worker cooperative is Vio.Me, a building materials factory in Thessaloniki. In May 2011 when the owners could no longer pay their bills and walked away, the workers decided to occupy the factory. By February 2013, after raising enough funds and community support, the workers started democratically running the company on their own. (They do not intend to buy out the owners, since the company owed the workers a significant amount of money when it abandoned the factory.) They established a worker-board, controlled by workers' general assemblies and subject to recall, to manage the factory. They also changed the business model, shifting to different suppliers, improving environmental practices, and finding new markets. Greek law currently does not allow factory occupations, so the workers are seeking the creation of a legal framework for the recuperated factory, which may enable more such efforts in the future. Vio.Me has received support from SYRIZA and the Greek Green party, from workers at recuperated factories in Argentina (see sidebar), as well as from academics and political activists worldwide.

Whither Europe and the Euro?

As Europe faces this ongoing crisis, it is also grappling with its identity. On the right are the neoliberal attempts to dismantle the welfare state and create a Europe that works for corporations and the wealthy—a capitalist Europe more like the United States. In the center are Keynesian calls to keep the EU intact, with stronger Europe-wide governance and institutions. These involve greater fiscal integration, with a European Treasury, eurobonds (rather than separate bonds for each country), European-wide banking regulations, etc. Keynesians also call for softening the austerity policies on Greece and other countries.

Proposals for European consolidation have inspired criticism and apprehension on both the far right and far left. Some on the far right are calling for exiting the euro, trumpeting nationalism and a return to the nation state. The left, meanwhile, voices concern about the emerging power of the European parliament in Brussels, with its highly paid politicians, bureaucrats, lobbyists, etc. who are able to pass legislation favoring corporations at the expense of workers. Unlike the far right however, the left has proposed a vision for another possible united Europe—one based on social cohesion and inclusion, cooperation and solidarity, rather than on competition and corporate dominance. In particular, socialists call for replacing the capitalist structure of Europe with one that is democratic, participatory, and embodies a socialist economy, with worker protections and participation at all levels of economic and political decision-making. This may very well be the best hope for Europe to escape its current death spiral, which has it living in terror of what the next stage may bring. ❑

Sources: Amitabh Pal, "Austerity is Killing Europe," Common Dreams, April 27, 2012 (commondreams.org); Niki Kitsantonis, "Greece Resumes Talks With Creditors," *New York Times*, April 4, 2013 (nytimes.com); Mark Weisbrot, "Where I Part from Paul Krugman on Greece and the Euro," *The Guardian*, May 13, 2011 (guardian.co.uk); Alberto F. Alesina and Silvia Ardagna, "Large Changes in Fiscal Policy: Taxes Versus Spending," National Bureau of Economic Research (NBER), October 2009 (nber.org); Geert Reuten, "From a false to a 'genuine' EMU," Globalinfo, Oct. 22, 2012 (globalinfo.nl); David Jolly, "Greek Economy Shrank 6.2% in Second Quarter," *New York Times*, Aug. 13, 2012; Joseph Zacune, "Privatizing Europe: Using the Crisis to Entrench Neoliberalism," Transnational Institute, March 2013 (tni.org); Mark Weisbrot, "Why Greece Should Reject the Euro," *New York Times*, May 9, 2011; Ronald Jannsen, "Blame It on the Multiplier," *Social Europe Journal*, Oct. 16, 2012 (social-europe.eu); Landon Thomas, Jr., and David Jolly, "Despite Push for Austerity, European Debt Has Soared," *New York Times*, Oct. 22, 2012; "German Public sector workers win above-inflation pay rise," Reuters, March 9, 2013 (reuters.nl); Liz Alderman, "Greek Businesses Fear Possible Return to Drachma," *New York Times*, May 22, 2012; Landon Thomas, Jr., "In Greece, Taking Aim at Wealthy Tax Dodgers," *New York Times*, Nov. 11, 2012; Rachel Donadio and Liz Alderman, "List of Swiss Accounts Turns Up the Heat in Greece," *New York Times*, Oct. 27, 2012; Landon Thomas, Jr., "Greece Seeks Taxes From Wealthy With Cash Havens in London," *New York Times*, Sept. 27, 2012; Niki Kitsantonis, "Ex-Mayor in Greece Gets Life in Prison for Embezzlement," *New York Times*, Feb. 27, 2013; Sam Bollier, "A guide to Greece's political parties," Al Jazeera, May 1, 2012 (aljazeera.com); Alexis Tsipras, "Syriza London: Public talk," March 16, 2013 (left.gr); Amalia Loizidou, "What way out for Greece and the working class in Europe," Committee for a Workers' International (CWI), March 19, 2013 (socialistworld.net); Richard Wolff, "Yes, there is an alternative to capitalism: Mondragón shows the way," *The Guardian*, June 24, 2012 (guardian.co.uk); Peter Ranis, "Occupy Wall Street: An Opening to Worker-Occupation of Factories and Enterprises in the U.S.," MRzine, Sept. 11, 2011 (mrzine.monthlyreview.org); viome.org.

CONTRIBUTORS

Sylvia A. Allegretto is an economist at the Institute for Research on Labor and Employment at the University of California, Berkeley.

Nicole Aschoff is a sociologist and writer living in the Boston area. She is a contributing editor at *Jacobin* magazine.

Dean Baker is co-director of the Center for Economic and Policy Research.

Drucilla K. Barker is professor of economics and women's studies at Hollins University.

William K. Black is executive director of the Institute for Fraud Prevention and teaches economics and law at the University of Missouri at Kansas City.

Darwin BondGraham is a sociologist and journalist who writes about political economy. He lives and works in the San Francisco Bay Area

Jim Campen is professor emeritus of economics at the University of Massichusetts-Boston and is former executive director of Americans for Fairness in Lending. He is also a *Dollars & Sense* Associate.

Jessica Carrick-Hagenbarth is a graduate student in economics at the University of Massachusetts-Amherst.

Molly Cusano is a former *Dollars & Sense* intern.

Gerald Epstein is a professor of economics and a founding co-director of the Political Economy Research Institute (PERI) at the University of Massachusetts, Amherst.

Susan F. Feiner is a professor of economics and women's studies at the University of Southern Maine.

Max Fraad Wolff teaches economics at the New School University graduate program in International Affairs.

Ellen Frank teaches economics at the University of Massachusetts-Boston and is a member of the *Dollars & Sense* collective.

Gerald Friedman is a professor of economics at the University of Massachusetts-Amherst.

Kevin Gallagher is an associate professor of International Relations at Boston University, and a senior researcher at the Global Development and Environment Institute, Tufts University.

Armagan Gezici, co-editor of this volume, is an assistant professor of economics at Keene State College, Keene, N.H.

Howard Karger is professor of social policy at the University of Houston.

David Kotz is professor of economics at the University of Massachusetts-Amherst.

Rob Larson is assistant professor of economics at Tacoma Community College in Tacoma, Wash.

Arthur MacEwan, a *Dollars & Sense* Associate, is professor emeritus of economics at the University of Massachusetts-Boston.

John Miller is a member of the *Dollars & Sense* collective and teaches economics at Wheaton College.

Fred Moseley is professor of economics at Mt. Holyoke College.

Doug Orr (co-editor of this volume) teaches economics at City College of San Francisco.

James Petras is an activist-scholar working with socio-political movements in Latin America, Europe, and Asia.

Robert Pollin teaches economics and is co-director of the Political Economy Research Institute at the University of Massachusetts-Amherst. He is also a *Dollars & Sense* Associate.

Steven Pressman is a professor at Monmouth University and a co-editor of the *Review of Political Economy*.

Alejandro Reuss (co-editor of this volume) is co-editor of *Dollars & Sense* and author of *Labor and the Global Economy* (Dollars & Sense, 2013).

Zachary Santamaria is a former *Dollars & Sense* intern.

Adria Scharf is executive director of the Richmond Peace Education Center in Richmond, Va., former co-editor of *Dollars & Sense*, and a *Dollars & Sense* Associate.

Abby Scher is a sociologist and journalist who was co-editor of *Dollars & Sense* in the 1990s. She is now a *D&S* Associate and an Associate Fellow of the Institute for Policy Studies.

Katherine Sciacchitano is a former labor lawyer and organizer. She teaches political economy at the National Labor College.

Robert Scott teaches in the Department of Economics and Finance at Monmouth University.

Orlando Segura, Jr. has worked for an Atlanta-based global management consulting company that consults for private equity firms, and for a private equity firm based in Boston.

William E. Spriggs is a senior fellow with the Economic Policy Institute and was the former executive director of the National Urban League Institute for Opportunity and Equality.

Chris Sturr (co-editor of this volume) is co-editor of *Dollars & Sense*.

Marjolein van der Veen is an economist. She has taught economics in Massachusetts, the Seattle area, and the Netherlands.

Ramaa Vasudevan is assistant professor of economics at Colorado State University and a member of the *Dollars and Sense* collective.

Jeannette Wicks-Lim is an economist and research fellow at the Political Economy Research Institute at the University of Massachusetts-Amherst.

Marty Wolfson (co-editor of this volume) teaches economics at the University of Notre Dame and is a former economist with the Federal Reserve Board in Washington, D.C.

CPSIA information can be obtained
at www.ICGtesting.com
Printed in the USA
FSHW020904151220
76714FS